Social Division

Social Division

ALAN H. CARLING

VERSO

London · New York

First published by Verso 1991

Verso
UK: 6 Meard Street, London W1V 3HR
USA: 29 West 35th Street, New York, NY 10001-2291

Verso is the imprint of New Left Books

British Library Cataloguing in Publication Data
A catalogue record for this book is available from the British Library

Library of Congress Cataloging-in-Publication Data
A catalogue record for this book is available from the Library of Congress

ISBN 0 86091 290 6
ISBN 0 86091 506 9 Pbk

Typeset in Times by B.P. Integraphics, Bath, Avon
Printed in Great Britain by Biddles Ltd

Dedicated to the lives of
David and Freda Carling

Contents

Figures and Tables

Tables

Figures

Acknowledgement

I should like to thank all those who have contributed comments on various parts of the manuscript at various stages of its preparation: Perry Anderson, Michael Banton, Brian Barry, Anthony Buckley, John Carling, Jerry Cohen, Mary Cooper, Norman Geras, Peter Halfpenny, Jeff Hearn, Bill Jordan, Steve Joseph, Jane Martin, Philip Pettit, John Roemer, Philippe Van Parijs and Erik Olin Wright. Philippe Van Parijs's invitation to Louvain-la-Neuve gave rise to much of Chapters 15 and 16, and Erik Wright's invitation to Madison, Wisconsin, enabled me to crystallize Chapter 7.

I owe a great deal to the initial support and subsequent patience of the editorial boards of *New Left Review* and Verso, and especially Robin Blackburn; but my greatest intellectual debt remains to the staff and students of a remarkable academic outfit – the Department of Interdisciplinary Human Studies at the University of Bradford. In this connection I would especially like to thank my present or former colleagues, Roger Fellows, Graham Macdonald, Jenny Bourne Taylor and David West.

Anne-Marie Robinson, Jeanette Stevens and Beverly Toulson have tolerated my mania for textual revision with unfailing good humour, ably assisted in the latter stages by Davinder Kaur Singh.

The life I've always wanted
I guess I'll never have
I'll be working for somebody else
Until I'm in my grave
I'll be dreaming of a life of ease
And mountains
Oh mountains o' things . . .

Sweet lazy life
Champagne and caviar
I hope you'll come and find me
Cause you know who we are
Those who deserve the best in life
And know what money's worth
And those whose sole misfortune
Was having mountains o' nothing at birth

Mountains o' Things, Tracy Chapman

Introduction

People differ in a thousand ways, and it is good that this is so. Among these differences are some less good perhaps, sharing at least the following features: (i) they occur in one form or another in many different historical and cultural settings; (ii) they are fateful for the lives of individuals; (iii) they are institutionalized in formidable ways (often although not always entrenched by legal codes); (iv) they are associated with large and/or pervasive inequalities of condition; (v) they are linked in various ways with major processes of social change; (iv) they are at once material and social, in various senses to be explored; (vii) they are widely, but not universally, thought to give rise to injustices which ought to be rectified.

Differences of this kind I will call *social divisions* and the process through which they occur, *social division*. The three major social divisions on which I shall concentrate are those of social class, gender and ethnicity. Others might be cited, especially age and disability, but also those relating to wealth and health, region and religion, the country and the city, the rulers and the ruled or the leaders and the led. Age and disability are excluded not because the topics lack importance but because the author lacks competence. Several aspects of liquidity, theology, geography and authority are implicated in the treatment of the three major divisions.

In Parts I and II of the book, I deal with social class through an exposition of Analytical Marxism, as this term and school of thought has come to be known over the last few years in connection with the names especially of Jerry Cohen, Jon Elster, John Roemer, Erik Olin Wright, Robert Brenner, Adam Przeworski, Philippe Van Parijs and Robert Van der Veen. The distribution of subject matter between the first two Parts respects a distinction between what may be called the general and special theories of historical materialism – namely, the long-run theory of historical change and the theoretical critique of capitalism.

1

Parts III and V aim to extend the class analysis to apply within the
private, in the sense of domestic, domain. Several economic models of
household interaction are proposed, including the exchange model, the
short commons model and the Chicken model. Chapter 8 investigates
the conditions under which either market exchange or domestic exchange
are ever possible. The household models are then subjected to a critical
experimental test which draws upon Susan McRae's study of the *Cross-
Class Family*: a nuclear family in which, crudely speaking, ideological
and economic factors pull in opposite directions. The upshot is that ideology wins the battle, but it may be that economics wins the war. At all
events, gender difference appears to enjoy an explanatory role beyond
that given by rational choice on the basis of inequalities in the distribution
of resources between the genders. This finding is held to imply that sociology is required, beyond economic theory.

Such a dual approach – of considering the way in which ideological
processes frame economic interactions – is continued in Part VI, where
questions are explored concerning the genesis and consequences of ethnic
and racial division. What makes a given division into an ethnic or racial
division is the belief by large sections of a given population in an often
unbelievable story about the origins and descent of particular social
groups.[1] The preferences which such stories legitimize establish social
contexts to which apply a variety of explanatory theories. These theories
divide roughly into special theories, dealing with the incentives faced
by individuals to affiliate to, or switch allegiance between, ethnic or racial
groups that are already formed, and general theories, dealing with the
formation of the groups themselves, including their sustaining narratives.
Michael Banton's contribution to the respective types of theory is the
springboard of discussion in the two chapters of Part VI.[2]

Part VII of the book attempts to look beyond social division to socialism, conceived as a form of society without social division. In the Utopian
part of Marx's vision of the future, social division is no problem, because
both human individuals and their social arrangements have changed to
such an extent and in such a way that the historic occasions for social
division simply never arise. In the more practical component of his vision,
scarcity still constrains human possibility, and it is a difficult problem
to ensure that social division does not arise even in conditions under
which the distribution of resources has been radically equalized. It is
a problem for socialists if, as I shall maintain, resource equalization is
necessary but not sufficient for socialism.

This leaves Part IV to provide, I hope, the keystone of the arch. It
extends the variety of property systems introduced in connection with
social class in Parts I and II by asking about public systems of property;
in doing so it calls into question the distinction between the public and

private domains which assigns the traditional subject matter of social class to the public domain while domestic labour languishes behind closed doors. Chapter 9 tackles the generic confusions which have existed even in the technical economic literature, first, over the distinction between the material and social dimensions of what is public and what is private about systems for the production and distribution of goods and, second, over the gist of the distinction between public and private goods themselves. These clarifications are intended both to assist the applications of the economic models of the household whose discussion straddles Part IV, and to inform the analysis of socialism in the penultimate Part of the book.

Despite these linkages of underlying theme, the several Parts of the book are designed to be relatively self-contained discussions that the reader may sample independently. I have attempted to keep the treatment at the lowest level of mathematical difficulty necessary to make points of theoretical importance – there is, for example, no matrix algebra in the book – and to help the non-mathematical reader by confining the technical discussion to a few chapters or sections within a chapter. The most technical chapters are 8 and 16, and sections 4.1 to 4.3, 5.1 to 5.3, 7.2, 9.2, 10.3, 11.2, 14.3 and 17.1.

There is a more detailed structure to the argument than that outlined above, but rather than describe that structure, I will attempt to motivate the whole treatment of social division offered below by means of a personal confession.

I am a socialist by political conviction; an individualist by intellectual training, and – who knows – by temperament; a sociologist by profession. By background, I belong to a family which has been dispersed fairly comfortably through the middle reaches of the English class system.

I am a child of this family, but I am more particularly a child of the 1960s. I belong to that generation which was formed at a moment when the world seemed made anew. No doubt this is part of the experience of every eighteen-year-old, but it is less common for this natural feeling to be amplified with feedback from unprecedented cultural changes, and to find some answering endorsement from the disoriented powers that be. For people like myself the university was at that moment a discovery that became a spiritual home: a phase of life which in my case seems to have become a life. Opposition to the university authorities in those days arose from a passionate if inarticulate belief in the values from which we believed the universities had departed: mine was truly a protestant awakening.[3]

I do not feel that I have ever repudiated the vision of the sixties. True, there were great failings in the vision of the times. It was believed that certain problems had been solved once-and-for-all: the economic problem, for example, and the problem of war. It was time for humankind to enter a new inheritance. Part of the emotional reaction to Vietnam, and also to Northern Ireland, was I suspect not so much that these conflicts were brutal, imperialist or unjust, but that they were so dreadfully old-fashioned. Feelings like these were no doubt extraordinarily naive, but they were animated by a breadth of purpose and a warmth of spirit that cannot be condemned. And I see in hindsight that what I have been doing is in some respects working out for myself what the vision of the sixties means, given the naivety of an original belief that the causes of social division and social conflict could magically be willed away.

My initial difficulty was that of someone beginning work in social theory in the mid seventies, at a time when the intellectual left was dominated by Althusserianism. It would be false to say that I was ever out of sympathy with Althusserianism, for that presupposes I understood what it was trying to do sufficiently clearly to form a judgement upon it. I am sure that the longer-term impact of Althusserian theory will have done nothing but good, leavening the rude mechanic arts of the English-speaking toilers in the field with a touch of high-class speculation from the French. But there is equally no doubt that in the short term it depressed the native tradition of outhouse sociology which had formed one of the intellectual mainsprings of a previous generation. In the 1970s, there were fifty social theorists condemning the very idea of consulting the facts to each one theorist collecting the facts that would be damned.

And this lesion in social inquiry perhaps had a political counterpart in my generation. No one I knew in their right minds – socialists to a person – would have dreamed of joining the Labour Party, any more than they would have contemplated a career in industry or commerce. "Local Government" was, I remember, a particular term of abuse among us. As Ken Livingstone records in his no doubt interim memoir, he was in 1969 nearly overrun as he placed his foot on the first rung of the Labour gangplank by rats pouring past him out of the ship.[4] The seventies on the left in Britain were not a time especially propitious either for theory or for practice, and especially the fusion of the two.

The political aftermath – I will not say consequence – of this is well enough known, as I write this on the very anniversary of a certain famous decade in office. A historical personage from Grantham appeared, and, Lo!, deprived my generation of what we had over-confidently believed was our political birthright. All the questions which the sixties had settled once-and-for-all were declared reopened, and, worse, resettled on the other side. Thatcherism has sometimes been held to be a reaction against the sixties by an English middle class which had flirted briefly with the best side of its character, and returned to a more comfortable moral groove of mean-minded vindictiveness; resuming, after a brief vacation, its historic mission to kick the proletariat on behalf of the aristocrats of high finance.

But this view has the generations slightly out of kilter. It is equally plausible to regard Thatcherism as the revenge of the Young Conservatives of the fifties for missing out all round: they did not have the opportunities for historic deeds grasped by their predecessors of the forties, nor did they have the untroubled social vision of their successors in the sixties, and this explains why she for them has been so strident in elbowing to be heard. They were just emerging from the shadow of Winston Churchill, poor lambs, when they were plunged back into the shade by John Lennon. Yet they did have things to say, and the left was in poor shape to receive them.

My earliest saviour in theory was Jerry Cohen. I was overwhelmed at first by the style more than the substance of his famous book: *Karl Marx's Theory of History: A Defence*. It was a revelation to know that it was possible to do Marxist Theory in his irreverent yet fastidious fashion; and that it was possible to apply analytical philosophy to important subjects. I initially gained from Cohen one indispensable key to reading Marx – the distinction in Marx's use of terms between the material and social properties of things – but I was otherwise thoroughly intimidated by Cohen's work. It seemed impossible to add anything worthwhile to his definitive account of the theory of history, especially as I then admired that account more for the ingenuity than the historical truth of his defensive reconstruction. If Cohen showed magnificently the sort of thing that might be done, his work did not show me much that I myself might do.

The effect of Jon Elster's work was even more ambiguous. Elster has been the Calvin of Analytical Marxism. He applies the scourge and the lash to Marx and his disciples with unremitting ferocity; indeed, he is to contemporary Marxist Theory somewhat as Mrs Thatcher has been to contemporary British industry. The slightest deviation from strict methodological individualism; the merest hint of indulgence in teleological modes of reasoning, or smidgeon of departure from the most austere canon of non-cooperative game theory; all these are held up naked to the public gaze. There is no doubt that all this rigour is very good for the theory; what is less clear is how much is left standing by the end.[5]

I was very receptive to Elster's general line of attack, because I had been fortunate enough to encounter in the early seventies a very fine teacher, Michael Taylor, who remains probably the only rational-choice Anarchist in the whole wide world. Yet I had since strayed from the path, willingly persuaded by Pradeep Bandyopadhyay into the pages of *Capital*, from which few souls return unscathed. So I was keen to hear

from Elster that one should bring the rational-choice approach to bear
on Marx, as part of the process of bringing it to bear on everything
else. What I found less easy to accept was the verdict that Marx barely
survived the application.

And this is how John Roemer engineered my salvation. For his astonish-
ing work showed that it was possible to place Marx's central insights
regarding class in a capitalist society on a theoretical foundation which
must satisfy the most stringent methodological individualism. His work
showed politically how one could make the socialist case compatible with
individualistic behavioural assumptions, and it showed professionally how
one could treat fundamental topics of sociology using the theory of rational choice. I quickly realized – or rather, I sensed tantalizingly without
then being able to prove – that the generalization Roemer had made
of the concept of exploitation in connection with the various circumstances
of social class, could be generalized yet further to apply to circumstances
of gender and ethnic relations. I had taken for granted that Marxism
could not stand alone as a theory of social class, and that it must live
in close relation with theories of gender and ethnicity. Having glimpsed
in Roemer's work the possibility of such a general theory of social division
based on rational-choice assumptions, I started out writing a book entitled
Rational Choice and Social Division.

And now I come to the nub of my confession. This book has been
written from the inside out. Much of the material in Parts III and IV
had been written in substantial draft before I began work on what became
Part I. The case I intended to put forward was that the defensible part
of Marxism was what I had called "Rational-choice Marxism" in a review
article of that title published in 1986.[6] This centred primarily on Roemer's
work: the pillar on which the viable claims of contemporary Marxism
were, I thought, resting almost entirely. Cohen's version of the theory
of history, while extraordinarily elegant in conception, was in substance
less impressive, and somewhat vulnerable on the one hand to Elster's
methodological anathemas and on the other to Robert Brenner's critical
historiography.

As I developed the argument, and also as I pursued the theoretical
strategy of applying rational-choice theory to gender and ethnicity, my
views began to alter. Put simply, I became more aware of the limitations
of rational-choice theory, and, simultaneously (not a logical consequence
of the first awareness), I became more aware of the strengths of competing
types of explanation – especially functional explanation – and of the theoretical claims both of collective action and of supra-individual systems
of perception and belief transmitted directly in a process of socialization
rather than attained through lengthy procedures of ratiocination. I came,
then, to surrender in part to my fate as a sociologist, and to begin to

understand what being a sociologist might mean. In particular, I came to conclude that Marxist theory might well rest on two pillars more substantial than I had thought, involving both the general and the special theories of historical materialism. It seemed that the way to proceed in social theory as a whole was to try and combine as sensitively and as explicitly as possible several styles of explanation at several levels of aggregation. Elster's micro-foundational programme of seeking individual-level explanations for all social phenomena, heavily skewed towards rational choice as the privileged mode of explanation, was too puritanical by half.

Since I have come to this view from a puritan background, and I am moving in a catholic direction, this makes me, I suppose appropriately in view of my social origins, an anglican among social theorists, who does not I hope carry his anglicanism so far as to abandon completely his faith in rational choice. Yet in view of this partial conversion, I put forward this book under its less sectarian and I hope more comprehensive title: *Social Division*.

Notes

1. I owe the phrase "unbelievable beliefs" to Anthony Buckley.
2. Michael Banton, *Racial and Ethnic Competition* (Cambridge: C.U.P., 1983).
3. I recognize as true of myself the critique of the student movement of the 60s given by Barbara and John Ehrenreich, "The Professional–Managerial Class", in Pat Walker, ed., *Between Labour and Capital* (Hassocks, Sussex: Harvester Press, 1979).
4. Ken Livingstone, *If Voting Changed Anything, They'd Abolish It* (Glasgow: Fontana, 1988).
5. See Jon Elster, *An Introduction to Karl Marx* (Cambridge: C.U.P., 1986), Ch. 10. I have put one sentence in this paragraph in the past tense, to signal a slight change of tune by Elster which occurs in *The Cement of Society* (Cambridge: C.U.P., 1989).
6. *New Left Review*, 160 (1986), reprinted in Mark Cowling and Lawrence Wilde, eds., *Approaches to Marx* (Milton Keynes: Open University Press, 1989), in which the present volume is advertised under its original title as *Rational Choice and Social Division*.

PART I

The Theory of History and the Logic of Class Struggle

1

A Theory of History

1.1 Marx, Engels, Cohen and Brenner

Marx and Engels once claimed that "the history of all hitherto existing society is the history of class struggles". A few pages later, apparently in summary of the intervening explication they had given this resounding claim, they wrote:

> We see then: the means of production and of exchange, on whose foundation the bourgeois built itself up, were generated in feudal society. At a certain stage in the development of these means of production and of exchange, the conditions under which feudal society produced and exchanged, the feudal organization of agriculture and manufacturing industry, in one word, the feudal relations of property became no longer compatible with the already developed productive forces; they became so many fetters. They had to be burst asunder; they were burst asunder.[1]

It has subsequently seemed less obvious to their supporters, and a lot less obvious to their opponents, that a narrative of class struggle tells the same story as a narrative of development of the forces of production. It is certainly not a logical truth that a history of class conflict is a history of technological development. So what is the relationship between technology and class in the Marxist conception of history?

The terms of any answer to this question have been massively clarified in recent years by the contributions of G.A. Cohen and Robert Brenner.[2] Cohen has given the most coherent – probably the only coherent – account of the Marxist theory of history. He has emphasized – indeed, almost

11

single-handedly reinstated – the level of development of the forces of production as the key explanatory variable in Marx's treatment of long-run historical change. Brenner, on the other hand, has written the most systematic comparative history of the transition from feudalism to capitalism, and has appealed for explanatory primacy to the variable incidence of class struggle between lord and peasant in late medieval Europe. Brenner has in the process explicitly denied that his approach is compatible with Cohen's account of the general theory of history. It follows that the theoretical question posed by the opening pages of the *Communist Manifesto* comes down these days to the question whether Cohen's technological determinism can be reconciled with Brenner's class struggle.

This is a question between two *orders* of explanation – whether one should look by and large to technology or class for the source of fundamental social change – but it becomes at the same time a question between two *modes* of explanation. For Cohen has argued not only that the level of technological development is for Marx the fundamental explanatory factor in history; he has argued that for Marx, technology explains history functionally. Brenner's reconstruction relies instead on a more conventional mode of intentional explanation, according to which history is the resultant of strategies pursued by actors in determinate class situations.[3]

To ask whether Cohen and Brenner can be reconciled, and therefore whether the twin emphases in Marx and Engels' historical materialism are compatible, is thus to ask, first, whether there is a single composite order of explanation which somehow synthesizes class factors with technical factors; and second, whether it is somehow possible to incorporate the intentional logic of class struggle within the functional logic of the theory of history. Here and in the following chapter, I outline Cohen's version of the theory of history, some objections of principle and substance to which it has been subject, and the alternative account put forward by Brenner. I will find that Cohen fails to persuade regarding the truth of the functional theory of history, and Brenner and other critics fail to persuade regarding its falsity. In Chapter 3, I sketch a synthesis of the desired kind between the two approaches, which adds I believe to the plausibility of both, and suggests that Marx and Engels might be able to have their historical cake and eat it too. The conclusion, briefly stated, is that if the task of the general theory of history is to show why it is that "the history of all hitherto existing society is the history of class struggles", then a functional explanation from technology is not an impossible candidate for that task.

1.2   Cohen on the Theory of History

Karl Marx's theory of history: an exposition

The building blocks of Marx's theory of history are forces of production, economic structures (composed of relations of production) and super-structures. "Forces of production" denote means of production and labour-power under a material description, including within "labour-power" productively useful scientific knowledge; "relations of produc-tion" denote relations of effective access to and control over forces of production and products; "superstructures" denote, minimally, those legal or political relations which are necessary to stabilize relations of production.[4]

Marx observes that as history proceeds, the forces of production tend to develop to ever higher levels, which means that the productive power of society expands, and with it the capacity of society to generate a physical surplus of production above the amount necessary to satisfy a relatively constant datum of human subsistence needs for the whole population. The fact that this development occurs enables history to be divided into four great eras according to the surplus-generating capacity society has achieved: virtually no surplus above subsistence for the whole population; some surplus; moderately high surplus; and massive surplus.[5] If in the first era there is virtually no surplus, there cannot be class division, because there is no product out of which a non-producing class could be supported. In the next two eras, there are pre-capitalist and then capitalist forms of class society. It is not just that the existence of some surplus allows the existence of a non-producing class in these two cases; it is that the two successive versions of class society exist because they are successively adapted to the prevailing levels of development of the forces of production. These first three terms of the historical sequence exhaust "all hitherto existing society".

In the fourth and final era, capitalist development has brought society to the point at which it can generate a massive surplus: it is then either the case that a society without class division is best adapted to any techno-logy capable of sustaining such a massive surplus, or it is the case that forms of social organization are no longer required to adapt to technologi-cal imperatives. In the latter interpretation, there has been a technological breakthrough, in the sense that human progress is no longer constrained by technology, and "the history of class struggles" has come to an end. It is then consistent with Marx's treatment of the question in the *Critique of the Gotha Programme* to regard the first interpretation as defining an initial, socialist, phase of the post-capitalist Era 4 (call it 4a) while the second governs a subsequent, communist, phase of the same era (call it 4b).[6]

It is worth noting about this sequence that in one era (number 1), there is nothing to explain, or rather, it is a nothing (the non-existence of a surplus-consuming dominant class) which is easily and directly explained (by the exceedingly low level of development of the forces of production); while in half of another (number 4b) there is also nothing to explain, or rather, there is probably no longer a claim being entered for explanation from technology to social form. It follows that the heartland of the theory of history is the stretch running from Era 2 through to Era 4a, beginning socially with pre-capitalist and capitalist class societies, and ending with the immediately post-capitalist non-class society; and beginning technologically with intermediate levels of surplus-generating capacity, lately verging on the massive.

All societies within this range consist of a package including a particular type of technology (technology at a certain generic *level* of productivity) together with particular forms of economic possession and legal or political institutions. In so far as the theory of history is intended as a general theory, it is evidently restricted to a rather small number of cases (societies of types 2, 3 and 4a) involving an even smaller number of transitions between them. Moreover, since the transition from Era 1 to Era 2 is lost in the mists of time, and the transition from 3 to 4a may not have taken place, it is not clear how easy it will be to test the claim to generality.

What is certain is that the theory must at least leap the hurdle presented by the boundary between Eras 2 and 3 – between feudalism and capitalism – since this is the only transition sufficiently distant for the dust to have settled and sufficiently close to appear within the historical record.[7] Successful clearance of this hurdle would be necessary but not sufficient for the general truth of the general theory, for it might be that the conditions which made for the truth of the theory in relation to the transition from feudalism to capitalism included historically variable conditions which would not obtain in relation to the prior transition to feudalism or the prospective transition from capitalism. It does not follow, as Marxists would prefer to have it, that any lessons learned from early capitalism are automatic lessons for early socialism. And even this relatively modest degree of empirical ambition will be frustrated if, as many critics have complained, the theory is incapable of presenting itself before its first empirical hurdle in fit logical shape. This is where Cohen's greatest contribution lies.

According to Cohen, Marxism reaches the starting blocks if and only if the relevant forms of historical social organization are conceived as explicable in two tiers of functional relationship. If we regard the base (consisting of the forces of production at a given level of development) as metaphorically lower than the economic structure (consisting of rela-

tions of production), then the lower tier of explanation goes from forces
to relations, and the second, upper tier, goes from relations to superstructures, which are metaphorically poised above the structure. Reading now
from top to bottom, the literal claim is that the existence (or form) of
significant non-economic institutions is functionally explained by the configuration of the social relations of production, which is functionally
explained in turn by the (level of development of the) forces of production.
That this is a functional explanation means that, in each case, the existence
(or form) of the explained item (explanandum) is explained by a propensity
the explained item has to affect the explaining item (explanans). Relations
of production of a certain kind exist because of their propensity to promote
the further development of given forces of production; superstructural
institutions of a certain kind exist because of their propensity to stabilize
given relations of production. If functional explanation is transitive, there
will be an induced explanation from the base via the structure to the
superstructure, so that whatever the superstructure contains (strictly
"whatever is superstructural") is allegedly explained ultimately by (something about) technology.

One can see how this double-decker layout justifies Marxism's reputation for being a theory of both continuity and change. If superstructures
are the way they are because of their propensity to stabilize relations
of production, it follows that relations of production would be less stable
than they are in the absence of superstructures, so that the theory predicts
the relative durability of relations of production. In this upper tier, functional explanation accounts for continuity.

In the lower tier – in the engine room, so to speak – matters are a
little different. It is true that the relations of production are adapting
to something constant, but the constant feature in question is the tendency
of something else (that is: the forces of production) to change constantly
– to change their level in one direction only: ever onwards and upwards.
This constant pressure, supplied metaphorically from below, brings about
a change in the economic and political package suspended just above,
and these successive revolutions of the economic structure and associated
superstructures lend history the overall pattern it has. So whatever name
functionalism has gained in the social sciences for its conservative habits
is unwarranted by Marx's theory of history in its dynamic aspect, supposing that the use of functional explanation in some theoretical context
always renders the theorist guilty of "functionalism".

Construed in this fashion, the Marxist theory of history claims to
explain why different types of relations of production, each type conserved
by appropriate political institutions selected for that very purpose, tend
to follow each other in an orderly succession over historical time: the
reason is that forces of production are first fettered, then fester and are

later fostered.

It is a feature of this explanation in its functional version elucidated by Cohen not only that there may be backwards, or rather downwards, counter-causation (from superstructure to structure and from structure to base) but that the functional explanation positively depends on the existence of such counter-causation. If the superstructure did not have the stabilizing effect it allegedly does on the structure, it could not have been selected by virtue of having just that effect on the structure; if relations of production did not have the force-enhancing effects they allegedly do, it would be incoherent to say that they exist when and because they tend to enhance the forces of production. This is why Sean Sayers' criticism of the "undialectical" character of Cohen's reconstruction is misguided.

> The development of the productive forces is made into the *sole* active force in historical development. Marxism is reduced to a form of technological determinism. Historical change is portrayed as a linear causal process. Movement always comes from "below", as it were, from the material level; and it is transmitted "upwards" in a causal and mechanical fashion. "The productive forces," writes Cohen, "strongly determine the character of the economic structure while forming no part of it". The economic structure in turn determines the character of the political superstructure. Economic relations and political forms are the mere effects, the mere outcome of a particular level of development of the productive forces. The relations of production and the superstructure are thus regarded as "inactive results" with no independent life or dynamic of their own.

Historical materialism is indeed "a form of technological determinism." But precisely because relations of production and superstructures enjoy "independent life" of the requisite kinds, they are enabled to contribute to their own determination by technology, given that the mode of determination is a functional mode of determination. This may well be an unfamiliar way of looking at things, which requires some getting used to. But once the novelty of the functional dialectic has sunk in, it can be seen that Cohen has found the only way in which Marxist historical theory might survive the time-honoured procedure by which distinguished critics on the political right mount an apparently unanswerable refutation of historical materialism by listing the sorts of undeniable effects the superstructure has upon the structure, and the structure has upon the base.[9] The demonstration of these effects actually helps to make the case in favour of functional explanation, since the demonstration of the "downwards" link would be part of any successful functional explanation.

Yet the fact that the functional theory of history neatly sidesteps some prevailing tactics of counter-exemplification does not imply that it will evade all other attempts at falsification. It may still be the case either

that functional explanation fails for reasons of principle or that it fails
in its application to the theory of history at its key moment: the transition
from feudalism to capitalism. The exchanges between Cohen and Jon
Elster have concentrated on the first issue; the disagreements between
Cohen and Robert Brenner have centred on the second.

The viability of functionalism

To explain how something happens is to give one version of why it happens: it happens because of the sequence of events recorded under "how".
Functional explanation is different, in that it tries to give a why-explana-
tion without commitment to a detailed account of "how". If it is said,
for example, that capitalism supersedes feudalism because it has a greater
propensity to raise the level of development of the forces of production,
then this is an explanation doing without a history of the transitional
process: a "why" without a "how". Granted that a full explanation of
anything should cover both the how and the why of the thing, then functional explanation may be incomplete explanation. So much is agreed
between Cohen and Elster. The difference between them has arisen over
the significance to be attached to the potential incompleteness of functional explanation.

For Elster, proper functional explanation always requires the specification of the (non-functional) feedback mechanism showing how the propensity of the explained item to affect the explaining item explains the
form or existence of the explained item. In Darwinian theory, which is
the paradigm for this discussion, natural selection supplies the feedback
mechanism. Birds have hollow bones because hollow bones facilitate the
flight of flying animals, yet hollow bones have come about as a causal
result of the naturally selected mutations of genes. Gene mutation is a
kind of generalized "how" to support the "why" of reproductive advantage. Cohen admits that functional explanation is strengthened by what
he prefers to call causal elaboration (his term for the demonstration of
Elster's causal mechanism), but he denies that functional explanation
requires causal elaboration to count as valid explanation.[10]

The crux of the disagreement is that for Elster, functional explanation
is always parasitic on non-functional (causal or intentional) explanation,
since functional explanation is valid if and only if an equivalent causal/
intentional explanation is provided, and if the causal/intentional explanation has been provided, then the equivalent functional explanation is
redundant. For Cohen, on the other hand, a functional explanation can
in principle stand in its own right, whether or not an equivalent causal/
intentional explanation is forthcoming.[11] Elster's strictures are directed
in the first instance not against Cohen so much as against what Elster

perceives to be a long-standing shortcoming of sociological theorizing
within and beyond the Marxist tradition. It will help to identify the kind
of target Elster has in mind if we consider an influential study by Paul
Willis published in 1977 under the title *Learning to Labour*.[12]

Willis was interested in how the education system works to allocate
individuals to positions within the overall division of social labour. He
wanted to know in particular how people come to accept the worst jobs
(in terms of conditions, pay and general status) without being forced
to do so. Willis focused his attention on a small group of somewhat
unruly and completely unteachable young white men in their last year
at a single-sex comprehensive school with 600 pupils in the heart of a
working-class housing estate in industrial Birmingham.[13] This handful
of students – in effect a right handful of non-students – styled themselves
"the lads", in sharp contrast to those they called "ear 'oles", who sometimes took school work seriously, and the "semi ear 'oles", who were
aspiring lads with suspect ear 'ole tendencies.

The lads rejected the official culture of the school to such an extent
that they reversed the conventional status ranking of intellectual and
manual work and consequently anticipated as their best careers those
manual occupations everyone else connected with the school rejected as
the worst. In this way, their transition from the school room to the shop
floor was considerably smoothed (remember this is the mid-70s, when
such transitions did occur), and the problem was solved of where Birmingham business would find its unskilled labour. Although the teachers
were frequently resigned to the academic indifference shown by the lads,
and sometimes had theories – like the bone idle theory – to account
for it, no teacher in the school wanted the lads to freewheel as completely
as they did.[14] So although it was an undeniable consequence of the fact
and the form taken by the lads' academic uninvolvement that the lads
were at once destined for and suited to unskilled manual labour, this
consequence was foreseen but not intended by any official action performed within the school.

Willis claims nevertheless that one can explain the educational failure
functionally, via the consequence it has of suiting pupils such as the lads
for the unskilled section of the capitalist labour force. The lads fail because
otherwise capitalism would collapse, and the education system, despite
its official avowals to the contrary, must ensure that a certain proportion
of those going through the system utterly reject its values. Willis' commentary often suggests that in rejecting the school the lads evince an understanding of the nature of class society better than that possessed by a
teaching staff taken in by a superficial liberalism and thus prone to promul-
gate an unsustainable ethic of personal advancement through scholar-
ship.[15] Judgements of consciousness aside, he has evidently offered a why

explanation for educational failure (the lads fail because capitalism requires of its education system that someone fail) without offering a how explanation (how does it come about through the regular operation of the school culture that an appropriate proportion of pupils utterly reject that culture?).

The problem of method raised by this want of a how is that the demonstration that there are consequences unintended by some parties to a given state of affairs does not of itself prove that the state of affairs obtains because of those consequences. After all, most states of affairs have myriad consequences, and they cannot all be explicative consequences. It is true that if there is a functional explanation of a given state of affairs, there will be *some* set of (intended or unintended) consequences of the state of affairs in virtue of which the state of affairs exists, but the specification of a plausible set of consequences is only a necessary step and never a sufficient step toward the successful accomplishment of that functional explanation. And it is this tendency to take a necessary condition of functional explanation for a sufficient condition that in Elster's view invites slipshod social science, wherever functionalism is espoused. Formally speaking, one is warranted in making the inference from the mere observation that some phenomenon A has a positive effect on some phenomenon B (A is functional for B) to the conclusion that phenomenon B explains phenomenon A functionally (A obtains because of its function for B) only if a consequence law exists of the form "If [If A then B] then A".[16]

For example, given that it can be shown that having hollow bones facilitates flight in animals that can fly and that being able to fly confers reproductive advantage on animals, it is a good bet that it is the flight facilitation function of hollow bones which explains why animals that do fly have hollow bones. This is because there is a generalized consequence law of evolutionary theory to the effect that whatever conduces to reproductive success in a species is explained by this conduciveness. The belief in the consequence law comes from the conviction that this type of explanation has been successful in similar cases (i.e., the belief arises from induction: a procedure to which ordinary causal laws no less than functional laws are subject, and indeed, vulnerable), or from the supposition of a general mechanism – such as natural selection – which would give the theorist plausible grounds for expecting this type of explanation to be successful in a new application. Without the backing of a well-established consequence law, or an attempt to specify in some detail the feedback mechanism whereby the function a thing has explains something about how the thing is, a functional connection is not by itself any kind of explanation at all.

Applied to Willis, the criticism comes to this: suppose that in the

Birmingham area of England, there are a variety of different schools. Suppose it happens that they all have prodigiously gifted and enormously enthusiastic teaching staff, magnificently supported by a sensitive and resourceful Government (we have moved into the eighties, the reader will note). The result is that even the most recalcitrant student comes out with a raft of formal qualifications. Employers in the Birmingham area now find it impossible to recruit unskilled workers. They even try to encourage immigration to meet their difficulty, but since the education system is so good, they find that pretty soon the children of immigrants are as overqualified as their native colleagues. So the firms go out of business, either because they just can't get the paid help, or because they have to put people with 20 years of schooling on the day shift, and these downwardly mobile graduates get so disgruntled that they start sabotaging production. So industry in Birmingham grinds to a halt, the taxes are no longer paid, the school system deteriorates, teachers suffer a crisis in morale, the kids cease to bother, no-one cares about education, and there is soon once again a stream of teenagers willing and able to take on unskilled manual work at ridiculous rates of pay. The economy of Birmingham therefore starts to revive with the sudden access of cheap labour and the whole process begins again. It might then be said that this economic pedagogo-cycle goes back and forth, working itself out in different ways in different parts of Birmingham, until there is an equilibrium distribution of schools in the city, or rather, an equilibrium distribution of pupils in class rooms, correlated with school, some of whom are educable and some of whom are not. This outcome – a split-level school system with well- and ill-motivated pupils – has then been explained by the function education has of supplying labour at various grades to the surrounding economy.[17]

To have established some such feedback mechanism is to have answered Elster's prayer. Without it, Elster would say, Willis has mistaken what is at best a more or less plausible hypothesis for an explanation of the facts. In particular, without some such elaboration Willis cannot justifiably superimpose upon the lads' fates a vast Althusserian superstructure of ideological transformations. How can we possibly tell if it is true that:

> A reverse polarization of a too well-learned distinction [of mental and manual labour – AC] neatly complements the dominant ideology and gives it a sounding board for the subjective creation of identities in labour for all those factions [sic] above the lowest. Without this clinching inversion of the ideological order at its lowest reach in relation to the giving of labour power the system would not be stable.[18]

Willis might of course defend himself against Elsterian scepticism by citing a consequence law to the effect that anything which is functional for capitalism exists because it is so functional. In that case, observing the function would be sufficient to warrant the functionalist conclusion. He might point out that the consequence law in question is part of the Marxist theory of history, in its superstructural manifestation, so that being ready to accept such an inference helps to define a Marxist outlook, just as a sociobiological outlook is partly defined by the preparedness of a person to accept that whenever a given social practice is shown to confer reproductive advantage, this latter fact serves to explain the practice.

An Elsterian rejoinder would nevertheless be swift: first, since it is a universal tendency to relax inquiry into findings which conform to one's theoretical presuppositions, the theorist should be especially suspicious of conclusions with which she or he agrees; second, it is not the case that the relevant part of the Marxist theory of history has been established in even a few central cases beyond such shadow of a doubt as would make inescapable the extension of the relevant consequence law to cover cognate cases. If we knew for sure why the army or the judiciary were there, we would be well advised to make the same sort of argument for the teaching profession; unfortunately we don't. It would therefore follow, third, that rather than deduce specific explanations from a not-yet-founded consequence law, it would be better to consider cases, with a view perhaps to founding such a law. In the meantime, the assumptions enshrined in a general commitment to a "Marxian" style of social inquiry are liable to make one settle too quickly for bogus explanations.[19]

Elster's most insistent point is well taken: functional explanation requires more work than is sometimes devoted to it. It is not enough to point truthfully to a function phenomenon A has for phenomenon B, and think that A is thereby explained by B. But how much explanatory work is enough? How elaborate must the causal elaboration be, and was Elster right to demand that it must go all the way: to the point at which a complete causal/intentional explanation is capable of supplanting the alleged functional explanation?

Functional explanation is going to be most useful in cases in which two rather complex entities – systems, if you will – are adapting to each other, and in particular, when the less powerful entity, or perhaps it is the less stable entity, is adapting to the more powerful or stable entity. (Without some asymmetry of powerfulness, stability or whatever, there would be a set of different, functionally specialized organs complementing each other within a whole larger than the sum of its parts, but there would be no basis for functional *explanation* of one part or organ by another.)[20] If the two interacting systems are so complex that it is almost impossible to grasp all the details of their operation, then functional explanation may be the only plausible resort, so that in demanding a full causal elaboration, one is essentially demanding much more than is reasonable to expect, and cutting off the only possibility one has of some kind of explanation, unsatisfactory as that explanation may be by the standard of full causal specification. This, at least, is one pragmatic line of defence of functional explanation, which I will regard as the *weak* defence.

A more principled line of defence of functional explanation is that the causal sequence can occur at too low a level of abstraction, so that functional explanation might remain superior to any particular causal explanation because it allows for the existence of functionally equivalent microscopic causal sequences leading to the macroscopic entity which is being explained. This I will regard as the *strong* defence. The strong defence maintains that while it may be true that any minutely specified causal sequence establishes a "why" through establishing a how, it need not succeed in establishing the "why" we want: the "really why". The finest grain of explanation need not be the best. Take, for example, the explanation of why I have written the previous sentence. Granting materialism, my neurons, or some of them (not enough, no doubt), were firing away creating the thought which another bunch of neurons then tried to turn into seamless prose by sending frantic messages to my writing hand. Now it is obvious that no-one will ever be able to recover the facts about the causal micro-sequence of brain states responsible for the sentence in question. It is even very unlikely that anyone will ever be able to do anything of the sort in the case of anybody else's sentences. In practice, then, one would always settle for incomplete causal chains in this domain, which means, of course, that one settles for incompleteness in any intentional account of human behaviour. The pragmatic defence of functional explanation is thus in good company, universal company, in fact.

The point, though, is whether we would really *want* such an explanation from brain states, even if we could get one. The real explanation we want for the occurrence of that sentence might be that it is there because of the luminous contribution it makes to the debate between Cohen and Elster, or because the point made in it impressed me greatly when I first heard a version of it from Graham Macdonald, and I have only just now understood what he meant. Either reason or Macdonald or both, since they are not mutually exclusive, are the real reasons why that sentence gets to be what and where it is. The conclusion, then, is that Elster's "ideal of a continuous causal chain" is not only not attainable, it is not necessarily an ideal.[21] To say of functional explanation that it falls short of something less than ideal is not an altogether telling criticism.

Recently, Elster has made a concession to the viability of functional explanation, which has served to all intents and purposes to close in Cohen's favour the debate on the question within Analytical Marxism.

What is slightly less clear is whether it is a concession to the weak or the strong defence of functional explanation. While pondering an example concerning the socially stabilizing effects of upward social mobility, Elster came to think it possible sometimes to improve upon a functional explanation with another explanation which is still functional. Elster elucidates the concession wrought from him by this new awareness as follows:[22]

> The functional explanation can be improved and still remain functional if we extend the causal chain *almost* the whole way back to the explanandum. Yet one difference between causal and functional explanation also follows. The limiting case of an improved functional explanation is a causal explanation – if the chain of consequences is extended the whole way back to the explanandum. In this sense functional explanation is, as I said, second-best.
>
> [An] answer to the question [about the admissibility of functional explanation – AC] is that for a functional explanation to be valid we must indeed provide the full feedback loop. In the light of what has just been said, *this response is excessively purist, at least on the level of principle.* I remain convinced, however, that for practical purposes [the attempt to fill in the causal story] is the only viable research strategy. In any case, it is vastly preferable to the first, naive brand of functionalism. I am not really concerned in this essay with the sophisticated defences of functionalism that have been proposed in recent years, but with the form of Marxist functionalism that has been historically important and that remains central in some quarters.

Elster says, at the end of the first cited paragraph, that functional explanation is still second best, so that it seems that he retains his enthusiasm for a complete causal account as the asymptotic ideal of functional explanation. He seems therefore to resist, not concede, the strong defence of functional explanation. This makes it a little odd for him to imply in the crucial concessionary words italicized by me in the second paragraph that the concession he has made is a concession in principle. What he means is presumably that in practice it is too purist to insist on the specification of a complete feedback mechanism, despite the advice he would still always deliver to budding research students: you have nothing to lose and a world of explanation to gain by lengthening your causal chains.

If Elster has abandoned any *principle* of explanation, it must be the principle that the *only* alternative to a functional explanation is a causal explanation. Now although this admission does not reprieve functional explanation in so many words, I think it does amount to a concession of what is most important in principle in the debate between Elster and Cohen: namely, the ability of functional explanation to stand alone in certain circumstances as legitimate explanation. For if functional explanations can be improved upon by other functional explanations in the

absence of full causal elaborations, then there are better and worse functional explanations among those without full causal elaborations, and
to be a better explanation entails being *some kind* of explanation. So
there are at least some functional explanations without full causal elaborations which are some kind of explanation. And this is all Cohen needs
to mount his defence in principle of Karl Marx's theory of history, as
Cohen reconstructs it. Since I think it is fair to construe Elster as having
made this concession in the quoted remarks, I think it fair to record
as consensual the following verdict on the theoretical status of the theory
of history:

(i) There *is* one and *only* one way in which the logic of the theory
of history can be watertightened. This is by interpreting the explanatory
claims of the theory as functional claims.[23]

(ii) It follows from (i) that if functional explanation is impermissible
explanation, then the theory of history is invalid, without any need to
consult the historical record. But functional explanation is permissible;
the objection in principle is false at the level of principle. Hence the theory
of history is not fatally weakened by being cast in the only form which
would make it logically tenable.

(iii) Functional explanation in the social (or natural) sciences is
nevertheless a difficult feat to accomplish, subject to all manner of traps
for the unwary. The traps loom especially large for Marxists because
they have especially powerful functional expectations derived from an
ambitious general theory whose central claims rely on the controversial
interpretation of a small number of historical cases.[24]

Satisfied by the conclusion of (ii) that it is possible in theory to proceed
with the functional theory of history, I hope to avoid the traps mentioned
in (iii) by raiding Brenner for the feedback mechanism in virtue of which
the functional theory of history might succeed in explaining history.[25]

Notes

1. K. Marx and F. Engels, *Manifesto of the Communist Party* (Moscow: Progress Publishers, 1953), p. 40 and pp. 48–9.
2. G.A. Cohen, *Karl Marx's Theory of History: A Defence* (Oxford: Clarendon Press,
1978) (hereafter *KMTH*); Robert Brenner "The Origins of Capitalist Development", *New
Left Review*, 104 (1977); T.H. Aston and C.H.E. Philpin, eds., *The Brenner Debate* (Cambridge: C.U.P., 1985) and the articles by both authors in John Roemer, ed., *Analytical
Marxism* (Cambridge: C.U.P., 1986). See also Claudio J. Katz, *From Feudalism to Capitalism*
(New York: Greenwood Press, 1989).
3. Brenner's work is an early example of the shift detected by Graham Crow, "The
Use of the Concept of 'Strategy' in Recent Sociological Literature", *Sociology*, 23, no.
1 (1989), and pursued relentlessly in the present book.
4. This paragraph condenses much discussion in *KMTH* Chapters 2 and 4 and refers

in its last clause to the more restricted construal of the superstructure pursued by Cohen in "Restricted and Inclusive Historical Materialism" in E. Ullmann-Margalit, ed., *The Prism of Science* (Dordrecht: D. Reidel, 1986). In Cohen's preferred usage, to say that something is part of the superstructure is to say that it is explained by what is structural. So the question is not "what explains the superstructure?"; but "what is superstructural?"

5. *KMTH*, p. 198.

6. Karl Marx, *Critique of the Gotha Programme* (Peking: Foreign Languages Press, 1976), p. 17. Related passages are subject to further analysis in Sections 6.3, 10.2. and Chapter 15.

7. I am unimpressed by Roemer's view regarding the transition from feudalism to capitalism that it is too soon to tell. *Free to Lose* (London: Radius, 1988), p. 123.

8. Sean Sayers, "Marxism and the Dialectical Method: A Critique of G. A. Cohen", *Radical Philosophy*, 36 (1984), p. 11.

9. See for instance the vacuous attack made against Marxist theory by Karl Popper on p. 43 of his *Unended Quest: An Intellectual Autobiography* (Glasgow: Fontana, 1986).

10. Cohen considers three major kinds of elaboration: the purposive, the Darwinian and the Lamarckian (in *KMTH*, pp. 287–30, reprinted in *Analytical Marxism*, pp. 227–30). My understanding of functional explanation owes more than I can disentangle to my colleague Graham Macdonald, whose forthcoming book on *Special Explanations* (Oxford: Basil Blackwell) is warmly recommended to the reader. I have also derived great benefit from discussion with Paul Wetherly, Alan Carter, Mark Cowling and other contributors to the Political Science Association Marxism Specialist Group, whose collective volume is forthcoming as Wetherly, ed., *Marx and History*. Alan Carter's view of Cohen is also given in *Marx: A Radical Critique* (Brighton: Wheatsheaf, 1988) and three other recent contributions are Derek Sayer, *The Violence of Abstraction* (Oxford: Basil Blackwell, 1987); Alex Callinicos, *Making History* (Oxford: Polity Press, 1989); and S.H. Rigby, *Marxism and History* (Manchester: Manchester University Press, 1987).

11. The Elster-Cohen exchanges are contained in Elster, "Review of Cohen", *Political Studies*, 28 (1980); "Marxism, functionalism and game theory", *Theory and Society*, 11, no. 4 (1982), reprinted in Alex Callinicos, ed., *Marxist Theory* (Oxford, O.U.P. 1989); *Making Sense of Marx* (Cambridge: C.U.P., 1985) (hereafter *MSM*), esp. ch. 1; and "Further thoughts on Marxism, functionalism and game theory"; in *Analytical Marxism.*; Cohen, "Functional explanation, consequence explanation and Marxism", *Inquiry* 25 (1982); "Reply to Elster on 'Marxism, functionalism and game theory'", *Theory and Society*, 11, no. 4 (1982); and "Reply to Four Critics", *Analyse und Kritik*, 5 (1983). For an assessment see Andrew Levine, Elliott Soper and Erik Olin Wright, "The Limits of Micro-Explanation" *New Left Review*, 162 (1987). The exchanges are in part a Marxian manifestation of the debate between individualism and holism. A perspicacious account of the larger debate and a defence of a "concessive holism" which is close in spirit to Cohen's position is given by Susan James, *The Content of Social Explanation* (Cambridge: C.U.P., 1984).

12. Paul E. Willis, *Learning to Labour: How Working-Class Kids Get Working-class Jobs* (Aldershot: Gower, 1978).

13. Willis, p. 4. I have identified "Hammertown" with Birmingham.

14. Examples of leaving reports and teacher attitudes are given in Willis, p. 62 and pp. 70–71, 78.

15. "The perspective on work offered by the counter-school culture really is superior to that supplied officially by the school": Willis, p. 136 (and cf p. 145).

16. See *KMTH*, p. 260, and Elster, "Further Thoughts", in *Analytical Marxism*, pp. 202–7.

17. On the split-level outcome: "The division between conformism and non-conformism is experienced as a division between different kinds of future, different kinds of gratification, and different kinds of jobs that are relevant to these things": Willis, p. 97.

18. Willis, p. 148.

19. The debate may be pursued through Michel Foucault, *Discipline and Punish* (Harmondsworth: Penguin, 1975); R. Dale, et al., eds, *Schooling and Capitalism* (London: Routledge and Kegan Paul, 1976); Samuel Bowles and Herbert Gintis, *Schooling in Capitalist America* (London: Routledge and Kegan Paul, 1976); the contributions of John Lea and

Dario Melossi to Bob Fine et al., eds., *Capitalism and the Rule of Law* (London: Hutchinson, 1979); and Robert G. Burgess, *Sociology, Education and Schools* (London: Batsford, 1986), ch. 4.

20. This is the nub of a distinction between functionalism in the sense of a commitment to functional explanation, and functionalism in the rather inchoate sociological sense that "When all institutions are functional each is maintained as part of an ongoing system by all the other institutions": *S.V.* "Functionalism", *Macmillan Student Encyclopedia of Sociology* (London: Macmillan, 1983). For Cohen's view of the distinction, see *KMTH*, pp. 283/4 and for Graham Macdonald's see "Philosophical Foundations of Functional Sociology" in Wetherly, ed., *Marx and History*.

21. Elster, "Further Thoughts" in *Analytical Marxism*, p. 205.

22. Elster, "Further Thoughts" in *Analytical Marxism*, p. 206, emphasis added.

23. "If the intended explanations are functional ones, we have consistency between the effect of A on B and the explanation of A by B, *and I do not know any other way of rendering historical materialism consistent*": Cohen, "Forces and Relations of Production", in *Analytical Marxism*, p. 15.

24. "I do not defend the sloppy functional explanatory theorizing in which so many Marxists engage": Cohen, "Forces and Relations", p. 18. Cf. the thoroughly Elsterian warnings already contained in *KMTH*, pp. 280–3. An early and systematic discussion of the strengths and weaknesses of functional explanation was given by Philippe Van Parijs, *Evolutionary Explanation in the Social Sciences* (Totowa, N.J.: Rowman and Littlefield, 1981).

25. No one has given good answers to the [how] questions ... about historical materialism. This seems to me an important area of future research for historical materialists": Cohen, "Forces and Relations", pp. 17–18.

2

Brenner on the Transition to Capitalism

2.1 Rationality through Thick and Thin

Brenner's point of departure is not a functional, or any other, version of a general theory of history, but a general theory of action. This theory is the rational-choice theory, which is sufficiently the backbone of this book to deserve a special word of introduction.

I take it that the indispensable feature of rational-choice theory is the assumption that *actors decide what to do by applying principles of optimization to a set of alternatives for action.* In what follows, I will always assume that the actor is a single locus of decision and action. I will usually assume also that the actor is a human individual, and that any actor's preference schedule only contains arguments making reference to (dis)satisfactions gained (suffered) by the actor whose schedule it is. I regard the individualism assumption as good discipline for a sociologist and the self-interest assumption as good discipline for a socialist, but neither of these frequently made interpretations of the theory is fundamental to the theory itself, as I conceive it.[1]

So conceived, rational-choice theory is, I guess, a branch of cognitive social psychology, and rational-choice explanation is intentional not causal explanation.[2] In the case of collective agents, the intentions will be virtual intentions attributed to the collective agent. Such virtual intentions will stand in some relation to the real intentions of the human individuals who are said to comprise the collective agent. What matters, at all events, is not the character of the agent, but the character of the agent's comprehension.[3]

If, for example, it is our unacknowledged deepest passions or our genes or our unreflective habits which are urging on us a course of action which happens to be optimal, or, more interestingly, if such passions, genes or habits exist because of their propensity to generate urges which inspire optimal actions, then this is not an application of rational-choice theory in the approved sense. It may be true that one can illuminate the configurations of predators and prey in animal species by using game theory to show that their behaviour corresponds to what their best strategies would be if the animals in question were able to pursue strategies. And it would not be surprising if this were true, given that the formal apparatus of game theory deals with the logic of interacting benefits, so that the benefits might be aspects of personal or group advantage which evolution could select, rather than aspects of personal or group satisfaction which a conscious actor might be able to choose. Yet these truths, supposing they are true, do not make seagulls and snails into rational-choice actors, and a similar point applies to human psychopaths, addicts and sleep-walkers. The term "alternatives for action" is therefore understood to mean that the alternatives are in some way alternatives for the actor, and this restricts the scope of the theory, so far as I know, to certain kinds of individual or collective human agents.[4]

On the other hand, I am not sure quite how aware the agent needs to be for rational choice to have taken place. It is certainly too much to ask that the agent is continuously scanning a sharply delineated set of disjoint and exhaustive possibilities for action, with precise pay-offs attached, personal computer in hand to calculate the odds. But, from what has been said, it will be asking too little if the actor is not expected to be able to call a couple of options to mind, to be free and able to pursue more than one, to weigh their attractions and reason what is best.[5]

That the actor reaches a decision in this way is what gives the theory its predictive bite, and the optimization assumption is indispensable because it is optimization that leaves the bite-mark.[6] But what decision any given actor reaches depends on many other components of the actor's overall cognitive equipment than the ability simply to optimize. The decision will certainly depend on the preferences the actor has among the alternatives the actor finds in what Elster calls her or his or its "feasible set", just as it will depend on the composition or extent of the feasible set, and maybe the availability of special techniques of deliberation upon the content, composition or extent of the feasible set.[7] The actor's preferences may be obvious, normal, regular, idiosyncratic, bizarre, difficult to detect and so on. Whether or not you think they are a topic for rational-choice theory depends on the width of your concept of rationality: thin rational explanation takes preferences for granted, while the thicker variety inquires also into the rationality of preferences.

This distinction between thick and thin rationality can be illustrated by the first application of the theory in this book. It was claimed above, as part of Willis's alleged functional explanation of the behaviour of his Birmingham lads, that their reaction to the school had the effect of smoothing their transition from school to factory floor. Suitably unpacked, this claim means that their exposure to the school created preferences which led them to seek unskilled manual work. The theory of action is implicit, and the fact that it usually goes unnoticed suggests how close is the link we customarily make between preferences and actions.[8] Speaking thinly, the lads' action is certainly rational, because if one loves manual and hates mental labour (or at least, if one thinks one does) the optimum decision is to seek manual over mental work.

Yet it is also sensible to ask whether the preferences the lads have are irrational, for actions that would be rational ways of implementing irrational desires can hardly be described as rational actions. It is clear, in fact, that the lads' preferences were formed under a serious misapprehension about what manual work was going to be like, and in the absence to boot of any experience of either type of work.[9]

There are solid grounds, then, for thickening the concept of rationality, to embrace aspects of the process through which beliefs, wants, desires and preferences are formed and translated into intentions for action. If, to take a simple case, we think we have an optimal action in an existing feasible set, it might well be rational, on some thicker, more balanced view, to devote effort to a search for neglected possibilities, or to the critical examination of the considerations which made the chosen action seem the best action, all things considered.

Yet thickening has its disadvantages too. It is not clear that the acme of autonomy is someone who's in this sense completely thick; they may be suffering instead at the apogee of indecision. For once we bring beliefs about the world into the equation, and begin to apply pressure to the theories we hold which enable us to foresee outcomes and weigh the consequences of our actions, the demand for total thickness seems to converge on the requirement for total knowledge of the world.[10] In most but not, as we shall see, in all applications with well-defined alternatives and payoffs to the various actors, we are at least able to say what is the thin rational action for every actor.[11] But if rationality *qua* thick rationality requires a consensus on what would be the findings of a rationally grounded natural-cum-social super-science, we would be waiting for a judgement from here to Kingdom Come.

These are issues whose depths I am frankly unable to plumb but I do not think the remainder of my argument requires their resolution.[12] First, the preference schedules attributed to actors all the way up to Part V will be of a straightforward variety; they are assumed to derive from fairly basic needs for food, clothing, shelter, warmth, leisure, entertainment and so on in social contexts containing a well-known and limited number of avenues for satisfying the needs. The assumption is, for example, that people will want to seek the best means to physical survival, or that people will wish to minimize the kind of effort that almost anyone in their right mind would regard as irksome.

Much more problematic are some of those cases treated in Parts V and VI, whose topics include social discrimination based on perceptions of difference by ethnicity, gender and race.[13] Thin rationality will want to accept the discriminatory preferences without comment, and explore the logic of discriminatory behaviour, taking the preferences theoretically for granted. The effect will be to rationalize the behaviour, in the thin sense of rationality. Yet I wish to emphasize at the outset that a commitment to rational-choice styles of explanation of such states of affairs in no way implies a judgement on the ultimate rationality of those states of affairs, given a fuller, a thicker and a more balanced conception of what rationality might be.[14]

2.2   The Logic of the Class Situation

In Brenner's world view, all actors are thin rational, but they do not all do the same thing, because they are in different situations, which open different opportunities and offer different constraints to their actions. In particular, they are in different class situations, given by the different relationships they have to forces of production. In each class situation, the rational-choice logic demands a different response, so that one understands the class specificity of action by understanding the character of the class situation in which the action takes place. History is explicable, to the extent it is explicable, only as the outcome – the resultant – of such class specific action of all the relevant class-situated actors, extending no doubt over considerable numbers of actors, periods of time and regions of geography.[15]

Brenner's actors are also conservative, in that their overriding aim is usually conceived to be the preservation of their existing class position. Brennerian persons therefore act rationally when they act in the best way to preserve their respective class positions, given the options made available to them by their respective class situations. If what it is rational to do depends in this way on the class situation of the actor, it will be helpful to rough out next the Marxist view of what distinguishes class situations – for what history records will vary with the distribution of such class situations, according to this theory.

It has been established by Cohen that the two key taxonomic variables of Marxian class situations involve the amount of ownership possessed by direct producers of the two sorts of basic item which comprise the forces of production – namely labour-power and means of production. The degrees of ownership of each sort of item are confined to three – namely ownership of *all*, *some* or *none* of the amount of that item the direct producer must set to work to acquire the wherewithal to provide the direct producers' means of life.[16] It follows that there are nine possible configurations for the class situation of the direct producer, given the analytical independence of the two variables concerned with the ownership respectively of labour-power and means of production.

Yet some of these nine possibilities – five, according to Cohen – describe either incoherent conjunctions of powers of possession or are of transitional or marginal practical importance. In particular, the ownership of labour-power enjoys a certain priority, in that a slave without effective control over her or his person, and therefore her or his labour-power, which is an aspect of the person, cannot coherently be said to have effective control over means of production, because one needs some degree of control over oneself before one can control anything besides oneself. This and the other deletions set aside, there remain four principal class situations for the direct producer, furnished with their equivalent and more familiar names as follows: ownership of all of both labour-power and means of production = independent producer; all labour-power and no means of production = proletarian; some labour-power and some means of production = serf; none of either labour-power or means of production = slave.

This is a taxonomy of class situations, yet it converts readily into a taxonomy of class *relations*. Ownership, in the list just given, refers to control over what the direct producers must set to work to provide for their own means of life. The direct producers have probably always constituted a majority of the population, and historically they have of course constituted the overwhelming majority. If the direct producers own less than all they need of either kind of force of production, this has to be because some minority group of non-producers owns what the producers lack.[17] By printing the taxonomy in the negative, so to speak, one finds as the obverse of the proletarian a non-producer who owns all the means of production but none of anyone's (anyone else's) labour-power: viz the capitalist. Similarly, the feudal lord and the slave owner are the counterparts of the serf and the slave. In these cases, the definition of the situation of the direct producer is sufficient to define a class relationship, and a society with class division: capitalism, feudalism, slavery.[18]

In the case of the independent producer, the negative is blank, photo-metaphorically, because there is no deficit of ownership from what the producers need to sustain the producers' life. This is what it means to be independent. In this case, we can say that there is a class society, but it is a one-class society: a class society without a class division. The

reason for adopting this terminology is that the members of the one-class
society all hold exclusive sway over all the productive forces they need
as individuals, or perhaps family units, but the quantity of forces of production each unit possesses obviously comprises only a small part of
the total resources of labour-power and means of production of the whole
society.[19] There is private ownership, in the sense of exclusive ownership,
and a property distribution in the society among a large number of separate property-owning units. However these are all alike, and in that sense
components of the same class, in that each unit has enough of all the
kinds of property it needs to survive on its own resources.

This arrangement is different in principle from a set-up in which there
is collective ownership of all the resources of the society by everyone
in the society, and it is this latter condition which corresponds to classless-
ness. As Cohen patiently explains, there are two senses of part-ownership
of a thing: the first sense, deployed in the taxonomy given above, is that
a part-owner has exclusive control over part of the thing; the second
sense, useful in the definition of a classless society, is that a part-owner
has part control over the whole of the thing.[20] The taxonomy refers to
the first sense of partial ownership: when feudal lords and serfs are defined
as having some ownership of both the labour-power and the means of
production that must be set to work to ensure the survival of the serf,
it is not because lord and serf have equal voting rights in the management
of a collective farm, but because the farm is divided into two, and each
of the two parties enjoys exclusive control over one of its parts: the lord
lords it over the lord's domain and the serf serfs it over the serf's plot.

The whole taxonomy, in short, is based on a concept of private, in
the sense of exclusive, ownership – and one should not imagine that private
ownership, in this sense of private, is confined to capitalism. It also follows
that public, in the sense of collective, ownership is not yet covered by
the theory. I return in Part IV to the vexed question of what the distinctions
between private and public ownership might be, and it will turn out,
unsurprisingly, that the current "highly idealized" taxonomy is a first
approximation only, though a sound one, to a much greater variety of
possible relations of ownership.[21]

Since sets of ownership relations just are "economic structures" in Marxian parlance (construing ownership as "effective control"), this cursory
taxonomy of ownership relations describes the main varieties of jam in
the Marxian sandwich of technological base/economic structure/political
and ideological superstructure. Given Brenner's methodological commitments, and the acceptance of such a Marxian taxonomy of economic
structure, his approach to the question of the transition between feudalism
and capitalism implies the development of two standard models, dealing
respectively with the interacting logic of the class situations of feudal

classes and of capitalist classes – that is, of rational actors placed in the "typical" situations of lord and peasant on the one hand and of capitalist and worker on the other.

Consider the model of capitalism first. Capitalism is, as the taxonomy says, characterized above all by wage labour free in the double, ironic sense used by Marx: the proletarian is free of means of production (because owning none) and free to supply labour-power (because owning all).[22] How then does this producer attain the means of life? According to the assumptions envisaged by the model for the ordinary operation of capitalism, the proletarian is unable to expropriate the capitalist's means of production. All the proletarian is left to do is either to hire out her labour-power (she continuing to own it) or rent the means of production which continue to be owned by the capitalist.

The fact that the proletarian thus has two symmetrical options of going to market has rarely been noticed by Marxists and hardly ever appreciated by them. The question is raised directly by Roemer's work, as we will see in Chapter 5. At the moment we pursue the argument, as Brenner does implicitly, on the usual Marxist assumption that the proletarian has no alternative but to hire out her labour-power for a wage. In this line of thought, it is characteristic of capitalism, indeed a consequence of the existence of capitalist relations of production, that labour-power becomes a commodity, and this helps to explain why capitalism is associated historically with an efflorescence of commodity exchange outshining all previous regimes of production, none of which compel their direct producers to join the labour market.[23]

Yet this dependence of the direct producer on the market, important though it is, is exceeded in importance for Brenner by the dependence of the capitalist productive unit on the market or, rather, the markets – the market for its output as well as for its inputs, including its labour input. According to Brenner, the logic of the class situations of all actors under capitalism is to economize, because failures to economize will eventually lead to failures in bringing the product to market at competitive prices. This insistent pressure to economize in Brenner's view generates a systematic tendency within capitalism to *specialize* production, to *accumulate* resources in the productive unit and to introduce technological *innovation*.

Specialization occurs because of the economic advantages of the division of labour both within and between productive units, made possible by the extension of market relations. This point is Adam Smith's. It applies to the management of the productive unit, including its taste for the specialization of labour, and it also applies to the wage labourers themselves, whose failures to adapt their labour-power to the demands of the market will leave them out of a job. Under capitalism, all actors

are forced to specialize because no one can afford not to do whatever
they are best placed to do by talent, skill, geographical location, climate,
access to raw materials and so on. It is not just that there are mutual
advantages to every actor trading on their strengths in this way (mutual
advantage from given situation is the very basis of commodity exchange);
the point is that trade forces actors to trade on their strengths in this
way, for there is, under the economic structure of capitalism, no salvation
outside the market place.

Capitalist actors likewise accumulate because in the market place one
must run to stand still; to guarantee one's position, one must invest,
and one must accumulate last week to invest this week in order to secure
the return for next week. (This is true everywhere except contemporary
Britain. In Britain one lives on last week and hopes this week that somehow
something will turn up for next week.) And actors innovate because this
is the only way to get their retaliation in first, to keep one jump ahead
of the competition. But the more you innovate the more you need to
accumulate, given the need to invest in the technology required in many
fields to raise productivity so as to give the productive unit the edge
it needs to sustain its presence in the markets for its products.

In short, and in keeping both with what Marx said loud and clear,
and with something that the functional theory of history in one of its
parts requires to be true, capitalism is a system of class relations that
especially fosters the development of the forces of production. According
to the form-content metaphor, it is a social form whose inner logic involves
the restless transformation of its material content.[24]

This link between capitalist economic structure and technological development is so important to Brenner's case that it deserves a full quotation
in Brenner's words, a title and a section of its own.

2.3 Brenner's Axiom

Only where labour has been separated from possession of the means of production, and where labourers have been emancipated from any direct relation
of domination (such as slavery or serfdom), are both capital and labour-power
"free" to make *possible* their combination at the highest possible level of technology. Only where they are free, will such combination appear *feasible* and *desirable*. Only where they are free will such combination be *necessitated*. Only
under conditions of free wage labour will the individual producing units (com-
bining labour power and the means of production) be forced to sell in order
to buy, to buy in order to survive and reproduce, and ultimately to expand
and innovate in order to maintain the position in relationship to other competing
productive units. Only under such a system, where both capital and labour

power are thus commodities – and which was therefore called by Marx "generalized commodity production" – is there the necessity of producing at the "socially necessary" labour time in order to survive, and to surpass this level of productivity to ensure continued survival.[25]

Brenner's Axiom, then, is that (short of socialism) *capitalist economic structure is necessary and sufficient for technological development*. Such technological development leads in turn to "development", in the larger modern sense which exists in contrast with "underdevelopment". I consider the sufficiency claim, which depends on the performance of capitalism, before the necessity claim, which depends on the non-performance of non-capitalism. Why then does capitalism promote the development of the forces of production? I think it is fair to say that the answer seems obvious to Brenner: the class situations of capitalist actors are such that specialization, accumulation and innovation are the rational responses. We observe these responses occurring in capitalism, and they occur because they are rational. For Brenner, the thin rational construal of the axiom is almost as axiomatic as the axiom itself.

I now show that the question is not so easily settled, by displaying four distinct readings of the sufficiency claim of Brenner's Axiom, only two of which are compatible with the position I have just attributed to Brenner as his obvious answer to the question I have raised. This will certainly clarify Brenner's argument (and may even strengthen it).

The four readings are presented in ascending order of rational-choice-ness. They offer variant interpretations of why capitalist actors are "forced" to undertake the capitalist activities of specialization, accumulation and innovation. They are, in order, the pure functionalist reading, the augmented functionalist reading, the historical rational-choice reading and the transhistorical rational-choice reading.

(1) *The pure functionalist reading*

In the first reading, actors are forced by the market relations of capitalism to specialize, accumulate and innovate because any actors who (which) have survived in the market must have specialized, accumulated and innovated in order to have survived. But the actions which had ensured their survival might have been inspired by luck, short-sightedness, pig-headedness or caprice. In that case, the idea of being "forced by the market", is a shorthand expression for a macroscopic process of social selection performed by the market, a process which envisages a functional explanation, not a rational-choice explanation, for the observed tendency of capitalist actors to specialize, accumulate and innovate.[26]

(2) *The augmented functionalist reading*

A second meaning of "forced by the market" is that actors are required by the market to act as if they were rational, whether or not particular actors do in fact act rationally, so that one can reliably predict what happens in market systems, especially over the long run, on the assumption that actors are acting rationally. In particular, since capitalist survival requires cost-effective specializations, accumulations and innovations, and since rational-choice theory would enable a person facing capitalist constraints to work out in advance what specializations, accumulations and/or innovations would tend to minimize costs, surviving capitalist actors must have acted more or less as rational actors would have acted in the same circumstances.

Rational-choice theory is here being deployed as a technical adjunct to a functional explanation, helping the theorist to make out what behaviour the market is liable to select by identifying what is functional for capitalism, and helping to identify thereby what patterns of specialization and so on a functional explanation would have to explain. This auxiliary, diagnostic role for rational-choice theory is similar to the role it might play in evolutionary theory, although here there is the added subtlety that the theory is auxiliary to action whose protagonists are sufficiently unlike seagulls and snails to be capable, one assumes, of rational choice (whether or not they indulge their capability). Capitalist actors might be rational actors, and are moreover forced by the market to act as if they were rational actors, without having to be rational actors. True, one might as well assume for some purposes that these capitalist actors are rational actors, but the fact remains that particular capitalist acts, though rational, may not have come about through rational action.[27]

(3) *The historical rational-choice reading*

A third reading of the axiom, which crosses the Rubicon into the domain of rational-choice explanation proper, is given by the idea that capitalist actors are acting with the requisite degree of consciousness, aware that they must find the best way to specialize, accumulate and innovate in order to survive under capitalism, but that this consciousness – call it the "market mentality" – is a cultural artefact of capitalist relations of production.[28] Because the only way to survive under capitalism is (in this view) to have a market mentality, all surviving capitalist actors possess the mentality in virtue of which they act in a manner explicable by rational-choice theory. It is not that capitalism forces a choice upon them, but it does cause them to be choosers.

This is a deeper claim than that there might be functional explanation of preferences, followed up with rational-choice explanation of action taking place on the basis of those preferences. It is rather a claim for a functional, sociological explanation of why it is that in a certain social domain – namely the market place – "economic" action occurs which "economic" theory is able to predict; a domain in which "each looks only to his own advantage", where Bentham *therefore* reigns.[29] In this domain, there is genuine rational-choice explanation of action, but functional explanation of what makes a rational-choice explanation appropriate.

This reading evidently delimits the pretensions of rational-choice theory and confines its application to a particular social domain – the market place – and therefore to a particular historical era – capitalism (granted the intimate connection noted between the market and capitalism).

This restriction will be congenial to those Marxists who are impressed by Marx's critique of commodity fetishism, those who find problematic the bourgeois subject and, of course, those who are fundamentally opposed to the market as a possible instrument of socialism. They will be joined by those Weberians who would limit the pretensions of utilitarianism for quite different reasons, seeing the "economic" behaviour in question not as a socially selected consequence of ownership structures and market relations, but as one expression of a largely unexplained drift towards rationalization inherent in Western culture.

Clearly, the restriction posited by this third reading will not restrict the application of the theory within the domain of capitalism and markets, so that Brenner's rational-choice explication of the claim that capitalism is sufficient for the development of the forces of production will not suffer at the hands of the restriction. Neither does the restriction embarrass Roemer's rational-choice theory of class division discussed in Part II, in so far as the theory applies to markets and capitalism.[30] But the third reading is not good enough for Brenner's claim that capitalism is *necessary* for the development of the forces of production. As Brenner formulates it, that claim requires:

(4) *The transhistorical rational-choice reading*

In this reading of the Axiom, which is fairly clearly the one intended by Brenner, capitalist actors are forced to act capitalistically, because actors are rational and capitalist acts are just what you get when you place rational actors in capitalist situations.[31] It seems that it is the situation which "forces" the behaviour, given a rational orientation to the situation; although the converse locution is equally available, it appears to me – that the actor chooses the behaviour, given the situation. The important point, though, is that according to the fourth reading *the actor is a rational actor independently of social context.* In the third reading, the socio-historical context created the actors, whereas the fourth reading requires the existence of a quasi-universal person, floating free, and ready to be plugged in as a constant component within different social contexts.

Brenner requires this transhistorical concept of the rational actor, because (i) his argument that capitalism is necessary to technological development depends on his claim that non-capitalism, so feudalism, cannot promote technological development; (ii) this conclusion is held to follow from his rational-choice model of feudalism; and (iii) the applicability of rational choice to feudal circumstances evidently requires that the applicability of rational-choice models not be restricted to either capitalism or the market domain. Brenner's defence of his Axiom requires the transhistorical reading of the Axiom, in sum, because that defence relies upon a rational-choice model of feudalism, which I proceed forthwith to examine.[32]

2.4   The Logic of Feudalism

Feudalism is characterized by a division of ownership in both labour-power and means of production between a non-producing class of feudal lords and a producing class of peasants tied to the land in the double sense of not being free to leave it and of not being easy to free from it; by a level of agricultural productivity therefore sufficient to support a non-producing class; by a relatively low level of penetration of market relationships into the agricultural economy; and by a decentralized political structure – Anderson's "parcellization of sovereignty".[33] The key difference from capitalism is that because none of the feudal actors is dependent on the market, none of them is subject to the logic which applies to actors who are dependent on the market – the logic of specialization, accumulation and innovation.

In particular, it is not rational for peasants to specialize their agricultural output, when markets are unreliable in respect of inputs and/or unreliable in respect of outputs. If markets are unreliable in respect of inputs it will be a foolish peasant household which will depend on the market to supply itself with essential means of production at prices it may not be able to afford. If markets are unreliable in respect of outputs, it will be a foolish household which will concentrate production in a line of agricultural produce that has to be sold at a good price in order to provide the wherewithal to purchase all the extra things the family is no longer producing because it has already committed its production to the line of produce in which it is specializing.[34] It is rational to specialize only after markets in basic products have become very reliable. But the development of reliable markets is a consequence of capitalism, including the increase in agricultural productivity which is (will be) a consequence of the capitalist tendency to specialize, accumulate and innovate. The preoccupation of the pre-capitalist peasant with self-sufficiency is not therefore an irrational prejudice; it is a rational adjustment to the peasant's class situation, at the general level of development achieved in a feudal, or other type of pre-capitalist, economy.

If the feudal peasant is not drawn by circumstances to engage in the syndrome of specialization, accumulation and innovation which leads to economic growth and development, then neither is the feudal lord. Although the feudal lord is a social animal with a considerable appetite for surplus produce, the form in which the surplus occurs creates a quite different structure of incentives for the feudal lord than for the agricultural capitalist.

As Brenner construes the feudal class relationship, the fact that there is an exploiting class (which requires productivity to be beyond a certain level), together with the fact that peasants enjoy direct access to their means of subsistence, implies that the peasantry must be *forced* to support the landlord class. No rational peasant class will give away what it is not required to give away, so if it does yield up a surplus which supports a lordly ruling group it must have been made to yield up the surplus by a coercive political system, a regime which is extra-economic in the sense that it does not operate via the market place.[35] (The phrase "extra-economic" identifies the "economic" with "the market".)

Seen in this light, the feudal system really is a protection racket: the landlord classes batten upon a peasantry which would rather be, and is quite capable of being, independent and self-sufficient, the landlords imposing by main force the part-ownership of the peasants' labour-power and means of production in virtue of which the landlords extract the landlords' revenue.[36] This is the special structure of exploitation better characterized as extortion, in that the would-be exploiter creates the adverse situation for the victim to which the victim's rational response is to comply with the extortionate demand.[37] Faced with a determined highwayman, it is better to give up one's money than one's life; and Marxism has often pictured the feudal system as daylight robbery.

The difficulty with this conception of the feudal class relation is that it seems to make the lords' ownership of (their parts of) the forces of production depend in an exceptional way on the unstabilized application of force – it is as if there is superstructural endorsement only for non-feudal ruling classes. Cohen expresses an alternative view in a complaint against a similar formulation to Brenner's put forward by Hilton:

[Hilton's] statement suggests that the serf is in secure control of his plot *indepen-*

dently of his fulfilment of his obligations to his lord. This is, however, untrue, since "the direct producer is not the owner, but only the possessor" of his personal plot. The rights he enjoys over it are tied to his performance of his duties: his enjoyments and obligations constitute a synthesis, neither part of which explains the other, contrary to what Hilton implies. The serf does not have burdens forcibly laid upon him *because* he controls his own little territory: they come with the territory.[38]

In this view, the structure of rights and duties, considered as a whole, is superstructural: it is what helps to stabilize feudalism. Indeed, it will be explained according to historical materialism by this stabilizing function it has. To conceive of feudalism simply as a protection racket is to miss this indispensable secret of its success.[39]

This account is markedly different from Brenner's. The difference is potentially troublesome, but I think there are at least two ways the two accounts can be reconciled. The first path of reconciliation pays attention to the specific character of feudal ownership relations.[40]

We are dealing in this period with a very peculiar form of rent. There is very little in the way of direct lease and contract. We have instead a theoretically fixed, but actually fluctuating, structure of customary rights and obligations that define landholding arrangements. These specify in the first place the regular (ostensibly fixed) payments to be made by the peasant to the lord in order to retain his land. But they often lay down, in addition, a further set of conditions of landholding: the lord's right to impose additional extraordinary levies (tallages and fines); the peasant's right to use, transfer and inherit the land; and finally, the very disposition of the peasant's own person, in particular his freedom of mobility.

What is peculiar about feudal ownership, then, is the latitude it allows to the feudal lord. This is an important part of what it means to say that the political and economic levels are inseparable under feudalism. It is implied by saying that not just power but *sovereignty* is parcelled out. The feudal lord enjoys a structure of rights which allows the lord to use coercive force, if need be, to vary the terms of the economic exchange between the classes. There is not therefore a simple counterposition of coercion with consent, but a distinction in the first instance among the coercive methods available to the lord between rightful and unrightful means of coercion. So if one freezes feudalism at a moment in time, the existence of coercion is quite compatible with a superstructural stabilization of property relations, and one would expect this superstructurally guaranteed latitude of lordly behaviour to lead to various levels of coercive practice, varying with the demands and incentives on the lords to optimize their surpluses in a given conjuncture.

Yet the peasants need not always take this lying down, and "the very distribution of ownership of the land between landlord and peasant was continually in question throughout the [medieval and early modern] period".[41] There is a struggle not only within the rules, about the distribution of the product between lord and peasant, but about the rules – a struggle which may, of course, be a struggle to change the rules in connection with a struggle to achieve a better outcome for one's own side under the rules. In this case, and especially in the longer term, Cohen's "synthesis" of rights and duties is a movable feast, and the role of coercion is not so much to implement rights of lords under the existing rules, with whatever latitude the rules allow, but to change the point of balance of rights and duties of one or other of the two sides within the existing synthesis.

The second path of reconciliation between Brenner and Cohen is thus to view the evolution of the exact synthesis which constitutes feudal relations of property as the result partly of coercive measures, not all necessarily extra-legal coercive measures.[42] Taken far enough in favour of the peasants, this process of adjusting feudal obligations can take the synthesis beyond feudalism altogether, and there may come a point in time, signalled by a sharp decline in the coercive latitude enjoyed *de facto* and *de jure* by the feudal lords, at which the peasants have achieved a structure of rights and powers akin to modern private property in land as well as effective powers of possession of their peasant persons. "Serfdom can be said to end only when the lords' right and ability to control the peasantry, *should they desire to do so*, has been terminated."[43]

Short of this eventuality, which historically just is the transition from feudalism to ... whatever follows feudalism ..., feudal lords retain the options which, according to Brenner, incline them, no less than their serfs, against a systematic development of agricultural productivity. Peasants don't specialize, accumulate or innovate; and neither do their lords. Instead, as, or if, the lordly consumption demands intensify, lords will optimize the agricultural surplus *product*. They can do this *intensively*, by taking full advantage of the latitude allowed by feudal relations of production to raise the level of exactions from their existing peasantry (or by exceeding this latitude with the use of legal or extra-legal coercion). Alternatively, the lords can increase their revenues *extensively*, by increasing the number of peasants under their control. The latter strategy is an option because of the decentralized, and somewhat unstable, political relations between lords (i.e. within the feudal ruling class). Lords will not specialize and innovate, nor systematically accumulate; instead they will militarize and expropriate.

It is true that there are other actors within the general run of feudal societies who are dependent on market relations, merchants being the prime example. But their efforts will not transform the situation unless they can induce the peasants to specialize their agricultural output. There may be long-distance trade on a large scale in physical surpluses, but this doesn't by itself touch the heart of the feudal economy, so long as both lords and peasants retain the option and the incentive to remain aloof from the market. And would-be specializers and entrepreneurs – e.g. those prepared to take the risk of cash crop production – are frustrated because most of the existing supply of their principal means of production – land – is already occupied for different purposes.

It follows, according to Brenner, that there is no automatic transition from either independent peasant production or a feudal class system to capitalist social relations. Indeed, the logic of the class situation of both peasants and lords is to *inhibit* technological development. What is required for capitalism to come into being is a class of direct producers already deprived of land, and a ruling group which can only survive through *economic* competition – a group that is profit-making rather than empire-building: an "economic" rather than a "political" ruling class. The fact that capitalism would make for economic development if it existed is not sufficient to bring about the existence of capitalism, especially given the fact that there is no-one within feudalism with the capacity and incentive to promote economic development. Quite the reverse, the major actors' capacities and incentives all lie in the reproduction of feudal relationships and concomitant economic stagnation.

The immediate intention of this argument of Brenner's is to clinch what I have identified as Brenner's Axiom: capitalism is necessary as well as sufficient for economic development, because neither feudalism, nor by implication any other of capitalism's pre-capitalist competitors, is capable of sustaining economic development.[44]

Once secured, the Axiom can be pressed into the service of Brenner's main purpose, the refutation of Adam Smith's explanation for the origins of development. According to Brenner, Smith's "fundamental proposition" is "that the rise of a trade-based division of labour will determine economic development through the growth of specialization and thereby the productivity of labour."[45] Brenner's rejoinder, making fundamental use of his Axiom, is that the spread of the market, in the sense of its growth in scale or geographical dispersion, is not sufficient to set in train the complex sequences of changes we know as economic development. It is only once productive units are dependent on the market and labour-power has become a commodity that the rational incentives of all the class actors lie in directions conducive to economic development.[46] To explain capitalist development, as Smith and all subsequent Smithians do, by the spread of the market is to put the cart before the horse. One has to explain first how capitalism comes about as a system of class relations which then has the effect, given rational behaviour in the context of markets, of promoting technological progress. And no hope of this explanation is to be found within feudalism itself, because the historical tendency of feudal relations lies neither in the transition to a capitalism which will promote technical progress nor in the promotion of technical progress on its own account.

Notes

1. The unitary actor assumption probably is indispensable, because it is probably entailed by the concept of optimization. It is also problematic in practice, although less so than it might be once it has been understood that the actor only needs to be unitary with respect to the social domain in which the theory is applied. This should disarm a criticism of rational-choice theory made by Barry Hindess, *Choice, Rationality and Social Theory* (London: Unwin Hyman, 1988), p. 89. In regarding the individualism assumption as dispensable I have distanced myself somewhat from Elster, and the way I described the distinctive presupposition of "Rational-choice Marxism" in *New Left Review*, 160 (1986), p. 26–7, now in Mark Cowling and Lawrence Wilde, eds, *Approaches to Marx* (Milton Keynes: Open University Press, 1989), p. 187. The idea that the self-interest assumption is indispensable to rational-choice theory is refuted by, for example, Michael Taylor's application of the theory to altruists in *The Possibility of Cooperation*, (Cambridge: C.U.P., 1987), ch. 5.

2. I have no wish to take part in the philosophical debate whether or how mental items like intentions and desires can bring into being other mental items or physical actions, so if intentional explanation is counted as a special variety of causal explanation, I mean that rational-choice explanation is not non-intentional causal explanation.

3. Hindess, p. 103, seems to criticize Elsterian methodological individualism for refusing to accept the existence of collective actors; he next suggests that even if Elster recognized the existence of collective actors, rational-choice theory would not be appropriate because "the decisions of corporations and other social actors should not be seen as the products of unitary consciousness" and then goes on to doubt that human individuals are unitary either, so concluding that the theory applies to them hardly any more than corporations. The point (see note 1) surely is that the actor must be unitary within the context of the action being explained, and that it is an empirical matter to what extent individual or collective actors qualify as sufficiently unitary. There are general grounds for thinking either that collective actors are less unitary (because they are bigger, physically dispersed and require coordination of a kind that a single mind does not) or that they are more unitary (because they are able to develop specialized monitoring and calculating departments, and unity-promoting, sanction-backed social norms which are the collective counterpart of unity-promoting conceptions of self for the individual – the superego of the firm). So in general I see no good reason to believe that rational-choice theory is more or less applicable to collective agents than individual agents.

4. These considerations are introduced to uphold a rather elementary distinction wilfully suppressed by Pierre L. van den Berghe: "The utilitarian choice model works with or without consciousness. Behaviour can be maximizing without being rational. Choice can be unconscious". See "Ethnicity and the sociobiology debate" in John Rex and David Mason, *Theories of Race and Ethnic Relations* (Cambridge: C.U.P., 1986), p. 260 and cf. Robert Axelrod, *The Evolution of Cooperation*, (New York: Basic Books, 1984) for similarly cavalier extensions of game theory to cover biology.

5. I do not regard as a compelling objection to rational-choice theory Hindess' p. 70 example that "I brush my teeth every morning but I do not normally calculate whether it is in my best interests to do so". The reason I don't make the calculation every morning

whether it is worth brushing my teeth is presumably my guess that I would get the same answer every morning. Habitual behaviour is not necessarily irrational behaviour. Shirley Dex makes the same point in an excellent survey of "The use of economists' models in sociology" in *Ethnic and Racial Studies*, 8, no. 4 (1985), p. 527.

6. The indispensability of the optimization assumption is thus tied to the falsifiability of the theory.

7. Elster, *Making Sense of Marx* (Cambridge: C.U.P., 1985) (hereafter *MSM*), p. 9. For "styles of reasoning" see Hindess, ch. 5, which considerably refines an idea floated in Anthony Cutler et al., *Marx's "Capital" and Capitalism Today*, vol. 2 (London: Routledge and Kegan Paul, 1978), Part II.

8. Elster distinguishes thin rationality from a broader rationality I am calling thick in *Sour Grapes* (Cambridge: C.U.P., 1983), p. 1.

9. Thick rationality "involves more than acting consistently on consistent beliefs and desires: we also require that the beliefs and desires be rational in a more substantive sense. It is not too difficult to spell out what this means in the case of beliefs. Substantively rational beliefs are those which are grounded in the available evidence: they are closely linked to the notion of judgment. It is more difficult to define a corresponding notion of a substantively rational desire. One way of approaching the problem is by arguing that autonomy is for desires what judgment is for belief, and this is how I shall in the main proceed": *Sour Grapes*, pp. 1–2. The distinction between thin and thick rationality is not the same as Graham Macdonald and Philip Pettit's distinction between behavioural and attitudinal rationality, upon which Hindess often relies. Behavioural rationality matches intentions appropriately with actions, while attitudinal rationality requires mutual consistency among beliefs and desires. See *Semantics and Social Science* (London: Routledge and Kegan Paul, 1981). Attitudinal and behavioural rationality are thus best regarded as the two dimensions of Elster's thin rationality. Thin rational choice is finally a subset of thin rational decision-making because not all consistent reasons for actions are optimizing reasons for actions.

10. Hindess, p. 86, criticizes the assumption that "action follows from belief and desire in much the same way that the conclusion of an argument follows from its premisses". This criticism makes the room for those different styles of deliberation which Hindess is fond of interposing between preferences and actions.

11. An exception is the Chicken game analysed in Section 11.1.

12. I can recommend two local plumbers: on the general problem see Richard Lindley, *Autonomy* (Basingstoke: Macmillan, 1986) and for a remarkable discussion of the formation of preferences undistorted by power, see David West, *Authenticity and Empowerment* (Hemel Hempstead: Harvester Wheatsheaf, 1990).

13. Gender discrimination in the labour market may well lie in the immediate background of the exchange model of the household discussed in Chapter 7, but the mechanism of discrimination is not a central concern there.

14. The charge that the application of rational-choice theory tends either to rationalize or to marginalize the problem of racism is made against Michael Banton's rational-choice theory of ethnic and racial competition by M.G. Smith, John Rex and Ralph Fevre in their independent contributions to "Rational Choice Revisited", *Ethnic and Racial Studies*, 8, no. 4 (1985), pp. 491, 559, and 576. I do not accept for a moment that Banton is guilty as charged, but I recognize that Banton might have made clearer the point I am here trying to clarify.

15. I am indebted to personal correspondence with Perry Anderson for the title of this section as an apt description of Brenner's general approach.

16. G.A. Cohen, *Karl Marx's Theory of History: A Defence* (Oxford: Clarendon Press, 1978), pp. 65–9 (hereafter *KMTH*). The words of this sentence are carefully chosen: the quantities of forces of production the direct producer must command for the purposes of the definition may exceed the quantity of forces of production necessary to produce the producers' means of life. In a class-divided society, the direct producer must produce a surplus destined for the dominant class in order to get the wherewithal for the producer's own survival. Subordinate producers must in a sense have access to more resources than they need.

17. Determining the proportions of producers to non-producers in a modern society is a controversial business, and it is conceivable that the producers are in a minority. The historical issue cannot however be in any doubt.

18. *KMTH*, p. 69.

19. The one-class/classless terminology is taken from C.B. Macpherson, *The Life and Times of Liberal Democracy* (Oxford: O.U.P., 1977), p. 12.

20. *KMTH*, pp. 63–4.

21. *KMTH*, p. 68, and cf. p. 65, n. 2. And from the horse's mouth: "Private property, as the antithesis to social, collective property, exists only where the means of labour and the external conditions of labour belong to private individuals. But according to whether those private individuals are workers or non-workers, private property has a different character. The innumerable different shades of private property which appear at first sight are only reflections of the intermediate situations which lie between the two extremes": K. Marx, *Capital*, vol. I (Harmondsworth: Penguin Books, 1976), p. 927. The idea that private and public systems of property can be arranged on a single dimension is found wanting in Chapter 9.

22. *Capital*, I, pp. 272–3, repeated almost verbatim on p. 874.

23. "Had we gone further, and inquired under what circumstances all, or even the majority of products take the form of commodities, we should have found that this only happens on the basis of one particular mode of production, the capitalist one": *Capital*, I, p. 273.

24. "The matter or content of society is nature, whose form is the social form": *KMTH*, p. 98. Cf. "everlasting uncertainty and agitation distinguish the bourgeois epoch from all earlier ones": K. Marx and F. Engels, *The Communist Manifesto* (Moscow: Progress Publishers, 1953), pp. 45–6.

25. Brenner, "The Origins of Capitalist Development", *New Left Review*, 104 (1977), p. 32 (hereafter "Origins").

26. A good case in point is the functional explanation of the size of capitalist enterprise due to economies of scale. See *KMTH*, pp. 280–81 and 288, and cf. James, *The Content of Social Explanation* (Cambridge: C.U.P., 1984), p. 174.

27. "There may be rational *conduct* even in the absence of rational *motive*": Schumpeter, cited in Elster, *Explaining Technical Change* (Cambridge: C.U.P., 1983), p. 115. Here is a case relevant to the Davidsonian argument, much canvassed in the literature, that the reasons which make the action rational must also be the actor's reasons for the action, if the action is to count as a rational action. See Elster, *Sour Grapes*, ch. 1, among many discussions.

28. The actors do not have to believe that they must specialize etc. *because* they live under capitalism. (They need not know anything about "capitalism".) They must nevertheless know that they *are* specializing etc. and it is a slightly open question whether they must know they are doing it to survive, rather than just for the hell of it, say. On the related theme of the connection between capitalism and individualism, see C.B. Macpherson, *The Political Theory of Possessive Individualism* (Oxford: O.U.P., 1962) and Nicholas Abercrombie, Stephen Hill and Bryan S. Turner, *Sovereign Individuals of Capitalism* (London: Allen and Unwin, 1986).

29. *Capital*, I, p. 280.

30. Roemer extends his theory backwards to feudalism and forwards to socialism, but its home base undoubtedly lies in capitalism.

31. There is at least one passage in his 1977 article which might indicate Brenner's sympathy for the third reading. At one point, he takes Adam Smith to task for "his connection of the rise of labour productivity to the *individuation of production*, and especially his attribution of a process of accumulation via innovation to individuals' *'self-interest'* manifested in 'profit maximization' and 'competition on the market'. This is how things are, 'how they really are' under capitalism. But this is only because the specific functioning of the individual components (productive units) of the system – their 'self-interest' profit maximization in order to compete on the market – is structured by the system of capitalist class relations." So it is by the end of the passage not self-interest, or even "self-interest", which is historically specific, as one might have thought from the start of the passage, but rather the system of capitalist class relations: the fourth reading has come out on top. Shortly

afterwards, Brenner confirms the transhistorical status of rationality by asking of the feudal lords, expecting the answer "No": "Does this mean that the lords were 'irrational'?"

By the time of his 1986 article, there is absolutely no doubt that we are dealing with "the rationally self-interested actions of *individual* pre-capitalist economic actors" and "the rationally self-interested action of social *classes* in pre-capitalist economies". Indeed, the assumption is rather rammed down our throats. See "Origins", pp. 37-8 and 42, and "The Social Basis of Economic Development", in John Roemer, ed., *Analytical Marxism* (Cambridge: C.U.P., 1986), p. 26 (hereafter "Social Basis"). Ellen Wood radically underestimates Brenner's attachment to rational-choice assumptions and therefore overestimates his theoretical distance from Roemer. See "Rational Choice Marxism: Is the Game Worth the Candle?", *New Left Review*, 177 (1989) and my response "In Defence of Rational Choice", *New Left Review*, 182 (1990).

The question of whether one can apply the rationality assumption within the pre-capitalist "natural economy" of the peasantry is one strand of the mainstream debate about pre-capitalist individualism, on which see Abercrombie et al., ch. 4.

32. A position intermediate between readings 3 and 4 might be the somewhat transhistorical reading: that both feudalism and capitalism create rational actors, perhaps for different reasons, but other modes of production do not. I take this possibility to be totally implausible. I likewise ignore the possibility that the Axiom is grounded in habitual action. If habits are unreflective, they fall under reading 1; if they are reflective, they fall under readings 3 or 4.

33. Perry Anderson, *Passages from Antiquity to Feudalism* (London: New Left Books, 1974).

34. Brenner, "Social Basis", p. 29. The peasant actor in the subsequent account is either an individual peasant or the peasant household considered as a unit of both production and consumption. I am not troubled by this departure from methodological individualism.

35. "In consequence of the direct producers' possession, the members of the class of exploiters (if one existed) were obliged to reproduce themselves through appropriating a part of the product of the direct producers by means of extra-economic coercion": Brenner, "Social Basis", p. 27.

36. Cf. Brenner's general characterization of classes: "Classes ... may be said to exist only where there is a surplus-extraction or property relationship in the specific sense implied here – that is, in the last analysis non-consensual and guaranteed either directly or indirectly by force." See "Agrarian Class Structure and Economic Development" in T.H. Aston and C.H.E. Philpin, eds., *The Brenner Debate* (Cambridge: C.U.P., 1985), p. 11–12, n. 4.

37. So I argue in "Exploitation, Extortion and Oppression", *Political Studies*, XXXV, no. 2 (1987), reprinted in Peter Abell, ed., *Rational Choice Theory* (Upleadon, Glos.: Edward Elgar, 1991).

38. *KMTH*, p. 84.

39. Whether this change of emphasis also changes the characterization of feudalism as extortionate is a delicate point. I think that the demands of feudal lords on peasants are still extortionate, despite the web of mutual obligations which unite them, on condition that (a) the peasants would always prefer to do less than more work to meet any given obligation and (b) there is a sufficient asymmetry in the steps the lords and peasants respectively must take to create and/or maintain either the obligations themselves or the contributions received by the lords from the peasants in satisfaction of the obligations. If condition (b) fails, feudal extortion reverts to feudal exploitation, and the reciprocal feudal obligations become analogous to the binding terms of a capitalist wage labour contract, entered into by parties who are "free" outside the terms of the contract.

40. Brenner, "Agrarian Class Structure", p. 19.

41. Brenner, "Agrarian Class Structure", p. 15.

42. For more on the distinction between property rules and the rules for changing property rules, see Chapter 9.1.

43. Brenner, "Agrarian Class Structure", p. 27.

44. Brenner deals only with feudalism. For arguments on the incompatibility of slavery with technological progress, see *KMTH*, pp. 190–2.

45. Brenner, "Origins of Capitalist Development", p. 37.

46. Brenner's response to Smith is a novel one within the Marxian tradition. Roughly speaking, if we start from the idea that Smith was correct to say that if you put capitalist people in capitalist circumstances, you get capitalist behaviour, there are two possible routes to the welcome Marxian conclusion that you don't always get capitalist behaviour. The first route is to say that you only get capitalist people under capitalist circumstances: Smith's error therefore consisting in the tacit universalization of the bourgeois conception of the human actor. Brenner's different response is that the "bourgeois" actor (alias the rational chooser) really is universal, but Smith was wrong to make capitalist behaviour (the tendency to truck and barter) universal, because rational individuals only truck and barter faced with the incentive structures provided by capitalism. Smith's error in this case lay in the tacit universalization of capitalist social relations.

The Logic of Class Struggle

3.1 Brenner contra Cohen

Joust the first

Brenner had originally entered the lists against the Smithian development theorists, including such Marxist, or Marxian, thinkers as Immanuel Wallerstein, and the Paul Sweezy of the celebrated 1950s exchange with Maurice Dobb in the pages of *Science and Society*[1]. But in a footnote of remarkable length Brenner aims the same argument as a glancing blow, clearly intended to be mortal, against Cohen's version of the theory of history. The footnote reads in part:

> One could not, I think, conceivably argue that individual pre-capitalist economic actors would seek to separate the pre-capitalist producers from their means of subsistence and break up the lord's institutionalized relationships with the producers which allowed them to extract a surplus by extra-economic compulsion in order to install a system where the individual actors had, as their rule for reproduction, the maximization of profits ... especially when such a system had never previously existed.
>
> Nevertheless, only if we could conceive of the economic actors as making such an unlikely move, could we accept the theory that the growth of the productive forces was primary in the march of history – that history was driven forward, in the last analysis, by the growth of technical knowledge and its application.[2]

Now it is true that the move Brenner describes is highly unlikely, but it is false that the unlikeliness of this move damages the theory of history, for the theory of history would be so damaged only if it were a conspiracy theory. Cohen's version of the theory does not require any conspiracy, so it is not damaged by the observation that no conspiracy exists. What the theory of history requires is the plausibility that over a long period of time new economic structures arise and persist which promote the development of forces of production, structures which (possibly) arise and (certainly) persist because they do promote that development.

A functional explanation of these phenomena does not require that anyone intends to establish the relevant structure, either for its own sake or because the existence of the structure has some consequence which it is intended to bring about (e.g. that capitalism is established because capitalism will lead to economic development). It is even unlikely that an economic structure, such as capitalism, is brought about at all, as capitalism. Something like capitalism is more plausibly the unintended outcome of independent acts of several actors, finding themselves in situations in which consenting adults tend to get engaged in capitalist acts, without anyone intending to establish the situation in which consenting adults would be likely to engage in capitalist acts, let alone intending to establish such a situation because it would lead to capitalist acts taking place. It may not even be necessary to a functional explanation that there *be* any intentional action, with or without unintentional consequences.

When the boy licked the pig that had been burned and liked the taste, it was an accident that the pig had roasted, but the roasting led to culinary innovation. What a functional explanation needs are claims of the kind: there will be pig-roastings and pig-lickings and, when there are, then there will be roughly predictable social consequences of the inevitable roasting and licking. Functional explanation does not depend on claims of the kind: the boy burned the hut, to trap the pig, to taste the flesh, to be able to institute capitalist social relations, to make a fortune running the first take-away outlet for bacon-burgers, to encourage the general development of fast food technology for the ultimate good of humankind.

Brenner regards Cohen's version of the theory of history as unsustainable because it conflicts with his own view of feudal society. I think he is able to reach this conclusion only because he apparently holds a rather facile view of what Cohen's theory involves. In the next section I make a general comparison of the two approaches before asking what light Brenner's own account of the historical transition from feudalism to capitalism throws on the theory of history, once it is fully appreciated that the theory of history deploys a functional logic of explanation.

Joust the second

Brenner is working with two ideal types: rational-choice models of pure feudalism and pure capitalism. The crucial difference between the models is that feudalism implies technological stagnation whereas capitalism implies technological development. His fundamental contention is that the tendency towards technological development under feudalism is so paltry that one could not conceive of so small a development leading to another system – capitalism – marked above all by its tendency to promote technological development.

In assessing this contention, it must be borne in mind that the respective tendencies (stagnation, development) are deduced in the first instance from the ideal typical models – models which take as given the respective social relations of feudalism and capitalism. It does not follow from the appropriateness of the two models to these contexts that an appropriate model of the transition from feudalism to capitalism simply places these two models end-to-end, so to speak, so that the only way capitalism can come about is through a tendency which is inherent in feudalism – in the sense of a tendency deducible from the ideal type of feudal relations. In fact, the ideal types are not really designed to illuminate this question as they stand because each of them treats as a premise what needs to be explained in a model of the transition – namely, the replacement of one set of social relations by another set of social relations. This is precisely what I have suggested elsewhere is the difference between special theories of each mode of production (the ideal typical models of feudalism and capitalism) and the general theory of history.[3]

In so far as there is a model of the *transition* from feudalism to capitalism, it is given by the relevant set of functional propositions summarized in Section 1.2 above. (Whether a set of general propositions in functional form is properly regarded as a model is a moot point I will not pursue.) How do these propositions relate to Brenner's models? Let us assume, first, what is most favourable to Brenner's position, that according to his model there is absolutely no tendency to cumulative technological development under feudal relations of production.[4] This is a useful statement of one element in the functional explanation – namely, that feudal social relations fetter the development of forces of production, given the level of development already reached under feudalism. Does this statement contradict the claim essential to the theory of history that the level of development of forces of production tends to increase throughout history?

It does not necessarily do so, because there is a distinction between the scope of application of an ideal typical model of feudalism and everything that goes on in a society legitimately described as a feudal society. There may be absolute stagnation according to the model, and yet there may be technological developments of a sort crucial to the success of the theory of history taking place in parts of the feudal world the model does not reach. There are at least two general considerations which somewhat increase the plausibility that sufficient technological progress is taking place to satisfy the general theory of history.

The first is that feudalism as a political system is highly decentralized partly because of a feature it shares with all pre-capitalist – or perhaps I mean pre-industrial – societies. In such societies, no ruling group has the economic or technical means to supervise or control directly a population scattered over any reasonably large area. According to Michael Mann's packhorse theory of history, the absolute limit of self-sufficient military control in pre-capitalism is about three days' horse distance, or at most 90 km radius. (A packhorse can apparently carry at most three days' worth of its own fodder, so that the military payload falls to zero if the staging posts are as much as three days apart.) Just because feudal control was extra-economic and *perhaps* heavier handed than is routine in some modern states does not mean that it was either uniform or universally efficacious. Mann goes so far as to say: "Before [the seventeenth and eighteenth centuries, the state] was tiny in relation to the resources of the economy and marginal in relation to the life experience of most of its inhabitants."[5]

Since it is easy to overestimate the powers of any pre-capitalist political formation, it is easy to underestimate the occurrence of interstitial zones of social action to which the pure model of feudal relations will hardly apply. There are simply more opportunities in pre-capitalist than modern political systems to escape or evade political control. This was perhaps particularly so under European – and especially Western European – feudalism than other pre-capitalist regimes because it was extremely decentralized politically.

The second general consideration intends to explain why actors somewhere, somehow will take technical advantage of the opportunities which are available, to innovate in ways which will – perhaps gradually and patchily – raise the level of development of the forces of production. This consideration is introduced by Cohen, and I will call it *Cohen's hand-waving argument*. Thus: "We do not claim for history as a whole that unbroken development of the productive forces which is peculiar to capitalist society. Instead we predicate a perennial tendency to productive progress, arising out of rationality and intelligence in the context of the inclemency of nature."[6]

To increase productivity in the approved Marxist sense is to reduce the (direct and indirect) labour time devoted to the production of a good. Rational people who want to enjoy the good and dislike the burden of producing it will therefore always wish to raise productivity – virtually by (Marxist) definition of productivity. Because people are thus rational across history – or at least, to some degree rational in this way – there is some good reason to think that some people, somewhere within the general run of a feudal society, will take advantage of the looseness of the society to innovate against the usual grain of the same society. And technological change is like a ratchet. Once it occurs the index of development clicks forward and it is very difficult to put back the clock. This is because technological change is fundamentally growth in technological knowledge and it is difficult to completely destroy or suppress knowledge. At least, it is difficult to do so under pre-capitalist social and technical conditions, because wholesale knowledge suppression requires a degree of cultural control – and therefore political control – which we have suggested that pre-capitalism is unable to sustain.

Now, although it would be stretching the usage too far to regard this hand-waving defence of the thesis that forces of production are bound to develop as a rational-choice defence of the thesis, the defence nevertheless appeals to the same general principle of rational economic motivation which characterizes rational-choice theories in general, including, of course, Brenner's models of feudalism and capitalism. At a crucial point in his reconstruction of the theory of history, Cohen appeals to rationality as a background variable – or, rather, a background constant – so that his theory is functional/rational not just functional.[7] Rationality occupies the place in his theory taken by genetic mutation in the theory of evolution, because it is used to instil a general confidence in the proposition that new varieties and combinations of forces of production will always be popping up, new combinations fit for evolutionary social selection. Rationality is the fuel which runs the motor of history and motoring occurs because the rolling resistance of (feudal) society is not everywhere so great as to prevent sufficient forward movement taking place.

I think it is fair to say that Cohen acknowledges that there is a weakness in this particular appeal to rationality. Acknowledged or not, weakness there certainly is. The appeal is in particular vulnerable to the kind of challenge Brenner directs against the whole Smithian tradition: where are the actors located whose interests incline them towards innovation? Cohen is certainly aware of this problem: "it is not evident that societies are disposed to bring about what rationality would lead men [sic] to choose. There is some shadow between what reason suggests and what society does. Further considerations are required to show that the shadow is not unduly long."[8]

One such consideration, hesitatingly entered, is that ruling classes are usually those whose socially located interest in innovation coincides with the general human interest – or the interest of "society" – in reducing average labour times. Brenner's argument certainly casts doubt on this claim, as far as feudal ruling classes are concerned, because his whole point is that feudal ruling classes have easier ways than technical innovation of realizing their socially located ends.

In any case, to confine the discussion to the technology-sponsoring dispositions of various ruling groups is to miss one of Brenner's other main points – namely that the historical fact requiring explanation is the occurrence of new social relations, not the behaviour of the various groups once the new social relations are established. And if it may be plausible that rationality might always lead to innovations in technique, it is less plausible that rationality would lead to the adoption of new social relations. As Chris Wickham puts the point: "The bounciness of twelfth-century Europe, which can be found in all aspects of its history (there's even some class struggle, with village communities establishing communal rights against landlords), did not entail qualitative development in the *relations* of production; mills and heavy ploughs, simple technological change, are scarcely going to do this on their own."[9] Indeed, the more Cohen's hand-waving argument looks as if it relies on the claim that rational people somehow, somewhere are going to contrive capitalist relations of production (especially if it is hinted that they do so because of their appreciation of the fact that capitalism is a better system than feudalism), the more it looks like the kind of conspiracy theory against which Brenner's opening sally would be decisive.[10]

Now there is a functional version of the hand-waving argument which might come to Cohen's aid at this point, an application, in fact, on a somewhat larger canvas of the view described in a previous section as the functional reading of Brenner's Axiom. That reading suggested that the productive units which survive under capitalism are those which have most adroitly specialized, accumulated and innovated. The analogous application to Cohen's hand-waving argument would contend that the units which will survive in the transitional conditions between feudalism and capitalism are those which are capitalist, and it is because the capitalist productive units have greater survival value that capitalism supersedes feudalism. And a plausible selection mechanism certainly is at hand to back up this contention.

If we assume the existence of a world market, and we assume dependence upon it, then it is plausible that the market acts as an economic selection mechanism for more highly productive techniques. Backward producers eventually go to the wall. So, if more highly productive techniques are associated with existing capitalist relations, and are more productive because of this association, then the world market in its ordinary role of economic selection will be acting simultaneously as a selection mechanism for capitalist social relations, in the way that would appear to be required for a successful functional explanation of the transition from feudalism to capitalism.[11]

The weakness of this argument is nevertheless apparent. One of its premises is that the relevant actors are dependent on the world market, and Brenner's whole point is that such dependence is what distinguishes the result (i.e. capitalism) from the starting point (i.e. feudalism). To the extent that feudal classes are able to insulate themselves from market forces, the world market will not act as a selection mechanism in favour of capitalist relations. (This is precisely Brenner's criticism of the Marxian neo-Smithians such as Wallerstein.)

To save the functional argument from this criticism, one would need to add an auxiliary selection mechanism of a political/military kind, to the effect that eventually the capitalist states will defeat the feudal states and overturn feudal class relations, and be able to do so because of the strength the capitalist states derive ultimately from the development of their capitalist economies. But suppose such a functional explanation were successful, in the sense of demonstrating the processes of economic (and probably political/military) selection through which capitalism was bound to supersede feudalism once capitalism had appeared. Even this would not be an explanation of why feudalism was bound to have been superseded, unless there is an argument for the likely appearance of capitalist social relations. And since the only argument of this kind would at the moment seem to be the original hand-waving argument, unrelated to any account of the prior evolution of, say, feudal social relations, the claim for the virtual inevitability of the transition is, to say the least, an uncompelling one.

I pause to summarize the argument so far, counted roughly as a stalemate between Cohen and Brenner.

(i) Brenner thinks he has a knockdown argument against Cohen's theory of history, which Brenner interprets as a conspiracy theory. The argument does dispose of the conspiracy theory, but not of Cohen's theory, which is not necessarily a conspiracy theory.

(ii) It is not the case that a functional explanation of the transition from feudalism to capitalism has to find a tendency included within an ideal typical model of feudal social relations that points feudalism in the direction of capitalism by internal evolution. Instead, the functional explanation could in principle rely on the plausibility of feudally corrosive developments appearing in areas of the feudal society bypassed by the ideal typical model.

(iii) Cohen's hand-waving arguments supporting the plausibility of such feudally corrosive developments are in general weak and in particular vulnerable to some of the points Brenner makes in his own analysis of what distinguishes feudalism from capitalism. Cohen relies on the rationality principle to argue for the existence of sufficient technical progress. This is a socially unlocated type of rationality, which might at a pinch account for a trend in favour of technical progress, but is much less plausible as an account of how capitalist relations of production come about, generating in their train the *systematic* tendency towards technical progress which is the mainspring of economic development.

(iv) The world market acts as an economic selection mechanism, and a powerful and important one, once people are dependent on the market. It may not be a sufficient selection mechanism of capitalist over feudal social relations, because the great feature of feudal social relations is their insulation from market forces. Without additional political/military selection, market forces might have insufficient feudal material to work upon.

At the end of round two, the functional theory of history is neither falsified nor shown as particularly plausible. We are still a bit at sea in the long-running debate: did feudalism fall, or was it pushed? And Brenner is not much further forward. His theoretical problem is to build a bridge between two special theories – his model of feudalism and his model of capitalism. Indeed in his emphasis, contra Cohen, on the eventful but essentially closed and historically static nature of feudal society, he has left rather a large problem for himself of explaining how and why capitalism succeeded feudalism.[12] I will now argue that his manner of resolving this problem in fact strengthens the claims of the functional theory of history, bringing Cohen and Brenner closer together in the process, Brenner's protests notwithstanding.

3.2   Brenner pro Cohen

Demography and class struggle

Brenner's model of feudalism is static, in the sense that technological change is not an inbuilt tendency of the model. However, there is another kind of dynamic to feudal society, which arises precisely because (agricultural) productivity is relatively constant, given the level at which productivity *is* constant. The dynamic in question is the Malthusian cycle of demographic boom and slump. Under feudalism the land is fairly productive so it supports a healthy population. Healthy populations tend to increase, but the quantity of land and its productivity are limited, so the total output of the land is limited, and its marginal product eventually decreasing. Rather than adjust in a precise, continuous fashion to these relatively fixed material constraints, the population density tends to increase to the point at which subsistence is threatened, the population becomes vulnerable to starvation and disease, there is a catastrophic collapse of numbers and the cycle begins all over again.

In the neo-classical models of this process which Brenner intends to reject, this demographic cycle causes a corresponding cycle of social and economic power. As the peasants become more numerous (i.e. their supply increases), their value tends to drop, so that wages and prices move against the peasants in the demographic boom. After the Black Death or some other disaster has struck, peasants become scarce and their bargaining position improves. Indeed, it may become so good that they are able to bargain themselves right out of their feudal obligations.

The incompleteness in this view, according to Brenner's now familiar general line of argument, is, first, that the people who benefit from fluctuations of supply and demand in the market place are the people who already have advantageous positions of ownership of the resources being traded in the market place. (If peasants own the land, land scarcity benefits peasants; if they don't, it benefits the land owner.) So the effect of movements of supply and demand depends upon the class structure. Second, the supply and demand mechanism only works for those subject to a (competitive) market, and the social context of feudalism isolates actors from the market.[13]

Brenner's criticism of the neo-classical explanation of the origins of capitalism is that it fails to set the impact of the supply and demand mechanism in the proper context of the class structure of the society out of which capitalism was evolving. It fails to take account of the actual incentives facing the relevant actors, thereby misjudging the impact of the demographic cycle. In fact, the class character of feudal society worked to restrain the up-swing of the demographic cycle somewhat, because the peasant population did not increase at the rate it could have increased if its relative affluence were not being taxed to such an extent by the lords and/or the state.[14] And the class structure exacerbated the effects of the down-swing, because if the reaction of the lords to declining revenues was to intensify their exactions, these exactions tended to worsen the already dire situation of the peasantry by, for example, depriving them of all sources of investment in the subsistence sector of agriculture. This explains why it could take centuries to clamber out of the trough – a much slower process than one would expect purely on the basis of the dynamics of market prices.[15]

What happened in particular in Eastern Europe with the cyclical demographic crisis of the fourteenth century was not the emancipation of scarce serfs, but the imposition of the second serfdom – an intensification of the feudal relationship and a resurrection of the barrier that segregated the lord-peasant complex from the market. Peasant communities were not sufficiently well-organized and historically rooted and perhaps not sufficiently scarce to prevent this outcome.[16] This development was quite compatible with the fact that one of the major motives for the lords to intensify the burdens they placed on the peasantry was the sale of produce in the embryonic world markets developing on the Atlantic seaboard. But European society was decentralized and diverse, so luckily this "Polish" outcome was not universal.

The place in which the peasantry were happiest was France. According to a rather startling claim made by Marx about the French case "the state power is not suspended in midair. Bonaparte represents a class, and the most numerous class of French society at that, *the small-holding peasants*" and Marxist criticism has tended ever since to treat France, both before and after the transition to capitalism, as a three-horse race: the monarch, noble and peasant are all in the field.[17] The nature of this three-person game is not specified in sufficient detail to know exactly what its equilibrium outcomes would be, but the general outline of the argument is clear: the three actors have definite interests to pursue in a context of alternatives which are partly decided by the actions of, and especially the relationships between, the other two parties. Thus, the peasant interest is to maintain property in the land, and, which is part of what it means to maintain property in the land, to limit both the current amount and the extent of possible variation of taxation from both the monarch and the noble. Both the crown and the landlords are interested in various circumstances in increasing both the amount of taxation and the certainty of being able to collect however much taxation they require. They are poised together against the peasants, who are the object of their tax-raising desires, but they are poised against each other as competitors for the taxes they desire. How this conflict is resolved determines the character of the state power.

Thus if taxation is already controlled by the nobles, the state may find it difficult, even if it wished, to open up a separate tax route bypassing the nobles. The monarch will then tend to be dependent on the nobility and gentry. This, very approximately, is the "English" and probably also the "Polish" case. But if the nobles are weak relative to the peasantry or, perhaps better, weak relative to the state, the state may be able to open up the direct tax route, partly by offering the peasantry greater security against its local nobility. If this partial collusion between peasant and monarch develops, as it arguably did in France, the peasant could secure possession of the land and resist arbitrary impositions from the lords.[18] Faced with this relationship between Crown and people, the lords, unable to oppress their peasantry in the old way, would turn to the state for help and try to extract from office their share of the taxation which they could no longer collect directly on their own behalf. Hence the "French" resolution: an absolutist monarchy on which the nobility and gentry are dependent.[19]

Although the French and Polish cases are very different in their forms of state and balances of class power, they are alike, according to Brenner, in one decisive respect. In Poland technological stagnation prevailed

because the ruling group could increase its income by reducing the peasantry to starvation. In France stagnation prevailed because the mass
of direct producers who were in possession of their means of subsistence
had no need or incentive to be drawn into production for the market,
and the state in effect supported them in this position.

Only in England did things differ. In England, the reaction to the demographic collapse was intermediate between the Polish and French cases:
the peasantry were well enough organized and/or sufficiently scarce to
escape the clutches of the lords and so resist reduction to a new status
of unfreedom. The feudal lords, on the other hand, were sufficiently cohes-
ive and opportunist to prevent the land falling into the possession of
the peasants.

There are two sides to the English argument and it is a nice matter
balancing the sides correctly. On the one hand, it is necessary to stress,
in comparison to the French case, how well organized our Norman rulers
were: "The extraordinary intra-class cohesiveness of the English aristocracy was thereby manifested simultaneously in their formidable military
strength, in their ability to regulate intra-lord conflict, and in their capacity
to dominate the peasantry."[20] But on the other hand, one should not
go too far in this direction, because otherwise it will be difficult to explain
why it was that the English ruling class, unlike the Polish, was unable
to dominate the peasantry so well that it could reduce the peasantry
to servile status. This weakness is especially important in the failure of
the English seigneurial reaction to the demographic crisis of the fourteenth
century, because this failure created the fundamental conditions for all
subsequent developments: an end to serfdom, the creation of a class of
yeoperson farmers without ownership of land, and the beginnings of an
agricultural proletariat.[21]

This was only the first phase in the development of capitalist social
relations, but it must be the crucial one in Brenner's view, for it was
the severance of the direct producers from their conditions of production,
forcing them to become either competitive-rent-paying tenants or competi-
tive-wage-earning labourers, that left them to the tender mercy of the
market. This dependence on the market set in train the technological
improvements – including the consolidation of holdings – which led eventually to the class differentiation of the labouring masses from the non-
working tenant farmers, and thus the tripartite class structure (labourer/
tenant/land-owner) which was so characteristic of the English rural landscape.

This differentiation would have probably came about "naturally" –
i.e. socially – as a result of the tendencies of a market system left to
its own devices, but it was aided in historical fact by the continuation
of the process Marx discussed under the heading of "primitive accumu-

lation": the enforced freeing of the direct producers from their existing rights over means of production, an expropriation "written in the annals of mankind in letters of blood and fire."[22] Initially, perhaps, this process involved a simple greed for land. But it became increasingly class-conscious, and conspiratorial. The glory of the Glorious Revolution consisted in part in the thefts "on a colossal scale – of state lands which had hitherto been managed more modestly. These estates were given away, sold at ridiculous prices, or even annexed to private estates by direct seizure ... The bourgeois capitalists favoured the operation, with the intention, among other things, of converting the land into a merely commercial commodity, extending the area of large-scale agricultural production, and increasing the supply of free and rightless proletarians driven from their land."[23]

Thus the first schemes of privatization, and so the facts that the oligarchy and gentry increased their share of the cultivable land from the extraordinary proportion of 70 per cent they held at the time of King William to the staggering figure of 80 per cent by the end of the eighteenth century.[24] Yet these land-owners differed crucially from their Continental confrères in being subject to the market through the competitive pressures on their rent-rolls, just as their tenants and their tenants' labourers were subject to the market through the pressure on the prices of agricultural produce and agricultural labour respectively.

To sum up the development of centuries in a phrase, the result was a ruling class which was unable to increase its return from the land by the feudal expedient of screwing the peasantry, and a peasantry unable to survive on the resources it possessed. The land-owning ruling class had to offer inducements to the peasant to enhance lordly income, and the peasantry had little alternative but to accept the best inducement it could get. Both sides were thus enmeshed in market relations, and the dominant relation of production was established as wage labour in the context of highly unequal private ownership of the means of production: in a word, capitalism.

This canter through late medieval Europe, which does scant justice to Brenner's nuanced and intricate historical narrative, still less to the history itself, nevertheless suggests how class struggle can be accommodated within the theory of history. Let us first recap Brenner's "dynamic of feudalism". The incentive structure of feudal production relations makes everyone averse to systematic technological development. However, if we add to this system a propensity of human beings to multiply, and thence to survive at quite high population densities because the technological level of agriculture, though more or less static, is fairly high by previous historical comparison, then long-term demographic fluctuations around a constant technical axis will be the feudal norm.[25]

Given this pattern, we can expect there to recur periodically what might be called an "internal frontier" in the aftermath of catastrophic demographic collapse. Whole areas of waste land and derelict buildings and former communities and barely surviving livestock will be created.[26]

How will this recurrent vacuum be filled? It will be filled in a sense by class struggle. This is not a struggle between classes within an existing mode of production; it is a struggle of individuals or groups to gain the resources which will constitute them in class terms. Not a struggle as a class, in other words, but a struggle to be a class. The resources at stake are land and peasants. The outcomes involve ownership of land and peasants (effective control, backed sooner or later by legal sanction). The motive is always to maximize ownership and the range of possible outcomes goes from lord-most-favourable to peasant-most-favourable. The lord-most-favourable outcome is to secure ownership of the land and ownership of the peasants short of slavery (i.e. to be Polish, and impose a second serfdom). The peasant-most-favourable outcome is to secure complete ownership of self and virtually private ownership of land (i.e. to be French, free of arbitrary impositions, and enjoy proprietorship on a small scale). The intermediate outcome is the typically English class compromise under which each side gets some but not all of what it wants. The lords get the land and the peasants get – the peasants.

The English outcome has not of course happened as a result of a vast conspiracy of some mysterious historical actor plotting to establish capitalism for the sake of establishing capitalism, despite the fact that one should not entirely discount elements of conspiracy on a lesser scale. It has not even happened as a result of negotiation between the erstwhile lords and serfs regarding their new social statuses. At most, the outcome could be represented as a truce between two groups, reflecting the institutional stabilization of their hard-won powers of possession.

We know, though, that the "English" outcome only has to happen once; a fact whose significance I will exploit in the next section. The description of the outcome includes the idea that a political system has been created which recognizes full private ownership of means of production and labour-power (i.e. there are no political battles to be fought after the economic battle for resources is decided because the battle for ownership is both economic and political). And we know from Brenner that once these social relations have appeared they bring with them a systematic tendency for technological development, even though this was no part of anyone's intention in the struggle which gave rise to capitalism. This tendency in turn allows a society for the first time to break out of the feudal demographic cycle, and eventually to show its evolutionary fitness either in economic competition on the world stage, or in political and military defeats of pre-capitalist power centres.

There'll always be an "England"

It is now possible to pose the key question to the theory of history: did
an England have to happen? With one major proviso, the answer I shall
give is "Yes". Or at least, I shall argue that the plausibility of this claim
is much greater than it was when it relied on rather general hand-waving
arguments about the inevitability of technical progress in most pre-capitalist times and places, especially if the hand-waving idea has to be that
capitalist social relations would be introduced by intentional – say, rational – action. My confidence, such as it is, depends on guessing the probability distribution of various outcomes to class struggle in the wake
of feudal demographic decline. To this end, I will apply a theoretical
sledge-hammer in a manner which will rightly appal any self-respecting
historian. I will divide Europe (West and East) into a number of different
zones, say eleven, to which I will give suggestive names, as "Wales",
"France", "Poland", "Holland", "England", "Catalonia", "Pomera-
nia", "Scotland", "Flanders" and so on, which may or may not bear
a relation to real countries living or dead. I now impose a handful of
rules for zone membership.

   (i) Zones must be sufficiently small to fit several of them, say eleven,
into the surface geography of Europe.
   (ii) Zones must be sufficiently uniform in their internal social arrangements to have a specific character, perhaps suggested by the choice of
an appropriate name. These characters will tend to distinguish zones from
their neighbours.
   (iii) Zones must be capable of pursuing essentially independent paths
of development. This does not mean that there are no relations between
the zones (in particular, world market relations, infection relations and,
perhaps, military relations). What it does mean is that no zone can impose
a whole path of development on another zone or, conversely, frustrate
a whole path of development on which another zone would otherwise
be engaged.
   (iv) Zones are sufficiently large to support independently the paths
of development whose independence of other paths of development is
guaranteed by (iii). In particular, a zone must be large enough to contain
market relations of such an extent that the Brennerian syndrome of specialization, accumulation and innovation can begin to take place within
it, and it must be large enough to support its own superstructural political
institutions.

I am not sure which historical areas fall under the scope of these rules.

I think that Battle Abbey's manor of Marley, which had apparently established a technologically oriented capitalist agriculture by the early fourteenth century, is not large enough. So "Marley" is not a candidate for the transition to capitalism. I am fairly certain, though, that England, France and Poland are large enough to be candidates. I am less clear about Flanders, which perhaps remained too dependent on external agricultural products, and, most significantly, Catalonia, which might possibly have made the first transition to agricultural capitalism if it had managed to disentangle itself from the Spanish state.[27] Let us imagine nevertheless that we have our group of eleven, and they all start off as feudal. Indeed, they are the components of European feudalism.

These eleven zones are independent in their paths of development but they are sufficiently linked by trade, population movement, disease and war to go through a somewhat similar demographic cycle. In the trough of the cycle there has been a catastrophic decline in population and traumatic disruption of the economic arrangements in every zone. There are class struggles, because actors are motivated, depending on their class situations, to grab land or peasants, or both, or to escape the feudal lords. There must be *some* outcome to this struggle of class formation and all outcomes can be ranked on a scale whose extreme points we have labelled "France" and "Poland", with "England" somewhere in between.

How likely are these various outcomes? I have little idea, *a priori* (or even *a posteriori*!), but we can at least get some grip on the consequences of various numbers being involved. Let us say that the probability of "England" is 10 per cent. We are only interested in "England" in this theory ("England" is the name we give to the zone in which the transition to capitalism occurs: that zone might turn out to be Catalonia). I don't think the 10 per cent assumption is an unreasonable one, partly because I am impressed that "England" is in the middle of the range of possible outcomes of class struggle, and I have a general regard for the Central Limit Theorem, which implies that I would be very surprised if all the innumerable factors which are responsible for the outcome of class struggle all piled up either on one side or the other, but never clustered in the middle. It would be very bad luck on the peasants if all the factors in a given conjuncture happened to favour the lords, and conversely for the luck of the lords. To say that the outcome is very likely to be either "France" or "Poland", but very, very rarely "England", seems like saying that if you toss a ball blindfold into a long trench, you will nearly always land close to one of the ends, though you don't know which end it will be. On the other hand, I don't know how broad or narrow is the English stretch in the middle of the trench we have to hit to get capitalism started. So I hope that 10 per cent is a fairly conservative estimate for the likelihood of England, and it certainly makes England pretty unlikely – on one throw of the zonal die.

But there are ten zones, so that the probability of an England *not* occurring during the first demographic cycle is $(.9)^{11}$, or just over 31 per cent. (This derivation assumes stochastic independence, which rule (iii) is designed to ensure.) This is quite surprising, because it gives capitalism almost a 70 per cent chance of occurring on the first demographic cycle. If we allow a second cycle, corresponding perhaps to the history of the "long sixteenth century", the probability of capitalism *not* appearing is $(.31)^2$, or less than 10 per cent. (This derivation assumes that there is longitudinal stochastic independence, i.e. that the non-occurrence of capitalism in a given zone in the first cycle does not affect the probability of capitalism occurring in the same zone in the second cycle.)[28] But in that case, the probability of capitalism occurring before the end of the second cycle – or during the first, if we are able to double the number of independent zones to twenty-two – is more than 90 per cent. If these data are to be believed, and they are not incredible, this conclusion would be as close to a statement of the inevitability of capitalism, given feudalism, as it would be reasonable to expect from social theory: not of course the inevitability of England, but the inevitability of "England".

My major proviso concerns the assumption of independence in the evolutions of the several zones (strictly, the combination of demographic linkage between zones with their social and political separation). Some general grounds were discussed above as to why social variety will tend to exist in all pre-capitalist formations. But it may be an important clue as to why "England" happened in Europe – and in feudalism, if the term "feudalism" is mostly applied to Europe – that European feudalism was politically decentralized. This would prevent the political suppression of an "English" outcome of class struggle by either a "Prussian" nobility, or indeed a "Napoleonic" peasantry, intervening from beyond the immediate region in which capitalism was first established. Since it has not been explained why European society was especially fragmented, or indeed why it was feudal, this assumption might be an auxiliary condition for the success of the claim that an England had to happen, given feudalism, and therefore that capitalism had to arise from feudalism.

The point is also relevant to the explanation of the transition from the pre-capitalist second era to the third, capitalist era, as opposed to the explanation of the transition from *European feudalism* to capitalism. It looks as if an additional argument would have to be given for the likelihood of "Europe" rather than say "Asia" emerging among pre-capitalist formations, where "Europe" is taken to be a politically decentralized *set* of zones, in which the class relation of local state power intimately affects the land ownership of the peasantry, though differently in different zones.[29] I cannot assess this question, which is why the inevitability of "England" is claimed relative to feudalism, not to pre-capitalist class societies as a whole.

Karl Marx's theory of history: a vindication?

What has been said so far is that Brenner's argument about the process of development will benefit from being conducted at a macroscopic level – the level of "zones" within European feudalism – at which the plausibility of the transition between feudalism and capitalism can be rendered more apparent. The purpose in this context of distinguishing England (the geographically located society) from "England" (the name given to whichever geographically located society ends up with capitalist social relations) is to suggest that the English historical experience might have had, and indeed would have had, counterparts in other regions of Europe.

These are the other causal paths, too numerous to imagine, and too detailed to disinter from history, with slightly different admixtures of land-holding customs, class organizations, evictions, infections and invasions, which would have hit the "English" target with a probability I supposed to be 10 per cent. For we are not really interested in England for its own sake. We are interested in the "England" property, together with the conviction hopefully generated by the probabilistic argument – which is, of course, a hand-waving argument, but a tighter one, I submit, than Cohen's hand-waving argument – that there is going to be some zone, say England, with the "England" property. And I take it that this argument, if successful, will illuminate the transition to capitalism more than will the successful pursuit of the Elsterian research strategy of establishing how every peasant died whose death contributed to the exact level of underpopulation which triggered the land-rush which led to the end of serfdom in Western Europe in a form conducive in at least one place to the emergence of capitalist social relations. Once we have engendered the conviction that capitalist social relations are going to be thrown up somewhere in Europe, given feudal relations, then the fact that these capitalist relations eventually supersede feudalism can plausibly be explained by the effect capitalist relations have of promoting technological development.

But this argument has brought us to the brink of agreement with Cohen's statement of the theory of history. The synthesis I have attempted of Brenner with Cohen runs schematically as follows: (unexplained) origin of European feudalism as a system of decentralized, extra-economic extraction from a peasantry tied to the land → feudal technological stagnation → feudal demographic cycle → recurrent opening of "internal frontier" of opportunity to gain resources in land and control over peasantry

→ determinate range of outcomes of the struggle to acquire resources; outcomes depending on "balance of class forces" → likelihood of an "English" outcome sometime, somewhere (i.e. likely origination of a free but dispossessed peasantry) → class differentiation of the peasantry between tenant and labourer (i.e. likely origination of agricultural capitalism proper) → capitalist technological development → escape from the feudal demographic cycle → general supersession of feudalism by capitalism in a struggle for fitness which is both economic (via world market competition) and political/military (via inter-state conflict).

In rebuttal of Brenner's scepticism about the theory of history I think it is sufficient to point out, first, that it is precisely the technological limits imposed by feudalism – the sense in which feudalism fetters the development of the forces of production and exists, more generally, in the range of productivity alluded to in the Section 1.2. statement of the theory of history –that causes the demographic cycle to occur which gives rise through the mediation of class struggle with reasonably high probability to capitalist social relations.[30] And, second, that once capitalist social relations have appeared, it is the growing technological gap between capitalism and feudalism (the parting of the ways captured so well in the contrast between Brenner's ideal typical models of the two regimes) which is responsible for the eventual supremacy of capitalism. And a good way to gloss this argument is to say that capitalist relations obtain because they, rather than feudal relations, are most appropriately adapted to develop the forces of production, given the level of development already reached under feudalism. Far from being incompatible with the primacy of the productive forces, this gloss is close to a statement *of* the primacy of productive forces in the process of transition.

I am not claiming to know whether this synthetic view of the transition from feudalism to capitalism is correct. But it does seem historically plausible as well as theoretically possible. The synthesis adds to Cohen's account a fuller, more contextualized view of the role of rational action in the mechanics of a functional theory. It adds to Brenner's account greater confidence in the likelihood of the transition to capitalism, and so helps to strengthen a long-standing Marxist intuition about the overall directedness of long-term historical change.

Notes

1. R.H. Hilton, ed., *The Transition from Feudalism to Capitalism* (London: New Left Books, 1976) and Hilton's introduction to T.H. Aston and C.H.E. Philpin (eds), *The Brenner Debate* (Cambridge: C.U.P., 1985).
2. Brenner, "The Social Basis of Economic Development" in John Roemer (ed.), *Analytical Marxism* (Cambridge: C.U.P., 1986), pp. 46–8, n. 13 (hereafter "Social Basis"). A very

similar line of anti-Cohen criticism is pursued in Andrew Levine and Erik Olin Wright, "Rationality and Class Struggle", *New Left Review*, 123, 1980, reprinted in Alex Callinicos, *Marxist Theory* (Oxford: O.U.P., 1989).

3. "Rational Choice Marxism", *New Left Review*, 160 (1986), p. 32.

4. It is a somewhat open question whether Brenner means to imply that feudalism was absolutely stagnant, or only stagnant relative to capitalist dynamism. Jerry Cohen has drawn my attention to one occasion on which Brenner agrees that "it is reasonable to expect, even in pre-capitalist economies, significant, though varying amounts of technical progress": see "Social Basis", p. 41. For Cohen's published thoughts on the matter see *Karl Marx's Theory of History: A Defence* (Oxford: Clarendon Press, 1978) (hereafter *KMTH*), pp. 194–6, and cf. the discussion of feudal technical progress in Michael Mann, *The Sources of Social Power*, 1 (Cambridge: C.U.P., 1986), pp. 399–413, which even locates the technological breakthrough before Domesday.

5. Mann, pp. 139, 511. Mann's remarks apply specifically to the central apparatus of the pre-capitalist state, which was at the hub of a decentralized political formation, so that the exercise of political power as a whole was less tiny that the exercise of state power strictly conceived. The emphasis nevertheless seems appropriate.

6. *KMTH*, p. 155.

7. It was in recognition of this feature of his theory that I felt able to include Cohen within the ambit of rational-choice Marxism. For reasons discussed in the Introduction, I am less attached than I was to the rational-choice designation of Analytical Marxism. See also "In Defence of Rational Choice", *New Left Review*, 182 (1990) for more discussion of Cohen's relation to the rational-choice paradigm.

8. *KMTH*, p. 153.

9. Chris Wickham, "Historical Materialism, Historical Sociology", *New Left Review*, 171 (1988), pp. 73–4.

10. Peter Halfpenny has argued in similar vein that Cohen's historical illustrations of functional explanation in *KMTH* make the functional theory a conspiracy theory, because Cohen only puts forward purposive elaborations of his theory. This may be true, but Halfpenny is less persuasive when he argues that since purposive elaborations are the only generally intelligible elaborations of functional claims, functional explanation is always a version of conspiracy theory. See "A Refutation of Historical Materialism?", *Social Science Information*, 22, no. 1 (1983), reprinted in Paul Wetherly, ed., *Marx and History*, forthcoming.

11. A similar line of argument is pursued by Christopher Bertram in "International Competition as a Remedy for Some Problems in Historical Materialism", *New Left Review*, 182 (1990).

12. "Capitalist economic development is perhaps an historically more limited, surprising and peculiar phenomenon than is often appreciated": "Social Basis", p. 53.

13. "The peasant (proprietor) did not have to be competitive, because he did not really have to be able to 'hold his place' in the world of the market, either the market for tenants or the market for goods": Brenner, "Agrarian Class Structure", in *The Brenner Debate*, p. 60. For the general argument, see "The Agrarian Roots of European Capitalism", in *The Brenner Debate*, pp. 218–19. I think this argument makes slightly misguided a characteristically elegant contribution to the debate made by John Roemer, "History's effect on the distribution of income", *Social Science Information*, 26, no. 2, 1987. Roemer establishes that the same economic and demographic data are compatible with different equilibria of income distribution, so that the response to demographic decline is catastrophic in the technical as well as human senses. But the argument seems to assume that landlords and peasants are parties to a bargain in the market, and this, says Brenner, is precisely what cannot be assumed. I do however take up Roemer's valuable general point about the relation of history to its models at the end of Chapter 14.

14. "Merely maintaining subsistence was rarely easy for the peasantry, especially the large numbers with relatively small holdings. Demographic growth and the subdivision of holdings diminished the size of the peasants' productive base, either relatively or absolutely. Meanwhile, the growth of taxation, especially consequent upon war, meant that greater production was necessary merely to survive": Brenner, "Agrarian Class Structure", p. 60.

15. "As the peasants' surplus tended to reach its limit, and indeed to decline with the drop-off of population, the lords build-up of more powerful instruments to redistribute it via coercive extraction and warfare tended to quicken, thereby creating the conditions of catastrophic crises of the economy and society as a whole" and "population remained at a low point for quite an extended period, long after stable economic conditions had fully been restored". Brenner, "Agrarian Roots", pp. 242, 224.

16. Brenner, "Agrarian Class Structure" pp. 38–47; "Agrarian Roots", pp. 274–83.

17. Karl Marx, *The Eighteenth Brumaire of Louis Bonaparte* (Moscow: Progress Publishers, 1977), p. 105.

18. Brenner gives a definitive statement of this position in "Agrarian Class Structure", p. 55, but he reconsiders the position slightly in response to crticism from Guy Bois, to emphasize the community of interest between monarchy and nobility rather more, and emphasize rather less the implied collusion between monarchy and peasantry against the nobility. See "Agrarian Roots", p. 262, n. 87. It is significant that this is, so far as I can see, the only substantial concession Brenner makes to any of the voluminous historical criticism directed against him. For the contrasting case of the English state, see "Agrarian Roots", p. 270, n. 104.

19. The foregoing two paragraphs only scratch the surface of an important set of problems. The conclusion of Margaret Levi's study makes the Anglo-French comparison a matter of efficiency as well as (or perhaps because of) the balance of royal-noble power: "[English] Parliamentary approval, once given, ensured a high degree of quasi-voluntary compliance. Consequently, monarchs had considerable control over financial policy as long as they worked closely with Parliament. . . . In France, however, monarchical power blocked the development of a strong and centralized representative institution. Monarchs could impose almost any tax they could think of, but with little assurance of compliance . . . [This] led to a far more ad hoc and far less efficient revenue production system than in England". See Levi, *Of Rule and Revenue* (Berkeley: University of California Press, 1988), p. 176. The models of both Chapter 14 and Chapter 16 below are highly relevant to this discussion, but I have not pursued their application to the feudal context.

20. Brenner, "Agrarian Roots", p. 258.

21. "In England, as throughout most of Western Europe, the peasantry were able by the mid-fifteenth century, through flight and resistance, definitively to break feudal controls over their mobility and to win full freedom": Brenner, "Agrarian Class Structure", p. 46. See K. Marx, *Capital*, Vol. I (Harmondsworth: Penguin Books, 1976), p. 900 for Marx's view of the origin of the "class of wage labourers" in the later fourteenth century.

22. *Capital*, I, p. 875.

23. *Capital*, I, pp. 884–5. That the Marxist theory of history does not depend on the existence of a conspiracy should not lead Marxists to ignore a conspiracy when it does exist. On this overindulgence towards critics, see *KMTH*, p. 290.

24. The figures are from "Agrarian Class Structure", p. 61 and p. 48, n. 80. It is also highly significant for the capitalist character of the English state, and for its "minimalist" bias, that the English lords keenest on enclosure were often those most hostile to the largest warlord magnates. This proclaims their "bourgeois" character in the sense that they placed economic competition above political war. See "Agrarian Class Structure", p. 59.

25. This is not to regard demography as a kind of naturally occurring adjunct to the social relations of production: there is a complex interaction between social relations of production, inheritance and kinship customs, the incentives to have families of various sizes at various times, and the consequent effect on population growth. The sense is that these important sources of variation are nevertheless constrained by the overall productive level of the economy, given the level this has reached under feudalism.

26. Brenner describes the following as the universal general issues for the whole of the relevant period "first, of course, serfdom; second, whether lords or peasants were to gain ultimate control over landed property, in particular the vast areas left vacant after the demographic collapse". See "Agrarian Class Structure", p. 35. For one graphic English example, see Howell's study of Kibworth, cited in Abercrombie et al., *Sovereign Individuals of Capitalism* (London: Allen and Unwin, 1986), p. 101.

27. For discussion of the first and last cases mentioned in this paragraph see "Agrarian

Class Structure", p. 32 and p. 49, n. 81 and "Agrarian Roots", p. 320–21. I am guessing that what held Catalonia back was its relationship to the Spanish state: such a development-hampering relation as England might have had with France, but for the Channel.

28. I do not think that longitudinal independence is necessarily implausible. History need not have the kind of continuity which would falsify the assumption. There might, for example, be a "Polish" outcome in one cycle so oppressive and generating such resentment among peasants that the peasantry would take the first opportunity to overthrow their oppressors in the next cycle and establish France. Conversely, "French" peasants in one cycle might become so complacent that they became vulnerable to a "Polish" aristocracy in the next cycle.

29. This is my attempt to crystallize the contrast between European feudalism and the Asiatic mode of production. In Marx's fleeting remarks on the latter, "the structure of the fundamental economic elements of [Asiatic] society remains untouched by the storms which blow up in the cloudy regions of politics": see *Capital*, I, p. 479. This might be taken to imply that a variable superstructure rests on a constant structural base. On the contrary, I think it must mean that the Asiatic state is not superstructural. It would follow that "Europe" is characterized by contrast by the fact that the state *is* superstructural: the point I have tried to convey in the definition. On the general importance of fragmentation to Mann's European dynamic, see Mann, p. 510 (and cf. *KMTH*, pp. 247–8 for Cohen's unhappiness with Anderson's resolution of this particular problem).

30. The last paragraph of Brenner's record-breaking anti-Cohen footnote in "Social Basis", p. 48 contains a rather obscure argument which is apparently intended to supplement the main argument cited in Section 3.1 above. I do not believe that the supplementary argument adds enough to Brenner's case to justify a discussion of it here.

PART II

Market Exchange
and Class Division

4

Roemer on Wealth and Class

4.1 A Fistful of Models

The feature that marks out capitalism as a social system in addition to
its propensity to promote technological development is its tendency to
generate social inequality.

The most characteristic form of inequality in capitalism arises from
the connection between free-market competition and class division. This
second part of the book is devoted to an exposition of John Roemer's
work in this area, which more or less coincides in my view with what
is known to Marxist theory about this fundamental connection. Roemer's
models deploy the general equilibrium analysis often associated with the
political right to make the case of the political left.[1] The models depend
on a variety of restrictive assumptions about social actors, their situations
and their motivations, as follows.

(1) There is exclusive private ownership of labour power, money and
means of production. Each actor is usually held to own just one unit
of labour-power, but variable amounts of money. This assumption ensures
that we are dealing with capitalist relations of production.

(2) Money is never disliked.

(3) Labour is the name for material productive activity, and labour is
never liked.

(4) Actors optimize with respect to money and labour in a multi-actor,
multi-sector economy. The means in general that they seek to maximize
a utility function which, in view of (2) and (3), is increasing in net money
revenue and decreasing in labour. Roemer's theory evidently becomes

a rational-choice theory through this motivational assumption.

(5) The precise form of the utility function is left unspecified, except to note the following two polar cases:

(a) *subsistence preferences*. Actors work just so long as is necessary to reproduce themselves. They are indifferent to money. This can be characterized as an infinite preference for leisure; actors stop working the moment they can afford to do so.

(b) *accumulation preferences*. Actors are indifferent how long they work, which implies that the only argument of their utility function is net revenue. It might be said that such actors have zero preference for leisure or, equivalently, are obsessed with making money.[2]

(6) There are perfectly competitive markets in means of production and the output of every production process. Perfect competition requires, among other unlikely contingencies, perfect information and the absence of monopoly power. Roemer's theory concerns the comparative statics of the equilibrium price mechanisms in such circumstances.

(7) In addition to the markets mentioned in (6), other competitive markets may be opened in labour-power (labour market) or in finance capital (capital market).

(8) What options are available to actors for the realization of the optimization programme mentioned in (4) depend on which markets are available to them according to (7).

  If a *labour market* is open, an actor maximizes by adopting that combination of the following three activities which is optimum in respect of the utility function envisaged in (5):

(x) *self-employment* (on means of production bought with own cash);

(y) employment of others (on means of production bought with own cash, with wages paid either *ex ante* or *ex post*);[3]

(z) *employment by others* (on means of production bought with other's cash, and wages paid *ex ante* or *ex post*).

If a *capital market* is open, but not a labour market, actors face the analogous possibilities of:

(x) self-financing of their own productive activities;

(y) lending to others (at interest) to finance other's productive activities;

(z) borrowing from others (at interest) to finance own productive activities.

If neither of these additional markets is open, actors are limited to option (x) – self-financing of self-employment – with trade only in produced commodities, but not labour power or capital.

(9) In all cases, the solutions of the optimizing programme must involve reproducible economies. In particular, all resources available at the start of the production cycle must be replaced by the end, and no actor can commit more resources than the actor possesses at the outset of production. Roemer emphasizes that "time is of the essence, as what constrains production decisions is the fact that inputs must be paid for today, and revenues from output accrue tomorrow."[4] This is what will place those with resources able to pay today in such an enviable social position with respect to those without resources, who can only pay later.

(10) A linear technology obtains. In these models "technology" is the name for those features of the material world which set constraints on the process of production. If an actor wishes to produce a certain amount of a certain product to sell on the market at a certain equilibrium price to realize a portion of the actor's revenue requirement, then the actor must first obtain inputs of labour-power and means of production (at going prices, where appropriate) in amounts determined by the technological relation between inputs and outputs.

A linear technology is one that relates outputs to productive inputs in fixed proportions. This means that production processes can be scaled up and down continuously and smoothly: twice the output requires twice each input, and so on. It is the same as saying there are no indivisibilities and barriers or economies of scale in production.

Linear technologies recommend themselves less because the real world falls in uniformly with their presuppositions than because they suit the linear requirements of matrix algebra. However, since economists of all schools are forced for technical reasons to make the same assumption of linearity in models of general equilibrium, this is the one assumption over which the different schools are unlikely to squabble: its abandonment would more or less destroy the profession.

Linear technologies come under three main brand names: Leontief, von Neumann and convex cone. *Leontief* technologies are many-to-one: each discrete production process has in general many input commodities (including labour) but only one output commodity.

The restriction implies that there can be no fixed capital (i.e. capital, such as the factory building, which endures beyond one production cycle)

because fixed capital is dealt with by regarding a given production process
as jointly producing at least two outputs, namely, the product itself and
partly-used fixed capital such as second-hand buildings, partly-used
machines and so on.[5]

To cope with joint production, the production process must be conceived as many-to-many: many commodity inputs to each process are
now connected (still by proportional coefficients) with many commodity
outputs. This is the more sophisticated *von Neumann* technology, whose
mathematical analysis is correspondingly complicated. Completing the
set of technologies is the *convex cone* technology which allows factor
substitution and contains the von Neumann technology as a special case.[6]

Listing these assumptions in their variety makes clear that Roemer is
proposing not just one model but an arsenal of different models of increasing complexity. We note in particular that assumption (1) allows heterogeneity of labour; assumption (5) offers at least two behavioural
orientations – subsistence and accumulation; assumption (8) offers at least
three trading environments – trade in produced commodities only, trade
in produced commodities plus labour-power and trade in produced commodities plus capital; whereas assumption (10) offers at least three technological environments – Leontief, von Neumann and convex cone.

We will see that one of the remarkable features of the theory is the
robustness of its basic findings across this variety of contexts of application. We begin though with an exposition of the theory in its simplest
possible variation: a two-person, single-sector, Leontief subsistence
model.

4.2   The Capitalist Bare Essentials

Let there be a single-sector competitive Leontief economy, which produces
a commodity, corn, from inputs of labour and corn. The linear technology
of production is specified by two numbers: a and L. a is the amount
of seed corn it takes to produce (to grow) one unit gross of corn. We
assume $0 < a < 1$, meaning that the process requires some capital (a
> 0) and is productive (a < 1). L is the amount of labour it takes to
assist the growth of corn. That the economy is competitive means that
a single market price of corn p prevails throughout the economy, together
with a single rate of profit, r, on capital invested, and a single wage
rate which we normalize to unity. (The latter assumption simply means
that the unit of monetary account is chosen so that the money price
p is equivalent to the amount of labour with which one unit of corn
can be exchanged.)

We now possess two descriptions of the economy – a material description in terms of the technological coefficients a and L, and a social description in terms of the money variables p and r. These two descriptions can be brought together via the following *accounting identity for productive units.*[7]

$$pa + rpa = (1 + r)\,pa = (p - L) \tag{4.1}$$

Equation (4.1) says that the investment cost in corn at the start of the production cycle (the amount pa on the left hand side of (4.1)) plus the profit on this investment at the rate r (the amount rpa on the l.h.s.), must be financed by the proceeds of the sale of (one unit of) corn output (the amount p on the r.h.s.) net of the wage bill for L units of labour at unit wage rate (the amount L on the r.h.s.)

The effect of (4.1) is to specify the relationship between the two variables r and p induced by the technical coefficients a and L. Note that because of the way that the money wage has been chosen as the unit of account, r and p are positively related. Recipients of profits will want high profits and a high price of corn; recipients of wages will want the reverse. It is also clear from (4.1) that there is a maximum technically-feasible profit rate, as the price of corn tends to infinity and all the net output is devoted to profit. This upper bound of the profit rate is given by $r = (1 - a)/a$. So $0 < r < (1 - a)/a$ in a feasible economy. This is equivalent to the assumptions that there is at least some profit and that some wages are paid: capitalists and wage labourers could exist.

Assume next that each of the two actors in our microcosmic capitalist society have identical subsistence preferences for an amount *b* of corn in each production cycle: actors will do anything to get their weekly ration b, and do nothing to get any more than b. In order to sustain the population, the economy must therefore be run at a level which produces at least 2b units of corn as net output. The production of this level of net output requires seed corn input at least as large as the quantity $2ba/(1 - a)$. This quantity of means of production can be bought for the sum $p.2ba/(1 - a)$ at the prevailing corn price p. Hence $p.2ba/(1 - a)$ is the minimum aggregate wealth in money terms which will allow the society to function.

The aggregate wealth of society can evidently be parcelled out among its two members in various ways. Any such allocation of investment capital just is an ownership structure of the society, which we are now in a position to introduce as an explicit variable of the model.

Following the precedent of a previously published example, I will call the two individuals Friday and Crusoe and distribute the wealth of society to them in amounts W_F and W_C respectively, such that

$$W_F + W_C \geq 2pba / (1 - a) \tag{4.2}$$

and

$$0 \leq W_F \leq W_C \tag{4.3}$$

Equation (4.2) gives the aggregate wealth constraint of the whole society. (4.3) says that no-one has negative wealth, and that if there is a poorer person, the person in question is Friday.[8] (Crusoe and Friday may also be conceived as equal sized *groups* of individuals in like situation rather than literally as single individuals.)

It will be convenient to define

$$W_F = wpba / (1 - a) \tag{4.4}$$

where the parameter w is the index of Friday's wealth. If $w = 0$, Friday is totally poverty-stricken; if $w = 1$, she has a share of society's wealth equal to half the minimum needed by society as a whole to reproduce itself.

Assume next that a labour market is opened: it is possible for Crusoe to hire Friday as a day-labourer, or vice versa. Each person therefore has the options of self-employment, being an employer and/or being an employee. In general, actors divide themselves betweeen these three activities.

Introduce accordingly variables describing the allocation each individual makes between the three options. Let x_F and y_F be the amounts of *corn* Friday produces gross from self-employment and as an employer respectively. Let z_F be the amount of *labour* she sells on the labour market (which has to be sold to Crusoe, of course, in this model, if she does sell any). Define x_C, y_C and z_C analogously for Crusoe. The problem is to solve for the variables x_F, y_F, z_F and x_C, y_C, z_C given (4.1) and (4.2), and the behavioural constraints of the model.

The constraints are that each person must gain a subsistence income sufficient to purchase a quantity b of corn with a minimum of labour, but without investing more in seed corn that their current wealth allows, or offering more labour-power than they possess. Consider Friday's programme for ease of illustration, bearing in mind that Crusoe has an identical behavioural programme. (The difference between them lies in resources of wealth and therefore constraints, not in motivations.) Formally, Friday's programme is:[9]

$$\text{Minimize} \quad Lx_F + z_F \tag{4.5}$$

$$\text{subject to} \quad p(1 - a)x_F + rpay_F + z_F \geq pb \tag{4.6}$$

$$pax_F + pay_F \leq W_F \tag{4.7}$$

$$Lx_F + z_F \leq 1 \tag{4.8}$$

The first line (4.5) corresponds to subsistence preferences: actors are only interested in minimizing their effort. The minimand is composed of the amount of time Lx_F Friday spends working in self-employment to produce the physical output x_F and the amount of time z_F she spends day-labouring.

(4.6) is the revenue constraint: Friday must earn enough from all her different activities to be able to purchase at least the subsistence bundle b at the going price p. The components of Friday's revenue are the value of the net output from her self-employment ($p(1 - a) x_F$); her profit from investment as a capitalist employer ($rpay_F$) and her wages from labouring as an employee at unit wage rate (z_F).

(4.7) is the wealth constraint: wealth limits the extent to which producers can be self-employed (x_F) or an employer (y_F).

(4.8) is the labour constraint: workers are unable to work longer than some unit ceiling of work in a given production cycle – say – the "maximum working week".[10]

Facing this situation, what is Friday's best combination of activities: (x_F, y_F, z_F)? Note first that whenever Friday invests her wealth as a capitalist, the profit she gets helps to satisfy her revenue constraint (4.6) without adding to the burden of labour-time she is trying to minimize at (4.5) (assuming, of course, that the economy equilibrates at a positive profit rate according to (4.1)). It follows that *it is better to be a capitalist than to be self-employed.*

The next point concerns the relative attractions of self-employment and wage labour. The problem is to reach the revenue threshold pb set by (4.6) with as little expenditure of effort as possible. Now if Friday increases her labour in self-employment Lx_F by, say, one day, she is increasing her output x_F by $1/L$ units of corn, which increases her net revenue on the l.h.s. of (4.6) by $p (1 - a) / L$ units of money. Increasing her wage labour by the equivalent labour-time of one day on the other hand increases her net revenue by just one unit of money. (Recall that the wage is unity: z_F has a coefficient of one in (4.6).) Whether it is better from the revenue point of view for Friday to spend her extra day working in self-employment than to spend it in wage employment therefore depends on whether or not:

$$p(1 - a) / L > 1 \tag{4.9}$$

(4.9) can be rewritten

$$p(1 - a) - L > 0 \tag{4.10}$$

But the l.h.s. of (4.10) is equal to rpa, according to (4.1), so condition (4.10) is equivalent to

$$rpa > 0 \tag{4.11}$$

which is the condition that positive profits are made. It follows that *it is better to be self-employed than it is to be a wage labourer.*

These arguments apply equally to Crusoe, who faces the same incentive structure as Friday. The upshot is that everyone wants to be an employer rather than being self-employed, and self-employed rather than employed. So why doesn't everyone become an employer? Wouldn't that be an admirable solution all round?

The obvious reply is that this is a logical impossibility: employers have to have employees by definition, and so not everyone can be an employer, for if all were employers who would be left to become an employee? This obvious reply is in fact mistaken. It neglects the possibility that people in a society can act *simultaneously* as employer and employee.

Suppose for instance that Friday and Crusoe both have some wealth. One thing for them to do with their wealth is devote it to self-employment. But there is nothing to prevent Friday using her wealth instead to employ Crusoe and Crusoe using his wealth instead to employ Friday. This case of split roles has some theoretical significance, because it can be shown that the two alternatives (self-employment versus the split role) are indistinguishable in welfare terms at an equilibrium. To see this, assume that Friday, say, has a labour-minimizing solution – (x_F, y_F, z_F) – which involves some self-employment ($x_F > 0$). Suppose she opts instead to split her self-employment between being an employer and being an employee. If this is to remain a labour-minimizing solution it must evidently involve Friday working the same (minimum) time as before. So the time she is no longer working for herself (Lx_F) must be devoted instead to working for somebody else (who must of course be Crusoe in this special two-person world).

In ceasing to be self-employed, she has sacrificed net revenue equal to

$$p(1 - a)x_F \tag{4.12}$$

But she now has two new sources of revenue to compensate her for her loss. One source is the wage from employment for a time Lx_F at a unit money wage. The second source is the profit from investment of the capital sum – pax_F – she has withdrawn from her self-employment activity. This profit is $rpax_F$. Hence she loses revenue $p(1 - a)x_F$ and gains revenue $Lx_F + rpax_F$. But we already know that

$$p(1 - a) = L + rpa \qquad (4.1)$$

Friday's revenue is therefore unchanged under her new arrangements, as is her working time and total capital stock. It follows that whenever an equilibrium exists involving at least some self-employment there is an equivalent equilibrium (in fact, an infinite number of such equilibria) which splits (some part of) the self-employed component of the actor's activity into an "employer" component and an "employee" component. The gains relative to self-employment of being an employer exactly cancel out the losses of being an employee.

It is an intriguing question why the split role alternative to self-employment does not seem to be very well developed in practice. John Roemer certainly gives it short shrift as "redundant in a parsimonious representation of the class structure of an economy".[11] He is less interested in the reasons why actors might act as both employer and employee than in the reasons they are to be found taking on either of these roles to the exclusion of the other.

Here is the first clue on the latter question. Suppose Friday had zero wealth ($w = 0$). Then her wealth constraint (4.7) operates to exclude both self-employment and her ability to employ others. This implies $x_F = y_F = 0$. Equation (4.6) then implies $z_F = pb\ [> 0]$. *When Friday has no wealth, she must be an employee exclusively.* This suggests that actors find themselves in the exclusive roles as a result of *their position in a hierarchy of wealth.*

We pursue this insight to solve for the six variables in the two optimization programmes in the following order: $z_C, y_F, x_F, z_F, y_C, x_C$. Begin, then, with Crusoe's prospects of wage labour. Crusoe's wealth is at least as great as Friday's (by hypothesis) and their joint wealth is at least as great as $2pba / (1 - a)$ (by (4.2)). Hence

$$W_C \geq pba / (1 - a) \qquad (4.13)$$

It follows that Crusoe is always in a position to devote a quantity of wealth $pba / (1 - a)$ to self-employment. He can then use this wealth to purchase seed corn in physical amount $ba / (1 - a)$ and produce a gross output $x_C = b / (1 - a)$. But if $x_C = b / (1 - a)$, his net revenue from self-employment is pb (according to (4.6)), which already satisfies his revenue constraint.

Since we know that actors always prefer self-employment to exclusive wage labour, we deduce that $z_C = 0$. *Crusoe is sufficiently wealthy to avoid exclusive employment by Friday.* But this means that despite the fact that like all actors, Friday *wants* to employ Crusoe (without being employed by him) she is never *able* to employ Crusoe. Hence $y_F = 0$.

But if $y_F = 0$, we can go on to solve (4.7) in Friday's programme for x_F:

$$x_F = W_F / pa$$
$$= wb / (1 - a) \tag{4.14}$$

As long as $w > 0$ Friday has the option of self-employment, and she will prefer it to exclusive wage labour in Crusoe's firm. So she will devote all her capital to self-employment. But will this be enough? Can she survive this way? She can if and only if her net revenue from self-employment reaches her subsistence threshold pb. The condition is given from (4.6) as

$$p(1 - a). \, wb / (1 - a) \geq pb$$

or

$$w \geq 1 \tag{4.15}$$

Case 1: $w \geq 1$

Suppose that Friday can survive from self-employment alone. Then Crusoe is unable to induce her to become a wage-labourer for him (unless he also becomes a wage-labourer for her, which is a possibility we ignore). But this is to say $z_F = y_C = 0$.

Crusoe's only remaining option is therefore to become self-employed, using an amount of his money capital equal to pb / (1 - a): the same amount that Friday is using. Now it is possible that Crusoe (or indeed Friday) has more capital available than is used in their respective self-employments, but the capital remains idle because neither person is able to induce anyone else to be a wage-labourer and neither person can be bothered to work on it themselves, given that each of their subsistence requirements has already been met. (In these cases, the wealth constraints (4.7) may be slack.)

It follows that if and only if $w \geq 1$ the society is composed entirely of the self-employed (ignoring the "split role" equilibrium). The solution vectors $<x, y, z>$ can be represented in Roemer's standard notation[12] as

Friday: $<b / (1 - a), 0, 0>$

Crusoe: $<b/(1-a), 0, 0>$

Case 2: $w < 1$

If on the other hand $w < 1$, Friday is forced to work for Crusoe because of her poverty.[13]

Solving (4.6) for Friday's wage-labour commitment z_F gives

$$pwb + z_F = pb$$

or

$$z_F = pb(1-w) \tag{4.16}$$

But if Friday works time z_F for Crusoe then Crusoe's business can produce a gross output $y_C = z_F/L$, or

$$y_C = pb(1-w)/L$$

Substitution from (4.1) for the ratio p/L gives

$$y_C = b(1-w)/[1-(1+r)a] \tag{4.17}$$

We have seen that Friday works for Crusoe when and because she has no alternative. She works up to the moment her subsistence constraint is satisfied, and then she stops. Once she stops, Crusoe's capitalist enterprise ceases to function, and his income from investment dries up. The final question, then, is whether Crusoe's revenue from his investment in the business is sufficient to cover *his* subsistence requirement, and therefore preclude the necessity of him working himself (in self-employment).

From Crusoe's (4.6) we have

$$p(1-a)x_C + rpay_C \geq pb \tag{4.18}$$

Now if $x_C > 0$, we know that Crusoe has had to invest some of his capital in self-employment, and he doesn't like to do that, because of the disutility he incurs through labour. So at an equilibrium, (4.18) is satisfied with strict equality: Crusoe doesn't invest more than he has to. Substitution from (4.17) and rearrangement gives

$$x_C = rab[(1-a)/ra - (2-w)][1-a]^{-1}[1-(1+r)a]^{-1} \tag{4.19}$$

The only term in this rather unwieldy product which can be zero or negative is the term $[(1-a)/ra - (2-w)]$. Hence the condition for $x_C \leq 0$ is

$$(2 - w) \geq (1 - a) / ra \tag{4.20}$$

Consider this expression. If it is satisfied, Crusoe is not self-employed. Hence he is exclusively a capitalist employer. The expression contains two parameters, w and r, which are respectively an index of Friday's wealth and the rate of profit in the economy. The l.h.s. of the expression is decreasing in w and the r.h.s. is decreasing in r. It follows that:

(i) For a given rate of profit, Crusoe is more likely to be a capitalist the poorer Friday is;
(ii) For a given wealth possessed by Friday, Crusoe is more likely to be a capitalist the higher the rate of profit is.

In sum, *nothing is more conducive to the assumption of a capitalist role than poverty in the population and high profitability in the economy.*

The limits of Friday's wealth are given for the present purpose by $0 \leq w < 1$ (if $w \geq 1$, nothing will induce Friday to become an employee). The numerical range of the l.h.s. of (4.20) is accordingly

$$1 (2 - w) \leq 2 \tag{4.21}$$

i.e. the l.h.s. of (4.20) never exceeds the value 2.

Now if profits are sufficiently low that

$$(1 - a) / ra > 2$$

or

$$r < (1 - a) / 2a \tag{4.22}$$

the inequality (4.20) cannot be satisfied for any value of w in the range: $0 \leq w < 1$.

(4.22) can then be used to define *the low profit economy* as an economy which will not support Crusoe exclusively as a capitalist whatever the distribution of wealth within it. In this case, $x_C > 0$. We also know that because the revenue constraint (4.6) in both Friday and Crusoe's programmes are taut, the net output of the society is equal to subsistence 2b, and the aggregate wealth deployed in production is therefore p2ba $/ (1 - a)$. Friday's share of this wealth is pwa $/ (1 - a)$, so Crusoe's is p $(2 - w)$ ba $/ (1 - a)$. (Crusoe may have idle wealth in addition with a slack wealth constraint (4.7), but Friday cannot.)

In order for Crusoe to become a pure capitalist we require *a high profit economy* defined by:

$$(1 - a) / 2a \le r < (1 - a) / a \tag{4.23}$$

In this eventuality, there will be some values of w: $0 \le w < 1$ which imply the satisfaction of (4.20). Consider therefore a case in which Friday is sufficiently impoverished to allow Crusoe to be a capitalist. Consider in particular that (4.20) is satisfied with strict inequality. What has happened here is that Friday is so poor, and profits in industry are so high, that she must work for Crusoe longer than is necessary to provide for Crusoe's subsistence out of his profits. One can imagine Friday hammering at the factory gate, begging to be let in to work on Crusoe's means of production; asking him to expand his output and capital deployed in order that she can get a living from the abysmal wages that he pays. In the discussion of the model so far there is no limit to this process. As r tends to its maximum value, at which the whole of the net product is devoted to profit, the price of corn goes to infinity, and so therefore does the amount of work pb that a propertyless Friday has to perform in order to satisfy the constraint (4.6).

In these deleterious circumstances the labour constraint (4.8) comes into operation, for the price of corn cannot be so high that workers have to work longer than their physically or socially permitted maximum working week in order to secure their subsistence b. Since the labour time is pb and the maximum working week has been normalized to unity by (4.8), the maximum price of corn is 1/b. The twin pressures of subsistence and exhaustion of the worker combine in this way to set an upper limit to the proportion of net output which can go to profit at the expense of the worker's consumption.

This mechanism was much emphasized by Marx in *Capital*, but it is also fundamental to the so-called neo-Ricardian development of Marxian economic theory pioneered by Morishima, Steedman and Roemer himself in the 1970s.[14] To see this, we only need to regard the wage portion b as a *proportion* per unit of the gross output of the economy and assume that all labour is performed by proletarians (which implies $w = 0$). Then each unit gross of corn output requires L units of labour, whose pay at unit money wage rate must cover b corn units of subsistence at the price p.

Hence

$$L = pb \tag{4.24}$$

If we regard b as a physical constraint on production, then equation (4.24) determines the price p in terms of this constraint and the technological coefficient L. We can then substitute for p in (4.1) to obtain the profit rate r in terms of b, L, and the other technological coefficient a. In this

case, all the money variables are determined by the physical conditions
of production, as the neo-Ricardian approach also concludes. Indeed,
since the neo-Ricardian price system for this model consists just of the
equations (4.1) and (4.24), we have verified for this model that the neo-
Ricardian analysis is contained as a special case of the Roemerian equilibrium solution for w = 0.[15] The difference is that the neo-Ricardian analysis assumes the distribution of actors to class roles that Roemer is able
to deduce within the model. What Roemer has done, in effect, is to encase
the formal economics of the neo-Ricardian analysis in a formal sociology
of class division.

4.3   The Class Wealth Correspondence Principle

The foregoing results establish Roemer's *Class Wealth Correspondence
Principle* (CWCP) in its simplest possible environment – a single-sector,
two-person Leontief subsistence economy. The principle says that as the
relative levels of wealth of the parties varies, so does the level and kind
of the activities which compose the equilibrium solutions of the optimization problem that they face. In the two-person world, a single parameter
w suffices to describe the possible distributions of social wealth, where
w is an index of the wealth of the poorer person, called Friday.
    The CWCP then establishes:

(i) If $w = 0$, Friday is exclusively an employee;
(ii) If $0 < w < 1$, Friday is partly an employee, and partly self-
employed;
(iii) If $w = 1 = (2 - w)$, both Friday and Crusoe are exclusively self-
employed;
(iv) If $1 < (2 - w) < (1 - a) / ra$ Crusoe is partly self-employed
and partly an employer;
(v) If $(1 - a) / ra \le (2 - w) \le 2$ Crusoe is exclusively an employer.

Table 4.1 exhibits these conditions, together with the corresponding equilibrium values for the variables (x, y, z), and the names given to the corresponding classes in Marxian literature, in their industrial and rural
denotations.
    Figures 4.1 and 4.2 display the solutions <x, y, z> against the wealth
of the two parties for a low profit economy and a high profit economy
respectively. In reading the figures, note that the left-hand portion $0 \le
w \le 1$ applies to the poorer member of society, and the right-hand portion
$1 \le (2 - w) \le 2$ applies to the wealthier member. $(2 - w)$ is an index
of the wealth of the wealthier person, except in the case of the pure

Table 4.1 The Correspondence between Wealth and Class

Wealth Grade	Wealth Parameter	Friday's Solution $\langle x_F, y_F, z_F \rangle$	Crusoe's Solution $\langle x_C, y_C, z_C \rangle$	Rural Classes	Industrial Classes
Zero	$w = 0$	$\langle 0, 0, + \rangle$ (1)		Agricultural labourers	Proletarians
Low	$0 < w < 1$	$\langle +, 0, + \rangle$ (2) (3)		Poor peasants	Semi-proletarians
Adequate	$w = 1 = (2 - w)$	$\langle +, 0, 0 \rangle$ (4)	$\langle +, 0, 0 \rangle$ (4)	Middle peasants	Petty bourgeoisie
High	$1 < (2 - w) < (1 - a)/ra$		$\langle +, +, 0 \rangle$ (5)(6)	Rich peasants	Small capitalists
Enormous	$(1 - a)/ra \leq (2 - w) \leq 2$		$\langle 0, +, 0 \rangle$ (7)	Landlords	Pure capitalists

The variables (x_F, y_F, z_F) and (x_C, y_C, z_C) give respectively the output from self-employment, the output from employment of others, and the time spent in wage labour of the respective parties Friday and Crusoe.

The functional forms of the various positive entries in the solution of the two-person, single-sector subsistence model are
(1) $z_F = pb$; (2) $x_F = wb/(1 - a)$; (3) $z_F = pb(1 - w)$; (4) $x_F = x_C = b/(1 - a)$; (5) $x_C = rabp[(1 - a)/ra - (2 - w)]/L$;
(6) $y_C = bp[1 - w]/L$; (7) $y_C = bp[1 - w]/L$

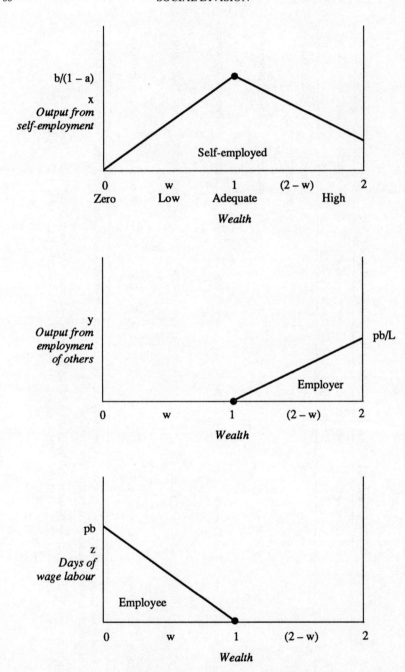

Figure 4.1 Wealth and Class in a Low Profit Economy

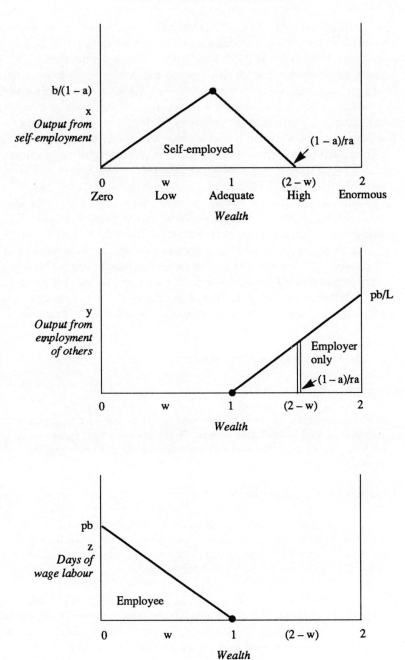

Figure 4.2 Wealth and Class in a High Profit Economy

capitalist whose wealth in general exceeds $(2 - w)$ when his poor relation has wealth w, for the reason given above that the economy is then generating a greater net output than the aggregate subsistence requirement $2b$.

The CWCP establishes that in a given material environment people facing an identical programme for survival will sort themselves neatly into one of five pairwise disjoint social classes. It has been shown that the classes are ordered top to bottom by the wealth of their incumbents. The better placed a person is, (in a sense which depends both on their wealth in relation to others and the profit performance of the economy) the higher their rank in a procession of class roles which runs: proletarian, semi-proletarian, petty bourgeoisie, small capitalist and pure capitalist.

The class status of each person in the society – and thence the class structure of the society – has been deduced on the basis of individualistic behavioural assumptions in the context of differential resource distribution. And the results accord to a remarkable degree with what Marx (and certain of his followers including Lenin and Mao) assumed but could not prove about what would happen in a competitive market society.[16] This is a remarkable demonstration of the classical theory of social class, conducted using the standard tools of modern mathematical economics.

4.4   On Marxian Class Confusion

At one point Roemer remarks:[17]

> In Marxism, class is not defined by wealth or status, but by how agents relate to the sale or purchase of labour-power. The three main classes are the bourgeoisie who hire labour, the proletarians who sell their labour, and the self-employed.

Elsewhere he says emphatically:[18]

> *A class is a group of people who all relate to the labour process in a similar way*. For instance, all those who sell their labour for a living form a class; and all those who hire labour form a class; and those who work for themselves and neither hire nor sell labour form a third class.

These definitions differ significantly. The first explicitly restricts Marxian class to the market place ("sale or purchase of labour-power"); the second takes a more ample view of "the labour process', which we might construe as referring to the material process of production in general. We may reject the first part of Roemer's first definition out of hand: Marxists cannot confine class relations to market relations, since if they did they could not regard pre-capitalist history as a history of class struggle.[19]

So the third clause of the first sentence of the first definition is strictly speaking false. But what of the second clause? Is it the case that "in Marxism, class is not defined by wealth or status"?

It is not the case according to Cohen. Monetary wealth is the kind of possession which commonly confers social access to forces of production. And it is ownership of forces of production which generates class positions in Cohen's view.[20]

A person's class is established by nothing but his [sic] objective place in the network of ownership relations, however difficult it may be to identity such places neatly ... *Not even his* [sic] *behaviour is an essential part of it.*

Cohen's definition counts as a *structural definition* of class, by contrast with either of Roemer's *behavioural definitions*. The major confusion in Marxian sociology is thus the confusion that lies between Cohen's having criterion and Roemer's doing criterion as the hallmark of a person's class position.[21]

One way to ease this confusion, proposed by Elster, is precisely to take advantage of the link between having and doing established by Roemer's CWCP. According to Elster, "*A class is a group of people who by virtue of what they possess are compelled to engage in the same activities if they want to make the best use of their endowments.*"[22]

Glance in the light of Elster's definition at Table 4.1. The various intervals of having in the left hand column translate one-to-one into the optimum doings recorded in the right hand columns. It is then possible to say of any agent observed engaged in any given behaviour: "They must be worth such-and-such". And it is possible conversely to say of any agent known to have a certain wealth: "They are bound to be doing thus-and-so". The effect of the existence of the CWCP appears to be that Marxists are conveniently relieved of the necessity of choosing between having and doing, because the link between the two dimensions has become so close.[23]

A first problem arises because the CWCP only holds as such in the tidy world of formal models, as Roemer would be the first to admit. The force of people being "compelled ... if they want to make ... best use" in Elster's definition is that the people in question would be so compelled if they were optimizers in a world adequately modelled by the formal theory.

One obvious departure of the model from reality lies in the assumptions it makes about perfect competition. More pertinent here is the problem of sub-optimization. Suppose that Mr Rockefeller takes a job on the assembly line (it isn't difficult for him to get the job, because he owns the plant). His behaviour makes him a proletarian and his wealth makes him a capitalist. Which is he?

I share Elster's intuition: "A Rockefeller cannot turn into a worker simply by taking a salaried job, unless he also gives away his fortune".[24] Elster's definition can accommodate – indeed, it is partly designed to accommodate – this point because in the stylized world of formal theory, Rockefellers just don't do such things. Since becoming a worker is not we suppose a rational response to Rockefeller's situation, his class position is defined by a combination of what he has (his wealth), and what it would be rational for him to do given his wealth (act capitalistically), whether or not he acts in fact as capitalists are invited to act according to formal theory.

This is a ruling in favour of formal theory, but it is not I think a formalistic ruling. It reflects the firm social and political conviction that even if Rockefeller is going through motions of work identical with his colleagues' on the line, his position remains fundamentally different from theirs so long as he retains the option they don't have of becoming a capitalist. There is a difference between being a worker and playing at being a worker which the structural definition of class respects, but the behavioural definition does not.

Neither does the Rockefeller point apply only at the upper end of the class scale. Consider workers who refuse to enter the factory out of principle, as some handloom weavers did in nineteenth- century Britain, with dire consequences for themselves and their families. The weavers were irrational perhaps, even silly, to resist the onward march of mechanical progress. But did they cease to be proletarian because they chose to starve to death? Surely not. In fact, they were becoming *proletarianized* because the productivity of the factory sector was undermining the commercial viability of self-employment in their homes. Industrialization elsewhere was narrowing their options, and this is of the essence of class position: *class position is about the range of options a person has as a result of the distribution of social access to forces of production.*[25] The role of the CWCP in this is to help us make sensible decisions about what range of behaviours a person is likely to have open to them on the basis of different kinds and levels of assets.

There are two main areas of difficulty with this approach. The first area occurs where we do not have something like the CWCP to link resources with behaviours, or where the slippage between the assumptions of the model and the arrangement of the real world seems especially drastic. The second area is where the model itself renders ambivalent judgements because the connection it makes between resources and behaviours is imperfect, even in the pristine world of theory.

Consider in this regard the basic triad: resources, behaviour, welfare.

The major thrust of the CWCP set out in Table 4.1 is that different resources lead to different behaviours, associated with different levels of welfare. Usually, we are firing on all three of these cylinders. So we have no difficulty in deciding that the discrete combinations of particular resources with particular behaviours with particular welfare levels establish discrete class groupings. But we have already encountered an exception to this general picture. Recall the split-role equilibrium. For any actor with some wealth there were two distinct behavioural options: (i) self-employment; (ii) being both an employer and an employee. The options were moreover indistinguishable in welfare terms. (This is why both options could lead to equilibrium.) Evidently we face an example in which equal resources are combined with different behaviours to generate equal welfare. How do we deal with this example?

Roemer is bound to assign the actors in this case to different classes on the basis of their different behaviours. Indeed, there is another example of the same kind of phenomenon about which Roemer is explicit that "the class structure differs" between two welfare-equivalent equilibria.[26] Strictly speaking, Elster's definition would render the same verdict, since it speaks of class members having "to engage in the same activities" in order to optimize. Self-employment behaviour and split-role behaviour are different activities, despite the fact that they lead to identical optima. So the self-employed and the split-role merchants are distinct Elsterian classes. But can the rather arbitrary choice of one action rather than an equally attractive one really give rise to a class difference, as Roemer and Elster are committed to saying?

In my view, the facts (i) that the options of the actors in the two putative classes (the self-employed and the split-rolers) are identical (i.e. their access to forces of production is identical) and (ii) that their welfare is the same are decisive against the view that they belong in different classes, notwithstanding the difference in their behaviours. The behaviours are simply different means of achieving the same result from the same starting point.

In such a case, where there is a set of different optimal behaviours linking similar resource positions to similar welfare outcomes, it seems appropriate to speak of *class fractions*. Thus, the self-employed and the split-role employer-employees are two distinct fractions of a single class: the petty bourgeoisie.[27] We end the chapter leaning towards a structural definition of class, and with a first piece of a theoretical jigsaw in place: equal resources, different behaviour and equal welfare imply equal class positions.[28] Further consideration of the link between behaviour and welfare will occupy the next chapter.

Notes

1. Such cross-dressing is bound to cause a certain intellectual turbulence within and between the Marxian and non-Marxian mainstreams. My purpose in this book is to expound and develop the theory rather than review its reception, but the interested reader may find a range of reactions from the sympathetic to the splenetic among Scott Lash and John Urry, "The New Marxism of Collective Action", *Sociology*, 18, no. 1 (1984); Adam Przeworski, "Marxism and Rational Choice", *Politics and Society*, 14, no. 4 (1985); Joseph McCarney, "A New Marxist Paradigm?", *Radical Philosophy*, 43 (1986); the contributions by Mike Taylor, Allen Wood, Scott Meikle, Cliff Slaughter, Douglas C. North and Elster to a symposium on "Making Sense of Marx", in *Inquiry*, 29 (1986); Donald Kieve, "From Necessary Illusion to Rational Choice?", in *Theory and Society*, vol. 15, no. 4 (1986); Michael Lebowitz, "Is 'Analytical Marxism' Marxism?", and W.H. Locke Anderson and Frank W. Thompson, "Neoclassical Marxism", both in *Science and Society*, 52, no. 2 (1988); Tony Smith, "Roemer on Marx's Theory of Exploitation", *Science and Society*, 53, no. 3 (1989); Bill Martin, "How Marxism Became Analytic", *Journal of Philosophy*, 86, no. 11 (1989); Ellen Meiksins Wood, "Rational Choice Marxism: Is the Game Worth the Candle?", *New Left Review*, 177 (1989); Thomas F. Mayer, "In Defence of Analytical Marxism", *Science and Society*, 53, no. 4 (1989/90); Alex Callinicos, "Introduction", in *Marxist Theory*, (Oxford: O.U.P., 1989); Jutta Weldes, "Marxism and Methodological Individualism", *Theory and Society*, 18 (1989); and Robert Ware and Kai Nielsen, eds., "Analysing Marxism", *Canadian Journal of Philosophy*, supplementary volume 15 (1989).

Close to the origins of the paradigm there is John Maguire's "Contract, Coercion and Consciousness" in Ross Harrison, ed., *Rational Action* (Cambridge: C.U.P., 1979) which raised many of its characteristic themes before John Roemer gave them definitive shape. The first authors to float the idea that Marx might be regarded fruitfully as a rational-choice theorist were, so far as I know, Anthony Heath, *Rational Choice and Social Exchange* (Cambridge: C.U.P., 1976), p. viii and Mancur Olson, *The Logic of Collective Action* (Cambridge, Mass.: Harvard University Press, 1965), pp. 102–10, who also cites C. Wright Mills and Talcott Parsons as precursors of this view (p. 105, n. 22).

2. John Roemer, *Value, Exploitation and Class* (Chur: Harwood Academic Publishers, 1986), p. 50. This monograph gives the most compact, though technical, statement of Roemer's theory. The fullest account remains *A General Theory of Exploitation and Class* (Cambridge, Mass.: Harvard University Press, 1982) (hereafter *GTEC*) while *Free to Lose* (London: Radius, 1988) is the most recent and most accessible treatment.

3. The timing of wage payments makes a difference to the arithmetic, but no difference to the fundamental conclusions of any of the models. See *GTEC*, p. 63/4 and Ian Steedman, *Marx after Sraffa* (London: New Left Books, 1977), ch. 8.

4. *GTEC*, p. 115.

5. Steedman, chs. 10–12.

6. *GTEC*, pp. 147–54.

7. Equation (4.1) assumes that wages are paid *ex post*. It is in fact the *ex post* version of the (single-sector) equation corresponding with Steedman's Equation (1), p. 51. I discuss below the intimate relationship between Roemer's models and neo-Ricardianism.

8. Friday and Crusoe appeared in "Rational-Choice Marxism" (on p. 144 of Mark Cowling and Lawrence Wilde. eds., *Approaches to Marx*, (Milton Keynes: Open University Press, 1989)) but it should be noted that they there enjoyed a choice of technique: Friday had access to a labour intensive technology to make good her subsistence, in case she had insufficient (direct or indirect) access to capital resources.

9. This programme corresponds to those set out in *GTEC*, p. 63; *Free to Lose*, p. 74; and "New Directions in the Marxian theory of Exploitation and Class" in John Roemer, ed., *Analytical Marxism* (Cambridge: C.U.P., 1986), p. 87 (hereafter "New Directions").

10. The existence of this constraint relates to the distinction Marx made between "absolute" and "relative" surplus value and to a consistent emphasis in *Capital* on the social and biological limits to capitalism's exploitation of the worker. See "Value and Strategy", *Science and Society*, XLVIII, no. 2 (1984), pp. 153–9.

11. *Free to Lose*, p. 76. I am not certain it is quite so redundant in practice: part of the intention of Thatcherite plans for popular capitalism is that employees should own shares while remaining employees of larger corporations, rather than leave the paid labour force to invest their capital in their own small businesses. In Thatcher heaven, the people's income would be drawn partly from wages and partly from profit on investment, precisely as envisaged in the split-role equilibrium. David Miller reports similar practices among members of nineteenth-century cooperatives in *Market, State and Community* (Oxford: Clarendon Press, 1989), pp. 87–8.

12. The notation, which is simply the conventional vector representation of the variables x, y, z, is explained in *GTEC*, p. 72; *Free to Lose*, p. 76; "New Directions", p. 89.

13. "Force" is the appropriate word, since in this model there is literally no alternative to Friday working for Crusoe, if she is to reach her subsistence constraint. As Ellen Wood has said "What compels direct producers to produce more than they will themselves consume, and to transfer the surplus to someone else, is the 'economic' necessity which makes their own subsistence inseparable from that transfer of labour" ("Rational Choice Marxism: Is the Game Worth the Candle?", p. 53.) This shows that Ellen Wood is wrong to offer this comment as a criticism of rational-choice Marxism. If, as she claims, hers is the classical position, then RCM is classical.

14. Michio Morishima, *Marx's Economics* (Cambridge: C.U.P., 1973); Ian Steedman, *Marx after Sraffa*; John Roemer, *Analytical Foundations of Marxian Economic Theory* (Cambridge: C.U.P., 1981); Ian Steedman et al., *The Value Controversy* (London: Verso, 1981).

15. Equation (4.24) is the single-sector version in our notation of Steedman's Equation (3), *Marx after Sraffa*, p. 51.

16. For textual references to Mao and Lenin, see *GTEC*, p. 73, n. 2.

17. *Value, Exploitation and Class*, p. 45.

18. *Free to Lose*, p. 5.

19. But note Elster's suggestion that "Marx was tempted by the idea of restricting classes to market economies" in "Three challenges to class" in *Analytical Marxism*, p. 144 (hereafter "Three Challenges") and the discussion of two relevant texts in Marx on pp. 148–9.

20. G.A. Cohen. *Karl Marx's Theory of History: A Defence* (Oxford: Clarendon Press, 1978), p. 73 and the last sentence with my emphasis from n. 1 on the same page.

21. I am not suggesting that the confusion lies within either of Cohen's or Roemer's positions, though it arguably did in Marx's. Compare, for example, the emphasis on the structural criterion of ownership (of labour-power, capital and land) in the tantalizingly incomplete final chapter of *Capital*, vol. III, with the following remark on socialism from the *Critique of the Gotha Programme* (Peking: Foreign Languages Press, 1976), p. 16 "[Equal right] recognizes no class differences, because everyone is only a worker like everyone else"; which implies that the behavioural criterion of working or not working is decisive for class difference. (See also n. 23 below.)

22. "Three challenges", p. 147 (original emphasis).

23. It is possible that Marx was getting round to a similar position by the end of *Capital*, vol. 3. He says: "The owners merely of labour-power, owners of capital, and landowners, whose respective sources of income are wages, profit and ground-rent, in other words, wage-labourers, capitalists and land-owners, constitute then [sic] three big classes of modern society based on the capitalist mode of production." He then answers his rhetorical question "What constitutes a class?" by "At first glance – *The identity of revenues and sources of revenue*. There are three great social groups whose members, the individuals forming them, live on wages, profit and ground-rent respectively, on the *realization* of their labour-power, their capital, and their landed property": *Capital*, vol. III (London: Lawrence and Wishart, 1974), pp. 885, 886, emphases added. "Sources of revenue" thus establish the structural positions of the individuals, which must be "realized" by the appropriate behaviour before the requisite revenues are forthcoming.

24. "Three Challenges", p. 144. Philippe Van Parijs thinks the Rockefeller case leads Elster's class concept into great difficulties. See "A Revolution in Class Theory" in Erik Wright, *The Debate on Classes* (London: Verso, 1989), p. 222, n. 14.

25. The wording is chosen to refer to the whole pattern of distribution of forces of production, not just the amount of given forces a certain person possesses. This choice

of words is intended to be consistent with the discussion of the Chicken equilibrium in Chapters 11 and 16, where the possibility of class division arises from the (public) character of the social access rule for products, not the (equal) amounts of productive resources available to individuals.

26. *Free to Lose*, p. 18. Discussion of the example is deferred to Section 6.1.

27. In the light of note 11 this ruling makes Thatcherite popular capitalism a thoroughly petty-bourgeois endeavour, which seems an appropriate judgement.

28. This is evidently the way to handle occupational differentiation within a Marxian framework. The jigsaw of class is not completed until the end of Chapter 11.

Roemer on Class and Exploitation

5.1 The Wealth Exploitation Correspondence Principle

Welfare is about the balance of goods and bads. In a subsistence setting, the ultimate good is survival, and other items – corn and so on – are goods in so far as they subserve this ultimate good. Goods that are necessary for survival satisfy a special class of wants called needs.

It is part of the intuition about needs that the utility which attends their satisfaction has the profile of a step function. If an agent consumes less of a subsistence good than they need, they are in a bad way. Ultimately, perhaps, they fail to survive. If on the other hand a person consumes more than they need, they are in approximately the same way as if they had consumed exactly what they needed, enough being as good as a feast.

This thinking lay behind the formulation of the revenue constraint (4.6), where "what a person needed" was given a unique value b, so that the step function for utility was sharply defined at the coordinate b in corn-space. It was therefore implicit in the model that all agents were alike in having needs (i.e. preferences over consumption goods whose utility profiles were step functions). It was further explicit that the step in each person's step function occurred at the same place in corn-space – namely b.[1]

We now assume, distinctly, that the height of each person's step function at the point b is identical. This is to say that at the point at which each individual is satiated, each individual is equally satisfied. These three assumptions are three different ways of saying that agents are *equally needy*. Taken together they establish a strong package of conditions on the uniformity of agents. Yet only if all three assumptions are made is it correct to conclude that the subsistence model is appropriate and that all agents at an equilibrium of the model have equal welfare from the viewpoint of their consumption of goods.

The point of imposing these uniformity conditions upon the utility from consumption is partly to concentrate attention on the utility from production. The welfare of agents at equilibrium will then differ only if they are differentially involved in production. Since the only welfare-relevant aspect of production is assumed to be labour, which is a bad, individual welfare depends inversely on the amount of labour performed. If we impose that all agents have identical (dis)utility functions over labour, then the comparative welfare of agents varies monotonically with the amount of labour they perform. The uniformity assumption over producer's utility may be interpreted as an assumption of *equal ability* to supply labour: each labourer is equally worn out by the same burden of work. The upshot is that the relative welfare of equally able, equally needy individuals at the equilibrium of a subsistence economy is given by the quantity of labour each performs.[2]

Ranking of agents by welfare now follows immediately from previous calculations. The amount of labour performed is simply the minimand $Lx + z$ of the programme (4.5)–(4.8). Recall that Lx is the time spent in self-employed labour, and z the time in wage labour. We find from the relevant entries in Table 4.1 and some manipulation that

$$Lx+z=pb[(1-a)-wra]/(1-a) \qquad : 0<w<1 \qquad (5.1)$$

$$=pb[(1-a)-(2-w)ra]/(1-a) \quad : 1<(2-w)<(1-a)/ra \qquad (5.2)$$

$$= 0 \qquad : (1-a)/ra \le (2-w) \le 2 \qquad (5.3)$$

Figures 5.1 and 5.2 display labour time $Lx + z$ as a function of the wealth index w for the low profit and high profit economies respectively. Labour time evidently declines monotonically with wealth. At $w = 0$, labour time attains its maximum value $[= pb]$. At $w = 1$, labour time is

$$pb[(1 - a) - ra]/(1 - a) = Lb/(1 - a) \qquad (5.4)$$

by substitution from (4.1). Beyond $w = 1$, labour time declines further, when it either falls to zero (in the high profit – high price economy) or does not (in the low profit – low price economy).

Given the connections assumed between labour time and welfare, we can deduce: *welfare declines monotonically with wealth*. Note that this finding is not a truism. Wealth *per se* is not an argument of any utility function (in fact, no money quantity enters any utility function in a subsis-

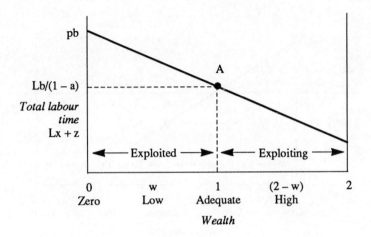

Figure 5.1 Labour Time and Wealth in a Low Profit Economy

tence economy). Wealth is merely a neutral means of positioning oneself with respect to non-monetary goods and bads. Yet it follows in a competitive subsistence economy that poor people are worse off than rich people. This is a Wealth Welfare Correspondence Principle.

We now envisage a slicing operation performed on the graphs of Figures 5.1. and 5.2. Some level of labour time is chosen (between zero and pb) and we separate the agents who are above and below the cut-off level. Any such line will split society into *a poor group* consisting of those people who (i) work longer than the cut-off time and (ii) have lower wealth than the wealth corresponding to the cut-off level; *a rich group* who (i) work less than the cut-off time, and (ii) have greater wealth than the cut-off level of wealth; and *a middle group* whose work time is exactly equal to the cut-off value, with corresponding wealth.

It should be stressed that we could slice at any level to generate a high wealth-welfare group distinct from a low wealth-welfare group, buffered by a middle group. Marxism in fact elects to make the incision at one particular level. I first describe and then explain that decision.

The Marxian cut off level is the labour time of producers in the dead

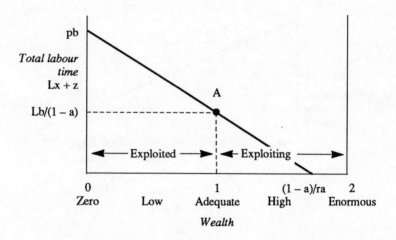

Figure 5.2 Labour Time and Wealth in a High Profit Economy

centre of the picture, for whom $w = 1$. The time in question is equal
to $Lb/(1 - a)$ (from (5.4)).

All those actors above this level of working-time, to the left of $w = 1$,
are then said to be *exploited* producers; all those below the level, to the
right of $w = 1$, are *exploiting*; while those poised exactly on the cut-off
line at $w = 1$ are exploitation neutral: *neither exploited nor exploiting*.

One reason for singling out this particular cut-off level is that the quantity $Lb/(1 - a)$ is fixed by the technical data alone. Indeed, its computation
relies on all the technical data (the labour input coefficient L, subsistence
level b and means of production coefficient a). A good way to visualize
the wealth–labour variation is then to regard the line-graph in Figures
5.1 and 5.2 as pinned down in the centre – at the technologically determined coordinates [1, $Lb/(1 - a)$] – and rotating about this fixed point
A as prices and profits rise (clockwise rotation) and fall (anti-clockwise
rotation).[3]

Another reason apart from its independence of price movements for
picking out $Lb/(1 - a)$ as a point of comparison for welfare purposes

is that it corresponds to the quantity of time a person would have to work if they were in a society all by themselves. If one therefore identified the quantity $Lb/(1-a)$ with the amount of labour a person had to perform to satisfy their subsistence constraint b on the basis of historically bequeathed forces of production [a, L], then $Lb/(1-a)$ is the *socially necessary labour time*.

Persons with wealth less than $w = 1$ are in this special sense working longer than is necessary; while persons with wealth greater than $w = 1$ are working less than is necessary. Persons with wealth equal to $w = 1$ are working just the time that is socially necessary. (Note that socially necessary labour time is not the social average of labour time. If the proletarian member of a two-person society works an infinite time, infinity divided by two is still infinity.)

These reasons may be good enough for singling out the cut-off level $Lb/(1-a)$ for some special attention. But are they good reasons for introducing the term exploitation to describe the relationship between the groups into which this particular incision divides society?

To exploit a person is, minimally, to gain some advantage at that person's expense. Gaining such an advantage involves taking advantage of something about the person or the person's situation. What grounds are there for saying that the wealthier Crusoes are taking advantage of the poorer Fridays?

Crusoe certainly gains an advantage from the presence of Friday. Were it not for Friday's work in his employ, Crusoe would have to work himself for a time $Lb/(1-a)$ no matter how much wealth he had. It is also a necessary condition of Friday's employment that Friday lacks wealth, since we have seen that the self- employment equilibria will occur if Friday has wealth at least equal to $w = 1$. It follows that Crusoe *is* taking advantage of an aspect of Friday's situation, namely Friday's level of wealth below $w = 1$.

One might go further, and say that what Crusoe is really taking advantage of is something about Friday herself. For it is Friday's neediness which mandates that she satisfy her subsistence constraint. It is this neediness which when she lacks wealth compels her to seek employment by Crusoe to his benefit ("compel" is appropriate: agents in the model become employees only to the extent that they have no other option).

If Crusoe is undeniably gaining as a result of what Friday does, is Crusoe *gaining at her expense*? This is a critical question, because the answer to it leads to the parting of the ways between neo-classical and classical Marxists, and thence between proponents and opponents of the capitalist system. I sketch the neo-classical argument for "No" followed by the classical Marxist argument for "Yes".

Neo-classical reasoning concedes that the capitalist gains as a result of the employment relation but argues that the worker gains as well. This is indeed self-evident: Friday would starve to death if the capitalist didn't give her a job. What we have in the employment relationship is therefore a case of mutually beneficial gains from trade. There is a net output in the production process which is the happy outcome of the union of the capitalist's capital with the labourer's labour. One can quibble about how this output is to be split precisely between the two parties to the union, but the mutual benefit of the general arrangement cannot be in any doubt. The employment relation has after all emerged as a consequence of an optimization programme. And what an equilibrium of an optimization programme means is just that everyone is doing better than they otherwise would – in this case, better than if the employment relation did not exist.

Given the mutuality of benefit, one could only say that the capitalist was gaining at the worker's expense by saying at the same time that the worker was gaining at the capitalist's expense. Yet that would be an absurd conclusion: mutual exploitation is a contradiction in terms.[4] So it must be that both are gaining, but neither is gaining at the expense of the other. Capitalism is an inherently non-exploitative system.

False, replies the classical Marxist. Capitalism is not only compatible with exploitation: exploitation is the very basis of its existence. The capitalist certainly does gain at the expense of the worker. To see this, one only has to consider the terms of the exchange between them. The only welfare-relevant items of this comparison are the subsistence goods b and the labour times $Lx + z$. Everyone is in equilibrium getting at least the subsistence b (the only person who ever gets more than b is the pure capitalist). What is this worth? Because labour time is the only real cost in the economy, subsistence must be worth the amount of labour it takes to create it. But it takes L units of labour to produce each $(1 - a)$ units of net corn output, so the (labour) value of each unit of corn is

$$L/(1 - a) \tag{5.5}$$

and the value (v) of the subsistence bundle b is therefore

$$v = Lb/(1 - a) \tag{5.6}$$

units of labour.

Every actor gets a bundle worth at least v (and every non-capitalist a bundle worth exactly v) but not everyone puts in the same contribution to attain it. The overall balance of what an agent receives to what an agent contributes is given by

Labour Balance $= v - (Lx + z)$ (5.7)

where the calculation (5.7) records the terms of a *virtual exchange* between each agent and "society", arising from the aggregate effect of all the real exchanges in the competitive market place.[5]

Substitution in (5.7) gives

Labour Balance $= Lb/(1 - a) - pb[(1 - a) - wra]/(1 - a)$

which reduces to

Labour Balance $= pb(w - 1). ra / (1 - a)$ (5.8)

We see from (5.8) that the net losers in the balance are just those agents with wealth $w < 1$, the net gainers are those with $w > 1$, and the neutrals have $w = 1$.

At an equilibrium of an economy with at least some poor agents, unable to survive on their own wealth, there will be some net losers. The reproduction conditions of the economy then ensure there will also be some net gainers. We know that the net gainers are gainers only because some others are net losers. We also know that the relation is asymmetrical: no-one can be both a net loser and a net gainer. This justifies calling the relationship between the two groups an exploitative relationship, according to Marxism.

Yet the point at which the balance tips between net loss and net gain is exactly the wealth level $w = 1$. This is the best reason for singling out that level of wealth, and its corresponding labour time $Lb/(1 - a)$, for the slicing operation. Given a certain conception of exploitation, this is the level of wealth which divides the exploiters from the exploited. The use of (5.8) has enabled us to defend a certain *Wealth Exploitation Correspondence Principle*.

5.2 The Labour Theory of Value

Nothing has been said so far about the labour theory of value, and as little as possible will be said hereafter. It may nevertheless be helpful to trace out its connection with the above.

Equation (5.5) shows that the value of the produced commodity, corn, depends only on the technological coefficients L and a. In this single-sector model, it is trivially true that prices are proportional to values, since there is only one price (of corn) to which the one value (of corn) is necessarily proportional. Labour value does not determine price nor does price determine labour value in this model, since both are determined by physical conditions of production (value by [a, L]; price by [a, L] (and [b], given the neo-Ricardian closure of the price system)).

In Marxian terminology, the *value of labour power* is the labour value of the subsistence bundle, which we have already calculated to be:

$$v = Lb/(1 - a) \tag{5.6}$$

This value is deducted as the worker's share from the *new value added* in each production cycle, leaving the capitalist's share as *surplus value*. Let the net value added be u and surplus value s. Then the Marxian value accounting identity is

$$s = u - v \tag{5.9}$$

Suppose that the class structure is simplified so that a proletarian faces a pure capitalist class. Then $w = 0$, and all labour is performed by proletarians. Hence

$$u = Lx + z \tag{5.10}$$

and we find that the Marxian accounting identity (5.9) is a version of the Labour Balance equation (5.7).

In particular

$$s = - \text{(Labour Balance)} \tag{5.11}$$

In words, the creation of surplus value involves the net extraction of labour from the direct producers. To be exploited in labour balance terms is therefore to have surplus labour extracted in the classical Marxian sense. But substitution of (4.24) and (5.8) (for $w = 0$) into (5.11) gives

$$s = r. \, La/(1 - a) \tag{5.12}$$

This equation usefully verifies the *fundamental Marxian theorem* for this model, that surplus value is positive if and only if the rate of profit is positive. This theorem is held to be fundamental to Marxism because if surplus value is connected with exploitation, the result grounds the Marxian contention that capitalism is inherently an exploitative system.

Steedman has said that the idea expressed in the fundamental Marxian theorem is "rather obvious". So long as profits are made, there is some physical output going to employers, and any physical output requires the expenditure of some labour to produce it. Since employers *qua* employers perform no labour, there must therefore be some net transfer of labour time to them when they acquire the ownership of their profits.[6] To the modern perception, it is differential wealth and its associated welfare differential which is crucial to the theory of exploitation, not the conception that every commodity is a congealed mass of embodied labour time.

5.3 The Class Exploitation Correspondence Principle

We have now made two decompositions of society, each keyed to the distribution of wealth. The *Class Wealth Correspondence Principle* (CWCP) relates behaviour to wealth. The *Wealth Exploitation Correspondence Principle* (WECP) relates wealth to welfare. If we bring the two principles together, we can form a composite principle which relates behaviour to welfare.[7] This is the *Class Exploitation Correspondence Principle* (CECP).

The derivation of the CECP is immediate, because of the pivotal role played by the wealth level $w = 1$ in each of its constituent principles. Taking care to find a form of words consistent with the possibility of split-role equilibria, we find:

Class Exploitation Correspondence Principle

(i) Every agent is exploited who can optimize by being an employee exclusively;

(ii) Every agent is exploiting who can optimize by being an employer exclusively;

(iii) Every agent who can optimize at exclusive self-employment is neither exploited nor exploiting.

This completes the exposition of Roemer's fundamental ideas in a two-actor, one-sector Leontief subsistence world, having indicated along the way how his theory subsumes in that context the neo-Ricardian analysis

of competitive price formation, the classical value theory of Marx, and
the fundamental Marxian theorem which links the two.

5.4   Psychology, Technology and Labour

Psychological profiles

To ask whether Roemer's theory generalizes is to ask whether the CWCP
and the CECP hold true as we move through the menu of alternative
assumptions set out in Section 4.1. We begin with possible variations
in the preference schedules – the psychological profiles – of actors.

Subsistence preferences involve the minimization of labour subject to
a net revenue constraint, but revenue *per se* does not appear in the agent's
utility function. Accumulation preferences are conceptually the exact
opposite of subsistence preferences. Accumulators maximize net revenue
subject to a labour constraint, but labour *per se* does not appear in the
agent's utility function. In classical notation, it is the difference between
the C-M-C and M-C-M′ chains of commodity production and exchange.

The logic of optimization nevertheless turns out to be similar. Accumulators will always labour as long as they are physically allowed (by the
labour constraint), since labour either in self-employment or for wages
generates revenue without incurring disutility. There are thus no non-
working capitalists in a pure accumulation economy. (The topmost position in the class hierarchy is empty.) Presented with the choice between
self-employment and wage labour, accumulators will moreover choose
self-employment (because they will not wish to sacrifice the profit payment
which goes to their employer if they opt for wage labour).

The overall picture is therefore as follows: agents will be self-employed
until either (i) their wealth runs out or (ii) their labour constraint is
reached. If agents' wealth runs out first, they will be seeking employment
in order to maximize net revenue from wage labour during the balance
of their allotted working time. Such agents will be in proletarian or semi-
proletarian class positions. If other agents reach their labour constraint
before their wealth runs out, they will wish to use the balance of their
wealth to employ the proletarians or semi-proletarians looking for work.
Since investment brings profit, all wealth will be used, if possible. Such
agents will be small capitalists (employers also engaged in self-employment). The remaining class of agents is composed of those whose wealth
runs out at exactly the moment their labour constraint is satisfied. These
are the exclusively self-employed petty bourgeoisie (or its equivalent class
fractions). The upshot is that the Class Wealth Correspondence Principle
generalizes to the pure accumulation economy.

It might be thought that if the CWCP holds for the polar extremes among possible preference schedules, then it must hold for all the other schedules in between. This is unfortunately not the case: it is possible to arrange preference schedules in which the wealthier agent ends up as the employee and the poorer agent ends up as the employer.

Suppose for example that a wealthy person has used up all his (say his) capital in self-employment. Then perhaps he would prefer to work just a little longer at an equilibrium as a wage labourer to gain some more revenue, even though he has to work for it (which incurs a disutility). This is a possible character sketch of a *rich agent who really likes to work*.

Now in order that our hero's taste for wage labour can be indulged he must find an employer. This could be a poorer person (still with some wealth) whose distaste for labour exceeds their taste for maximum revenue: *a poor agent who really dislikes work*. Such an agent may prefer to be an employer than to be self-employed, because what the agent loses in revenue at equilibrium from having to pay wages is more than compensated by what the agent gains in not having to perform the labour for which the agent is instead paying wages.

Given a wealthier person looking for work, and a less wealthy person looking to avoid it, a mutually advantageous deal can be struck in which the poorer person employs the wealthier person, contrary to the Class Wealth Correspondence Principle. There can even be a single schedule of preferences which includes the preferences of the poorer and the wealthier persons as two points on a single curve, so long as the relative preference for labour increases sufficiently as wealth increases.[8]

Roemer sets some store by this counter-example and illustrates it with his repeated story of the wealthy workaphilic Adam who ends up as the proletarian, employed by the poorer, workaphobic Karl.[9]

The significance one attaches to the counter-example depends on an empirical and a theoretical judgement. Empirically, it is probably unlikely that agents' propensity to offer labour increases sufficiently with wealth to generate the counter-example. As Roemer points out, "it is often believed that labor supplied decreases with wealth".[10] So the existence of the counter-example need not disturb the idea that the CWCP is a valid sociological, if not a logical, generalization.

But I do not think that the counter-example much disturbs the logic of the theory either. It is true, given Roemer's behavioural definition of class, that the Adam–Karl example exhibits the wrong direction of connection between class and wealth. Yet it is surely unreasonable to expect that a theory of social class should apply regardless of preference schedules – to cater for the saint, the hermit or the miser, as well as ordinary mortals. An ordinary mortal for this purpose is a person:

(i) who never likes labour;

(ii) who never dislikes revenue;

(iii) whose dislike for labour doesn't evaporate too quickly as wealth (hence net revenue at equilibrium) increases.

Since dislike of labour is not likely to evaporate with wealth at all, (iii) is not a very restrictive condition. It is then possible to say that the CWCP holds under a slightly restricted definition of the type of person to whom the social class concept applies, rather than say that the Adam–Karl counter-example falsifies the CWCP.

Variation of technology

If it is variation in preference schedules which spells trouble for the CWCP, it can be guessed that it is variation in technology which will cause problems for the CECP. This, because of the well-known difficulties surrounding the concept of labour content in increasingly sophisticated linear technologies.

In a single-sector Leontief technology, we have seen it to be trivially true that prices are proportional to values. As is known from discussion of the venerable Transformation Problem of values into prices in Marxian economics, values and prices are proportional in a multi-sector Leontief economy if and only if the organic composition of capital is constant across all sectors. This highly unlikely contingency effectively makes each industry a replica of every other industry from the value point of view (so it effectively reduces the multi-sector economy to a single-sector economy). Otherwise, and in general, prices diverge from values.

If we measure agents' welfare (hence exploitation status) by the labour balance method, the disproportionality between values and prices in a multi-sector economy presents no problem for subsistence preferences: each actor consumes the same given bundle of commodities b which has a *fixed* labour content at equilibrium. Since all agents have the same weekly shopping basket we can compute for all agents a balance between labour expended and labour content of goods received. (This is why the single-sector derivation of the CECP presented in the previous chapter offers an accurate summary of the position for a multi-sector Leontief subsistence economy.)

With accumulation preferences, on the other hand, agents' welfare will depend on the net revenue they receive. If values are not proportional to prices, the same net revenue can be spent by any given agent on commodities with different labour values. It follows that whether or not an agent is exploited in the classical labour balance sense is liable to depend on the particular bundle of use-values the agent chooses to consume.

Roemer sidesteps this problem by introducing a "preference-independent" generalization of the exploitation concept. It is no longer the value embodied in goods consumed which is relevant, but the maximum value that the putative exploited could command (if they bought only "high value" goods with their lower revenues) and the minimum value that the putative exploiters could command (if they bought only "low value" goods with their higher revenues).[11] This modification accords with the general argument in favour of structural definitions: we look at the relation between resource position and welfare regardless of the agent's preferences and behaviour as a consumer. Agents are being placed in the same welfare band however they choose to spend their money. Elster, who gives such a "modal" conception of class first place in his appreciation of Roemer's work, remarks that "if an agent could change from being exploited into being an exploiter simply as a result of a change of tastes, some of the moral connotations of exploitation would be lost."[12] But the consequence of the new definition is to introduce a "grey area" of agents whose exploitation status is indeterminate, since the range of labour values they can command by purchasing different bundles of commodities straddles the amount of labour they perform (in general by working for others or working on their own account).

This muddies the waters of the CECP, but Roemer is nevertheless able to retrieve a weaker version of the CECP which arguably preserves its essential point: it turns out that class position is still ordered monotonically by wealth and, more importantly, that all agents in the "grey area" of exploitation status are petty bourgeois (i.e. they have levels of wealth at which they optimize by pure self-employment). The converse does not, however, hold, so that there may be rich petty bourgeois who are exploiters alongside capitalists, and poor petty bourgeois who are exploited alongside proletarians.[13] On the other hand, if the organic composition of capital is uniform, the grey area shrinks to a point, so that the precision of the subsistence CECP is restored and "the existence of a nontrivial grey area is equivalent to the transformation problem."[14] The most general models in the sequence of technologies hold further surprises for the same problem.

In a convex cone technology, there are constant returns to scale, but joint production and factor substitution are allowed. This assumption admits fixed capital and turnover times of processes for the first time. The question is how to adapt exploitation theory to this more general context. The key problem is how to give sense to the notion of the labour embodied in commodities, given that different production processes are available and that more than one product may be produced in the same process. The procedure developed by Morishima is to define labour value according to the minimum direct labour required to produce a given net output. This definition preserves the fundamental Marxian theorem, that "exploitation is equivalent to profit-making".[15] Following through this "received" definition, Roemer finds to his dismay that the CECP is false for the cone technology.

There are two ways out of this dilemma. One must either accept that the CECP is false, and therefore fragile in depending on the restrictive assumptions of the Leontief technology (no fixed capital), or one must try to redefine the concept of value (in a non-arbitrary way) so that the CECP remains true for the cone technology. Roemer adopts the latter approach (which seems to give very little room for manoeuvre on the face of it). His solution is to posit a final definition of value which excludes from the determination of minimum labour inputs all those processes which cannot be operated at maximum profit rates, and which will there-fore not be operated by rational maximizers.

The CECP becomes true under this definition, and it is fortunate that the fundamental Marxian theorem survives (when it might well have been lost under any non-Morishima definition of value). The final definition also has a nice combination of features to recommend it and features which might condemn it in the eyes of Marxian tradition.

First, the two definitions (Morishima's and Roemer's) coincide for the Leontief technology, since all processes operated at all are operated at a single (maximal) profit rate in a reproducible solution of the Leontief economy.[16] From this point of view, either definition is an appropriate generalization beyond the Leontief case. But the difference between the two definitions in the more general context is that Morishima's depends only on the technological constraints, whereas Roemer's also includes a market constraint (on profitability).

Recommending itself to the Marxian tradition, Roemer's definition endorses the view (often held by the orthodox) that "value" is not a material category applicable to all regimes of production but a social category peculiar to capitalism, because the profitability constraint helps to determine what values are.[17] Set against this is the contradiction to the view (also dear to the orthodox) that values are logically prior to prices. We left this question with Steedman above in neutral gear, so that "labor values do not precede prices, but prices and values have a common ancestor – the technology and real wage."[18] With Roemer, equili-brium prices determine which processes capitalists will operate, and values are defined only with respect to this restricted universe of technique. Prices therefore precede values in the order of determination.

If attention were focused only on questions of price determination, there might not be so much to choose between Morishima's and Roemer's generalizations of the value concept. But the new element to consider is the CECP. If the CECP articulates the key Marxian insight about capitalism, then Roemer's definition must be preferred, since the Mori-shima definition makes the CECP false for the cone technology. Moreover, since the Roemer definition makes the CECP true for the cone technology, the CECP has been carried through to the most general context in which economic theory is usually conducted. Abandonment of the orthodox claim for the priority of values seems a small price to pay for such an achievement.

Heterogeneous labour

The problem of heterogeneous labour is perhaps the most vexed facing the classical theory of value, and the degree of vexation is peculiar to theories of labour value among economic theories generally. The underly-ing reasons for this are fairly obvious. Any theory which seeks to under-stand prices, and therefore market behaviour, in terms of labour value is bound to resort at some stage to a homogeneous standard of labour which is going to mirror prices.

Attempts to establish commensurability in the Marxian tradition are more notable for their ingenuity than their plausibility. The classically inspired attempt, for example, to look at skilled labour in terms of the amount of unskilled labour required to produce it raises more problems, both conceptual and technical, than it resolves.[19]

Roemer pursues the question using two conceptions of heterogeneity. The more radical conception is of a number of distinct, and mutually incommensurable, kinds of labour, each offerable in different amounts by producers. But it turns out that this assumption leads into a cul-de-sac, since even where a distinct class decomposition occurs, there is no coherent way to make welfare comparisons of agents located via their optimizing programmes in the separate universes constituted by different kinds of labour (only one universe exists under the assumption of homogeneous labour). For radically heterogeneous labour there is nothing into which a theory of exploitation can sink its teeth.[20]

Under another, milder, conception, labour power is homogeneous but unequally endowed to agents. This models a sort of homogeneous sort of heterogeneous labour. It may be interpreted either in terms of leisure preference (some agents are prepared to offer more labour than others) or as a proxy for skill differentials. In the former interpretation, it is subsumed under the case of psychological profiles discussed above. In the latter interpretation, the assumption is open to the same objection as any reduction procedure. It is not obvious that to be skilled is to have a bit more of something that everyone else also has. It may be to have something that others don't. If the average assembly line were to be operated by the average Marxist theorist, for example, the result is less likely to be lower output than total chaos.

With this conceptual reservation, the assumption of mildly hetero-geneous labour nevertheless generates some interesting results. The CECP is preserved, but the correlation of both class and exploitation status with wealth breaks down, to be replaced by a correlation with the wealth endowment/labour endowment ratio. Retrospectively, this may not be surprising. The mild heterogeneity assumption essentially counts each agent as several people from the labour input point of view, but still regards them as one person from the revenue receipt point of view. The situation of each heterogeneous person is therefore like the situation of a coalition of several homogeneous people each contributing a unit of labour-power. The collective wealth of the coalition would equal the wealth of the equivalent heterogeneous person, but the effective individual wealth of coalition members must be reduced in proportion to the number of people in the coalition. This is why the wealth/labour ratio takes the place held by straightforward wealth in the early models. The upshot is, however, that very handsomely endowed labourers may be wealthy but still be exploited by poor, but very poorly endowed, labourers, since the wealth/labour ratio of the wealthy individual is lower. Or putting it another way: "any agent with positive wealth can make himself into an exploiter by offering sufficiently little labour."[21]

The logic of this case is very similar to the logic of the Adam–Karl counter-example, and I think the same judgement applies. It is important to know that if either the taste or the capacity for labour increases suffi-ciently with wealth, the CWCP fails to hold, but this is an unusual eventua-lity which ought not to ruffle us unduly.

5.5   Market Options

Industrial and financial capital

The generalization of the theory from labour markets to capital markets is immediate.

If the options x, y, z in the model of Section 4.2 refer to lending activi-ties rather than employing activities, and the profit rate is replaced by a rate of interest on borrowed capital, then the optimization programme for aspiring finance houses is directly analogous to the programme (4.5)–(4.8) for aspiring capitalist employers. It can be shown that there is an *isomorphism* between on the one hand spending money to hire labour and on the other hand lending money for labour to hire itself: "it does not matter whether labor hires capital or whether capital hires labor."[22] It follows in particular that the equilibrium profit rate equals the equilibirum interest rate and that the class-equivalence set out in Table 5.1 obtains.

Table 5.1 The Class Isomorphism of Industrial and Financial Capital

Labour Market Classes	*Capital Market Classes*
Pure capitalist	Pure lender
Small capitalist	Lender plus own financing
Petty bourgeoisie	Solely own financing
Semi-proletarian	Borrower plus own financing
Proletarian	Pure borrower

Isomorphism implies that the CWCP and the CECP hold in exactly the same way when (i) a labour market is open; (ii) a capital market is open; or (iii) both markets are open, whatever other options from the menu of possible assumptions are chosen in respect of preference schedules, technology or heterogeneity of labour.

This finding of equivalence in class structure and welfare between the financial and industrial variants of capitalism reinforces the general emphasis Roemer's treatment places on resources above behaviour as the key focus of inequality: "given differential ownership, there are a variety of institutions all of which skin the cat in the same manner."[23]

Since this idea of the symmetry between the hire of labour by capital and the hire of capital by labour is a favourite theme of the political right, especially in its attacks upon the Marxian preoccupation with the dynamics of the labour contract, it might be thought that Roemer's result represents a major political concession. On the contrary, I believe it reinforces the conviction that it is difficult for agents to escape from initial poverty even if the extra option of borrowing capital is made available to them. For one's fate in respect of perfectly competitive capital markets is as predetermined by resources in these models as is one's fate in respect of perfectly competitive labour markets, leaving you in an identical position of exploitation whether you take the industrial employment route or the loan finance route.[24] This point is liable to become increasingly important as the workers of Eastern Europe and the Soviet Union emerge blinking into the harsh new dawn of international capitalist finance.

The industrial and financial segments of the classes at each level in Table 5.1 are clear examples of *class fractions*, as that term was introduced in Section 4.4. Thus, the industrial capitalists and the bankers are two fractions of the big bourgeoisie, and similarly for all the other classes lower down.

If there is an isomorphism between industrial and financial capitalism regarding the central facts of class formation, it is still possible that domination of workers by management on the industrial shop-floor is the basis of an important second-order distinction between the two main branches of capitalist enterprise.

Roemer says that "domination of workers is necessary because of imperfections in the technology for writing and enforcing contracts. Capitalists do not dominate workers at the point of production because they are malevolent, but because of the impossibility of writing a perfectly delineated, costlessly enforceable contract for labor."[25] Recall that Roemer's location of the causal origins of capitalist exploitation in the initial distribution of resources makes a considerable dent in a time-honoured strand of Marxian sociology that dwells on the bitter experience of factory work. His exploitation-centred concept of class differs from the domination-centred approach of shop-floor sociology. And it may be that Roemer is making a conciliatory gesture to the latter approach by accepting that there is something special about the enforcement of the labour contract, albeit that the terms of the contract are still in his view determined by the anterior distribution of resources. Yet the necessity of contract enforcement does not in fact distinguish industrial from financial capitalism, since the latter has analogous enforcement problems of its own: the personnel department in the factory finds its counterpart in the credit department of the bank.[26] The problem of contract compliance is in fact a universal problem for exchange transactions (and not only market exchange transactions). The general problem is raised in Chapter 8, and Chapter 17 goes on to ask why superstructures may be required to stabilize systems of exchange and how they may be provided. For the moment, it is enough to observe that the modern Marxist analysis makes no distinction in principle between financial and industrial capital.

Trade as imperialism

Suppose that we now close both the labour and capital markets, leaving open just the markets in produced commodities. Roemer shows rather surprisingly that class-like phenomena of differential welfare can arise even in this restricted context, with none of the institutions traditionally thought by Marxists to be responsible for exploitation. The mechanism of unequal exchange works as follows.

Assume first that each agent in the economy faces an optimization programme similar to that of the pure accumulator in the accumulation models. The agent must maximize net revenue by investing current wealth in appropriate productive activities, given a standard Leontief technology.[27] The difference from the previous models is that the agent is allowed neither to employ labour nor to borrow additional finance capital. These restrictions make it appropriate to regard the agents as distinct *nations* in an international economy linked only by trade in competitive markets for produced goods. The optimization problem of each agent-cum-nation is thus to maximize net national product.

Because international competition in labour supply and capital markets is excluded, there can exist differential wage levels and profit rates in different countries (corresponding to the competitive rates established by the *internal* labour and capital markets of each nation, shielded as these are from *international* competition). It can be shown that nations which are mutually isolated in this way will in fact enjoy different optimal internal profit rates (and associated internal wage levels). These differential optima depend on the capital-labour ratio: the higher the capital-labour ratio (i.e. the higher the ratio of national wealth to the national labour supply), the lower will be the maximum internal profit rate, and the higher the corresponding internal wage level.[28]

It is also true that a given nation is able to earn its maximum profit rate only in a sub-set of the industrial sectors available to it. Nations will thus specialize in producing certain products for the international commodity trade, while neglecting others as relatively unprofitable (i.e. unprofitable for the particular country, given its particular capital-labour ratio). In general, each nation will specialize in producing just two products, depending on the relation between the capital-labour ratio of the country and the capital-intensity of the technology for producing the various products: countries with higher capital-labour ratios will have to specialize in capital-intensive industries in order to realize their nationally specific maximum profit rates.

It should be noted that the variation in the equilibrium product-mix of the different countries has come about not because of a variation in technological know-how (since every process is available in principle to every country) but because of an optimization decision taken by each country against a background of differential resource distribution (different national wealth and labour supply conditions). Yet the effect of the decisions of each country to adopt different product-mixes for international trade, and therefore to develop an international division of labour in the production of the various goods, is to make it possible that given countries have different balances in the labour content of the goods they export (as industrial producers) and import (as industrial consumers).

One difficulty that arises in the calculation of such a balance is, of course, that the very condition under which it is possible for the phenomenon of an international division of labour to exist – namely, a variation in the capital-intensity (the "organic composition of capital") among technologies in the different industrial sectors – is also the condition which makes market price in general diverge from labour value.[29] But Roemer is able to deal with this problem by introducing a modal definition of exploitation (in the same way in which he dealt with the analogous problem in the accumulation economy discussed in 5.4). He is then able to show that a Resource Exploitation Correspondence Principle of the anticipated kind applies for the relations between the stylized national agents: at an equilibrium of the appropriate model "a country with a high capital-labour ratio is gaining from unequal exchange in the sense that its national income unambiguously commands more embodied labour, through the goods it can purchase than the labor that is expended by its population in production. Similarly, a country with a low capital-labor ratio is exploited in the sense that its national income cannot possibly command as much embodied labor, in the purchase of goods, as its population expended in production. We observe as well an international division of labor, although each country has knowledge of all the production processes."[30]

These results depend on the non-competitive character of the international supply of labour and capital. What happens if the economic walls are breached which surround either the nation's labourers or the nation's capital stock? Recall that the equilibrium wage rate within a given country *increased* and its equilibrium profit rate *decreased* with an *increase* in the country's capital-labour index. Thus, if free movement of labour is allowed, there will be labour migration from poor to rich countries (in search of higher wages), and if free movement of capital is allowed there will be capital migration from rich countries to poor countries (in search of higher profits).

These movements will lead directly to an international equalization of wages or profits respectively. It can be shown further, however, that equalizing wages will equalize profits and *vice versa*, so that the opening of either the international labour market or the international capital market is sufficient to equalize the equilibrium values of both wages and profits in every country. Indeed, there is a perfect isomorphism of the equilibria obtained from the labour market and the capital market options. (This should not surprise us, in view of the isomorphism results of Section 5.5.)

Once wages and profits are equalized internationally, the erstwhile international division of labour will also disappear, since all nations will be facing the same profit and wage decisions and each national economy will produce the same product-mix (sometimes with the help of either imported labour or imported capital). Yet this does *not* entail the elimination of the welfare differential between the asset-rich countries (with high capital-labour ratios) and the asset-poor countries (with low capital-labour ratios). Roemer shows that countries are distinguished at equilibrium in a systematic way *according as they export or import labour* (or, isomorphically, according as they import or export capital). Moreover, the character of countries as net labour exporters or net labour importers correlates perfectly with their position in a hierarchy of resources – poor countries tend to export labour (isomorphically, import capital) whereas rich countries tend to import labour (isomorphically, export capital). Table 5.2 sets out the relationship between the capital–labour ratio and the character of the country vis-à-vis its labour or capital imports and exports, where the entries in the columns show the decision a country with a given capital–labour ratio must make to optimize net national product.[31]

In keeping with his behavioural definition of class, Roemer regards such a character of a country as a social class characteristic, and Table 5.2 exhibits a Class Resource Correspondence Principle.[32] (Table 5.2 is directly analogous to the version of Table 4.1 which would apply to an accumulation economy with no pure capitalist class at the top end of the class scale.)

Table 5.2 The Class Resource Correspondence among Trading Nations

Labour Market National 'Class' Position	Capital/Labour Ratio	Capital Market National 'Class' Market
The import of some labour	High	The export of some capital
Neither the import nor the export of labour	Adequate	Neither the export nor the import of capital
The export of some labour	Low	The import of some capital
The export of all labour	Zero	The import of all capital

A final result connects behaviour with welfare: countries which must export labour (or import capital) to optimize are the victims of unequal exchange (from the modal labour content viewpoint). Hence there is, in effect, a Class Exploitation Correspondence Principle in international relations, and the basic results of previous discussions have been reproduced in the context of a competitive world economy, with the capital-labour index of a given country playing the role taken by the straightforward wealth index of a given actor in the earlier models of a capitalist economy.

A note on the place of formal models

The mathematical models summarized unmathematically in the previous section comprise a remarkable set of tools for understanding the ebb and flow of international trade. They pass three demanding tests, and a comment on this particular set of models may serve as a general appreciation of Roemer's formal work.

(i) The models are both logical and elegant. Logicality is a technically minimal property of any admissible mathematical model, yet it is sometimes only if a model is couched in mathematical language that its logical quality can be rendered apparent. Mere logicality is not to be sneezed at (especially within the social sciences). Elegance is a more elusive concept, since it includes an aesthetic element. But whatever mathematicians mean by elegance is by common consent possessed by Roemer's models, above and beyond their logical coherence.

(ii) The models draw into a single frame of reference a number of issues which have long been the subject of more diffuse attention within the Marxian tradition – unequal exchange consequent upon an international division of labour in production, imperialism (in Lenin's sense of capital export), and international labour migration (of a kind much discussed in the Marxian literature of ethnic division in the metropolitan countries).[33]

It is not just that the models serve to reorganize on existing fields of discourse: they genuinely add new knowledge. Thus, it was not so obvious in radical circles pre-Roemer that an imbalance in the international terms of trade was probably a function of the uncompetitiveness of labour and capital markets, whereas the existence of large-scale labour migration and/or capital exportation was the function of a countervailing competitiveness. And there were certainly no circles which connected these ideas so systematically with traditional Marxian concerns about class division and labour balance, opening the way for a rather precise comparative evaluation of a wide range of class-like phenomena.

(iii) The models generate an immediate sense of command over the relevant empirical material; they both make sense of and make sense in terms of well-known features of the international environment (such as those mentioned under (ii)).

Yet it is difficult to pin down precisely what it is about a given model that is responsible for generating this sense of grip upon the world. The cognitive effect of exposure to Roemer is not that one is immediately seized with the desire for example to compute the capital-labour ratio of Pakistan, and compare it with the ratio for Western Germany (although that is the sort of thing that Erik Wright might do!). The models do not work at that level of concreteness. Indeed, it is a curious fact that the more abstract and hence parsimonious a model is, and thus the further it is in one sense removed from empirical reality, the more – if it is well designed – it seems to illuminate its chosen domain of empirical reference. Perhaps this is part of what is meant by elegance of theory in any applied discipline.

It seems likewise true that comely models in the politically connected disciplines act to illuminate the larger possibilities of political action rather than prescribe in any detail the policies to be pursued. Thus, the message of the trade models is that, given rational choice of technique, lack of wealth is sufficient to explain technological backwardness. And further, that any attempt to overcome the problem by borrowing money from or lending labour to the metropolitan countries is unlikely to alter the situation fundamentally. This is not to say that a constraint on the ability of (would-be) developing countries to operate different technologies – because of poor education, lack of urban infrastructure and so on – is not an important factor in real life. The point is that it looks as if development requires wealth, even if it also requires education, and even if the theory cannot tell us exactly how development is done.[34]

Notes

1. In a multi-sector model, b would be a constant vector quantity of subsistence goods.

2. I am explicitly concerned in this book with individuals who have unequal personal capacities or requirements only in Sections 5.4, 6.3, 10.3. and 15.2.

3. It is clear that the "balance of class forces" is tipping more in favour of the propertied classes as the line rotates clockwise. If the rotation goes far enough (i.e. if prices and profits are high enough), Figure 5.1 gives way to Figure 5.2 and the role of pure capitalist becomes available for the first time. In the absence of some mechanism such as a biological limit of maximum work and/or minimum subsistence, the level of prices and profits is set by the bargaining power of the two classes, who might for this purpose be collective actors formed according to the process sketched in Chapter 17. Endorsement of Roemer does not therefore imply acceptance of methodological individualism.

4. Judith Farr Tormey, "Exploitation, Oppression and Self-Sacrifice" in *Philosophical Forum*, 5, nos. 1/2 (1973/4), pp. 212–3, which also contains outstanding early proposals for a generalization of the exploitation concept to apply to both the class relation and the household.

5. "Exploitation theory views goods as vessels of labor, and calculates labor accounts for people by comparing the 'live' labor they expend in production with the 'dead' labor they get back in the vessels": John Roemer, "Should Marxists be Interested in Exploitation?", in John Roemer, ed., *Analytical Marxism* (Cambridge: C.U.P., 1986), p. 261.

6. Steedman, *Marx after Sraffa* (London: New Left Books, 1977), p. 57, and see also G.A. Cohen, "The Labour Theory of Value and the Concept of Exploitation", in Steedman et al., *The Value Controversy* (London: Verso, 1981), p. 221: "It is neither the labour theory of value (that socially necessary labour-time determines value) nor its popular surrogate (that labour creates value) but the fairly obvious truth (that labour creates what has value) ... which is the real basis of the Marxian imputation of exploitation."

7. For a very thorough exposition of the variety of possible correspondence principles, see Peter Abell, "Rational Equitarian Democracy, Minimax Class and the Future of Capitalist Society", *Sociology*, 21, no. 4 (1987).

8. The formal condition is given in John Roemer, *Value, Exploitation and Class* (Chur: Harwood Academic Publishers, 1986), p. 50.

9. *Value, Exploitation and Class*, pp. 68–71; *Free to Lose* (London: Radius, 1989), pp.

129–31; "Should Marxists be Interested in Exploitation?", pp. 58–9; and for variations on a similar theme, "Are Socialist Ethics Consistent with Efficiency?", *Philosophical Forum*, 14, nos. 3/4 (1983).

10. *Value, Exploitation and Class*, p. 50, but note also the comment in *Free to Lose*, p. 131 that the conditions of failure of the CWCP "are quite rare, but not outlandish".

11. "In [this] definition, we do not consider an agent to be exploited if he [sic] *happens* to purchase a bundle of goods which embodies less labor time than he worked; he is only exploited if he could not feasibly have purchased a bundle of goods embodying as much labor time as he worked": *A General Theory of Exploitation and Class* (hereafter *GTEC*) (Cambridge, Mass.: Harvard University Press, 1982), p. 135. The results reported here depend on an "Assumption of a Large Economy", since the supply of "high value" and "low value" goods must be large enough to absorb the revenues of any individual agent.

12. Jon Elster, *Making Sense of Marx* (Cambridge: C.U.P., 1985), p. 174.

13. *GTEC*, Theorem 4.7, p. 130.

14. *GTEC*, p. 125.

15. *GTEC*, p. 148.

16. Since it was Roemer who generalized Morishima's definition for the convex cone technology, both definitions under discussion are in a sense his. I have used the term "Morishima definition" for the sake of distinctness and familiarity.

17. "Capital is ... not only a sum of material products; it is a sum of commodities, of exchange values, of *social magnitudes*": K. Marx, "Wage Labour and Capital", in R.C. Tucker, ed., *The Marx-Engels Reader* (New York: W.W. Norton, 1972), p. 177. Original emphasis.

18. *GTEC*, p. 150.

19. For an early statement of the reduction procedure in Marx, see "Wage Labour and Capital", p. 175. Some of the problems are outlined in my "Value and Strategy". I argue that the only admissible differentiating characteristics of abstract labour are time and intensity. The latter differentiation raises problems of its own, since, as Elster notes, "Marx never explains ... how more and less intensive labour can be reduced to a common standard of labour time": *MSM*, p. 192. It should be noted, however, that this problem is common to neo-classical and Marxian production functions.

20. *GTEC*, pp. 178–83.

21. *GTEC*, p. 178.

22. *Value, Exploitation and Class*, pp. 61–2.

23. *Value, Exploitation and Class*, p. 62.

24. See "New Directions" in *Analytical Marxism*, p. 93 and "Should Marxists be Interested in Exploitation?" p. 43.

25. *Value, Exploitation and Class*, p. 66 and *Free to Lose*, p. 86.

26. I am unclear whether Roemer thinks there are systematic differences between industrial and financial capital in this respect. The discussion in *Free to Lose*, pp. 96–8 suggests that he does, whereas the comment in *GTEC*, p. 95, n.1 suggests that he does not. The relation between domination and exploitation is explored by Erik Wright in "The Status of the Political in the Concept of Class Structure", *Politics and Society*, 11, no. 3 (1982), and his view is modified in *Classes* (London: Verso, 1985), pp. 56, 72.

27. The exposition will follow Roemer's "Unequal Exchange, Labor Migration and International Capital Flows", in P. Desai, ed., *Marxism, Central Planning and the Soviet Economy* (Cambridge; Mass: M.I.T. Press, 1983).

28. The initial statement of this point in "Unequal Exchange, Labor Migration and International Capital Flow", p. 38 contains a misprint: "internal wage rate ... decreases" should read "increases".

29. This is implicit in the proof of Theorem 1 in "Unequal Exchange", p. 42.

30. "Unequal Exchange", pp. 43–4.

31. "Unequal Exchange", Theorem 2, and *Free to Lose*, Section 7.5.

32. Table 5.2 synthesizes *Free to Lose*, Tables 7.2 and 7.3.

33. See also Arghiri Emmanuel, *Unequal Exchange* (London: New Left Books, 1972); Lenin, *Imperialism* (Peking: Foreign Languages Press, 1965); and Stephen Castles and Godula Kosack, *Immigrant Workers and the Class Structure in Western Europe* (Oxford: O.U.P., 1973).

34. See Alec Nove, *The Economics of Feasible Socialism* (London: George Allen and Unwin, 1983), pp. 186–95 for salutary discussion of the attempt to translate unequal exchange theory directly into economic policy for developing countries.

6

The Problem of Exploitation

6.1 The Baby and the Bathwater

In the third part of his major work, John Roemer introduced the general
conception of exploitation which gave its title to his book. This general
theory – also known as the *property relations* approach to exploitation
– was refined and sharpened in three subsequent articles, in the course
of which it was claimed that the property relations approach had "superseded" the labour theory conception which has filled the past two
chapters.[1]

Since Roemer set up the argument as if the two conceptions were at
loggerheads, and made clear his preference for the property relations
approach over its rival, the result was a rather strange gesture of auto-
iconoclasm which called into question the status of his monumental work
on the labour theory of exploitation. In this section, I describe the new
property relations approach before examining its relationship to the
labour theory view which gave it birth.

The fundamental idea of the general theory is to compare the welfare
of agents under two scenarios:

(i) The equilibrium under some current allocation of resources;
(ii) The equilibrium following a counterfactual resource equalization.

A coalition of agents is said to be *exploited* in the status quo only if
two conditions are met:

Condition 1: The agents' welfare would improve under the equalizing
dispensation.

Condition 2: The welfare of all other agents would deteriorate under the equalizing dispensation.

A coalition is said to be *exploiting* only if the converse adjustments occur, i.e. if the exploiters would lose out and the rest would gain.[2] The counterfactual equalization may be conceived as occurring when a given coalition withdraws from society with an appropriately equal share of society's resources and sets up on its own account. In technical language, the counterfactual opportunities available to various withdrawing coalitions can be expressed in terms of the characteristic function of a game, and Roemer's general theory becomes thereby a branch of cooperative game theory.[3]

The generality of the general theory resides in two of its features. First, the theory can refer to a range of possible resources and a variety of possible counterfactuals regarding the egalitarian redistribution of those resources. Second, the theory can refer to a variety of different dimensions of welfare for agents, and of psychological constructions placed upon those dimensions. In short, the description of both agents and agents' situations is left wide open under the definition. It follows that the general definition admits of a whole variety of types of exploitation, depending on the types of resources, redistributions and agent profiles one has in mind for a particular application of the general concept.

Roemer uses this flexibility of the definition to disambiguate the dispute mentioned in Section 5.1 between neo-classicals and Marxists about the exploitative status of capitalism. He suggests that the dispute hinges on which counterfactual to the status quo the parties to the dispute have in mind.[4] The neo-classical contention is that the capital–labour relationship cannot be exploitative, because both sides gain from trade. This is true only if the benchmark from which one measures gain and loss is the current distribution of resources. Thus, if the proletarian withdraws with only the proletarian's resources (i.e. full ownership of labour-power and zero ownership of means of production) then both the capitalist and the proletarian classes lose out, contrary to Condition 1 in the general definition. Hence the neo-classical judgement ("no exploitation") is consistent with Roemer's definition, given the nature of the counterfactual the neo-classical thinker is inferred to have in mind.

The Marxian thinker chooses a different counterfactual, under which the proletarian withdraws with some appropriate share of means of production, in addition to her or his existing ownership of labour-power. If this counterfactual share of resources is the wealth level dubbed "adequate" in the subsistence models of chapters 4 and 5 (i.e. $w = 1$), then any agent with inadequate current wealth ($w < 1$) will gain (in labour terms) from the counterfactual equalization, whereas an agent with more than adequate wealth (w > 1) will lose (again, in labour terms).[5] So those with less than adequate wealth are exploited and those with more than adequate wealth are exploiters according to the general definition.

We see that the choice of Marxian counterfactual skilfully achieves two objectives: (i) it picks out the same coalition of agents as exploiting and exploited under the general definition as under the classical labour theory conception; (ii) it makes plain that the Marxian charge against capitalism is tacitly premised on a demand to equalize assets in alienable means of production.

Roemer proposes that this test based on the equalization of alienable assets be regarded as the test for *capitalistic* exploitation, on the reasonable grounds that it is the test failed by capitalism, according to the Marxian perception.

A different test can however be applied which focuses on labour-power as the unequally distributed resource instead of means of production. To say that labour-power is unequally distributed is to say that some agents are not free to dispose of their own labour-power (equivalently – some other agent has the right to the uncompensated use of the agent's labour-power). The corresponding counterfactual test is to ask what happens when an agent withdraws with a full share of her or his own labour-power. In the case of capitalism, we know that the general definition is not satisfied (since each agent already owns a full share in her or his labour-power, and both proletarian and capitalist lose out if the proletariat withdraws only with its existing labour-power). In feudalism, on the other hand, if the serfs withdraw with full ownership of their labour-power, they gain and the lords lose, since the serfs no longer perform uncompensated feudal labour service (or give equivalent goods in kind). The test is therefore regarded as a test for *feudal* exploitation, because it is the test that feudalism fails (and capitalism passes). Feudal lords exploit their serfs' lack of freedom over labour-power, whereas capitalists exploit their workers' lack of wealth.[6]

Both Marxian and neo-classical thinkers regard feudalism as exploitative, because each rejects unequal distributions of labour-power (as an infringement of a bourgeois freedom), whereas only Marxian thinkers regard capitalism as exploitative, since only they reject unequal distribution in alienable means of production (neo-classicals accept unequal distribution of alienable assets as an expression of a bourgeois freedom!).

There is no doubt that Roemer's general definition is immensely clarifying and powerful. Indeed, it is the idea that more than any other inspired the writing of this book. However, while I shall refuse to bite the hand that feeds, I cannot resist a bit of a nibble.

The question is whether or in what sense the general property relations conception "supersedes" the classically inspired labour theory conception. Roemer argues:

> It is clear one can perform the [counterfactual equalization] tests [required by the general definition] regardless of how complicated the production specification is – that is to say, we do not require restrictions on the production set which are necessary to allow us to be able unequivocally to speak of embodied labour time. Thus the theory of exploitation is liberated from its dependence on the very special labour theory of value.[7]

It appears from this statement that Roemer believes the relation between the two approaches is rather like the relation between the theory of relativity and Newtonian mechanics, wherein relativity supersedes conventional mechanics by liberating its physics from the restrictive assumption that the speed of light is infinite.

In such a relationship, the superseding theory (i) is superior to the superseded theory in at least part of their common domain of application, and (ii) contains the superseded theory as a special case (note that (ii) implies that the superseding theory is nowhere inferior to the superseded theory).

To apply this frame of reference to the present case we must first establish which theory it is that Roemer claims is superseded. I have used the vague phrase "labour theory of exploitation" to cover three conceptions which I now distinguish.

To begin with there is the *labour theory of value* in the sense which asserts that prices are explained by labour values. This assertion is, in general, false, as Roemer's work abundantly shows. The labour theory of value is indeed superseded by the linear production models discussed above. But the labour theory of *exploitation* is thereby superseded only if the labour theory of exploitation depends on the labour theory of value, and in fact it does not, because there is a second conception – the *labour balance* conception of exploitation – which does not rely on the labour theory of value. Labour-balance conceptions compute a labour balance (as in Chapter 5) from the very production models which supersede the labour theory of value.

Now it is of course true, as Roemer says in the preceding quotation, that there are limits to the generalization of the concept of embodied labour-time which imply limits to the generalization of the labour balance calculation. (The chief limitations are imposed by the homogeneous labour and linear production assumptions.) Yet it is also true that Roemer's ingenuity has extended the concept of labour balance to accumulation models in which the link between labour-time and price breaks down. (I have in mind here the "modal" version of the labour

balance conception which can be applied when the labour theory of value
is false.) So while the property relations approach does indeed supersede
the labour theory of value in this domain, it does not *ipso facto* supersede
the labour balance conception of exploitation.

The third candidate for supersession is what Roemer sometimes calls
the *surplus-value* conception of exploitation.[8] His target here is the orthodox Marxist idea that exploitation arises when and only when surplus
value is extracted from workers through the labour contract at the point
of production (and perhaps through the credit market also). This is the
visceral conception metaphorically favoured by Marx when he writes of
surplus value being pumped out of the direct producers, sucking them
dry in the process. I have called it elsewhere the hydraulic view.[9]

Roemer's case against the surplus-value conception is that "the property
relations definition of exploitation renders better verdicts than the surplus-
value definition" in respect of several troublesome counterexamples. But
even if this is true it may or may not follow that the property relations
approach is superior to the *labour balance approach*, depending on what
verdict the labour balance approach renders in respect of the same counterexamples.[10] I will agree with Roemer's judgements as between the property relations and surplus-value approaches. But I will also argue that
the labour-balance approach is consistent with the property relations
approach in respect of those counterexamples, so that both of the latter
approaches therefore supersede the surplus-value approach.

The counterexamples are of two main kinds. *Series A* consists of examples in which there appears to be "extraction of surplus value" but there
is no exploitation. *Series B* contains the converse set of examples in which
there does not appear to be "extraction of surplus value" but there is
exploitation.

A prominent example in series A involves agents who have equal wealth,
but not enough wealth to gain their subsistence from the capital-intensive
sector of the economy (the "factory") alone. Resort must therefore be
had to the labour-intensive sector (the "farm"), but this resort can involve
either (i) each agent splitting time in equal proportions between Farm
work and Factory work or (ii) some agents being exclusively Factory
workers, hired part of the time for wages paid to them by capitalist Factory
employers who must thereafter work for themselves on the Farm, and
who work only on the Farm.

In all cases, there is equal welfare among all agents and hence there
cannot be any exploitation, even though there is "extraction of surplus
value" at the point of production in the Factory under regime (ii).[11] Roemer
has this case in mind when saying that the surplus-value conception takes
"too micro an approach".[12] It would be more accurate to say that it
takes too *narrow* an approach, since the problem arises from looking

only at the terms of the labour contract in the Factory sector, and thus neglecting the countervailing labour burdens that the Factory employers suffer when they work on their own Farms. (Those burdens are relatively higher because of the lower productivity of the Farm sector.)

Since these extra burdens of work exactly cancel out the surplus value extracted by the Farmers from their Factories, the net result is a perfect labour balance of all agents in every sector, which is why one judges that exploitation cannot be occurring. But given that a conception of labour balance is deployed to make the case against the surplus-value view of exploitation, this example can hardly be an embarrassment to the labour balance conception, and cannot therefore supply any reason to prefer the property relations conception over the labour balance conception.

A slightly different range of series A examples with "surplus value but no exploitation" involves the cases of children, invalids and other dependants cared for by able-bodied persons. Here there really is an unequal labour balance (the carers contribute disproportionately and the cared-for receive the benefit), but the unequal exchange is not usually adjudged exploitative.

The first point about these cases is that the resource inequality goes in the wrong direction – it is the "sufferers" from the labour balance viewpoint who are likely to have the superior resource position: adults over children, the healthy over the ill, the able-bodied over the disabled and the middle-aged over the elderly. It follows that one will have to strain a little to make the provision of caring an equilibrium of rational behaviour, because caring activity seems to be against the self-interest of the carers. Carers must either be endowed with altruistic preferences, or be subject to external incentives to care (where, for example, caring is the expected thing to do, as it is especially of course for women).

The second point is that since the abilities and/or needs of the respective parties differ, there may be good reason why the labour balance should be unequal. Perhaps the theoretical link that has broken in this case is the connection between labour and welfare, so that welfare balance implies labour imbalance. The egalitarian benchmark for the general theory will then be set by a certain labour *imbalance* and it will in fact make sense to speak of exploitation as a deviation from this point of imbalance.

Thus, if a carer is doing more for an elderly person (or a child) than we feel is justified by differential needs and/or abilities we can say quite intelligibly to her (or sometimes him): "You are letting your aged dependants (or teenaged children) take advantage of your good nature: they are exploiting you because they are not doing enough for themselves."

It is implicit in these remarks that if the hypothetical carer were of a less amiable disposition,then the carer would gain and the cared-for lose in comparison with the status quo, restoring an appropriate (im)balance to the caring relationship. Once it is allowed that personal identity (i.e. preference profiles) might be subject to counterfactual alteration, there is no inconsistency in principle with either the labour balance conception or the general theory of exploitation.[13] The only casualty of these series A counterexamples appears to be the surplus-value conception.

Series B counterexamples involve cases with exploitation but no "extraction of surplus value". These are cases in which the exploitative labour imbalance is caused by mechanisms other than the operation of standard capital ownership. The prime example here is of the international division of labour discussed in section 5.5, where labour imbalance was mediated entirely through the market in produced goods, in the absence of labour or capital market competition. The corresponding counterfactual equalization in the general theory is the equalization of the capital-labour ratio between countries.[14] Both the general theory and the labour balance conception rule that exploitation is taking place, even though there is no point of *production* at which surplus value might be siphoned off: another strike in favour of those two conceptions against the surplus-value definition.

So far, the conclusions are that (i) the labour theory of value and surplus-value conceptions of exploitation are inadequate from either the explanatory or the normative points of view, in comparison with both the property relations and labour balance conceptions; and (ii) the property relations and labour balance views coincide where they are both applicable, but the property relations approach has a larger domain of application (including, in particular, cases involving heterogeneous labour and non-linear production functions).

These conclusions invite the inferences (i) that the property relations and the labour balance approaches both supersede the other two approaches; and (ii) that the labour balance approach is indeed a special case of the property relations approach, just as Newton is a special case of Einstein.

Unhappily, the second inference is disqualified by an important fact. Relativity theory stands on its own as a theory, independently of classical mechanics; Roemer's general theory on the contrary continues to lean on the labour balance conception (strictly, on the models which generate the labour balance conception).

Indeed, it is not clear that the supposed general theory is a proper theory at all. A *theory* of exploitation says: "under such and such circumstances there will be a phenomenon which for the following reasons we may call exploitation" – for instance "under conditions of free market competition with differential access to means of production there will

be a distribution of labour times which . . . etc." All the general definition
says is: "If there is a phenomenon which satisfies the following conditions,
then for the following reasons we may call it exploitation".

This weakness of the general theory is revealed by a third batch of
counterexamples, in which the general theory as it stands is led astray
by the absence of models which display the appropriate causal connections
among agents' labour, and hence welfare.

The simplest example involves two agents with different capital
resources living alone on two different islands, running their respective
economies out of all contact with one another. If we apply the general
test for capitalist exploitation, we find that exploitation is supposed to
exist, since the poorer agent would undoubtedly benefit and the richer
agent lose out in an egalitarian redistribution of the pooled resources
of the two islands (or should we say lagooned resources?). Yet this verdict
offends our intuition. Exploiters must *derive benefit* from the exploitation
relation, whereas there is no inter-island connection in this example
between the welfare of the rich islander and any activity of the poor
islander.

Roemer tries to rescue the general definition from this counterexample
by adding to the definition a third condition designed to test for the
dependence of the exploiter on the exploited in the status quo.[15]

Condition 3: The welfare of the exploiting coalition would deteriorate
if the exploited coalition withdrew with its *current* resources.

In the two-island case, condition 3 fails to hold, since the welfare of
the rich islander would be quite unaffected by the putative withdrawal
of the poor islander. (The poor islander has in effect withdrawn already.)
Hence the rich islander does not exploit the poor islander – a verdict
that conforms with our intuition.

More significant examples of agents who satisfy the original conditions
1 and 2 of the general definition, but not the new condition 3, are the
unemployed and the poor peasantry. Roemer coins the cumbersome term
"Marxian unfair treatment" to describe their situation.[16] It is more
straightforward just to say that such agents suffer *differential exclusion*
from resources. This is the first step in their fate, and exploitation occurs
as a second step only if the exclusion from resources leads excluded agents
to act in a way which benefits their exploiter.[17] Yet even if the counterfactual grid in the general definition is now fine enough to catch the proper
distinctions among these various cases, the general theory still gives no
account of the circumstances under which exclusion will lead to exploitation.

I conclude that Roemer's general theory does not supersede what I have called the labour balance conception of exploitation. The relation between the two approaches is not that of general to special case; it is rather that of form to content. The general theory remains dependent on the labour balance conception. Without labour balance concepts, there is no measure of agents' welfare in the general theory (for the standard cases of Marxian concern); without the models which underlie the labour balance calculations, there is no causal story of agents' interactions.[18]

Perhaps the sharpness of Roemer's polemic against the labour theory of value and the orthodox surplus-value conception of exploitation may be excused by the need to rouse Marxists from their dogmatic slumber. There is some danger nevertheless in ejecting the labour-balance baby with the value-theory bathwater.

6.2   Antecedence and Entitlement

Exploitation is about welfare, but it is also about justice. The relation between the two gives rise to the greatest difficulty in Roemer's conception of exploitation.

Roemer says in one of his papers that "if I occasionally use 'exploitation' in its ethical as opposed to its technical sense, the word will be italicized" and this indicates his usual custom.[19] It follows that he mostly uses the word "exploitation" in its technical sense to describe allocations whose justice or injustice remains an open question.

I do not find this practice congenial. I agree with Judith Farr Tormey, G.A. Cohen, Jon Elster, Robert Van der Veen, Philippe Van Parijs and David Miller that the word "exploitation" is morally loaded whenever it is applied to human interaction.[20] It is not the case that exploitation is sometimes justified and sometimes unjustified; it is always unjustified. Unequal exchange is the morally neutral term, and we say that exploitation occurs if and only if a given unequal exchange is also an *unjustified* unequal exchange.

Compare another brace of terms: exclusion and oppression. Where exclusion is specifically unjustified, we can speak of *oppression*, which is the morally loaded term reserved for unjustified varieties of exclusion.[21] Thus, I am claiming, oppression is to exclusion what exploitation is to unequal exchange. I will use the morally neutral term unequal exchange in what follows for what Roemer usually calls exploitation, and I will use the term exploitation for what Roemer occasionally sets in italics.

This point is relevant to the interpretation the reader must make of a disconcerting answer Roemer gives to his question "Should Marxists be interested in exploitation?" Here is the writer who has done more than any other to advance our understanding of exploitation. And yet he says: "There is, in general, no reason to be interested in exploitation theory."[22]

I will dissent from this conclusion, but it is necessary first to realize that what Roemer means by his answer is that "there is, in general, no reason to be interested in exploitation in the technical Marxian sense relating to labour balance calculations." And part of his reason for thinking that such reasons are lacking is that he thinks labour balance calculations do not enjoy any direct relation with any question of justice. It follows in his view that if one is ultimately interested in exploitation in his moralized, italic sense, it will be a mistake to proceed by way of exploitation in plain script.

He reaches this conclusion by considering four reasons why one might be morally interested in labour balance calculations, and rejecting them each in turn. The reasons correspond with four time-honoured strands of Marxian thinking, concerned with accumulation theory, domination theory, alienation theory and inequality theory respectively. I summarize the first three of Roemer's rejections, with which I agree, before concentrating on the fourth, from which I dissent.

The accumulation theory draws on the classical Marxian claim that labour is the sole source of value, and that surplus-value is the secret of profit and accumulation in a capitalist economy. This claim is false, because labour is not the only input to the production process with the apparently magical property of being able to create more of itself at the end than there was at the beginning.

In fact, all commodity inputs to a productive economy have this property. In the single-sector model the labour value added to produce one unit of gross output is L, and the (indirect) labour input required for the (re)production of this labour is the labour content of the labourer's consumption, alias the value of labour power. According to (5.6), the value of labour power is $Lb/(1 - a)$. Consider in this light the condition

$$Lb/(1 - a) < L \qquad\qquad\qquad (6.1)$$

When (6.1) is true, two facts are being expressed: first, that surplus value is positive because value added (L) exceeds the value of labour power; second, that the labour-equivalent quantity of input on the l.h.s. of (6.1) has the apparently magical property of delivering a greater amount of labour as output (r.h.s.). So far so good for the classical perception: labour creates surplus value; profit is possible if and only if labour is exploited (in the technical Marxist sense).

But now ask what is the *corn* value of one unit of gross output. How much corn is embodied in corn? Each unit of produced corn requires a direct corn input of amount a (as means of production) and an indirect input of amount b (to feed the labourers who work for time L on means of production a to produce an output of one unit of corn). Hence the corn embodied in corn is (a + b). Corn has the magical property of self-expansion if and only if the corn embodied in one unit of corn is less than one unit. This requires

$$(a + b) < 1 \qquad\qquad\qquad (6.2)$$

But the reader may check that (6.2) is an identical expression to (6.1): corn and labour-power have equally magical properties. The fact that profit is possible if and only if corn is exploited should give us pause when assessing the significance of the equally valid statement that profit is possible if and only if labour is exploited (in the technical Marxist sense, in both cases). There is no reason to single out labour for a privileged explanatory role in production, and defend labour balance theory on that account.[23]

The domination theory holds that domination is connected with the extraction of surplus-value at the point of production, so that the analysis of labour imbalance helps one to determine how and why reprehensible forms of domination on the factory floor occur. The short answers are (as we have seen) (i) that domination relates imperfectly to labour balance (because of industry–finance isomorphism and other counter-examples); (ii) that domination in the labour process is theoretically a second-order effect and (iii) that if domination is the morally objectionable aspect of production, it would be better to observe and challenge it directly rather than infer it in a roundabout way from tricky labour balance calculations.

A third contender is alienation theory. Alienation theory makes the moral turpitude of capitalism arise from selling one's labour-power to produce boring regulation goods for an anonymous end user, an act incurring the "prostitution of a deep aspect of the self".[24] I think a shorter answer is available than Roemer gives concerning the possible connection of alienation theory with labour balance theory. The whole of labour balance theory depends on the analysis of the outcome of market transactions. Alienation theory on the other hand condemns the market *tout court*, in favour of some other form of social organization. So alienation theory presumably condemns an equal and an unequal labour balance with the same fervour, when both are arrived at through market transactions. A moral interest in alienation cannot motivate a moral interest in labour balance: they are quite independent grounds of criticism of market societies.[25]

Inequality is the last and most promising source of possible motives for taking a moral interest in labour balance theory. Roemer discusses this connection and then rejects it, for reasons which I will argue are mistaken.

Roemer begins by noting that the Wealth Exploitation Correspondence Principle makes labour imbalance "essentially equivalent to initial inequality of assets." In cases in which the WECP holds, moral interest in labour imbalance is motivated because labour imbalance "is a measure and consequence of the underlying inequality in the ownership of means of production, an inequality which is unjustified."[26]

It transpires that Roemer means by this statement that labour imbalance in the standard models is morally wrong if and *only* if the antecedent resource distribution is morally culpable: "When exploitation is an injustice, it is not because it is exploitation as such [i.e. not simply because it is unequal exchange], but because the distribution of labour expended and income received in an exploitative situation are consequences of an initial distribution of assets that is unjust."[27]

I suspect that one reason Roemer adopts this view is its connection with the property relations definition of exploitation which we have seen him prefer to the labour balance conception. Ethical interest is directed at the distribution of assets rather than at the outcome of interaction because the counterfactual tests in the general theory involve the redistribution of initial assets. In particular, the counterfactual redistribution "embodies one's notion of what is ethically preferable and non-exploitative."[28] The various equal shares with which agents withdraw in the various applications of the general theory are regarded also as *equitable* shares.

The different withdrawal tests therefore embody various conceptions of justice: feudal justice makes feudalism appear just, capitalist justice makes feudalism appear unjust but capitalism just, socialist justice makes both feudalism and capitalism appear unjust, and so on. The counterfactual withdrawal option establishes both a positive standard (a benchmark for relative gain and loss in welfare terms) and a moral standard of assessment for the status quo. And Roemer concludes that "the clear statement of an alternative regime of property relations makes the game-theoretic definition superior in an ethical theory."[29]

Whether or not Roemer was led to his opinion on justice by his preference for the property relations conception of exploitation, he seems wedded to the belief that the injustice of an outcome must be caused by the injustice of the outcome's cause. I give Roemer's view a formal rehearsal as:

Antecedence Principle: Injustice in the outcome of a set of transactions arises if and only if the antecedent distribution of resources is independently unjust.[30]

Let us apply the antecedence principle to a sequence of transactions in a literal-minded fashion. Suppose we are interested in whether some outcome in the here and now is just – at the end, say, of day one. Then the antecedence principle makes this question turn on the justice of the resource distribution at the dawn of day one. But the resource distribution at the dawn of day one is derived from the distribution at the start of day zero ... and thence day minus one, minus two ... back to the dawn of time at day minus infinity. The antecedence principle draws us back into the pre-history of property in order to establish the status in justice of some current allocation.

I now argue that the antecedence principle is untenable. Let us suppose that some grounds have been established for distinguishing just from unjust titles to assets. Let it happen that I possess some large sum of money from ancestors who acquired it and bequeathed it to me with uncanny propriety. Absolutely everything they did conformed with the moral standards we have just established. My moral title to these assets is utterly unimpeachable. Suppose that I now use the money to pay someone to rob a bank, and use more of it to bribe the police so that the crime goes undetected. (If the reader has a soft spot for bank robbers, imagine instead that I use the money to reduce a poverty-stricken rural population to debt peonage, hiring bandits to enforce my exorbitant rates of interest.)

Are these outcomes justified? I guess not, and the examples are easily generalized so that the argument applies in respect of any moral code. For suppose that there is at least some action involving the use of money which a given moral code prohibits – bribery, murder, extortion, racketeering, prostitution, you name it. Then I can choose to use my justly acquired money with uncanny impropriety to violate whatever moral code you nominate. (If your preferred moral code prohibits none of my possible actions, it isn't much of a moral code.) And any distributive outcome which follows on my unworthy deed is bound to be unjustified (by your moral standards) regardless of whether or not the initial distribution of resources was justified.

This argument is intended to establish that there is an irreducible moral distinction between the acquisition and the use of resources – justice of use cannot be inferred from justice of possession. To make this explicit, I reformulate the antecedence principle as

Historical Entitlement Principle: Injustice in the outcome of a set of transactions arises if and only if the antecedent distribution of resources is independently unjust and/or the transactions are unjust.[31]

The explanatory aspect of Roemer's work leads us to believe that unequal distribution of forces of production will cause labour imbalances. The latter may be unjustified under the historical entitlement principle, we now see, either because the initial resource distribution is unjustified or because the transactions are unjustified (or both). I try to elucidate Marx's views on these questions, before comparing them with Roemer's. I also serve notice of later challenge to the comprehensiveness of the historical entitlement principle.

6.3   Marx on Capitalist Injustice

That Marx thought capitalism inherently unjust

It is well known that Marx condemned capitalism because it came into the world "dripping from head to toe, from every pore, with blood and dirt".[32] This is the claim documented at length in Part 8 of the first volume of *Capital*. But did Marx also, and independently, condemn capitalist *transactions* for their injustice?

The question is significant for several reasons. Suppose that capitalist transactions are exonerated. Then the moral status of current capitalism depends entirely on the history of its origin. If what Marx says about blood and dirt is literally true, then capitalism is altogether culpable, because of its utterly detestable origins. The verdict on actually existing capitalism is the same as if all capitalist transactions were condemned.

But it is perhaps unlikely that Marx is literally correct. Indeed, since we saw in Part I that the tendency of Brenner's historiography is to locate the decisive origin of capitalism somewhat earlier than the events recorded in *Capital*, I, Part 8, the emphasis shifts somewhat from primitive accumulation – extra-capitalist methods of forcible accumulation – to intra-capitalist processes of profitable accumulation.[33]

If we were to accept that forcible accumulation was dirty and assumed for the sake of argument that unforcible accumulation on the basis of just initial possession was clean, the effect would be to give capitalism two distinct moral personae. The unacceptable face of capitalism would include everything consequent upon the original bloody expropriation (and, presumably, all effects of intervening bank robberies and so on). In particular, unequal exchanges of labour would be unjustified exploitations if they took place against a background distribution of unequal assets ultimately traceable to criminal activity.

The acceptable face of capitalism would include by contrast everything consequent upon the immaculate part of the historic collection of assets. In particular, unequal exchanges of labour would be justified if the unequal distributions of assets responsible for such unequal exchanges had themselves arisen from normal capitalist acts related to property holdings with an immaculate social pedigree.

I notice first that it will be a mighty empirical problem to determine on this basis which current labour contracts are exploitative and which are not. But I also remark that this bi-focal view of capitalism is a strange one for a Marxist to adopt, because it makes exploitation a merely contingent feature of capitalist relations. Capitalism in this view is exploitative only in so far as it has non-capitalist origins of a particularly murky variety. For any existing dirty capitalism, there might have been a clean capitalism with exactly the same unequal distribution of resources, and exactly the same trajectory of subsequent development, yet the first would be culpable and the second would not.

I think this implication alone makes it unlikely that Marx restricted his moral condemnation of capitalism to the tacky circumstances of its origin. And I think it is not difficult to show from the text that Marx condemned capitalist transactions regardless of the moral history of capitalist property. In this sense, the magnificent polemic at the end of Volume One of *Capital* is misleadingly conclusive. What remains less clear is *why* Marx condemned the capitalist transactions he undoubtedly did condemn. I treat these questions in turn.

At the very beginning of his analysis of "how capital is itself produced," Marx discusses the morality of capitalist accumulation. His numerical example concerns a cotton spinner who has advanced £10,000 for labour and raw materials, and made £2,000 profit. He continues:

> The original capital was formed by the advance of £10,000. Where did its owner get it from? "From his own labour and that of his forefathers", is the unanimous answer of the spokesmen of political economy. And, in fact, their assumption appears to be the only one consonant with the laws of commodity production.
>
> But it is quite otherwise with regard to the additional capital of £2,000. We know perfectly well how that originated. There is not one single atom of its value that does not owe its existence to unpaid labour. The means of production with which the additional labour-power is incorporated, as well as the necessities with which the workers are sustained, are nothing but component parts of the surplus product, parts of the tribute annually exacted from the working class by the capitalist class. Even if the latter uses a portion of that tribute to purchase the additional labour-power at its full price, so that equivalent is exchanged for equivalent, the whole thing still remains the age-old activity of the conqueror, who buys commodities from the conquered with the money he has stolen from them.[34]

Note in this passage the moral contrast drawn between the "original capital" of £10,000 and the "additional" or accumulated capital of £2,000.

The original capital originated, according to "the unanimous answer of the spokesmen of political economy", "from [the owner's] own labour and that of his forefathers". The pointed reference to the political economists might suggest that Marx believes the justification of current capitalist wealth by the past labour of the capitalist to be a spurious, ideological justification. But the fact that he says "it is quite otherwise with regard to the additional capital of £2,000", must imply that he is prepared to let go the argument advanced by the political economists in respect of the original £10,000. Why otherwise say "otherwise"? The justificatory argument of the political economists, true or false, is let go because it is irrelevant to the point Marx is most concerned to make about the additional capital of £2,000 – namely, "there is not one single atom of its value that does not owe its existence to unpaid labour". And there follows one of Marx's least inhibited denunciations of capitalism as a species of theft.

According to the subsequent argument, the £2,000 profit, when capitalized, is used to buy both additional means of production and additional labour-power for production on a larger scale the next time round. These are the two "parts of the tribute annually exacted from the working class by the capitalist class". And each part of this swollen treasure chest of tribute consists of "money [the conqueror] has stolen from [the conquered]". What was stolen from workers at the end of the last round of production is what enables the capitalist to repeat the crime the next. And the capitalist can go on repeating the robbery indefinitely. As he does so (say, he), his total capital grows exponentially, and yet the only part of his capital which he owes (possibly justifiably) to his original labour is the original capital sum of £10,000. It follows that "in the flood of production the total capital originally advanced becomes a vanishing quantity (*magnitudo evanescens* in the mathematical sense) in comparison with the directly accumulated capital, i.e. the surplus value or surplus product that is reconverted into capital."[35] And thus it happens that "the ownership of past unpaid labour is ... the sole condition for the appropriation of living unpaid labour on a constantly increasing scale."[36] It is a corollary of this view that the question is more important whether the £2,000 profit represents a species of theft than the question whether the original £10,000 was acquired by theft, since the effects of the former appropriation eventually overwhelm the effect of the latter appropriation.

And it is clear from Marx's language that he thinks the extraction of profit to be unjust, though perfectly legal: the capitalist becomes entitled to something to which the capitalist is not truly entitled. Thus "property turns out to be the right, on the part of the capitalist, to appropriate the unpaid labour of others or its product, and the impossibility, on the part of the worker, of appropriating his own product"[37] and "the value of [the] product includes, apart from the value of the capital advanced, a surplus-value which costs the worker labour but the capitalist nothing, and which none the less becomes the legitimate property of the capitalist."[38]

What is wrong with capitalism is that it is a system wherein it is legitimate for social wealth to become "to an ever-increasing degree the property of those who are in a position to appropriate the unpaid labour of others over and over again."[39]

The implication of these key passages seems inescapable: (i) Marx thought capitalism an unjust system; and (ii) Marx thought that the injustice of the system arose directly from the character of capitalist transactions, among other sources.

Why Marx thought capitalism inherently unjust

The passages cited in the previous section involve three suggestions as to why Marx thought the thoughts I have ascribed to him. The suggestions concern *freedom*, *rights* and *welfare*.

Lack of freedom is implicit in the references to the capitalist theft of surplus value and explicit in "the impossibility, on the part of the worker, of appropriating his own product", and we shall see in the next section that this line of thought is powerfully expressed in other parts of Marx's work. In the *Capital* discussion, however, references to freedom are less prominent than references to *unpaid labour*. The frequency of such references might suggest that Marx adhered to a Ricardian socialist position, giving labour the *right* to the whole product.[40] The first difficulty is to specify in what the whole product of labour might consist. How much labour is unpaid? If we stay with Marx's numerical example, the whole product of the production process is £12,000, £14,400, £17,280 – and so on per subsequent rounds of production. It is clear that Marx is graciously allowing the capitalist to replace the original cleanly-acquired investment fund of £10,000. So the labourer is not entitled to the full proceeds of labour, if full proceeds are identified with total output.

Yet what Marx says is mostly consistent with the view that labour has the right to the whole *net product* of labour, and thereafter to the *full product of the capitalized net product* of labour.[41] This implies that the rightful share of labour in total output is everything minus the original £10,000. So labour deserves £2,000, £4,400, £7,280, and so on per subsequent rounds of production.[42] The proportion of the whole product belonging to labour evidently tends to one hundred per cent as time goes by, because current production depends more and more on capitalized surplus value and less and less on the continually recycled investment of the original £10,000. The moral face of capitalism becomes more and more filthy as accumulation proceeds. Notice that this is worse news for capitalism than is given by an antecedence principle which fixes the proportion of dirt on the face of capitalism at the birth of property for ever more.

The moral judgement against the extraction of unpaid labour might derive from the idea that whatever creates value has a right to the value it creates, read in conjunction with the thought that "labour-power possesses the peculiar use-value of supplying labour and therefore of creating value".[43] One might then construct the following argument for Marx's position. Persons have self-ownership, so they own their own labour-power (this is one of the defining characteristics of capitalism as a mode of production). Labourers put their labour-power to use in the production process, creating all the new value in the production process. Owners are morally entitled to the things created by what they own. Therefore labourers are morally entitled to the whole of the net output: surplus-value is theft.

There are two problems with this argument. First, it is not clear that labourers are indeed the persons with beneficial ownership of labour-power at the moment labour-power allegedly creates new value, because at that moment labour-power is on loan to the capitalist (as a consequence of the labour contract).[44] Second, even if it is the labourer who owns the labour-power at the decisive moment, the unpaid labour argument is premised on a factual contention which was shown above to be false. One could run the argument of the previous paragraph with equal plausibility, merely substituting "corn" for "labour-power" and "owner of corn" for "owner of labour-power", to reach the opposite conclusion that capitalist owners of corn rather than proletarian owners of labour-power are entitled to the entire product net of depreciation and wages.[45]

The upshot is rather unsatisfactory. It does appear that Marx was putting forward an argument about unpaid labour with a rights flavour in *Capital*, but the argument is poorly served by one of the main contentions Marx seems to urge in its support. There is worse to come. Any attempt to rebuild the *Capital* argument would have to take account of the withering attack Marx levelled against the version of the unpaid labour theory promulgated by the unfortunate Lassalleans who wrote the *Gotha Programme*. This attack is so scathing that it raises the question of whether Marx abandoned the very idea of a rights-based critique of capitalism, including the treatment he had earlier given of unpaid labour in *Capital*.

The first point of the *Gotha Programme* reads: "Labour is the source of all wealth and since useful labour is possible only in society and through society, the proceeds of labour belong undiminished with equal right to all members of society."[46] After he has delivered a few ranging shots, Marx focuses his criticism on the concept of the undiminished proceeds of labour:

> What are "proceeds" of labour? The product of labour and its value. And
> in the latter case, is it the total value of the produce or only that part of
> the value which labour has newly added to the value of the means of production
> consumed?[47]

This criticism obviously reiterates the distinction apparent in the *Capital*
discussion between the gross and the net proceeds of labour. It follows,
and Marx shortly makes the point, that the Lassallean proceeds of labour
must be diminished to take account of the depreciation of means of production, including "reserve or insurance funds against accidents, disloca-
tions caused by natural calamities etc." This conforms fully with the
argument in *Capital*.

More puzzling is Marx's inclusion in the same series of deductions
of a deduction in respect of "expansion of production". This is a part
of net revenue (i.e. revenue net of asset depreciation). It is reinvested
surplus value, which in the *Capital* discussion clearly belongs to the
labourer. Marx did not there criticize capitalists only for the private consumption they made out of profit; his clear intention was to criticize
them for their accumulation activities, irrespective of their consumption
activities. The obvious implication of the *Capital* discussion, which Lassalleans were fully entitled to draw, is that under socialism, the decision
on the division of the net product between accumulation and consumption
would be taken by workers instead of capitalists, as an expression of
the workers' newly established right to the whole net product. In Marx's
Critique the investment ratio has on the other hand been determined
in advance by "economic necessity", and the workers are left with the
full proceeds of labour minus asset depreciation minus the necessary funds
for accumulation.

This is a very odd position for Marx to adopt. It might be true, given
Marx's views on the objective laws of a capitalist market economy, that
while capitalists enjoyed the right of expropriation of the surplus, capitalists do not have the power to determine the dimensions of the surplus
they receive. But it is very odd to apply parallel reasoning to the case
of the investment decision "within the co-operative society based on common ownership of the means of production." For in such a society, "the
producers do not exchange their products [nor] does the labour employed
on the products appear . . . as the value of these products, as an objective
quality possessed by them." Such a socialist society exists "in contrast
to capitalist society" and "individual labour no longer exists in an indirect
fashion but directly as a component part of the total labour."[48] Socialism
in such a conception is supposed to have moved the investment decision

from the realm of external constraint to the realm of collective decision, in which case the amount to be deducted for investment purposes should not be a matter of economic necessity. So the investment fund is not a prior deduction from the amount of the social product available for distribution, contrary to what Marx says. In his apparent anxiety to find new ways of diminishing the proceeds of labour, the Marx in the *Critique of the Gotha Programme* is inconsistent with the Marx in *Capital*.

Marx then goes on to criticize the Lassalleans for their formula which states that the (by now relatively diminutive) consumption fund belongs "with equal right to all members of society". Marx has trouble with "equal", with "right" and with the membership of society.

I have argued in the previous section that the Marx of *Capital* must be understood to condemn capitalism for its abrogation of just entitlements. This is not to say that Marx's attitude towards moral issues is free of tensions – for instance, when he follows his *Gotha Programme* description of the rights workers would enjoy under socialism with the remark that the notion of a fair distribution is "obsolete verbal rubbish".[49] I am nevertheless prepared to advance the claims that in the *Critique of the Gotha Programme*, Marx asserts (i) that the notion of rights has validity only under certain historically specific circumstances; and (ii) that the Lassalleans had misidentified what it is that workers have a right to, given the existence of historical circumstances making talk of rights appropriate.[50]

I will return to the first claim in the chapter on Communism. All I wish to point out here is that assertion (i) entails that the concept of rights certainly is valid under *some* historical circumstances, and that the relevant historical circumstances include the historical circumstances principally addressed by the authors of the *Gotha Programme*. So Marx would be inconsistent with the positions he adopted in both *Capital* and *The Critique of the Gotha Programme* to criticize those authors just on the grounds that their programme speaks of the *rights* of labour.

But what is it that workers have a right to, given that they have a right to something? Marx is certainly correct to criticize the ambiguities in the *Gotha* formula. Even if we have agreed what is the total amount left for consumption out of our diminished proceeds of labour, distribution of this amount "with equal right to all members of society" can mean different things. It could mean equal unconditional distribution per head of population, or equal unconditional distribution per worker, or equal distribution per work (which implies that distribution to persons is conditional upon work).

Marx resolves these difficulties, famously, in favour of what I will call a disjoint needs/contribution principle. He divides the population into two groups. The first group (let us call them group A) consists of equally able, equally needy adult individuals (who are also male breadwinners in the public domain, according to Marx's Victorian sociological imagination).[51] The second group (group B) consists of completely disabled persons, or at least, people who cannot be expected to make a contribution to production (probably being in Marx's imagination persons unsupported by a male breadwinner belonging to the first group). Applied to this disjunction, Marx's needs-contribution principle says:

Contribution element: In group A, there is equal distribution per work (i.e. per productive contribution).

Needs element: In group B, there is distribution in recognition of group B membership (i.e. per need, given that group B is defined as having needs but not having the means to fulfil them).

Although these rules fall some way short of an adequate set of principles for a welfare state, the introduction of the needs element nevertheless entails a significant shift in the moral ground. For it suggests the intrusion of a patterned, or end-state, conception of justice, as opposed to a libertarian conception consistent with the historical entitlement principle. In particular, able-bodied workers are not entitled to the proceeds of their labour regardless of the needs of those people around them who for one good reason or another cannot or do not contribute to social production.

To what then are members of society entitled, when they do not enjoy libertarian property rights in the proceeds of their labour? The rationale for any needs-contribution principle is, essentially, that each individual has *an entitlement to equal welfare*. Since welfare depends on the satisfaction of needs, the needs-oriented element of the principle will tend to imply an unconditional distribution of goods in proportions which recognize that those who cannot work require a share of the goods of society to attain the same welfare level.

But the equal welfare criterion also demands that any person who makes a contribution is entitled to compensation for the effort they have expended, in such a way that their welfare is restored to its pre-contribution level. This gives rise to the contribution element of the principle. If effort is measured by output, then contributions are rewarded in proportion to output, although this first approximation to a contribution principle glosses over the problem caused by unequal abilities. If part of what it means to have greater ability at some activity is to be able to produce the same output with less effort, then equal compensation requires that higher rewards go to the *less able* persons among those contributing the same tangible output.[52]

If it can be agreed on the strength of such considerations that Marx's discussion of socialist distribution rules in the *Critique of the Gotha Programme* is animated by his commitment to some form of welfare egalitarianism, the question arises of whether the shift from a rights criterion to a welfare criterion makes the *Critique of the Gotha Programme* inconsistent with *Capital*. I do not think it does, for the appearance of inconsistency evaporates once it is recognized that the sociological world of *Capital* contains only able-bodied group A individuals, whose needs are identical, and whose relative welfare depends only on their relative labour contributions. We know in particular from the arguments of section 5.1 that under these assumptions *labour balance theory is a special case of welfare theory*. In a world of equally needy, equally able persons welfare egalitarianism would stipulate, in the words of the *Critique*, that "the same amount of labour [a person] has given to society in one form he [sic] receives back in another."[53] What is wrong with capitalism is that it systematically violates this principle. In the words of *Capital* quoted above, the problem is that surplus-value "costs the worker labour but the capitalist nothing." It is unfair that burdens should be shared out in this way among equally capable individuals just because of the distribution of property.[54]

But now it is easy to give a different answer than Roemer to Roemer's question: Why should Marxists be interested in exploitation? Marxists should be interested in exploitation because labour imbalance is unfair (given certain assumptions about the equality of the individuals among whom labour comparisons are made). And labour imbalance is unfair because under the relevant assumptions, labour imbalance is welfare imbalance. Roemer is quite mistaken to think that we need to find a moral interest in labour imbalance in something other than labour imbalance: the thing is inherently of moral interest. In searching for injustice far afield, Roemer seems to have missed something under his nose.[55]

6.4   Capitalism: The Bedrock Case Against

We have supposed that there is an initial distribution of resources, on the basis of which various transactions occur, leading to an outcome of some kind. Criteria of justice can be applied independently to the initial distribution, the transactions or the outcome. The libertarian position enshrined in the historical entitlement principle allows considerations of justice to impinge only on the initial distribution and the transactions. Welfarist positions apply moral principles directly to outcomes.

Capitalism is largely unjustified if, as Marx argued so fiercely, primitive accumulation is largely a matter of force and fraud. Yet even if it were not, there is another source of capitalist injustice, which was conceded by Locke, insufficiently emphasized by Marx, and has been explored more recently by Cohen.[56] According to Locke an appropriation into private hands of some unowned resource is justified only if "enough and as good" is left available to second comers. I will clarify in chapter 9 which kinds of goods satisfy the proviso, but it can be said at once that they are very few. It is doubtful these days that even the atmosphere of the Earth is included in their number. For the vast majority of goods which fail to satisfy the Lockean proviso, private appropriation is unjustified unless, as is usually argued, compensation is paid to all those whose use of the common share of the resource is precluded by the private appropriation of the resource. Capitalists are simply not free, in general, to use initial resources until they have paid a stiff tax to all non-users.[57] I doubt, then, that much of current capitalism survives both branches of its first test: justice of acquisition.

The second test concerns transactions. We have discussed the fallacy in one Marxian argument for the rights of labour to the whole net product. Marx would have been better advised to make more prominent in *Capital* the argument from freedom he dwelt upon elsewhere:

> From the fact that labour depends on nature it follows that the man who possesses no other property than his labour power must, in all conditions of society and culture, be the slave of other men who have made themselves the owners of the objective conditions of labour. He can work only with their permission, hence live only with their permission.[58]

Capitalist transactions are unjust, then, in so far as they are *coerced*. And a libertarian must agree with this verdict, because libertarians require that a justified transaction be a voluntary transaction, and a coerced transaction is not a voluntary transaction.[59]

To what extent then is capitalism a coercive system? One part of the answer is clear: to at least the extent that the subsistence model applies. The point of the subsistence model was to portray the programme each individual has to solve under capitalist social relations in order to satisfy each individual's fundamental human needs. Every Friday was forced by the existence of these needs, and her lack of access to means of production, to seek employment by some Crusoe. She was coerced, even if it was not any particular Crusoe who coerced her. She was unjustly treated in the contract of labour exchange precisely because she had no viable alternative to conforming with its unequal terms.[60]

Where the argument from freedom goes, the argument from welfare follows close behind. The role of labour-time has been progressively eroded in contemporary Marxist thinking. Theorists have tried to kick the habit of seeing physical things as lumps of clotted effort. They have abandoned the explanatory economics of the labour theory of value and

Roemer has finally come to recommend a complete evacuation: "[Labour balance] theory is a domicile that we need no longer maintain: it has provided a home for raising a vigorous family who now must move on."[61]

I say to Roemer 'leave the kids alone'. Labour-time retains an indispensable role as an index of welfare, and Marx's distinctive concern in the matter of distributive justice lies directly with welfare, not with property rights or transactions. He did not judge labour imbalance to be wrong because property distributions were unethical, but almost the reverse. He judged property distributions unjustified when and because they arose from, and thereafter served to perpetuate, unjustified allocations of toil – when "a class is called forth, which has to bear all the burdens of society without enjoying its advantages, which, ousted from society, is forced into the most decided antagonism to all other classes."[62]

The Marxian welfare case against capitalism is strongest where the connection is most direct between labour-time and welfare. And this occurs once again under the assumptions of the subsistence models, because the minimization of labour-time acts there as at once the sole motive of each actor's conduct and the sole criterion of their success.

The bedrock case against capitalism comes down to this. Capitalism is an economic system of dubious historical provenance, under which private owners have assumed the legal right to use resources belonging to us all in ways they are not entitled to do; it has forced great masses of people on pain of misery to support and extend this system of injustice, and by its very nature it has unfairly imposed on one class alone among the able-bodied population the burden of providing for the basic needs of all.

As we consider the important complications of theory and society which arise as property distributions become minutely graduated, human motivations more sophisticated, personal needs and abilities more finely differentiated, and the economy oriented more to choice than necessity, we should not overlook the bedrock case. For it is a powerful one, and by it capitalism stands condemned.

Notes

   1. "New Directions in the Marxian Theory of Exploitation and Class" and "Should Marxists be interested in exploitation?" appear in John Roemer, ed., *Analytical Marxism* (Cambridge: C.U.P., 1986) while "Property Relations vs. Surplus Value in Marxian Exploitation" is in *Philosophy and Public Affairs*, 11, no. 4 (1982) (hereafter "Property Relations vs. Surplus Value"). The supersession claim occurs on p. 313 of the last article.

   2. This definition is based on John Roemer, *A General Theory of Exploitation and Class* (Cambridge, Mass.: Harvard University Press, 1982) (hereafter *GTEC*), p. 194 and the first two conditions in "Definition PR", in "Property Relations vs. Surplus Value", p. 285. A predecessor exists for Roemer's definition: "[Exploitation] may be defined as *any regular*

profiting of one element in society at the expense of other elements which would be abolished if the elements came to be equal in power": Edward Alsworth Ross, *Principles of Sociology*, 3rd Edition (New York: D. Appleton-Century, 1938), p. 172 (original emphasis). Ross's larger-than-life influence on inter-war social science in the USA is recounted in Julius Weinberg, *Edward Alsworth Ross and the Sociology of Progressivism* (Madison, Wisc.: State Historical Society of Wisconsin, 1972).

3. Cooperative game theory is introduced in Section 7.2. The property relations conception is cooperative because it assumes that any withdrawing coalition can cooperate to distribute the available utility appropriately between its members.

4. This is the "non subtle" disagreement between neo-classicals and Marxists, according to *GTEC*, pp. 205–8. The more subtle disagreement includes consideration of the incentive effects of workers' collective withdrawal from capitalist relations.

5. Strictly, a wealthy agent will lose only if some poor agents exist who will gain.

6. *GTEC*, pp. 199–202, and see also Wright, *Classes* (London: Verso, 1985), pp. 77–82. Section 2.4 above considers the question whether the feudal relationship is extortionate, rather than exploitative.

7. "Property Relations vs. Surplus Value", p. 302.

8. Perhaps I am being charitable. One of my complaints is that Roemer's usage is ambiguous among the three different conceptions of labour theory I am trying to distinguish.

9. "Value and Strategy", *Science and Society*, XLVIII, no. 2 (1984), p. 142: "The economy so conceived resembles less a finely tuned mechanism than a playful contraption of tubes and pumps, sinks and pipes."

10. "Property Relations vs. Surplus Value", p. 302.

11. This example is presented in *GTEC*, pp. 10–11 and pp. 234–5; as Examples 1 and 2 in "Property Relations vs. Surplus Value" and in John Roemer, *Free to Lose* (London: Radius, 1988), pp. 16–20. Since Roemer consistently applies the behavioural criterion to distinguish the "class structure" at the division of labour equilibrium of (ii) from the class structure at the autarchic equilibrium of (i), he concludes that "a class structure is not *ipso facto* associated with inequality of final welfare" (p. 20). This case is analogous to the split-role equilibrium discussed in Section 4.2. My view is that the behavioural difference generates class fractions, not distinct classes.

12. "Property Relations vs. Surplus Value", p. 302.

13. Roemer has tried to cope with the carer examples by using a condition of "dominance" as an additional criterion of the general definition. The attempt was begun in *GTEC*, p. 195 and petered out in "Property Relations vs. Surplus Value", p. 304, n. 12 with the words: "A completely satisfactory analytical definition of exploitation is an open question." More recently, Roemer has tried another condition: "that there be no consumption externalities between the coalitions S and S', and that all agents be utility maximizers." "Second thoughts on Property Relations and Exploitation" in Robert Ware and Kai Nielson, eds., "Analyzing Marxism", *Canadian Journal of Philosophy*, Supplementary Volume 15 (1989), p. 259.

14. The relation between the capital-intensive countries and the labour-intensive countries therefore involves exploitation, according to Roemer, but not a class difference, since both sets of countries behave in the same way with respect to the market for produced commodities. So class difference is for Roemer neither necessary to exploitation (by this note) or sufficient for exploitation (by note 11). My proposal at the end of Chapter 12 implies a class difference between capital-intensive and labour-intensive countries, and therefore restores the correlation between class difference and an exploitative relationship.

15. "Property Relations vs. Surplus Value", p. 285.

16. "Property Relations vs. Surplus Value", p. 292. Examples 3, 4, 6, 7 and 8 discuss permutations of "Marxian unfair treatment". Examples 1, 2 and 5 belong to series A while example 9 represents series B. See also Philippe Van Parijs's pioneering discussion of the nature of a possible class distinction between the employed and unemployed in "A Revolution in Class Theory" in Erik Olin Wright, ed., *The Debate on Classes* (London: Verso, 1989), pp. 230–41.

17. The distinction between one-step and two-step transactions is introduced in my "Exploitation, Extortion and Oppression", *Political Studies*, XXXV, no. 2 (1987).

18. This position is close to the one adopted by Elster in his initial response to Roemer: "Roemer versus Roemer", *Politics and Society*, 11, no. 3 (1982).

19. "Should Marxists be interested in exploitation?", p. 263, although there are other formulations, such as in "Property Relations vs. Surplus Value", p. 310, which suggest a closer connection between exploitation and injustice in Roemer's mind.

20. Judith Farr Tormey, "Exploitation, Oppression and Self-Sacrifice", *Philosophical Forum*, 5, nos. 1/2 (1973–4) Condition 4, p. 208; G.A. Cohen, "The Labour Theory of Value and the Concept of Exploitation", in Ian Steedman et al., *The Value Controversy* (London: Verso, 1981), p. 206; Robert Van der Veen, "Can Socialism be Non-exploitative?" in Andrew Reeve, ed., *Modern Theories of Exploitation* (London: Sage, 1987), p. 108, n. 5, citing Elster, *Making Sense of Marx*, p. 228 to similar effect; Philippe Van Parijs, "Exploitation and the Libertarian Challenge", in Reeve, p. 112, and David Miller, *Market, State and Community* (Oxford: Clarendon Press, 1989), p. 175.

21. Unjustified exclusion is oppression, but not every case of oppression involves unequal treatment: a whole population could be unjustly excluded from some resource or opportunity without any other person having preferential access to the same resource. This point is related to the fact that the term "oppressor" is reserved for the person who *causes* the oppression, not the person (if any) who benefits from it. (This is unlike the relation between the exploiter and the exploited.) Tormey gives the essential distinction between exploitation and "oppression which may exist without anyone's gaining from it" (p. 207), but her subsequent discussion of oppression relates it rather too closely to states of mind – to feelings of being put down – especially through her condition OC_2 (p. 216). In the light of these definitions, Roemer's category of persons suffering "Marxian unfair treatment" contains excluded persons who may or may not be oppressed (depending on whether the exclusion is unjustified or justified). See also Erik Wright, *Classes* (London: Verso, 1985), pp. 74–75 for similar use of the oppression concept to sort out Roemer's terminology.

22. "Should Marxists be Interested in Exploitation?", p. 262, and the sentiment is repeated in *Free to Lose*, p. 131.

23. The above adapts *GTEC*, Appendix 6.1 to the model of the previous chapters. The result is also relevant to the Roemer-Wolff controversy: John E. Roemer, "R.P. Wolff's Reinterpretation of Marx's Labor Theory of Value: Comment" and Robert Paul Wolff, "Reply to Roemer" both in *Philosophy and Public Affairs*, 12, no. 1 (1982).

24. "Should Marxists be Interested in Exploitation?", p. 271.

25. Though they can be brought together, as in Section 15.2.

26. "Should Marxists be Interested in Exploitation?", p. 261.

27. *Free to Lose*, p. 57, and see equally explicit statements on p. 130 and in *Value, Exploitation and Class* (Chur: Harvard Academic Publishers, 1986), p. 67.

28. "Property Relations vs. Surplus Value", p. 285. Note that Roemer is using the term "exploitation" in an evaluative sense in this quotation.

29. *GTEC*, p. 236.

30. In our terminology, the Antecedence Principle states that exploitation exists if and only if the antecedent resource distribution is oppressive.

31. "Whatever arises from a just situation by just steps is itself just", Robert Nozick, *Anarchy, State, and Utopia* (Oxford: Basil Blackwell, 1974), p. 151.

32. Karl Marx, *Capital*, Vol. I (Harmondsworth: Penguin Books, 1976), p. 926.

33. But compare Marx's contention that "the [English] genesis of the [capitalist] farmers is . . . a slow process evolving through many centuries": *Capital*, I, p. 904.

34. *Capital*, I, p. 728. The central theoretical portion of *Capital*, 1 is divided between two basic questions, as follows: Parts Three to Six (containing Chapters 7–22) are about the production of surplus value, given capital; Parts Seven and Eight (containing Chapters 23–25) are about the production of capital, given surplus-value. Marx establishes this contrast slightly melodramatically at the end of chapter 6 as the twin aspects of the "secret of profit-making" that he is going to conjure in turn from the "hidden abode of production" where "we shall see, not only how capital produces, but how capital is itself produced" (pp. 279–80). His narrative branches at this point, and the discussion of the second branch is only resumed several hundred pages later, at the start of part 7 on p. 709. Since the issue of justice in capitalist accumulation is the very first substantive question raised by

Marx in his treatment of the second branch of his main argument, the passages discussed above are given pivotal significance by the architecture of the whole volume. For this reason, I regard them as privileged texts.

35. *Capital*, I, p. 734.

36. *Capital*, I, p. 729.

37. *Capital*, I, p. 730.

38. *Capital*, I, p. 731.

39. *Capital*, I, p. 733. This quotation is from a passage "added by Engels to the fourth German edition on the basis of a similar passage included by Marx in the French translation of 1872" (p. 730, note). I have not been able to consult the French original.

40. On the various Ricardian socialist positions, and the question who precisely counts as a Ricardian socialist, see Andrew Reeve, "Thomas Hodgskin and John Bray: free exchange and equal exchange", in Reeve, *Modern Theories of Exploitation*.

41. It is unclear what quantity Ricardian socialists generally intend by "full proceeds of labour", and whether they generally have an exact concept in mind.

42. I have claimed only that what Marx says is *mostly* consistent with attributing these quantities as labour's rightful reward, because there is an aberrant paragraph on p. 729 of *Capital*, I, beginning "The accumulation of the first additional capital of £2,000 ...", which is apparently inconsistent with these attributions.

43. *Capital*, I, p. 731.

44. Self-ownership implies the right to make a contract, not necessarily to benefit in certain pre-ordained ways from particular contracts.

45. The argument is complicated by the problem of defining "wages" in this context.

46. Marx, *Critique of the Gotha Programme* (Peking: Foreign Languages Press, 1976), p. 8.

47. *Critique*, p. 12.

48. *Critique*, pp. 14–5.

49. *Critique*, p. 17.

50. For the justice debate, see especially N. Geras, "The Controversy about Marx and Justice", in Callinicos, ed., *Marxist Theory* (Oxford: O.U.P., 1989) and Allen Wood, "Marx and Equality", in John Roemer, ed., *Analytical Marxism* (Cambridge: C.U.P., 1986).

51. See *Capital*, I, p. 655 for one of many examples of this imagination at work in Marx's economics.

52. Marx's awareness of the complications inherent in a more comprehensive type of needs-contribution principle is evident from the rather evasive discussion about the "bourgeois limitation" with which "equal right is perpetually burdened": *Critique*, p. 16. I dip my toe in these troubled waters sufficiently in Section 10.3 to show that the connection between needs, contributions and welfare is not at all straightforward when needs differ. It is however interesting to note that the rationale for the Lockean theory frequently invoked by libertarians may in fact be contributionist: see Miller, *Market, State and Community*, p. 55.

53. *Critique*, p. 15.

54. Cohen makes the same point in a rather different way in "The Labour Theory of Value and the Concept of Exploitation", p. 220, n. 21.

55. This oversight is especially surprising, given the radical welfarism espoused by Roemer in "Equality of Talent", *Economics and Philosophy*, 1 (1985) and "Equality of Resources implies Equality of Welfare", *Quarterly Journal of Economics* (November 1986). Maybe the following passage provides a clue: "It is perhaps ironical, that although exploitation is proposed as a non-welfarist theory of ethics, as it makes calculations in terms of labour and not in terms of utility, it nevertheless must eventually take preferences seriously in reaching a verdict as to the significance of the exploitation accounting it makes" (*Value, Exploitation and Class*, p. 72).

56. G.A. Cohen, "Nozick on Appropriation", *New Left Review*, 150 (1985) and "Self-Ownership, World Ownership and Equality: Part II" in Ellen Paul et al., eds., *Marxism and Liberalism*, (Oxford: Basil Blackwell, 1986).

57. See Hillel Steiner, "Three Just Taxes", in Philippe Van Parijs, ed., *Arguing for Basic Income* (London: Verso, 1992).

58. *Critique*, p. 9.

59. Cohen demolishes Nozick's pro-capitalist argument on this point in Section III of "The structure of proletarian unfreedom", *Analytical Marxism*, p. 238, and Part 1 of Miller, *Market, State and Community* gives a comprehensive critique of the libertarian case.

60. Cohen has argued in "The structure of proletarian unfreedom" that most proletarians in a country such as Britain have the option of leaving the proletariat within a period of, say, five years, by setting themselves up in business after the model of the immigrant corner shop-keeper. Possession of such freedom by each individual nevertheless depends on the fact that not many proletarians take advantage of it, so that the proletariat still suffers from a collective form of unfreedom. Casual observation of my Asian neighbours in Bradford makes me think it is a longer haul for a whole family out of the proletariat than Cohen seems to think it is, but if his argument is accepted, then references to freedom in this section must be understood as referring to collective freedom.

61. "Should Marxists be interested in exploitation?", p. 262.

62. Marx and Engels, *The German Ideology* (London: Lawrence and Wishart, 1970), p. 94. Norman Geras supports this quotation with several more to like effect from Marx's work and concludes that Marx's "critique of capitalism is motivated by distributive considerations, at least among others. Do those who claim that he did not think capitalism unjust have any persuasive answer to this apparent evidence against their claim? None that I have been able to discover" ("The Controversy about Marx and Justice" in Alex Callinicos, *Marxist Theory* (Oxford: O.U.P., 1989), pp. 248–51).

PART III

Domestic Exchange and Household Division

7

The Exchange Model of Households

7.1 The Personal and the Political

If the personal is political, the idea cuts both ways. It means first that what are ordinarily called personal relationships are not exempt from the critique of power. And since personal relationships are also private, whereas the critique of power has been centred historically on the public domain, the feminist adage invites us to open the private domain to inspection from the public. In so doing, the constitution of the "public" and "private" is called into question from the public side.

Since I have largely adopted the "economic" assumptions of rational-choice theory, I will be following the lead established by pioneers such as Margaret Reid and Hannah Gavron, and pursued more recently by writers such as Sheila Allen, Michèle Barrett, Veronica Beechey, Leonore Davidoff, Jean Gardiner, Ann Oakley and Jan Pahl in the UK and Sarah Fenstermaker Berk, Richard Berk, Johanna Brenner and Maria Ramas, Heidi Hartmann, and Joseph Pleck in the USA, of treating the household in its economic aspect.[1] In particular, I will be concerned to argue that one who accepts at least the outline of the previous treatment of class division will find it hard to resist some conclusions on the economic aspects of gender division which look feminist. It follows, of course, that one who is not inclined to accept the previous treatment will not be much moved towards feminism by the analogy; even if the case for the analogy is sound. I should also make it clear that I will not be arguing for a perfect analogy: a point at which the analogy fails is a useful diagnostic for the difference between class division and gender division. The exploration of the analogy is a main purpose of the three central parts of this book.

But this purpose may be undermined by a second reading of the phrase "the personal is political", given by the sense in which the political is personal. We seem to be at a stage of development in the theory of gender division which bears some resemblance to the state of class theory in the middle of the last century. At that time, the experience of those at the receiving end of capitalist industrialization had been articulated in a variety of different ways and given rise to a range of political movements and demands. Marx and Engels gave this experience a decisive representation – decisive in the sense that it has fixed the image of the experience ever since, for their serious opponents as much as their friends.

What is happening now is surely that feminism has given a decisive representation to the experience of women. There is, of course, no guarantee that the second wave of feminism will not break and recede, but the signs point to the irrevocability of the changes now in train: there has been a massive, if complicated, development of women's participation in the labour force, and it seems as if some of the conventional forms of heterosexual marriage are breaking down, without the appearance of any widely endorsed successor.[2] In so far as feminism articulates these changes from the viewpoint of women, it has had a greater, more consistent impact than any of the social movements whose proximate origins lie in the 1960s. It is not going to go away, and it demands a response from men, however uncomfortable it makes us feel.

But what kind of response? Feminism articulates women's experience as *women's* experience. So too, it might be thought, Marx and Engels articulated the experience of workers as workers. And both feminism and Marxism have sometimes projected this experience as universal, so that women and workers appear as privileged subjects of historical process.[3] But classical Marxism at least combined this vision with an epistemology that gave those excluded in person from the putative universal subject potential access to the universal experience. How could it do otherwise, given the personal formation of the founders of historical materialism, in which they have been followed faithfully by most Marxist leaders of subsequent generations?[4] Here the theory recapitulates, systematizes, and eventually returns the experience of the working class to the class. At least it does so in theory, for in theory the theory is not supposed to substitute for the experience.

While it would be impertinent to speak by contrast of *the* feminist epistemology, there is nevertheless some inclination within feminism towards an experiential epistemology: a position arising historically in reaction against the tendencies discerned in male-stream social theory, including Marxism.[5]

In the strongest statements of this position, men are altogether denied understanding of women's experience. Even when men use the same words as women, their meanings must differ.[6] Thus, if I argue that women are oppressed or exploited – terms whose prevalence within all varieties of second-wave feminism constitutes *prima facie* evidence for the existence of some analogy between class division and gender division – I cannot mean by these terms whatever it is that feminists mean when they use the same terms. Worse, my use of the same terms must be an attempt to expropriate their feminist usage, since, deprived of access to their proper reference, the only meaning I can give them will rely on masculine experience, or male-stream forms of expression. What appear to be public expressions are really private to women, and the distinction between the public and the private is called into question from the private side.

The consequences of this position are plain to see.[7] Leave aside the question of how I could have apparently had communicated to me the impossibility of communication with me. If it is true that words carry a dual reference then I lack the words which would speak to feminist concerns. I might develop the words which would speak of a masculine experience – and they might even be the same marks on paper that I see in feminist writing – but I could gain no understanding from any feminist uses of the words, and I could not know if I were reproducing in their use by me the forms of expression or the meanings which feminists criticize in men. So I might choose silence. Yet the silence of men on these questions has been deafening, and helps to reproduce the partial standing of the gender question in social theory and academic practice.[8]

It seems then that silence would be an evasion, and speech without reference to feminism would be an affront, so I cannot accept the strongest interpretation of how the political is personal. But all interpretations bar the strongest are still in the field, and they will bear upon the terms in which an analogy between class division and gender division is now proposed.

7.2   A Contract of Marriage

Two kinds of game

The formation of households and their internal arrangements will be viewed as the outcome of either a cooperative or a non-cooperative game. The distinction between these two approaches is first outlined. In a cooperative game, binding agreements are possible, and some such agreement is the outcome of the game. A bargaining process of some kind is envisaged, but cooperative game theory usually studies properties of the outcomes without regard to the process by which the outcome would or should be reached. In particular, cooperative game theory identifies those

outcomes which are *Pareto-optimal*. An outcome is Pareto-optimal when
no other outcome under consideration leaves at least one person better
off and no-one else worse off than the Pareto-optimal outcome. The theory
then expects or directs actors to make an agreement which is Pareto-
optimal: "A cooperative outcome can be defined as an outcome that
is Pareto-optimal in a game where not all outcomes are Pareto-optimal".
Commonly, however, a large number of outcomes have the Pareto property, which suggests the requirement for solution concepts in addition
to Pareto-optimality in order to refine the predictions of the theory. A
variety of proposals have been made, but as Friedman concludes, these
"are quite diverse and no one commands the field; yet each has appealing
features."[9] It follows that cooperative game theory can often be somewhat
indeterminate. It does not offer clear guidance concerning outcomes in
the Pareto-optimal set which generate direct clashes of individual interest
among the players.

In non-cooperative game theory, the players do not look for agreement:
they pursue strategies instead. The outcome is conceived as a combination
of the strategies chosen by each player. The choices are made independently by the players, but they are still interdependent in two senses:
(i) The choice I make will in general affect the benefit you enjoy, whatever
you choose; (ii) the choice I make can take into consideration the choices
you face, including the effect my choice will have on your choice, and
the effect this choice of yours will have on my benefit.[10] The motive for
choice is to maximize benefit, and each player will make the choice which
is going to achieve this result, all things considered. Game theory thus
falls squarely within the domain of rational-choice theories identified in
Section 2.1.

The fundamental solution concept of non-cooperative game theory is
that of *equilibrium*. An outcome (i.e. a set of strategy choices) is an equilibrium if it is true for each player that they have no incentive to change
their choice of strategy, given the choice of all other players. The concept
of equilibrium may be interpreted in two ways. On the one hand, a player
wondering which strategy to choose will know that all players (including
herself or himself) have some incentive to choose the equilibrium strategies, since the equilibrium outcome cannot be the worst possible outcome
for any player (if it were, then some player could certainly do better
by choosing another strategy at equilibrium, contrary to the definition
of equilibrium). An equilibrium may, of course, be much better for me,
or for everybody, than "not quite the worst". The more nearly the equilibrium approaches the best of all possible worlds for me, the greater my
incentive to choose an equilibrium strategy. Thus an equilibrium may
result from a common cognitive process of the players: each of them
uses non-cooperative game theory to analyse all the interactions between

players' choices, and each player spontaneously and independently comes to a similar conclusion – choose my equilibrium strategy. The equilibrium is the outcome that occurs because everyone intends that it occur.

There is another way of looking at a non-cooperative equilibrium which does not appeal so strongly to the cognitive acumen of the players. Suppose the players are slightly myopic. They do not consider all the choices everyone might make: this is too complicated. Or perhaps the players lived before game theory was invented in 1945.[11] Instead, each player singles out some particular choice they expect each of the other players to make. These expectations compose the situation each player conceives herself to be facing. A natural guide to this situation is the set of choices other people have made in the past. The myopic player then wonders which choice to make, perhaps whether to change her own past choice – assuming that her situation does not change (i.e. assuming that other players' choices remain the same). The definition of an equilibrium then ensures that no player will change their choice at equilibrium, so that all players are justified in their tacit, myopic assumption that their individual situations will not change. Myopic players might also converge on an equilibrium in the following fashion. Your choice places me in a certain situation: I make my choice in that situation: this changes your situation and maybe therefore your choice: but this changes my situation and I change my choice ... Once an equilibrium is reached, this process comes to a stop as an unintended consequence of myopic action. (It does not always come to a stop: in some games, we go round and round in circles).[12]

Notice that the first interpretation of equilibrium treats all players as equally strategic game-theorists. The second takes a slightly loftier portmanteau view of the social process which results from microscopic (myoposcopic) decision making. The observer *qua* game theorist is out of the game, and aware of people's situations, whereas the players are just in their situations.[13]

Under either interpretation of its major solution concept, it is clear that non-cooperative game theory gets closer to the dynamics of interaction than its cooperative counterpart. It is then not surprising to find that it tends to make more definite predictions about outcomes. But the equilibrium concept is not without its own problems. There may be no equilibrium, or many equilibria (analogous to the typical situation of cooperative game theory), or the equilibrium may be thought unsatisfactory for a variety of reasons.

The most celebrated, although not as I shall argue the deepest, example of the latter occurs in the Prisoner's Dilemma, which is rare among two-person binary choice games in having a single non-cooperative equilibrium which happens to be the only outcome excluded from the Pareto-optimal set of cooperative outcomes.[14] The Prisoner's Dilemma poses the distinction between cooperative and non-cooperative game theory in the sharpest terms: rational actors should agree to a joint course of action which is better for everybody; and yet rational interactors will under certain assumptions (subject to investigation in Chapter 8) adopt the independent courses of action which end up being worse for everybody.

In the following two chapters I will first analyse households as the outcomes of cooperative games, and then switch to the non-cooperative perspective. It turns out that the formation of households does involve a Prisoner's Dilemma. But the problem may not be fatal, since there are ways of treating the Prisoner's Dilemma which lead to a modification rather than an abandonment of the results of the cooperative analysis. In the course of the discussion, I will be interested in the extent to which the contrast between the cooperative and non-cooperative approaches sketched here can become attenuated, and the related possibility of treating the two approaches within a single theoretical framework.

Domestic exchange

Imagine a woman and a man who are bound to sell their labour-power to obtain their means of life, or more moderately, are bound to sell their labour-power to satisfy their attainment of means of life. The first case corresponds to the proletariat of pure capitalism, and the second to capitalism with a welfare net or a socialist system with wage labour in the public domain. The woman and the man face individual and equal subsistence constraints of two kinds: they must work outside the home to bring in an amount of money at least as great as some constant k; they must work in connection with the home at least as long as some constant time t. These "musts" are imperious: it is just as impossible to avoid the housework constraint by migrating to a fully commodified economy of take-away outlets (one might speak of "McDonaldism") as it is to avoid the earnings constraint by manufacturing all your subsistence goods in a do-it-yourself peasant economy at home.

For the rest of this part of the book, the household is treated by analogy with a market exchange between private owners. Each party who works, either in public or private, is thought to dispose of the product of that work, where "product" is either money drawn from wage working or use-values derived from domestic labour. These products can either be consumed directly or traded for a partner's product. Trade involves a product passing from the exclusive jurisdiction of one person to the exclusive jurisdiction of another.

In terms of the systems for the allocation of money reported in the sociological literature, the household so described is closest in spirit to Pahl's "allowance system" and Barrett and McIntosh's "wife's wage".[15]

One should nevertheless bear in mind that there is a distinction, relevant to the full classification of allocation systems but irrelevant to the current context, between bearing the responsibility for undertaking a task and gaining the benefits of the task being undertaken. If, for example, a husband hands over all his money at the end of the week for his wife to manage under Pahl's "whole wage system", then what matters for the present model are (i) the amounts of that money spent on behalf of the husband and wife (i.e. spent on goods which the respective individuals consume individually) and (ii) the amounts of time spent in the activities of buying the goods which the husband and wife will subsequently consume individually. These quantities of money and time will count towards the satisfaction of the money and time constraints of the individuals for whom the relevant goods are destined. The shopping is thus divided between "His" and "Hers", and when she is doing his shopping, she is working on his behalf, and giving him her time, rather than he giving her his money. And this is true, even if she is doing her shopping in the same store with money that used to be his.

If such a model of the household looks unrealistically individualized, or privatized, I can only appeal to the reader's patience. The notion of what is "private" and "public", or, relatedly, what is "individual" and "collective" about allocation systems is an elusive one. It appears to have escaped the specialized economics literature, and the conceptual clarification of chapter 9 will be required before the issue can be properly addressed in chapter 10. An interpretation of the foregoing exchange model will then be offered that makes it look considerably less privatized, and a quite different model of household arrangements developed which is unequivocally "public". Indeed, the latter model will treat the nuclear household as a two-person microcosm of a socialist society. An additional reason for making a careful analysis of households is thus the general light it throws on the problems of socialism.

Perhaps I should anticipate one general line of criticism of my approach, without claiming in the least to settle it. While it is presumably uncontroversial that people go in for market exchange largely for economic reasons, it is presumably controversial that people go in for marital exchange for the same sort of reason, as opposed to emotional or sexual or procreative or conventional reasons.[16] Even where marriage is conceived in the image of an exchange transaction, the items of exchange might more obviously include emotional dependence, or an exchange of the woman's scarce sexual resources for the man's scarce financial resources.[17]

In the current model, it is economic resources that both partners have, and economic resources with which they bargain. Indeed, the model is almost sex-blind, and deliberately so. The two individuals will be subject to the same constraints and have similar opportunities for satisfying them;

they will be said to have the same domestic skills and obey the same principles of behaviour. The point of such assumptions is not to deny the great inequalities which separate the sexes, nor the number of different respects in which inequalities may arise. The point is to see how far one can go in explaining the tendency for women to be distributed to the private realm and men to the public realm by a suitable choice of one attribute in which women and men differ, when they are treated as alike in every other respect. If, as I shall hope to show, such an explanation goes surprisingly far, then *an* explanation of a general phenomenon has evidently been offered, without there being a claim thereby to offer *the* explanation of the general phenomenon. That economics *can* explain something need not imply that it *does* explain something, let alone that it can explain everything. It is only towards the end of chapter 12 that I hazard how economics does explain something in the gender field, and I will claim there that economics does so not by economics alone. For now, on with the model.

A model of cooperation

Suppose that the wage rate any individual faces is w money units/time unit. Optimizers with no other option work a total time k/w + t: a total made up of k/w time units of paid work and t time units of domestic work. We might imagine this situation as the starting point of independence from which a person negotiates a relationship. It envisages a society in which everyone initially lives alone and is both a wage-worker and a domestic worker.

But what from one point of view is the starting point of a relationship is from another point of view the threat point in recurrent bargaining in a household already formed. Under the privatized construal of what each household member owns, independence is an instantaneously available resort, or refuge, from the other household member. In particular, no one need, and no rational person will, work longer in any domestic arrangement than the time applicable to them when the person is living alone, namely the time k/w + t, where w is the wage rate the person can command in the public domain. This is Thatcherite family life, in which society does not exist. Persons are not constrained in their choices, according to this model, by extraneous loyalties or commitments.

(i) *An egalitarian society*

In an egalitarian society, there is the same wage rate – say w – for each member of any cross-gender couple. What bargain will they reach? The total working time of the couple cannot be changed from 2 k/w

+ 2t. So this can only be split 50:50, since otherwise one partner would be working longer than k/w + t, and no partner is going to accept that, when they would only work k/w + t living by themselves. But so long as the working time is split 50:50, the partners are indifferent to the composition of this time – it might be composed of waged work or of house work. It follows that the partners are indifferent between independence, and joint household arrangements with any division of labour of the two partners that leaves aggregate working times unchanged. This is directly analogous to Roemer's case of split-role class equilibria, discussed in Section 4.2.

The absence of positive economic incentives to form a household in such an egalitarian society might be taken to imply that households will not form, or taken more plausibly to suggest that whatever households are formed will have been formed for non-economic reasons. A welcome by-product of equalizing access by women and men to economic resources might be that relationships will be established for the "right" reasons, undistorted by the economic pressures on household formation which arise inevitably within:

(ii) *An inegalitarian society*

In an inegalitarian society, the woman and the man face different wage rates for paid labour w_1 and w_2, where $w_1 < w_2$. The woman is paid less than the man.

This is by no means an arbitrary assumption. On the basis of British data for 1980, it would be reasonable to assume that 80 per cent of randomly chosen cross-gender couples in the full-time labour force would show a difference in the direction indicated. An index of the great dispersion of the two distributions is that approximately 75 per cent of women then earned below £91 a week while approximately 75 per cent of men earned above the same figure. The pattern of dispersion in earnings for all employees (full and part time) is surprisingly similar for the year 1911/12, when the pay level was around £1 a week, and if anything the disparity had moved further in favour of men by 1958–9, at a pay level of £8 a week.[18]

International comparison of average hourly rates confirms that despite some proportionate improvement in most OECD countries since the 1960s (notably excluding the USA), women's rates have usually existed in a range between 60 and 80 per cent of men's rates.[19] Wright's US sample data is certainly consistent with the lower figure. If one looks at the matter from the point of view of households which have formed, it is likely that fewer than ten per cent of couples at the 1971 UK Census were "cross-class" in the sense used by Susan McRae in her recent study

– a figure borne out for the 1980s by her difficulty in finding a suitable sample of couples to study.[20]

The wage differential posited in the model may have come about for a variety of different reasons, including the following:

(i) Differentiation in wages paid to women and men for exactly the same kind of work, perhaps as a result of a deliberate and rational divide and rule strategy by an employer, given a particular distribution of preferences of men for working with women and an interest of the employer in avoiding unity among workers and hence costly strike action.[21]

(ii) Differentiation in wages paid in different but comparable jobs (in some sense difficult to determine) as a result of a definition of those jobs as women's and men's work, possibly as a part of the response of trade unions to the demand for equal pay or a change in the climate of opinion which makes discrimination of the kind specified in (i) more difficult to sustain.[22]

(iii) Differentiation in wages paid in making the same product using two different technologies, one of which is introduced partly in order to attract as workers women whose domestic circumstances restrict their mobility and increase competition among them for paid work.[23]

(iv) Differentiation in wages because of skills or organizational experience which have been acquired in the past in circumstances which would have made it more difficult for women than men to acquire the same skills or organizational experience, or because what is defined as a "skill" or experience relevant to the organization are skills or experiences which are as a matter of fact easier for men than women to acquire in a given society, or more likely for men than women to have acquired on the basis of autonomous choice.[24]

(v) Differentiation in wages as a result of an autonomous choice by a woman not to acquire certain skills or experience when these were available to her, because, for example, she preferred to raise children, when raising children does not qualify as relevant experience in connection with a seniority system or career structure.[25]

(vi) Differentiation in wages as a result of some rare talent in the man that the woman could under no circumstances have acquired.

These possibilities, which are well documented in the literature (except perhaps the last), are not intended to be exhaustive, nor are they mutually disjoint. They are introduced to indicate the variety of routes by which a wage differential may occur. Starting with the second case, it might also be open to argument – especially perhaps in the fifth and sixth cases – whether the situation described is unjust. In all cases there is an exclusion (a lack of access to a higher paid position), but in some cases it may be possible to argue in historical entitlement mode that none of the relevant antecedent conditions is unjust, because where unequal treatment has occurred, it has occurred on a justifiable basis – such as skill, talent or organizational experience. In other words, the excluded situation in which by our hypothesis the woman is placed (access to a lower wage) may be oppressive or not, and where it is oppressive, it need not be an instance of gender oppression. (If the situation of those without property is oppressive, we already know that the propertyless woman and man in this model may be oppressed in this fashion.) Still, it is the woman and not the man who is in the worse market position, and it is this fact, rather than the justice of the fact, that is required for the next stage of the argument.

If the woman and the man remain independent of each other, with wage rates w_1 and w_2 respectively, then they will work total times $k/w_1 + t$ and $k/w_2 + t$ respectively to meet their subsistence constraints, where $k/w_1 + t > k/w_2 + t$, since $w_2 > w_1$. That is, the woman on her own will work longer than the man on his own.

Following Pleck, any differential of this kind in total working times will be called an *overload*.[26] Can they both do better than this? Suppose they decide to form a joint household in which the woman agrees to do housework for the man for a time s and the man agrees to give the woman money m from his earnings. Are there values of s(> o) and m(> o) which make such an arrangement – think of it as a contract of proletarian economic marriage – advantageous to both?

(a) *The woman's decision*

Let the times spent working inside and outside the house be t_1 and t_2 respectively. Then the woman wishes to minimize $(t_1 + t_2)$ subject to:

$$t_1 \geq t + s \tag{7.1}$$

and

$$w_1 t_2 \geq k - m \tag{7.2}$$

The first inequality says that the woman must work in the home on her own behalf for a time at least t beyond the time (time s) she has contracted to work in the home on the man's behalf.

The second inequality says that she must work outside the home at her going wage rate (w_1) for at least the time required to make up the difference between her overall requirement for money and the amount she receives from the man. In view of this constraint, $m \leq k$ (i.e. no deal will be made that involves the man contracting to provide more money for the woman than the amount of money she requires someone to provide). Minimizing $(t_1 + t_2)$ implies that both inequalities are satisfied with strict equality, so that

$$(t_1 + t_2) \min = (t + s) + (k - m)/w_1$$
$$= (t + k/w_1) - (m/w_1 - s) \tag{7.3}$$

Were the woman on her own, she would have to work a total time $t + k/w_1$. According to cooperative game theory she will accept any deal (any values of s and m) which will reduce the total working time. These are values of m and s such that

$$m/w_1 - s > 0$$

or

$$m/s > w_1 \tag{7.4}$$

(b) *The man's decision*

Again, let the times the man works inside and outside the home be t_1 and t_2. The man will minimize $(t_1 + t_2)$ subject to:

$$t_1 \geq t - s \tag{7.5}$$

$$w_2 t_2 \geq k + m \tag{7.6}$$

The first inequality says that the man will work in the home for at least as long as required to make up the difference between his domestic labour requirement and the amount of labour the woman performs on his behalf. In view of this constraint, $s \leq t$ (i.e. no deal will be made which requires the woman to work longer on the man's behalf than the man requires somebody to work on his behalf).

The second inequality says that the man will work outside the home at his going wage rate (w_2) for at least as long as is necessary to cover his own requirement for cash in addition to the amount he has contracted to give the woman.

Solution of (7.5) and (7.6) yields

$$(t_1 + t_2) \min = (t + k/w_2) - (s - m/w_2) \tag{7.7}$$

and the man will make the deal if and only if

$$s - m/w_2 > o$$

or

$$w_2 > m/s \qquad\qquad (7.8)$$

The deal will be in the interests of both parties if and only if both (7.4) and (7.8) are satisfied, i.e.

$$w_2 > m/s > w_1 \qquad\qquad (7.9)$$

where $o < s \le t$ and $o < m \le k$.

The necessary and sufficient condition for the existence of values m and s satisfying (7.9) is

$$w_2 > w_1$$

The wage differential postulated at the outset is necessary and sufficient for rational actors to enter a contract of proletarian economic marriage. The ratio m/s, which has emerged as a primary statistic of household formation, is evidently the amount of money paid by the man for the performance of each time unit of housework. In other words, it is the *shadow wage rate* for housework.

Inequality (7.9) says, in effect, that a household will form when and only when it is in the interest of the man to subcontract housework at a wage rate less than he commands in the public domain, and simultaneously in the interest of the woman to accept housework at a higher wage rate than she can command in the public domain. Since the opportunities of the two partners differ, the opportunity costs of their respective alternatives can make it in both partners' interests to clinch the deal.

It is possible to see from this interpretation the political ambiguity inherent in the demand for wages for housework. On the one hand, the demand discloses the nature of the economic contract of marriage, at the same time as it insists that housework is work in a society which tends to identify work with paid work, and indeed, to identify pay with work. On the other hand, a wage for housework will be paid only under conditions of inequality, and a woman's housewage would never be as high as a man's breadwage. Wages for housework would not *per se* overturn inequality, nor, as we shall see, prevent exploitation.[27]

The formation of households

A complete specification of a household is given by the set of external parameters and the internal deal, written $<k, t, w_1, w_2, m, s>$. Usually this description will be shortened to $<m, s>$. Condition (7.9) specified those joint households which can form because they are Pareto-preferred to the maintenance of separate, individual households. Call such a joint household a *formable household* (the term "household" will subsequently denote an arrangement between two able-bodied adults unless otherwise specified).

As the values m and s vary it is possible to distinguish formable households by their division of labour – as s increases, the woman is providing more of the domestic labour and as m increases, the man is contributing more to the money income of the household. A disjoint and exhaustive classification of formable households is obtained as follows:

(i) *Symmetrical households* (the households of "symmetrical families") are those in which the partners share both paid work and domestic work (though they do not necessarily share each kind of work equally).[28] This implies $m < k, s < t$.

Among non-symmetrical households, there are

(ii) *Houseworker households*, in which all the domestic work is performed by the (lower paid) woman, and paid labour is shared ($s = t$, $k < m$).
(iii) *Breadwinner households*, in which all the paid work is performed by the (higher paid) man, and domestic work is shared ($k = m$, $s < t$).
(iv) *Traditional (or houseworker/breadwinner) households*, in which there is a complete division of labour, and no work is shared ($k = m$, $s = t$).[29]

This decomposition of household by type is analogous to Roemer's class decomposition. We know that all formable households are Pareto-preferred to separate living arrangements (this is what Condition (7.9) ensures). But are some formable households Pareto-preferred to other formable households? To answer this question, rewrite (7.3) and (7.7) as

$$(t_1 + t_2) \min = (t + k/w_1) - m (1/w_1 - s/m) \tag{7.3}$$

$$(t_1 + t_2) \min = (t + k/w_2) - m (s/m - 1/w_2) \tag{7.7}$$

where the equations refer respectively to the woman's and the man's optimization problem.

Observe that for constant s/m both parties can improve their position by increasing m (since $1/w_1 - s/m > 0$ and $s/m - 1/w_2 > 0$ by definition of formable households). It follows that if the constraints on the maximum values of m and s are both currently slack (m < k and s < t), it is possible to increase both m and s consistently with s/m remaining constant so that both partners' positions improve: *symmetrical households are never Pareto-optimal.*

Moreover, all the households which satisfy at least one of the constraints with strict equality (k = m, and/or s = t) are Pareto-optimal. (If m is constant (= k), the interests of the partners are directly opposed over s; if s is constant (= t), their interests are directly opposed over m): *All formable non-symmetrical households are Pareto-optimal.*

But all types of non-symmetrical household are not always formable, so that the set of Pareto-optimal households need not include representatives of each type. To see this, consider whether the traditional household (m = k, s = t) is formable. From (7.9), the condition is

$$w_2 > k/t > w_1 \qquad\qquad (7.10)$$

With this relationship of the parameters, the Pareto set does include representatives of all types, since there are houseworker households < m, t > with m < k and $m/t > w_1$ satisfying (7.9) and likewise breadwinner households <k, s> with s < t and $w_2 > k/s$. On the other hand, if $k/t \geq w_2$ all the Pareto-optimal households have a houseworker (but no breadwinner) and if $k/t \leq w_1$, they all have a breadwinner (but no houseworker). Figure 7.1 displays the set of formable households in (m,s) space, with its frontier of Pareto-optimal households, under one of the three relevant configurations of the parameters $[w_2 > k/t > w_1]$. Note that the woman's position improves relative to the man's the higher her wage for housework, which increases moving anti-clockwise in the Figure. Given the assumptions of the model, she would prefer her partner to act as breadwinner, while he, conversely, would prefer her to act as houseworker. (Recall that both are motivated to minimize working time, not to take on particular types of work for their own sake.)

Household variations

It has already been said that cooperative game theory allows one to conclude that any household which forms will be at a point on the Pareto frontier, without offering much guidance about which point on the frontier this is likely to be. It follows that the impact of variation in the parameter

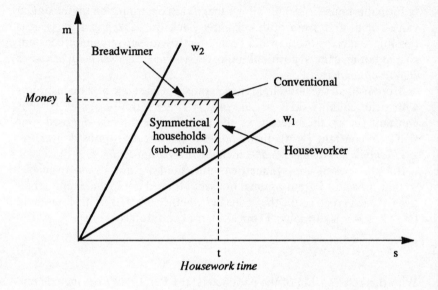

Figure 7.1 Domestic Exchange and Household Division

values upon the configuration of households can only be predicted indirectly, via the effect such variation has on the *range* of households available on the Pareto frontier. Four such effects are worth mentioning: the basic effect of variation in real wages and the more complex effects of variation over historical time, variation by life-cycle and by social class.

If the woman's wage w_1 decreases, she is "more likely" to be a dual-earning housewife (i.e. there are more houseworker households on the Pareto frontier, all other things being equal). The reason is that the lower her wage in the public domain, the lower is the shadow wage for housework which she will still find acceptable. This shadow wage may be so low that she finds herself doing all the housework and having to go out to work to earn the money to make up her financial subsistence requirement. Graphically, the effect of decreasing the parameter w_1 (and so rotating the ray w_1 clockwise in Figure 7.1) would eventually be to open up the range of houseworker households on the vertical segment of the Pareto frontier.

Likewise, if the man's wage w_2 increases, he is more likely to be a breadwinner who also performs household chores. If this conclusion sounds counterintuitive, in that the man's bargaining power seems to have increased with his wage yet the outcome seems less in his interest, recall that the new possibilities of households involve those in which the man can afford to pay his partner a new, higher wage for housework, close to his own, and ultimately pay her so well that she does not have to do all his chores to obtain her whole financial subsistence.

If the wage movements are in the other directions, then so are the tendencies of household formation: higher-paid women are less likely to be housewives, lower-paid men less likely to be breadwinners. If the pay *differential* grows (or narrows), the effect is difficult to predict. Essentially the range of formable households is expanding (or contracting) at both ends, and with it the scope for bargaining over the shadow wage for housework. Perhaps if men's wages rise as women's fall, or vice versa, the division of labour will remain pretty much the same, although the *joint* incentive to form *some* kind of household increases with the differential (all this assuming, of course, that the other parameters, k and t, remain unchanged in the process).

Although there have no doubt been complicated changes in real wages, in wage differentials and in the associated "historical and moral" elements in the subsistence parameters k and t over the longer run, the clearest secular tendency of capitalist development is towards the commodification of the household: the transfer of basic provision from direct household labour to external wage labour and the market place. Some sociologists have made this tendency a fundamental feature of the industrialization process; feminists have often observed how the growth of women's paid labour found them undertaking tasks in the factory they had formerly undertaken in the home, and Barbara and John Ehrenreich among others have made "consumerism" important to the stabilization of U.S. monopoly capitalism at the turn of the century.[30]

If consumerism involves a straightforward gain of exchange-values at the expense of use-values (i.e. a straightforward substitution of cash purchases for items formerly produced in the home), the effect will be to increase the parameter k at the expense of the parameter t. This will lead to an unequivocal increase in the ratio k/t, regardless of the exact dynamics of substitution of the newly purchased consumption items for their home-made predecessors. The ratio k/t is therefore a useful index of commodification of the household.

The same index will also reflect the effect of the substitution of money expenditure for the domestic labour requirement which occurs indirectly via household "capital" investment in labour-saving devices. Whatever one thinks of the wilder horizons of domestic gadgetry, and however one criticizes consumer capitalism for promoting inauthentic needs, there can be little doubt that the core innovations in domestic technology – washing machines and washing-up machines, stainless steel cutlery, vacuum cleaners, synthetic fabrics, furnishing and furniture-making materials, mains water and drainage, electric lighting, gas and electric cooking and heating, refrigeration, emulsion paints and motor transport – are all significantly labour-saving as well as significantly money-taking.[31]

If relative wages remain unchanged, the effect of an increase in the ratio k/t will be to make the breadwinner household less likely. We are then more likely to see the configuration that has been thought typical of twentieth-century development: the dual earning couple in which the woman continues to perform all the housework. Before being carried away completely by the apparent success of this prediction, we need however to reckon with the fact that "in 1850, 1911 and 1951 alike, 31 per cent of the employed labour force in Britain was female" as well as the facts that "in 1911, one in ten married women had a job; in 1951, one in five; in 1976, one in two."[32] Overall, it seems plausible that the effects of changes in real wages and the gender wage differential, together with sectoral changes – especially the decline in domestic service – offset the long-run tendency in favour of commodification of the household as this appears in employment statistics.

It may be, for example, that in the earlier phases of the industrial revolution men's and women's wages were low and dual earning households therefore more frequent; at a later stage, men's wages rose absolutely and/or relatively to women's wages, leading to more breadwinner households and an associated "ideology of domesticity"; later still, the tendency towards consumerism and a rising standard of subsistence led once again to dual earner households, but at a much higher level of consumption than during the earlier throes of industrialization.

Every household forms one element in an envelope of historical change; but each household has a history of its own. This history will be in part a history induced by the movement of wages available to the two partners at different stages of the life cycle. Here the basic rule is that an increase in either the woman's or the man's wage will make a breadwinner household more likely, in the first case by removing from the "bottom end" of the formable set those houseworker households which are the worst for women, and in the second case adding to the "top end" of the formable set those breadwinner households that are best for women. If the idea sounds counterintuitive that women whose position in the public realm improves are more likely to end up dependent on a breadwinner, recall that in this model no-one *wants* to work, so that having a superior external option creates a bargaining chip which *enables* a person to avoid working as much as possible. (Think of the pure capitalist, whose possession of property enables him or her to avoid working altogether.)

Since it is quite likely that what also happens during the life cycle of the couple is a change in the subsistence parameters (better conceived in this context maybe as aspiration levels rather than subsistence indices, strictly speaking), one might find the following sorts of pattern:

(i) A woman has a job with a "working-class" trajectory of earning power, which peaks early and low, and she lives with a man in a job with a "middle-class" trajectory which peaks later and higher.[33] The couple will tend to move from the dual-earner to the breadwinner configuration, recapitulating in their life history something of the putative general history of the nineteenth century.

(ii) Both members of a couple – a yuppie couple let us imagine – have middle class career trajectories, but their aspiration level of money income (k) rises as quickly as their wages, so they remain a dual earner household. This type of motivation is not incompatible with the behavioural assumptions of the model. The couple still don't like working for its own sake, but they have to work ever more frenetically in order to satisfy their demands for ever higher material standards of living. This is why higher wage rates become an obsession for them, because the only way for non-capitalists to maximize income while minimizing effort is to maximize the rate of return from effort.

(iii) A manual working man initially earns more than his non-manual working domestic partner. But her earning power rises as his remains static: the range of formable households closes with the improvement of her bargaining position. Eventually her earning power may exceed his, so that the couple becomes "cross-class", with consequences discussed in Section 12.2.[34]

Such possibilities – of the two members of the couple having differential trajectories of earning power – do not exhaust the range of class variation, even in its most basic outline. When Marx and Engels wrote that "the bourgeoisie has torn away from the family its sentimental veil, and has reduced the family relation to a mere money relation", they meant, I think, exactly what they said: it was the marriages of the bourgeoisie which were thus reduced, not all marriages contracted in a bourgeois society. What is important to the economic configuration of bourgeois marriages in the literal sense – including the power struggles within them, in so far as these are conducted economically – is the differential property holding of the two partners, and the way in which legal property arrangements and inheritance customs discriminate between the sexes. I have no thoughts to offer on this important topic: the exchange model concerns persons whose only property is earning-power.[35]

There is, however, another set of class-relevant circumstances to which the existing model applies directly – indeed, it may apply here rather better than it applies to the typical couple. The exchange model of this chapter predicts that a person will subcontract housework only at a wage lower than the wage the domestic employer can command as an employee in the public domain. It was natural to think of the domestic employer as a "him", and to regard the exchange model as a model of that *virtual* cash transaction which forms with imperfect explicitness the economic thread of the tangled skein which constitutes the typical domestic partnership. But the model will apply equally to the real cash transaction in which a higher-paid person employs a lower-paid person to perform domestic duties as nanny, mother's help, cleaner, maid, au-pair.

Here the model applies on two sites, not one. The houseworker is doing all the housework (or, at least, more than half the housework) for two separate homes: her own and her employers'. The money she earns from domestic employment is then used to satisfy her personal financial constraint for the things she needs to buy for her own home. The model is especially appropriate to this case because resource ownership is explicitly privatized.[36]

In this arrangement, the identity of the "employer" is variable: it might be a single person, or it might be a couple considered as a unit, or it might be the lower earner, statistically the woman, in a cross-gender couple. At all events, the transaction will occur, according to the model, if and only if there is a class of potential domestic workers whose earning power is lower than the wage the relevantly defined domestic employer could command as an employee outside the home.

Perhaps one can describe the transformation of domestic service between the nineteenth and the twentieth centuries as follows: in the nineteenth century, the disparity between the incomes of middle or upper class households (derived from employment and/or property) and the wages of working class women was so enormous that it enabled households placed relatively modestly in the whole social scale to conduct a somewhat pretentious domestic establishment. Recall the progression: the key transition within Booth's working class is that the wife no longer works outside the home; the next big break-point on the scale arrives when the wife becomes the domestic employer.[37] Mrs Beeton's book is not the Housewives' Charter; it is a book on *Household Management*, not Household Labour.

In the twentieth century, the extremes of this economic disparity tend to narrow (at least *within* the First World). Non-domestic kinds of paid employment become more attractive to working class women, although they may find themselves working in the jam factory producing the jam which is bought by the household whose employment they have just left, and which feels unable to make jam for itself because it no longer has their help as servants. But as far as the uncommodified portion of household provision goes, the domestic burden shifts from one group of women (or, rather, women in one guise) – domestic servants – to women in another guise as housewives. A good way to pass this burden back again is for the burden which has already been passed down once, we will suppose, from a man in a couple to a woman with lower earning power in the couple, to be passed on a second time to a third party – to a second woman with earning power lower than the earning power of the woman member of the couple.

This would make sense from an economic point of view even if the woman in the couple hated to go out to work. There will be an even greater incentive for her to subcontract domestic work if her preferences have changed from those assumed by the model to make external work preferable in itself, or preferable in the manner of the yuppie couple, while domestic work remains to be avoided. And it still seems possible to find women who will be domestic employees under these circumstances, even if the English middle class have to go beyond Ireland and the North these days, to recruit from the Philippines.[38]

I come now to the final domestic contingency, one which destroys all previous calculations. As every parent knows, and every intending parent should be told, the arrival of children in a household increases the parameter t overnight to previously unimaginable levels. (The parameter k will no doubt increase somewhat, and eventually quite a lot, but initially not so much.) In Margaret Reid's Oregon study of the 1930s, for example, the average weekly domestic work load of farm and non-farm families without children – 49 and 50 hours respectively – increased to 66 hours in both cases with children, and 81 and 94 hours respectively when the youngest child was under a year old. And this finding has been duplicated in every study since.[39]

The effect of a dramatic increase in t will be to decrease the number of dual-earner households and increase the number of breadwinner households. If the increase is large enough, no dual-earner household will be Pareto-optimal. This is certainly consistent with a familiar pattern of wives' withdrawal from paid labour following childbirth. As Johanna Brenner and Maria Ramas have argued trenchantly against Michèle Barrett, one may not have to invoke explanations from hegemonic gender ideology in the public domain, or even the excluding tactics of male trade unionists, to account for the economic consequences for women of a continuous cycle of child-bearing throughout a large proportion of their adult lives: "when women spent much of their married life bearing and

nursing children, as they did throughout the nineteenth century, the logic
of the sexual division of labour embodied in the family-household system
was overwhelming".

Brenner and Ramas suggest that the order of determination is from
biology to child care to withdrawal from waged work (because of "the
incompatibility of child care and work outside the home") and thence
to a less advantageous labour market position: "women's skills are less
'valued' not because of an ideological devaluation of women, but because
women are less likely to be unionized, less mobile in making job searches,
more constrained in general by their domestic duties." Barrett's response
is not I think to deny the importance of the child care constraint, but
to emphasize the social context in which the biological events occur, making the constraint more an outcome of choice than a matter of biological
necessity, strictly speaking. Why not marry later, have fewer children,
share child care, pool nursing, lobby for adequate state provision?[40]

The logic of the exchange model is slightly different from either of
these accounts. The exchange model postulates the following sequence
of events: (i) couples have children, subject to all the biological/social
pressures analysed by both Brenner/Ramas and Barrett. (ii) The couple
in effect take responsibility for the children by admitting the children
to membership of the household. (iii) This increases the constraint t which
applies to each member of the couple (in this sense, the responsibility
is shared: if the increase is only in the woman's constraint, there is no
scope for bargaining and she is already regarded as saddled with the
lot). (iv) Given the existing wage differential, which may well be caused
either by the kind of ideological/political factors emphasized by Barrett
or by the kind of economic/"biological" factors emphasized by Brenner/
Ramas (for instance a woman who already has children has not gained
the working experience to command a higher wage), the economic logic
is for the woman rather than the man in the couple to take on the
additional child care – depending on the precise outcome of the "rebalancing" of the partnership bargain consequent upon a sudden increase in
the parameter t.

And when, for a complex series of reasons including to some degree
the economic incentives to have families of different sizes, the birth rate
and family size have declined sufficiently to begin to create periods free
of child care, it would become more typical that the parameter t would
lessen at some points in the life-cycle of the household, with a concomitant
tendency for the wife to resume paid work: a pattern consistent with
the well-known bimodal distribution of women's paid employment by
age in Britain.[41]

What is more difficult to explain is why men remain so much apart
from the domestic role, as public health and social services improve, the

number of births per couple declines, and nursery education and bottle-feeding become options available to, or at least conceivable by, the couple – when it becomes less easy for men to deny there is a choice who holds the baby. The explanation awaits, I believe, the Chicken kept for later in the book.

7.3 Domestic Exploitation

Unequal exchange

The exchange model applies with variations to a range of different domestic circumstances. But it is a feature of the model across all these variations that *the exchange it predicts is an unequal exchange*. The lower earner (the woman, on our basic presumption) is always working longer *in toto* than the man within any formable household. The formation of a household may reduce the wife's overload, but the overload vanishes only in an extreme case.

To see this, calculate from (7.3) and (7.7) the difference between the woman's and the man's working times. The woman's overload is

$$Ov = [(t + k/w_1) - (m/w_1 - s)] - [(t + k/w_2) - (s - m/w_2)]$$

$$= k/w_1 - k/w_2 + 2s - m/w_1 - m/w_2$$

$$= (k - m)(1/w_1 - 1/w_2) + 2(s - m/w_2) \qquad (7.11)$$

The first term of this expression is non-negative (since $m \le k$ and $w_2 > w_1$) and the second term is strictly positive (since $w_2 > m/s$). So the woman is always working a longer time than the man, although if $m = k$, the difference can become vanishingly small as s tends to k/w_2 from above.

For this inequality to constitute exploitation, the outcome must be compared to some counterfactual alternative, according to Roemerian general theory. In this case, the counterfactual evidently involves the abolition of the wage differential, so that both have access to an equal wage rate, say w_0. Here we must distinguish two games which are implicit in the model. In the first game, the couple as a unit are playing against the world by performing paid labour in the public domain at wage rates w_1 and w_2. It is in the joint interest of the couple to substitute the man's higher paid for the woman's lower paid labour in order to meet their joint cash requirement (2k) with greatest efficiency. The quantity m is the index of this substitution, and as m increases, the relationship of the couple to the world improves. This is the point that Jane Humphries has emphasized in defending the logic of proletarian household forma-tion.[42]

But this does not mean that the household will always have a breadwin-ner, since there is a second game being played between the partners in the couple, and here it is in the man's interest to use the fact that it is he who has access to the higher wage (a preferential relation to the external world) as a bargaining counter in order to raise the value of s. If he is successful in this respect, and his partner is a wage-earning housewife, then $k < m$ and the outcome is inefficient from the point of view of the couple as a unit (and from the viewpoint of Becker's neo-classical theory of marriage).[43]

If we wish to focus on the second game – the situation internal to the couple – it makes sense to choose as a counterfactual equal wage rate (w_0) that wage rate which leaves unchanged the relationship between the couple and the world, so that the world at large is indifferent between the status quo (the household $<m,s>$) and the situation portrayed in the counterfactual. The requirement is met when the total paid labour time both individuals would work under the counterfactual at an equal wage rate w_0 is the same as the total paid labour time they work under their current domestic arrangements with wages w_1 and w_2. The value of w_0 is thus given by

$$w_0[(k - m)/w_1 + (k + m)/w_2] = 2k \tag{7.12}$$

We know that if this equal wage rate obtained, the couple would not form a joint household and each would work a total time $k/w_0 + t$. $2k/w_0 + 2t$ is, by hypothesis, equal to the total working time of the couple in their current household arrangements and it has been shown that the woman will work longer than the man in any formable household satisfy-ing (7.9). So the woman is currently working longer than $k/w_0 + t$ and the man working less than $k/w_0 + t$. Her position would improve and his deteriorate under the counterfactual alternative envisaged above. The man is taking advantage of the woman, according to this test.

The argument as it applies to the standard cross-gender case can be summarized as follows:

(i) A proletarian economic marriage will form if and only if the prospec-tive partners have access to different wage rates.

(ii) The partner with access to the higher wage will take economic advantage of the other partner in any marriage that will be formed.

(iii) The man has access to the higher wage rate.
Therefore
(iv) The man will take economic advantage of the woman.

In order to complete the discussion of exploitation, we now turn, as usual, from the political economy to the moral sociology of the situation.

Domestic injustice

By analogy with the discussion of property class injustice in chapter 6, we ask whether injustice arises in an antecedent distribution of resources, or in relation to transactions or outcomes.

The relevant antecedent inequality is the wage inequality. Suppose first that this differential has come about unjustly because, for example, it has come about through gender discrimination. Then it is by taking advantage of an unjust state of affairs that the higher earner is able to maintain an unequal position within the domestic relationship. This unequal domestic exchange is clearly a case of exploitation, strictly parallel to the class exploitation, dealt with by Roemer, which occurs when an injust distribution of private property causes an unequal outcome of working effort through the operation of the market.

This is from the theoretical point of view the easiest case, and it may well be the most common one. Yet to commit oneself to the proposition that every wage differential between any two potential domestic partners has come about unjustly is to commit oneself to a very strong historical claim (the analogous claim in the history of private property is: all capitalist accumulation is primitive). We can in any case afford to be slightly relaxed on this subject, because we rejected on very general grounds in Section 6.1 what we took to be Roemer's antecedence principle, so that even if it is agreed that some wage differential has clean origins, the justice of the subsequent transactions and outcome remains an open question.

The domestic transaction might, for example, be unjust because it is a coerced unequal transaction, as we argued was true of the capitalist subsistence transaction. Now one difference between the situation of the woman here and the poor person there is that the poor person literally had no alternative but wage labour if the person was to reach her or his subsistence datum. The woman here has the alternative of survival without domestic exchange, since she can satisfy her subsistence constraint by her own wage labour at the wage rate w_1 in the public domain. The propertyless are therefore forced to be proletarians in a sense that women are arguably not forced to be houseworkers on a man's behalf.

However, there are circumstances in which the woman's position vis-à-vis domestic exchange is not all that different from the propertyless person's position vis-à-vis wage labour exchange. If the woman's wage is sufficiently low that she cannot in fact meet her money subsistence constraint k without working beyond some physical maximum of labour time (given that she also has domestic work time t), then she is in effect forced into dependence on some man, just as the propertyless are forced into dependence on some property owner. This will also cover the case in which women are so culturally discouraged from wage labour in the public domain that their wage rate w_1 is effectively zero. If the woman is thus coerced by her need for money into an unequal domestic contract, then this state of affairs must be condemned by a libertarian under the historical entitlement principle, regardless of the justice of the wage differential (though it seems empirically unlikely that an extreme wage differential by sex would ever in fact have non-sexist origins).

And we are not finished yet. Even if the wage differential is just and the domestic exchange is not coerced, there may be reasons to disapprove the exchange. The strongest approach is to follow what I concluded was Marx's line vis-à-vis the justice of capitalism, and to apply a (disjoint) needs-contribution principle to the *outcome* of the domestic exchange. We have shown in the previous section that the existence of home life never overcomes the inequality of earning power in the public domain. All formable households thus fall foul of the needs-contribution principle, and one reason for being against wage differentials is precisely because they imply overall arrangements which violate this principle. This judgement applies, indeed, whether or not a household is formed, because its egalitarianism deplores the inequality in the aggregate labour times of two unequal earners living separate lives.

If this degree of egalitarianism is too much for the reader to take, two proposals of more moderate stamp are available which suggest that a justified wage differential can lead nevertheless to an unjust domestic outcome.

The first proposal says that the outcome is unjust only in so far as the higher wage earner has used his bargaining power to *increase* the amount of inequality – the abuse of the differential consisting in any use of the differential which makes the differential worse. The difficulty here is evidently to quantify the idea of "making the differential worse".

Throughout the range of formable households the woman's overload is greater than zero, yet in only some parts of the range is it worse than the overload which would exist if the two partners were living in separate establishments. This counterfactual overload is

$$(k/w_1 + t) - (k/w_2 + t) = k\,[1/w_1 - 1/w_2] \qquad (7.13)$$

where the two terms on the l.h.s. are the respective aggregate working times of a woman and a man living as single persons.

It might be said, then, that there is unjust unequal exchange in formable households with overloads greater than this amount. These are overloads in the range: Ov contained in $[k\,[1/w_1 - 1/w_2],\ (k + m)\,[1/w_1 - 1/w_2]]$

where the upper bound occurs in the formable household which is worst for the woman, in which $m/s = w_1$. Since m is positive in all formable households, this range is non-empty. *For all parameter values, there will be some formable households in which the inequality becomes worse.* It can be shown that these households correspond to shadow wage rates in the range: m/s contained in $[w_1, 2[1/w_1 + 1/w_2]^{-1}]$.[44]

Arrangements in this range are arguably unjust, therefore exploitative, because the man has used an existing – let us say justified – inequality to worsen the relative inequality from the woman's point of view, despite the fact that the situation has improved absolutely from the woman's point of view compared to her initially unequal situation. (If it had not improved according to the latter comparison, the household would not be formable.)

What remains a delicate issue on this argument is whether the woman is conversely abusing the man, morally speaking, whenever the man enters a household on terms which reduce the initial inequality between the two partners, granting as before that the initial inequality is justified because of the superior talent, skill, experience, seniority, contributions of hard work in the past, or other meritorious quality the man is held to possess.

The second general approach to the possible unfairness of a domestic arrangement caused by a justified wage differential is suggested by an argument of Richard Norman that "principles of equality are properly applied to those distributions of powers and of benefits which are the concern of a co-operative community."[45] Norman's meaning is that principles of equality are *only* to be applied in such circumstances. I take a possible application of this idea to be that when two people are living apart, not in a co-operative community, it might be improper to apply a principle of equality, such as some needs-contribution principle, to the inequality which exists by hypothesis between them. They dwell in quite distinct universes, morally speaking, as well as living apart. What a domestic contract between the two people achieves is to link them not only economically but morally.

After they have come together, the two individuals form a miniature cooperative community, and it is intolerable within such a community not to apply principles such as a needs-contribution principle to the welfare of its participants. The domestic outcome would then count as unjust, even though the same or even perhaps a worse degree of inequality between the two individuals would not have been unjust when the two individuals lived under different roofs.

I am not sure if I would advocate the Norman approach. I am sure that it does correspond to a fairly widespread moral feeling, albeit one which is difficult to express in public, since it sets up rather explicit and narrowly circumscribed boundaries to a moral concern whose charity ends outside the home. At all events, it offers one way of defending the view that a domestic outcome is unjust despite the fact that its antecedent conditions are all just.

In this section, I have argued that the domestic exchange might be unjust because:

(i) The antecedent wage differential has unjust origins
and/or
(ii) The exchange transaction is unjustly coercive
and/or
(iii) The antecedent wage differential has unjust distributive consequences
and/or
(iv) The consequent welfare differential is unjustly greater than the welfare differential existing between two individuals living apart under a just and antecedent wage differential
and/or
(v) The consequent domestic differential is to be judged by a different, more egalitarian, standard than the antecedent wage differential.

In such cases there is domestic exploitation as well as domestic unequal exchange. I note in particular that the strong principle which seems required in order to condemn capitalist unequal exchange as inherently exploitative (namely a needs/contribution principle as it applies among equally needy, equally able individuals) will make out domestic exchange also to be inherently exploitative (by route (iii) above). This support for an analogy between class division and (one aspect of) gender division may be compared with the qualified rejection of the analogy voiced by Erik Wright:

> I do not think it is transparently true that husbands universally exploit their wives within domestic production, and the case has certainly not been rigorously established. From a labour-transfer point of view it is not clear that there is a net transfer of surplus labour from housewives to their working husbands. From the game-theoretic perspective it is even less clear that working class men would be worse off and women better off *within given families* if there was a completely egalitarian division of tasks in both the home and the workforce. This would depend upon how the total wages obtained by a family with two workers is allocated within the family and how the total amount of labour performed by the two would change under the counterfactual conditions. It is entirely possible that both spouses would be materially worse off under the counterfactual conditions, given the existence of gender discrimination in the labour market.[46]

The cooperative bargaining model strengthens the contention of the last sentence in all but one respect. The model suggests first that it is not just entirely possible, but in fact the case that both partners would be materially worse off were there to be a "completely egalitarian division of tasks in both the home and the workforce." Such a division defines a perfectly symmetrical household, and all symmetrical households are Pareto sub-optimal "given the existence of gender discrimination in the labour market."

The respect in which the last sentence is misjudged is the description of such a comparison between Pareto-optimal and sub-optimal households as involving a counterfactual condition. It has been argued that the most relevant fact is the existence of the wage differential, and a condition running counter to this fact cannot take for granted the existence of the wage differential. It is rather like saying that workers cannot be exploited because they would be worse off (and the capitalists too!) if the workers opted out of wage labour with no redistribution of property in the means of production. With a correctly specified counterfactual it is the case that "husbands universally exploit their wives within domestic production." At least this conclusion follows if we grant the special assumptions of the model, an unfavourable moral judgement along one of the lines pursued in this section, and the general approach to social division which Wright endorses in his enthusiastic adoption of the Roemeresque treatment of social class.

Notes

1. Margaret G. Reid, *Economics of Household Production* (New York: John Wiley, 1934); Hannah Gavron, *The Captive Wife: Conflicts of Housebound Mothers* (Harmondsworth: Pelican, 1968); Ann Oakley, *Housewife* (Harmondsworth: Penguin, 1974); Sheila Allen and Diane Barker, eds., *Dependence and Exploitation in Work and Marriage* (London: Longman, 1976); Michèle Barrett, *Women's Oppression Today* (London: Verso, 1980); Sarah Fenstermaker Berk, ed., *Women and Household Labour* (Beverly Hills: Sage, 1980) and Veronica Beechey, *Unequal Work* (London: Verso, 1987) are milestones in a wide-ranging debate.

2. On labour force developments, see especially Rosemary Crompton and Michael Mann, eds., *Gender and Stratification* (Cambridge: Polity Press, 1986). On marriage rates, see C.C. Harris, *The Family and Industrial Society* (London: George Allen and Unwin, 1983), ch. 11.

3. "The cultural revolution, like the economic revolution, must be predicated on the elimination of the (sex) dualism at the origins not only of class, but also of cultural division ... What we shall have in the next cultural revolution is the reintegration of the male (technological mode) with the female (aesthetic mode), to create an androgynous culture surpassing the highs of either cultural stream, or even of the sum of their integrations. More than a marriage, rather an abolition of the cultural categories themselves, a mutual cancellation – a matter-antimatter explosion, ending with a poof! culture itself." ... "The feminist vision of the world will not be realized in our lifetime, our century, or this millenium." The quotations are respectively from Shulamith Firestone, *The Dialectic of Sex* (London: Women's Press, 1979), pp. 179–82 and from Marilyn French, *Beyond Power:*

On Women, Men and Morals (London: Abacus, 1986), p. 530. On a future from which men tend to be excluded by their biology, see Mary Daly, *Gyn/Ecology* (London: Women's Press, 1979) and for doubts about the political implications of the radical vision see Lynne Segal, *Is the Future Female?* (London: Virago, 1987).

4. A partial list of Marxist paternal backgrounds – Marx: lawyer; Engels: manufacturer; Mehring: Junker; Plekhanov, Labriola: landowners; Kautsky: painter; Lenin: civil servant; Luxemburg: timber merchant; Trotsky: farmer; Hilferding: "insurance functionary"; Bukharin: teacher; Preobrazhensky: priest; Grossman: mine-owner; Lukács: banker; Benjamin: art-dealer; Adorno: wine-merchant; Horkheimer: textile-manufacturer; Della Volpe: landowner; Sartre: naval officer; Korsch, Althusser: bank managers; Colletti: bank clerk; Lefebvre: bureaucrat; Goldmann: lawyer; and Gramsci, "uniquely (of his generation of Western Marxists) brought up in conditions of real poverty". See Perry Anderson, *Considerations on Western Marxism* (London: Verso, 1979), pp. 1, 5, 7, 22, 26.

5. "For us experience and feeling must be at the heart of feminist research or it is not 'feminism' as we understand it": Liz Stanley and Sue Wise, *Breaking Out* (London: Routledge and Kegan Paul, 1983), p. 50. The rooting of science in experience, and the privileging of women's experience, are brought together in the position Sandra Harding attributes to "feminist standpoint theorists: Knowledge is supposed to be based on experience, and the reason the feminist claims can turn out to be scientifically preferable is that they originate in, and are tested against, a more complete and less distorting kind of social experience. Women's experiences, informed by feminist theory, provide a potential grounding for more complete and less distorted knowledge claims than do men's": Sandra Harding, ed., *Feminism and Methodology* (Milton Keynes: Open University Press, 1987), pp. 184–5.

6. "Inherent in this analysis of dominant/muted groups is the assumption that women and men will generate different meanings, that is, there is more than one perceptual order but that only the 'perceptions' of the dominant group, with their inherently partial nature, are encoded and transmitted": and later, "Women are beginning to name the problem as one of male control of society but, unfortunately, because they have not had access to the same experiences as women, many men are not in a position to hear, or to understand, what it is that women are saying": Dale Spender, *Man Made Language* (London: Routledge and Kegan Paul, 1980), pp. 77 and 95.

7. The argument follows Alison Assiter, "Did Man Make Language?", *Radical Philosophy*, 34 (1983), p. 26: "If language creates the world, and if there is a man's language (a man's set of senses) and a woman's one, and if the two do not overlap, it follows that there is a man's world and a women's world, and ne'er the twain shall meet."

8. "Intellectual [as opposed to political] separatism has many dangers. Chief among these, perhaps, is the fact that it requires *no change* from men, and nor does it confront the social organization of masculinity": Michèle Barrett, "The Soapbox" in *Network: Newsletter of the British Sociological Association*, no. 35 (1986), p. 20. A break in the silence on gender among men is reflected *inter alia* in the beginnings of academic study of men and masculinity, which received the imprimatur of the British Sociological Association at its first UK conference on the topic organized in Bradford in September 1988. A useful bibliography is David Ford and Jeff Hearn, *Studying Men and Masculinity* (University of Bradford: Department of Applied Social Studies, 1988) and early collections from two sides of the Atlantic are Andy Metcalf and Martin Humphries, eds., *The Sexuality of Men* (London: Pluto Press, 1985): Harry Brod, ed., *The Making of Masculinities* (Winchester, Mass: Allen and Unwin, 1988); and Rowena Chapman and Jonathan Rutherford, eds., *Male Order* (London: Lawrence and Wishart, 1988).

9. James Friedman, *Game Theory with Applications to Economics* (New York: O.U.P., 1986), pp. 20, 216.

10. It is in virtue of these interdependencies that Elster states: "Game theory provides solid microfoundations for any study of social structure and social change." See "Marxism, functionalism and game theory", in Callinicos, ed., *Marxist Theory* (Oxford: O.U.P., 1989), p. 86.

11. This remark dates game theory to the publication of John von Neumann and Oskar

Morgenstern, *The Theory of Games and Economic Behaviour* (Princeton: Princeton University Press, 1945).

12. This will occur for example if two players are currently making different choices – say left and right – in the symmetrical binary choice game known as the Assurance Game (see section 8.3). The myopic left player will switch to right and the myopic right player will simultaneously switch to left, so that the original configuration is reproduced with the roles of the two players swopped around.

13. In *Explaining Technical Change* (Cambridge: C.U.P., 1983), pp. 74–7, Jon Elster distinguishes strategic from parametric rational choice, where parametric choice involves optimization in an environment treated as fixed, just as my myopic player treats as fixed an environment which includes (or presupposes) choices made by other players. Elster leaves the impression that strategic rationality distinguishes game theory as a whole. In my view, the distinction is rather between the types of cognitive orientation players are thought to bring to a given game. One can then give distinct strategic or parametric interpretations of the outcome of the same game. Strategic players of the Assurance Game, for example, are unlikely to tolerate the cycling behaviour described in the previous footnote. They will arguably be far-sighted enough to settle on one – hopefully the better – of their two equilibria (the argument is given in 8.3).

14. Two asymmetric two-person binary choice games with this same property are catalogued numbers 47 and 48 in Anatol Rapoport and Melvin Guyer, "A Taxonomy of 2 × 2 Games", *General Systems*, 11 (1966).

15. Jan Pahl, "The allocation of money within the household", in Michael D. Freeman, ed., *The State, the Law and the Family* (London: Tavistock, 1984), pp. 40–41; Michèle Barrett and Mary McIntosh, *The Anti-social Family* (London: Verso, 1982).

16. Should it be uncontroversial that market behaviour is economically motivated? Parity of treatment of the private with the public does not only invite an economic approach to marriage; it invites an emotional approach to the market.

17. "We are poorer than men in money and so we have to barter sex or sell it outright (which is why they keep us poorer in money). We are poorer than men in psychological well-being because for us self-esteem depends on the approval – frequently expressed through sexual desire – of those who have and exercise power over us": Andrea Dworkin, *Intercourse* (London: Secker and Warburg, 1987), p. 127. On relationships as an arena for games of mutual dependence, see further Susie Orbach and Luise Eichenbaum, *What Do Women Want?* (Glasgow: Fontana, 1984). On the aptness of marriage as contract see Jessie Bernard, *The Future of Marriage* (New York: Bantam, 1973); Barbara Ehrenreich, *The Hearts of Men* (London: Pluto Press, 1983), p. 43 – and on the inaptness of marriage as contract, Stephen Heath, *The Sexual Fix* (London: Macmillan, 1982). Carole Pateman's *The Sexual Contract* (Cambridge: Polity Press, 1988) is a critique of the Hobbesian contractarian tradition for its male-centredness. I am grateful to Tracy Johnson for the Ehrenreich reference.

18. Ivan Reid and Eileen Wormald, eds., *Sex Differences in Britain* (London: Grant McIntyre, 1982), calculated from gross wages, Table 6.9; Guy Routh, *Occupation and Pay in Great Britain 1906–60* (Cambridge: C.U.P., 1965) calculated from annual gross income of employees, Table 24. Since Routh's data include part-time as well as full-time wage earners, it seems quite possible that the dispersion of full-time wage rates between men and women has actually increased between 1911–12 and 1980, as well as between 1911–12 and 1958–9.

19. Pippa Norris, *Politics and Sexual Equality* (Brighton: Wheatsheaf, 1987), Figure 4.4. For a depressingly similar pattern going back as far as the 1560s for domestic and agricultural wage labour in the English counties, see Chris Middleton, "Gender divisions and wage labour in English history", in Sylvia Walby, ed., *Gender Segregation at Work* (Milton Keynes: Open University Press, 1988), Figure 5.1.

20. Erik Olin Wright, *Classes* (London: Verso, 1985), Table 5.10 gives women just under 60 per cent of the income of men in both the unambiguous working class and middle class categories of his analysis. This figure refers to total income from all sources but see Wright's comment on wage rates, p. 127. The proportion of UK couples in which the wife earns more than her husband may be as low as five per cent. See Susan McRae, *Cross-Class Families* (Oxford: Clarendon Press, 1986), and Section 12.2 below. Veronica

Beechey and Tessa Perkins report that "there is little evidence of part-time workers receiving different hourly rates of pay from full-timers, although a few cases of different hourly rates do exist": *A Matter of Hours* (Cambridge: Polity Press, 1987), p. 151. This is consistent with the assumption of the model that the wage rates w_1 and w_2 are independent of m and s.

21. John Roemer, "Divide and Conquer", *Bell Journal of Economics*, 10, no. 2, (1979) develops this argument in the context of racial division. It evidently applies equally to sexual division. Roemer's theory is discussed in Section 14.2.

22. Equal pay was introduced throughout the British Civil Service, and hence the British Post Office, in 1955. The response of the Union of Postal Workers to the enforced end of pay discrimination was to define postwomen "as a supplement to the male labour force". Men were hired preferentially, and on preferential security, to a job with equal pay. The result was that "For many postwomen, 1955 was the year they got equal pay shortly before losing their jobs", and the overall distribution of men and women to relatively high and low paid positions in the Post Office went unchanged, until the 1955 scheme finally fell foul of the Sex Discrimination Act in 1975. See Janet Siltanen, "Domestic Responsibilities and the Structuring of Employment", in *Gender and Stratification*, p. 105.

23. A particularly graphic example, which involves national as well as gender division, accompanied the introduction of lettuce-cutting machinery into Southern California farms. See Robert J. Thomas, "Citizenship and Gender in Work Organization: some considerations for theories of the labour process", in Michael Burawoy and Theda Skocpol, eds., *Marxist Inquiries* (Chicago: Chicago University Press, 1982).

24. On the gender constructions of "skill" in the British garment trades, and how this changed in conjunction with the technologically induced pressure of deskilling throughout the production process, see Angela Coyle, "Sex and skill in the organization of the Clothing Industry", in Jackie West, ed., *Work, Women and the Labour Market* (London: Routledge and Kegan Paul, 1982). See also Jane Gaskell, "Conceptions of Skill and the Work of Women: Some Historical and Political Issues", in Roberta Hamilton and Michèle Barrett, eds., *The Politics of Diversity* (London: Verso, 1986); Shirley Dex, *Women's Occupational Mobility* (London: Macmillan, 1987), p. 529; and Anne Phillips and Barbara Taylor, "Sex and Skill", in Feminist Review, ed., *Waged Work* (London: Virago, 1986).

25. "Another extremely effective move would be to give official recognition to the years spent looking after children as work experience. This may sound eccentric until we remember that it has been done before – for men, of course. Post-war Britain recognized the service years as relevant to the work experience of ex-servicemen. . . . It enabled men to enter jobs at levels which their actual experience would not have justified": Mary Midgley and Judith Hughes, *Women's Choices* (London: Weidenfeld and Nicolson, 1983), p. 178.

26. Joseph H. Pleck, *Working Wives/Working Husbands* (Beverly Hills: Sage, 1985), p. 30.

27. For a recent appraisal of the debate see Veronica Beechey, *Unequal Work*, Introduction and the comment that "many feminists felt it was reactionary to pay women wages for doing housework because this would institutionalize their position within the family rather than liberating them from it" (p. 7).

28. This usage is intended to conform with that of Michael Young and Peter Wilmott's *Symmetrical Family* (Harmondsworth: Penguin, 1973), p. 32: "There is some role-segregation along with a greater degree of equality than [was generally the case after the Industrial Revolution, roughly speaking]." The clause in brackets is my gloss on Stage 2 of their splendidly Whiggish scheme, in which progress towards equality filters forwards in time and downwards from the upper classes.

29. I will use the terms houseworker and breadwinner to designate household members who are the sole conductors of housework and paid work respectively. I have taken it that "housewife" is an irredeemably gendered term, whereas "breadwinner" is not, on the evidence that "male breadwinner" is a more common expression than "female house-wife". I will also be considering predominantly those households containing either (i) a single responsible adult with or without resident children, or (ii) two responsible adults with or without resident children. I will usually assume that the two adults are a cross-gender couple, and sometimes for the sake of verbal variety that they are married, but nothing

in the analysis hangs on the latter expressions. These various restrictions are not very restrictive, statistically speaking. About 92 per cent of non-institutional households in Great Britain contain at most two adults, according to the 1984 *General Household Survey*, Figure 3B.

30. Margaret Reid, *Economics of Household Production*, p. 75; C.C. Harris, *The Family and Industrial Society*, Part 2, Section 1; Barbara and John Ehrenreich, "The Professional-Managerial Class", in Pat Walker, ed., *Between Labour and Capital* (Hassocks, Sussex: Harvester Press, 1979), pp. 15–17; and Stuart Ewen, *Captains of Consciousness* (New York: McGraw-Hill, 1976).

31. I am not claiming that it is a straightforward matter to relate the index k/t to technological change, or, especially, that the index makes a complete ordering of every combination of household needs, labour requirements and labour-saving devices. I am claiming, I think, that whatever the ratio is precisely, it is liable to change in one direction only over the longer term.

32. Ann Oakley, *Subject Women* (Glasgow: Fontana, 1982), pp. 145–7.

33. Erik Wright drew attention some time ago in the case of students to the importance of the life-cycle perspective in allocating persons to class positions. See *Class, Crisis and the State* (London: New Left Books, 1978), pp. 92–3.

34. This is the route to the formation of a "cross-class" couple which McRae describes as "wife upwardly mobile", although she also records the somewhat surprising finding that the precise source of cross-classness makes rather little difference to what subsequently happens to the couple. See *Cross-Class Families*, ch. 3.

35. K. Marx and F. Engels, *Manifesto of the Communist Party* (Moscow: Progress Publishers, 1953), p. 45; and compare F. Engels, *The Origin of the Family, Private Property and the State* (London: Lawrence and Wishart, 1972), p. 142. Jane Humphries claims: "According to Marx there was ... no material reason for [the] existence of the working-class family, and he concluded without empirical evidence that it had already ceased to exist." See "Class struggle and the persistence of the working-class family", *Cambridge Journal of Economics*, 1, no. 3 (1977), p. 242.

36. See Jeffrey Weeks, *Sex, Politics and Society* (London: Longman, 1981), p. 65, for discussion of the sexual exploitation of domestic employees.

37. Class: "E. Regular Standard Earnings ... A large proportion of the artisans and most other regular wage earners ... As a rule the wives do not work, but the children all do: the boys commonly following the father (as is everywhere the case above the lowest classes), the girls taking to local trades, or going out to service ... H ... Upper Middle Class. All above G are here lumped together, and may be shortly defined as the servant-keeping class." Class E accounted for 42 per cent of the population in Booth's estimate and Class H for 5 per cent, almost "entirely due to Hackney". See *Life and Labour of the People in London* in Peter Keating, ed., *Into Unknown England 1866–1913* (Glasgow: Fontana, 1976), pp. 121, 124.

38. I hope this is fair comment. I have heard more recently of the systematic recruitment of young people from the North of England for domestic service in the nouvelle mansions of the South.

39. Margaret Reid, *Economics of Household Production*, Table XXI; Joseph Pleck, *Working Wives/Working Husbands*, Tables 2.5 through 2.8. A rule of thumb seems to be that the presence of children (of any age) increases the time work load by between 25 and 30 per cent.

40. Johanna Brenner and Maria Ramas, "Rethinking Women's Oppression", *New Left Review*, 144 (1984), pp. 52, 51, 55; and see the reply by Michèle Barrett, *New Left Review*, 146 (1984), p. 124.

41. On the birth rate, see Weeks, *Sex, Politics and Society*, chs. 3–4. The bimodal pattern of women's employment emerged rather later than a straight correlation with the declining birth rate would suggest: it was hardly evident as late as 1951 in Britain, and is not at all apparent in the US Census of 1930. Indeed, Britain may be somewhat exceptional in this pattern, because "the lack of state and indeed private facilities makes part-time work a more feasible option for women in Britain, thereby encouraging them to leave their full-time job at the time of child birth." Historical information on Britain and the USA is contained

respectively in Catherine Hakim, *Occupational Segregation* (Department of Employment, 1979); Margaret Reid, *Economics of Household Production*, Table 3; and the quotation is from Jill Rubery, "Women and recession: a comparative perspective", in Jill Rubery, ed., *Women and Recession* (London: Routledge and Kegan Paul, 1988), p. 276.

42. Jane Humphries, "Class struggle and the working-class family", p. 252. Excellent navigation through the reefs of the family wage is provided by Michèle Barrett and Mary McIntosh, "The 'Family Wage': some problems for Socialists and Feminists", *Capital and Class*, 11 (1980) and Veronica Beechey, *Unequal Work*, p. 43.

43. Gary S. Becker, "A Theory of Marriage", in T.W. Schultz, ed., *Economics of the Family* (Chicago: University of Chicago Press, 1974). The incentive to form households in this theory is the same as that in the exchange model, the number of variables is larger, and the utility functions are more general in form. The drawback is that the household has aggregate production and utility functions, so that the relationship between the married partners is missing from the theory of their marriage! This is analogous to the problem of the neo-classical theory of the firm, which is likewise wanting in methodological individualism.

44. The upper bound of shadow wage rates with this property is the shadow wage rate which leads to an overload equal to (7.13). This can be shown by substitution for m/s in (7.11).

45. Richard Norman, *Free and Equal* (Oxford: O.U.P., 1987), p. 105.

46. Erik Olin Wright, *Classes*, p. 129. I am happy to acknowledge that the exchange model of households presented in this chapter has been developed in the light of incisive criticism by Erik Wright of an earlier version of the model which inadequately expressed my intuition that a close parallel existed between domestic exploitation and class exploitation.

47. Wright, *Classes, The Debate on Classes* (London: Verso, 1989), and "What is middle about the middle class?", in John Roemer, ed., *Analytical Marxism* (Cambridge: C.U.P., 1986).

8

The Confidence Game

8.1 The Impossibility of Exchange

Assume that two parties, X and Y, have items x and y under their control, which they own and are free to dispose of upon any terms they respectively see fit. Assume that there is perfect information: X and Y know correctly everything they need to know about x and y. Assume that both x and y are valuable to both X and Y. This just means that both X and Y would prefer to enjoy the disposition of item x than not enjoying such disposition of item x, and likewise for both X and Y in respect of item y.

The final condition we impose on preferences is that X wants y more than X wants x, and that Y wants x more than Y wants y. While neither party wants to get rid of what they now possess, each party would prefer to substitute what the other party possesses for what each of them now has. The obvious solution to this problem is for the two parties to exchange the two goods: X hands over x to Y in return for Y handing over y to X.

These are the standard conditions for mutually beneficial exchange on the basis of prior ownership of resources. If either x or y is an amount of money (or perhaps, if X and Y are foreign exchange dealers, and both x and y are amounts of money), the exchange is a *commodity exchange*. Everything said so far obviously applies both to the market models of class division and to the exchange model of households (where the formable households are just those which pass the foregoing conditions of exchange).

The payoff structure for the two-sided giving game established by these preferences – the Exchange Game – is set out in Table 8.1, with a, b, c and d the payoffs to player X from the various outcomes.

Table 8.1 The Exchange Game

Strategy/Outcome	(X's) Payoff	Exchange configuration
(X) doesn't give x/(Y) gives y	a	'Gift' of y (better for X than exchange)
(X) gives x/(Y) gives y	b	Exchange of x for y
(X) doesn't give x/(Y) doesn't give y	c	No exchange
(X) gives x/(Y) doesn't give y	d	'Gift' of x (worse for X than no exchange)
	$a > b > c > d$	

The fact that X finds both x and y valuable implies respectively that: $a > b, c > d$ and $a > c, b > d$. This fixes the payoff structure, up to the assigment of rankings between the payoffs b and c. This last piece of the puzzle is supplied by the condition that X benefits from trade: $b > c$. It follows that $a > b > c > d$ and *the Exchange Game is a Prisoner's Dilemma*. The story has been told from X's point of view, but Y sees things the same way from Y's point of view, and the game has ordinal symmetry.

Now it is generally held that the Prisoner's Dilemma is insoluble – or, rather, that it is all too easily soluble. According to standard non-cooperative game theory, the dominant strategy of each partner is not to part with what each possesses at the start of the game. Norman Schofield has remarked that "if an individual has a dominant strategy available then there is no alternative to choosing that strategy. As far as I can tell within [the] framework [of non-cooperative game theory] there is no resolution to the paradox – indeed, I would hardly call it a paradox."[1] And John Watkins, who had mounted a rearguard action on behalf of a favourable resolution to the Prisoner's Dilemma, has more recently become "a chastened Johnny-come-lately, ... now [turned] orthodox: the Prisoner's 'Dilemma' presents rational Egoists with no dilemma: their strictly dominant strategies drive them infallibly, provided they act rationally, to a strictly Pareto-inferior state."[2]

Applied to the present context, this theoretical consensus implies that mutually beneficial exchange between beneficial owners of resources will not take place. *Neither households nor markets will exist.*

I will revel in my emphasis on this point, which appeals to my sense of fun as well as my sense of justice. Non-cooperative game theory is the theory *par excellence* of liberal individualism, yet the theory holds that *free-market individuals can't get it together in free-market relation-*

ships. Or, to choose a form of words which would ingratiate me among orthodox Marxists, if such hope were not by now in vain: *bourgeois persons don't behave in bourgeois fashion, according to bourgeois theory.*

It follows that although the Prisoner's Dilemma is often taken to be connected exclusively with the provision of public goods – indeed, that in this application it sounds the death knell of a socialist economy – in fact, it cuts just as deep within a private ownership market economy.[3] Regarding the Prisoner's Dilemma, we are all in the same boat. I ask next what sort of boat it is that all of us are in.

8.2   The Possibility of Exchange

The thin possibility

Markets and households are very widespread phenomena and yet non-cooperative game theory tells us that neither is possible. How do we square theory and phenomena?

One answer is that the choice faced by actors includes only part of the payoff structure given in Table 8.1. In the instant at which each party hands over the item x or y, each believes that this action is necessary and sufficient to secure their possession of the other item, y or x. The effect of this belief is to reduce the payoff structure to just two outcomes in each person's mind: either the status quo or reciprocal donation. Since each party now only compares payoff b to payoff c, and each prefers b to c, the exchange occurs.[4]

If, on the other hand, the parties believe that the donation of their own item is neither necessary nor sufficient to secure a reciprocal donation, neither will donate, and the exchange will not occur.

On this account of the matter, the key question is the character of certain beliefs held by the parties, in the light of which they interpret the payoff structure. These beliefs are not derived from the payoff structure, but reflect the relationship which each party thinks exists between various social actions – that is, the beliefs involve actors' theories about the social world. If we prescind for the time being from the *rationality* of these beliefs, we see that the cooperative outcome (exchange) is thin rational, given the belief that the two separate acts which constitute the exchange are suitably connected; whereas the non-cooperative outcome (no exchange) is also thin rational, given the opposite belief that the two separate acts are quite unconnected. For obvious reasons, we may call the first type of belief cooperative, and the second type of belief non-cooperative, and we suspect that it might be possible to reconcile cooperative with non-cooperative game theory by allowing explicitly for

variable beliefs about the connectedness of the relevant social acts. I first
establish the formal conditions under which distinctive beliefs lead either
to the cooperative or to the non-cooperative outcome, and then try to
understand what the conditions mean.

In the standard notation, the two options in the Prisoner's Dilemma
are C (for Cooperate, alias hand over your good in the Exchange Game)
and D (for Defect, in other words withhold your good in the Exchange
Game). We call the corresponding beliefs C-type beliefs and D-type beliefs
(non-cooperative ones, which we refrain from calling defective beliefs,
for fear of prejudicing the discussion).

Suppose then that one of the actors has beliefs which make the conditional probability of a positive response from the opponent to the actor's
cooperative move equal to the quantity p $[0 \leq p \leq 1]$. That is: pr [C/C]
= p. Suppose similarly that the conditional probability of a negative
response to the actor's non-cooperative move is held to be equal to q
$[0 \leq q \leq 1]$, so that pr [D/D] = q. Then, since the opponent's disjoint
positive and negative responses [C and D] exhaust the environment of
choice, we may deduce pr [D/C] = $(1 - p)$ and pr [C/D] = $(1 - q)$.

The assumption in the non-cooperative world is that the chances of
my opponent cooperating are unaffected by whether or not I cooperate.
Formally, this implies pr [C/C] = pr [C/D] or $p = 1 - q$. The condition
of pure non-cooperative theory is thus:

$$p + q = 1 \tag{8.1}$$

This is a formal statement of what it is to hold a pure D-Type belief.

Notice that this condition passes no judgement on what an actor believes
the other player is actually going to decide. It just says that the other's
decision is going to be (probabilistically) independent of what the actor
decides.

We now set out the actor's decision problem in its general form. The
actor's expected utility from the choice of C is

$$\text{Utility } [(C, C)]. \text{ pr } [C/C] + \text{Utility } [(C, D)]. \text{ pr } [D/C] \tag{8.2}$$
$$= b\,p + d\,(1 - p)$$

The actor's expected utility from the choice of D is likewise

$$\text{Utility } [(D, D)]. \text{ pr } [D/D] + \text{Utility } [(D, C)]. \text{ pr } [C/D] \tag{8.3}$$
$$= c\,q + a\,(1 - q)$$

So the actor chooses to cooperate if and only if

$$b\,p + d\,(1 - p) > cq + a\,(1 - q) \tag{8.4}$$

I now show how condition (8.4) embraces both the non-cooperative and the cooperative solutions.[5]

(a) *Purely non-cooperative world* [p + q = 1]

If p + q = 1, Condition (8.4) reduces to

$$p(a - b) + (1 - p)(c - d) < 0 \tag{8.5}$$

Since either p or $(1 - p)$ is strictly greater than zero and a > b; c > d by definition of the Prisoner's Dilemma payoff structure, (8.5) is never satisfied. Hence the actor will always choose D and non-cooperation will prevail (provided the actor's opposite number has the same sort of beliefs).

Notice that (8.5) is, in effect, a statement of the *dominance* of strategy D. Given (8.1), the probability p has become the unconditional probability that the actor's opponent plays C. Condition (8.5) can therefore be read as follows: regardless whether my opponent plays C (with unconditional probability p) or D (with unconditional probability $(1 - p)$), I will be better off, because in the first eventuality I will gain a over b, and in the second eventuality I will gain c over d. So I don't need to know the value of p, or, indeed, bother to perform the arithmetic in (8.5). *Dominance finesses the calculation of expected utility.*

(b) *Purely cooperative world*

The pure C-type belief was: "You cooperate if and only if I cooperate." The formal counterpart of this C-type belief is that

$$p = q = 1 \tag{8.6}$$

In this case, (8.4) reduces to

$$b > c \tag{8.7}$$

which is always true by definition of the Prisoner's Dilemma payoff structure. Hence players with type C beliefs will always cooperate.

(c) *Intermediate worlds*

A world is intermediate when

$$1 < p + q < 2 \tag{8.8}$$

In these worlds, an actor believes that the fact that the actor cooperates will increase the chances that the other player cooperates, without making the other actor's cooperation certain. (There is another somewhat perverse range of cases with $0 < p + q < 1$ in which an actor thinks her cooperation will *decrease* the chances of someone else's cooperation. I ignore these cases.)

This intermediate world is split down the middle by a line in (p, q) space depicted in Figure 8.1 such that

$$p(b - d) + q(a - c) = (a - d) \tag{8.9}$$

Along this borderline there is indifference between the two options

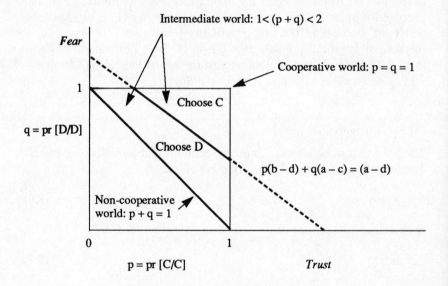

Figure 8.1 The Confidence Game

C and D. North-east of this line, C is preferred to D, and we are in the land of cooperation. South-west of this line, D is preferred to C, and we are in the land of defection. The Prisoner's Dilemma payoff structure ensures that this line makes a proper intersection of the open triangular area: $p + q > 1$; $p, q < 1$; $p + q < 2$. This means that for all values of a, b, c and d with $a > b > c > d$ there exist beliefs other than the pure D beliefs ($p + q = 1$) which lead to non-cooperative behaviour, and beliefs other than the pure C beliefs ($p + q = 2$) which lead to cooperative behaviour. What these beliefs are depends, through (8.9), on the particular values of a, b, c and d in the payoff structure, but this much can be said: The likelihood of cooperative behaviour, i.e. the likelihood that

$$p\,(b - d) + q\,(a - c) > (a - d) \qquad\qquad (8.10)$$

increases for given values of a, b, c and d with both p and q.

These are the *trust* and the *fear* elements respectively in my attitude towards my opponent. The higher p is, the more I hope that the fact that I cooperate will lead my opponent to cooperate. The higher q is, the more I worry that the fact that I don't cooperate will lead my opponent not to cooperate.

What I need in order to cooperate is a certain confidence in my opponent's positive and negative reactions, as quantified by (8.10). Indeed, were the existing usage not so entrenched as to make any proposal for a name change futile, I would advocate the Prisoner's Dilemma being called *the Confidence Game*.

The partition between cooperative and non-cooperative theory depicted in the figure evidently depends on the assumption that players optimize with respect to expected utility. This might be challenged, on the grounds for example that a risk-averse player will maximin, and cooperate only if the opponent is completely trustworthy – in other words, the cooperative world will shrink to the part of the line segment $p = 1$ north of the border line given by (8.9).

I am not very impressed by this challenge. No doubt Figure 8.1 is unrealistically clincial, as are all formalizations. Yet an actor would have to be extraordinarily nervous to forego the chance of a potentially large cooperative gain the first time there is *any* risk of being suckered. For this risk applies to all exchange transactions in practice, and it does not seem to discourage exchange.[6]

I claim, then, that we have made some progress towards a thin rational solution to the Prisoner's Dilemma, by envisaging the theories which actors might hold that imply their mutual cooperation. Under what circumstances, though, might these theories be held validly, so that exchange would be rational from some thicker point of view?

The problem of contract compliance

It would certainly be rational to hold C-type beliefs if there was mutual causation between the reciprocal donations of the two actors. But there cannot be mutual causation of the two donations, because it would then have to be true of each donation that it both followed and preceded the other donation. And if there cannot be mutual causation, it will be irrational to believe that there is mutual causation.

There is luckily another possibility which looks more promising. We are dealing here with circumstances in which there is likely to be a (perhaps not very explicit) *agreement* to exchange before exchange takes place. Could not the correlation between the two sides of the exchange arise from a common, prior cause – namely an agreement to exchange? In this view, the existence of the agreement is necessary and sufficient for the occurence of each side of the exchange, which are both thus necessary and sufficient for each other, in fulfilment of the required condition for cooperative exchange to occur between rational individuals.

But it is not quite enough to assume without further investigation that the agreement causes the exchange to occur, because a gulf is fixed between the word of agreement and the deed. Let us define as a *moral* person someone who performs her or his obligations for the sole reason that they are obligations (i.e. independently of any prudential considerations). Let us define conversely an *amoral* person as one whose attitudes are never determined by the existence of (what moral persons call) obligations. In particular, an amoral person experiences no pressure to do what she or he has promised to do as a result of the promise she or he has made to do it. We now place our moral and amoral persons in the situation which (i) follows an agreement to exchange, but (ii) precedes the acts which would fulfil the agreement to exchange.

The position of the moral person is straightforward. She or he keeps her word, and performs the act promised in the agreement. I believe it can be shown from an analysis of the concept of obligation that this occurs even if the moral person is let down by the other party: failure of someone else to fulfil an obligation they owe me cannot be deemed to delete the obligation I owe them, even if the respective obligations originated in the same agreement.[7]

Consider next the reaction of the amoral person in a similar situation. Since it is either the case or not the case that the amoral person's partner will in fact uphold their side of the bargain, the likelihood of the partner's donation is not conditional on whether or not the amoral party will abide by the terms of the agreement. But we know from the previous section that if the amoral party is also a rational party, she or he will have a dominant strategy not to donate in such circumstances. Since an amoral rational party is not bound by the terms of any agreement, her or his conduct will be determined solely by interests, which here dictate the violation of the terms of the agreement to exchange. We conclude that moral parties to an agreement will cooperate and amoral parties will defect when the time comes to implement the agreement.

This conclusion – which moral actors can work out for themselves – will make moral actors vulnerable to the worst possible outcome (C, D) whenever they face an amoral opposite number. So no rational moral actor will make an agreement with an amoral actor. But since a rational moral actor will make an agreement with another moral actor, each moral actor's choice hinges on her or his estimate of the morality of the other actor. But amoral actors will also know this, so their interest will be to disguise their amorality – to engage, as it is said, in a *confidence trick*, in order to induce their partner to make an agreement that they, the amoral actor, have no intention of upholding. The moral actor's estimation problem can be quantified from the results of the previous section.

Let a moral actor estimate that the opponent has a probability p of being moral. Then pr [C/C] = p, because the moral actor will only play C if there has been an agreement, which the moral actor estimates the partner will fulfil only with probability p. On the other hand, we find pr [C/D] = 0, since the moral actor will play D only if there has not been an agreement, in which case neither a moral nor an amoral opposite number will play C. It follows that pr [D/D] = q = 1.

Substitution of these probabilities in (8.4) implies that moral actors will make an agreement if and only if their trust in the morality of their partner is such that

$$bp + d(1 - p) > c \tag{8.11}$$

or

$$p > (c - d)/(b - d) \tag{8.12}$$

Since b > c > d, there will always be values of p [0 < p < 1] satisfying (8.12). This begins to look fairly optimistic for solutions to the Prisoner's Dilemma, because it looks as if a community of moral persons will be able to sustain cooperation indefinitely. If everyone in society abides by their agreements, then everyone will have an incentive to make agreements, and no one will ever receive any evidence which makes them revise their estimates of anyone else's propensity to honour agreements.

A cloud is nevertheless looming in this sunny sky. The problem is that *there is always an incentive to be an amoral person*.[8] To see this, suppose that an amoral person is facing an opposite number whose probability of being a moral person is p. If the partner is moral, the amoral person can con the partner, yielding the amoral payoff a. This event has probability p. If the partner is on the other hand amoral, each party will try unsuccessfully to con the other, yielding payoff c with probability $(1 - p)$. The expected payoff to the original amoral actor is therefore $ap + c(1 - p)$. Yet

$$ap + c(1 - p) > bp + d(1 - p) \tag{8.13}$$

since $a > b$ and $c > d$. Hence there is an incentive to be amoral.

I do not say that moral personae are like ordinary choices, which can be taken up and set aside at will. So I do not claim that all moral actors will become amoral at the drop of a hat, whenever it suits their purposes. That would in any case defeat the intention of the distinction between moral and amoral behaviour introduced above. But I do say that the existence of a sustained incentive to be amoral creates a pressure which will lead to a certain long-run migration from morality to amorality – not a torrent, perhaps, but a steady trickle. That is, I posit a long-run rational-choice theory of identity. And, in particular, I regard as unstable an equilibrium which requires a strong moral identity as the sole bulwark against self-interest.[9]

Under such long-run pressure, the proportion of moral persons in a society will decline, and with it the likelihood of finding morality in anonymous partners to a given two-person one-shot exchange, such as a market transaction. If this likelihood drops below the threshold set by (8.12), exchange becomes too risky for moral persons to undertake and the exchange economy will cease to function forthwith.

This process is depicted in Figure 8.2. If we assume that there are m moral persons in a given N-person society, and we ignore stochastic effects, each actor's payoff depends on the proportions of morality to amorality among those with whom the actor does business. For any moral actor, the proportion of moral partners in business is $(m - 1)/(N - 1)$, and we can write the payoff function (from (8.11)) as

$$f(m) = b(m - 1)/(N - 1) + d(1 - (m - 1)/(N - 1)) \tag{8.14}$$

If however the moral actor defects, there will be only $(m - 1)$ moral persons left in the society for each of the amoral actors to con, so that

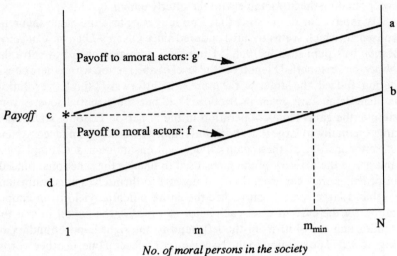

Figure 8.2 The Market Confidence Game

the payoff function in prospect for any moral actor who defects can be written

$$g'(m) = a(m - 1)/(N - 1) + c(1 - (m - 1)/(N - 1)) \qquad (8.15)$$

Figure 8.2 graphs these two functions in a form of Schelling Diagram.[10] The fact that the function g' is everywhere greater than the function f establishes the dominance of amorality (as given by (8.13)), and proclaims this N-person game to be an N-person Prisoner's Dilemma, with the single non-cooperative equilibrium indicated at the left-hand boundary of the figure. Without some outside assistance, the market exchange economy will therefore progressively collapse. Indeed, if the number of moral persons falls below the coordinate m_{min} in figure 8.2, no exchange whatever will occur, because condition (8.11) is violated.

Note that this game is a confidence game in a new, meta-level sense. It is a game about whether it is true of a large society that people on the whole comply with their contracts, not about whether it is rational to make a particular contract, given a prevailing level of contract compliance. And it might be thought strange to try and tackle the two-person

exchange dilemma by embedding it in a meta-game which turns out to
be an even larger version of the same dilemma. Is this not a case of
compounding the intractable with the utterly unmanageable?

My motive for doing so is that I no longer believe the game-theoretic
consensus which seems to have endured since Olson's *Logic of Collective
Action* was published in 1965.[11] I think it is straightforward to solve the
N-person Prisoner's Dilemma at the level of abstraction we are here considering. Indeed, the larger N, the more straightforward I think the solution
is. The details are given in Section 17.1, but the essential idea is very
simple: the gains from cooperation in the N-person Prisoner's Dilemma
are potentially so large that the moral majority can easily finance a system
of sanctions out of these gains which will ensure contract compliance,
and hence the delivery of the gains used to finance the sanctions. Indeed,
in principle they can even do so at no cost to themselves at equilibrium,
so that a large society can realize the entire potential yield from cooperation (in the current case, each actor can receive the payoff b, and the
equilibrium can shift from the left hand to the right hand boundary of
Figure 8.2). The solution to the N-person confidence game, in other words,
is to depend on moral individuals, whose moral stance is stiffened by
universally applied sanctions against immoral behaviour. And this, I submit, is the most plausible framework within which anonymous market
exchange becomes a rational possibility.

8.3 Household Games and Supergames

Assurance against confidence

What works for markets won't work for households, for the household
is too small. When N = 2, it only takes one person's defection to eliminate
all the cooperative gains which would have to exist to finance the sanctions
necessary to stop the person defecting.

The most plausible – perhaps the only – alternative source of sanctions
lies in the future of a game played not just once, but several times in
succession by the same two players. A game which thus strings together
a sequence of elementary games is called an iterated game, or a *supergame*.

Usually, a supergame is thought to be played over an infinite number
of time periods receding into an indefinite future, but I will introduce
a two-period game which illustrates the fundamental features of the solution without relying on such an unrealistic assumption.

The essential point is that supergame players can play conditional super
strategies, such that their choice of strategy – say C or D – in a later
period is dependent upon their partner's choice in an earlier period. This

enables them, in particular, to punish a non-cooperating partner by with-drawing later cooperation: to play tit-for-tat.

In the two-period context, a tit-for-tat player begins by cooperating in round 1, but then cooperates in round 2 if and only if their partner cooperated in round 1. Thus

$$\Pr[C_2/C_1] = 1 \tag{8.16}$$

$$\Pr[D_2/D_1] = 1 \tag{8.17}$$

where the strategy subscripts refer to the respective rounds of the game, and the notation C_2/C_1, say, makes one person's round 2 cooperation contingent on the other person's round 1 cooperation.

Suppose next that a two-period supergame consists of the tit-for-tat strategy together with the strategy of unconditional non-cooperation, which we label T and D respectively. Then the outcome (T, T) involves both players playing C_1 and C_2 (i.e. cooperating in both rounds). A D player always plays D_1 and D_2 (i.e. defects in both rounds), whereas a T player facing a D player starts with C_1 and then switches to D_2 (because (8.17) applies).

Notice that the effects of these alignments create a perfect correlation between the partners' choices in round 2. Players will only play C_2 or D_2 in circumstances in which their partners are playing respectively C_2 and D_2. Yet nothing in conditions (8.16) or (8.17) offends our sense of the temporal priority of causes over effects, since the causes C_1 and D_1 precede their effects C_2 and D_2.

The payoff from any of the superstrategies is the sum of the payoffs from the two rounds, which are weighted relative to each other in the ratio 1:k. The parameter k [0 < k < infinity] can be thought to measure the extent of future-orientation or far-sightedness of the players. (Please note that the symbol "k" is here used in a different sense than in the previous chapter.)

The expected payoff of a T player is then given by

$$[bp + d(1 - p)] + k[bp + c(1 - p)] \tag{8.18}$$

and for a D player it is

$$[a(1 - q) + cq] + kc \tag{8.19}$$

where

$$p = \text{pr}[C_1/C_1] = \text{pr}[T/T] \text{ and } q = \text{pr}[D_1/D_1] = \text{pr}[D/D]$$

The first term in each of (8.18) and (8.19) refers to the round 1 payoff and the second term to the round 2 payoff. T will therefore be chosen in the supergame if the expression in (8.18) exceeds that in (8.19); and conversely for D if (8.19) exceeds (8.18). As before, we establish the boundary line in (p, q) space along which players are indifferent between the two superstrategies T and D. From (8.18) and (8.19), indifference entails

$$p[(b - d) + k(b - c)] + (a - c)\,q = (a - d) \tag{8.20}$$

Comparison of (8.9) with (8.20) shows that, formally speaking, the effect of embedding the one-shot Prisoner's Dilemma in the supergame is to change the gradient of the boundary line depicted in Figure 8.1. As k increases, the line rotates clockwise around the intercept A on the q-axis, as depicted in Figure 8.3. If k is sufficiently large (which means that the second round payoffs are weighted sufficiently in comparison

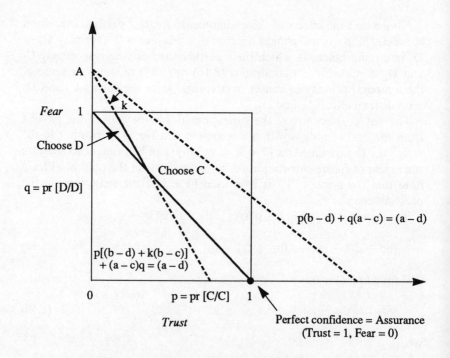

Figure 8.3 The Assurance Game

with the first round payoffs), the rotating boundary line will intersect the line $p + q = 1$ at some value $p < 1$ (this is the configuration drawn in Figure 8.3). The significance of this intersection is that unconditional defection is no longer a dominant strategy in the supergame (according to the argument attached to equation (8.5)), assuming that the supergame is played non-cooperatively (i.e. given that the choice of one player's superstrategy does not affect the other player's choice of superstrategy). This implies that the supergame no longer has the structure of a two-person Prisoner's Dilemma, and this in turn holds out the possibility that mutual cooperation can occur between rational actors who are (i) bereft of moral principles and (ii) unencumbered by a system of sanctions external to themselves.

The values of k which achieve this transformation of the payoff structure are easily found from (8.20) to be

$$k > (a - b)/(b - c) \qquad\qquad (8.21)$$

The supergame payoff structure – of strategy T played against strategy D – is then as set out in Table 8.2.

Table 8.2 The Exchange Supergame

Supergame strategy/outcome	Supergame payoff
(T, T)	$b^* = b(1 + k)$
(D,T)	$a^* = a + kc$
(D, D)	$c^* = c(1 + k)$
(T, D)	$d^* = d + kc$

$b^* > a^* > c^* > d^*$, where $a > b > c > d$, and $k > (a - b)/(b - c)$

What has occurred is evidently that the two highest ranked outcomes have been transposed compared with the one-shot exchange game, so that mutual cooperation (which is the effect of (T, T)) becomes the most favoured outcome in the supergame. The one-shot Prisoner's Dilemma has been transformed into another game called the Assurance Game.

It is easily confirmed that if the partner in an assurance game plays T, the best response is T (because (T, T) > (D, T)) whereas if the partner plays D, the best response is D (because (D, D) > (T, D)). There are thus two distinct equilibria in the assurance game ((T, T) and (D, D)) as against the single equilibrium in the Prisoner's Dilemma. Yet both players much prefer the equilibrium of mutual cooperation to the equilibrium of mutual non-cooperation because (T, T) > (D, D): (T, T) is the Pareto-preferred equilibrium outcome. The assurance game is thus the prototype of a game in which there are multiple equilibria, one (or some) of which are preferred by every actor to other, less satisfactory equilibria. It might be said that the outcome (T, T) is singled out by the joint application of the major solution concept of non-cooperative theory (which identifies the equilibrium outcomes (T, T) and (D, D)) and the major solution concept of cooperative theory (which applies the Pareto test among the set of equilibrium outcomes).

Facing such a payoff structure, (non-myopic) non-cooperative players will reason as follows: Although if I played T, I would be vulnerable to my partner playing D (and leaving me with the worst payoff $d*$), my partner would then get payoff $a*$, which is worse than they could get by playing T, for in that case we would both get the very best payoff $b*$. I can feel *assured* that my partner will play T because I can rely on their reasoning to this conclusion (this is the name of the game). Hence non-myopic non-cooperative players will play the conditional cooperative strategy T.

Although the argument in Sen's original presentation of the assurance game is not entirely unequivocal on this point, I take it that the crucial difference between the assurance game and the Prisoner's Dilemma – the extra ingredient which transforms what I have called confidence in the confidence game into the assurance of the assurance game – is that each actor in the assurance game can absolutely rely upon a rational partner making the cooperative response, even if the partner is also thought to hold what I have called non-cooperative beliefs.[12]

This point is well illustrated from Figure 8.3. If I have complete faith that my partner will play T, then $p = 1$, and therefore $q = 0$ in the non-cooperative world defined by $p + q = 1$. But if k is large enough to satisfy (8.21), the coordinate (1, 0) lies north-east of the boundary line in Figure 8.3 given by (8.20) and my rational response is to reciprocate by also playing T, despite the fact that T is not a dominant strategy. The conclusion is that if the shadow cast by the future is sufficiently long, two amoral actors will act in concert in the two-person exchange supergame.

The household supergame

I have presented the supergame as a two-period game partly to make the point that the solution does not depend on the more usual assumption that the supergame extends over an infinite number of time periods into the future, where the payoffs in each period decrease successively by some constant horizon factor $(0 < h < 1)$.[13] Applied to the case of the two strategies T and D, this more usual version of the supergame reduces essentially to two time periods: the first round followed by all rounds subsequent to the first round.[14] Thus, the payoff from the outcome (T, T) is given by

$$b^* = b + hb + h^2 b + \dots$$
$$= b/(1 - h) \qquad (8.22)$$

and similarly for all the other supergame payoffs.

Comparison with the entries in Table 8.2 gives

$$(1 + k) = (1 - h)^{-1}$$

or

$$k = h/(1 - h) \qquad (8.23)$$

as the weighting factor equivalent to a horizon factor h. After substitution of (8.23) in (8.21) and rearrangement, the condition for the assurance solution to the supergame becomes

$$h > (a - b)/(a - c)$$

or

$$h > t \qquad (8.24)$$

where the quantity $(a - b)/(a - c)$ is called the temptation to defect (t) in the elementary game. The temptation to defect is the ratio of the amount a player stands to gain from defection in a given period $(a - b)$, to the amount the player stands to lose from a partner's retaliatory punishment $(a - c)$.[15] Temptation increases with potential gain and declines with potential punishment. It is easily checked that with Prisoner's Dilemma payoffs (where $a > b > c$), the value of temptation ranges above zero less than one. We may then characterize an amoral player as a person who gives in to the slightest temptation, and thus plays D in the elementary game. But we have shown via (8.24) that in the super-game, such a person will cooperate so long as the horizon factor h exceeds the temptation to defect t. (Please note that the symbol "t" is here used in a different sense than in the previous chapter.)

To apply this analysis to the household exchange model, we assume that an agreement has been made to form a household $<m,s>$, in which the exchange period is one week, set against a time horizon stretching into the future with parameter h.[16]

Consider first the woman's temptation to defect in the one-period household game. If she withdraws her domestic labour, she gains time s. If her husband withdraws his contribution m, her opportunity cost is m/w_1 (it is the time she has to work to make up the contribution). Her temptation to defect is therefore

$$t_1 = s/(m/w_1)$$
$$= w_1 s/m \qquad\qquad (8.25)$$

where $0 < t_1 < 1$, since s, m > 0 and $w_1 < m/s$ for formable households.

The man's temptation to defect is the ratio of what he gains from defection (a time m/w_2) to the loss of time s from his partner's defection which he has to make up by house-working an equivalent time s.

$$t_2 = (m/w_2)/s$$
$$= m/sw_2 \qquad\qquad (8.26)$$

where $0 < t_2 < 1$ since s,m > 0 and $w_2 > m/s$.

These results confirm that the one-shot game has ordinal symmetry and is a Prisoner's Dilemma. Despite the fact that the woman's and man's payoffs differ, they are in a similar strategic situation. Next define $t_0 = (t_1 t_2)^{1/2}$ as the couple's joint temptation to defect and observe from (8.25) and (8.26) that

$$t_0 = (w_1/w_2)^{1/2} \qquad\qquad (8.27)$$

One rationale for the term "joint temptation to defect" is that if the individual temptations are equal, both values are equal to the joint temptation. Another rationale is that (8.27) makes the joint temptation a function of the couple's external situation alone (the wage rates w_1 and w_2). It is something they share, regardless of their internal household arrangements. (8.27) also implies that the greater the wage differential, the less joint temptation there is to defect from the household (i.e. there is a sense in which the greater the external economic inequality, the more are the partners trapped economically within the household).

As the actual household arrangements $<m,s>$ vary within the limits set by the external wage parameters w_1 and w_2, the individual temptations of the partners are inversely related because the product of the two temptations is constant by (8.27). As the ratio m/s decreases, and the household arrangements are less favourable to the woman, her temptation to defect

increases while that of the man decreases. Conversely, as m/s increases
and the household is less favourable to the man, his temptation to defect
increases and hers declines. In general, one cannot say whether the
woman's temptation to defect will be higher or lower than the man's:
it all depends on the particular household arrangements they make.

In the one shot non-cooperative game, this variation has no effect on
behaviour, since the temptation to defect is always greater than zero.
In the supergame this variation is the key to the type of game that exists,
and therefore the behaviour that can be predicted. The supergame allows
one to model a sense in which the partners cannot push each other too
far: to a critical point at which the temptation to defect *in the supergame*
is first positive. Whether or not long-term temptation exists depends on
whether a player's payoffs in the supergame have the Prisoner's Dilemma
or assurance game ranking.

(a) For the woman, the critical point separating these two cases is
$t_1 = h$ or $m/s = w_1/h$ (by (8.24) and (8.25)).

If $m/s > w_1/h$, then $w_1 s/m = t_1 < h$
and her supergame payoffs are A.G. $\qquad$ (8.28)

If $m/s < w_1/h$ then $t_1 > h$
and her supergame payoffs are P.D. $\qquad$ (8.29)

(b) For the man, the critical point is given by $t_2 = h$, or $m/s = w_2 h$
(by (8.24) and (8.26)).

If $m/s < w_2 h$, then $m/s w_2 = t_2 < h$
and his supergame payoffs are A.G. $\qquad$ (8.30)

If $m/s > w_2 h$, then $t_2 > h$
and his supergame payoffs are P.D. $\qquad$ (8.31)

The configuration of the supergame can now be ordinally symmetric
(with both players having either Prisoner's Dilemma (P.D.) or assurance
game (A.G.) payoffs) in which case the supergame has the same form
as the Prisoner's Dilemma or the assurance game respectively. These cases
will be called the Prisoner's Dilemma supergame and the assurance supergame.

Alternatively, the supergame can set a player with P.D. payoffs against
a player with A.G. payoffs. The inequality in the ordinally symmetrical
elementary game has duly reappeared as an ordinal asymmetry in the
corresponding supergame. Hegelians would no doubt welcome this evidence of quantity turning into quality. The conditions under which these

various supergame configurations occur are as follows:

(i) If $h < t_0^2$, both (8.29) and (8.31) are satisfied for all (cooperatively) formable households and the supergame is a P.D. supergame. Non-cooperative players will not therefore form households; and the supergame ploy has failed to resolve the problem of the elementary game.

(ii) If $t_0^2 < h < t_0$, it is either the case that both (8.29) and (8.31) are satisfied, or that only one of the conditions is satisfied. In the former case, the previous point applies and households will not form. In the latter case there is an asymmetrical game, in which the values $<m,s>$ are such that one of the partners has been "pushed too far": the woman in the direction of greater overall inequality or the man in the direction of greater overall equality. The partner pushed too far will face P.D. payoffs. Since the strategy D is dominant in the Prisoner's Dilemma, the first player will play D, and their assurance game partner is bound to respond with D also.[17] Supergame households will not form in these circumstances either.

(iii) If $t_0 < h$, it is either the case that both (8.28) and (8.30) are satisfied, or that only one of them is satisfied, as $<m,s>$ varies over the range of cooperatively formable households. In the former case, the supergame is an assurance supergame and households will form: in the latter case it is an asymmetrical game of the type analysed at (ii) and they will not. The condition for the satisfaction of both (8.28) and (8.30) is

$$w_1/h < m/s < w_2h \qquad\qquad (8.32)$$

Since $h < 1$, the condition (8.32) is more restrictive than the original condition of formability [(7.9)] given in the previous chapter. *The range of non-cooperatively formable households in the supergame is narrower than the range of cooperatively formable households in the corresponding elementary game.* Since it is also true that the supergame is only soluble at all if $h > t_0$, we note the parallel with the condition $h > t$ in the general case (condition (8.24)). This parallel supplies the best rationale for regarding the quantity t_0 as the joint temptation to defect.

How likely is it that this crucial condition $h > t_0$ will be encountered in practice? The general answer is unclear, but at least this much can be said. The value of h will tend to be fairly high, depending on the time periods over which supergame aggregation occurs. Thus, if the basic time period in the elementary game is one week (which means that tit-for-tat players will punish defection after one week by defection for one week), the discount parameter h will measure the weighting of next week's payoff compared to this week's. In such a perspective, h is likely to be as least as large as, say, 0.9. (It may even be as large as this in an annual perspective, corresponding to an 11 per cent annual rate of interest.)

The assurance supergame will then be found for at least some households if it is also true that $t_0 < 0.9$ or $w_1/w_2 < 0.81$. The wage rate data suggest that this order of wage differential by gender is very commonly found, so that the economic data will often be sufficient to predict the formation of supergame households among amoral players. On the other hand, if it is the case that future-orientation decreases (as some critics seem to believe is characteristic of the "me" generations of the 1970s and 80s) and, perhaps more significantly, that wage differentials are narrowing, one might expect more Prisoner's Dilemma supergames, and thus the breakdown of households containing non-cooperative players.[18]

Perhaps this offers a clue why one of the major social trends is the "increased numbers of parent surrogates in the employment of the state (police, teachers, doctors, social workers, etc)."[19] Could it be that the forms of social control characteristic of a personal relationship endowed with a sense of permanence are giving way to the forms of control previously associated with anonymous market exchange, among pairs of persons under outside surveillance from the agents of the public at large?

Notes

1. Norman Schofield, "Anarchy, Altruism and Cooperation", *Social Choice and Welfare*, 2 (1985), p. 209.

2. John Watkins, "Second Thoughts on Self-Interest and Morality", in Richmond Campbell and Lanning Sowden, eds., *Paradoxes of Rationality and Cooperation* (Vancouver: University of British Columbia Press, 1985), p. 72.

3. Here is a representative text-book statement: "First, prisoner's dilemmas involving two or more persons illustrate many of the problems that one is likely to encounter in applying non-cooperative game theory to politics. Second, the prisoner's dilemma itself models a great many key political situations, including the causes of market and governmental failure, the incentives for political participation, paradoxes of vote trading and the disincentives of people to reveal truthfully their demand for publicly provided goods and services": Peter C. Ordeshook, *Game Theory and Political Theory* (Cambridge: C.U.P., 1986), p. 203. The point I wish to emphasize is that the market is one big failure, from the orthodox perspective of non-cooperative game theory. See also Michael Taylor, *The Possibility of Cooperation* (Cambridge: C.U.P., 1987), p. 37 citing Dennis Mueller, *Public Choice* (Cambridge: C.U.P., 1979), ch. 2.

4. See Derek Parfit's discussion of reciprocity in "Prudence, Morality and the Prisoner's Dilemma", in Jon Elster, ed., *Rational Choice* (Oxford: Basil Blackwell, 1986), p. 35. Other signs of the faltering of the consensus on the inevitability of non-cooperation in the Prisoner's Dilemma are contained in David Gauthier, *Morals by Agreement* (Oxford: Clarendon Press, 1985), ch. 6; Jean Hampton, *Hobbes and the Social Contract Tradition* (Cambridge: C.U.P., 1986), esp. pp. 70–71; and Frederic Schick, *Having Reasons* (Princeton: Princeton University Press, 1984).

5. This is the moment at which I trip lightly around Newcomb's Problem, for my awareness of which I think I am grateful to Richard Lindley, as I am to Philip Pettit for correspondence touching on all the concerns of Chapter 8. I think I must be a one/two-boxer regarding Newcomb's Problem, depending as the (p, q) beliefs my actor entertains after Nozick's genie's high jinks are complete do not or do satisfy condition (8.4). Pettit's thoughts on the subject are available in "Free Riding and Foul Dealing", *The Journal of Philosophy*,

LXXXIII, no. 7 (1986) and "The Prisoner's Dilemma is an Unexploitable Newcomb Problem" *Synthese*, 76, no. 1 (1988), and Newcomb's Problem is discussed extensively in Richmond Campbell and Lanning Sowden, eds., *Paradoxes of Rationality and Cooperation*, Parts III and IV.

6. The challenge comes from Mike Taylor, against whose unyielding scepticism I have launched several versions of the current argument, to its successive improvement.

7. Consider a case in which you, say, let me down in the performance of your side of an agreement. Analysis suggests that your non-performance of your obligation to me cannot delete (i) just your obligation to me, or (ii) just my obligation to you, or (iii) both of our obligations. Non-performance therefore deletes (iv) neither of our obligations. So obligation is indefensible.

8. I suspect that this vitiates Gauthier's meta-level solution in *Morals by Agreement*. It is true that we all have an incentive that everyone be moral, but the trick is to con your partner into agreeing to be a moral person, while being secretly determined to remain an amoral person oneself. The Prisoner's Dilemma inherent in the exchange agreement is thus reproduced in the meta-level game about whether to be or not to be the kind of person who honours agreements.

9. The main application of this theory will be to the question of ethnic affiliation in Chapter 13, where the moral identity discussed in the present chapter will become a more general social identity.

10. See my two articles on the "Schelling Diagram" and "Symmetry and Social Division", *Behavioural Science*, 32, no. 1 (1987) and 34, no. 3 (1989) for discussions of Schelling Diagrams. Please note that the present Figure 8.2 is essentially the same as Figure 8 of the second article, but the notation has been changed, so that here the functions f and g' take the place of the article's functions g' and f respectively. The functions are further explained in Section 16.2. For analogous but uncritical use of Schelling diagrams, see Jon Elster, *Nuts and Bolts for the Social Sciences* (Cambridge: C.U.P., 1989), chs. 13 and 15.

11. Mancur Olson, *The Logic of Collective Action* (Cambridge: Harvard University Press, 1965), ch. 2.

12. Sen writes: "Given that each individual has complete assurance that the other will do [T], there is no problem of compulsory enforcement. Unlike in the case of the isolation paradox [a Prisoner's Dilemma], it is not in the individual's interest to break the contract of everyone doing [T]. In this case assurance is sufficient and enforcement is unnecessary and we shall refer to this case as that of the assurance problem." This seems clear, but Sen goes on rather unaccountably to deny that (T, T) is an equilibrium point and then quotes Baumol with approval to the effect that the individual will not play [T] "except if he has grounds for assurance that others, too, will act in a manner designed to promote the future welfare of the community." Elster has commented in similar vein that in the assurance game "solidarity can substitute for material incentives". In my view, the key point is that assurance in the assurance game derives from considering what it is in the *opponent's* interest to do, given that the opponent is a rational actor. This is a mechanism of pure rational choice, unadulterated by external considerations of solidarity, moral incentives and so on. Solidarity would after all solve the Prisoner's Dilemma very comfortably. See Amaryta K. Sen, "Isolation, Assurance and the Social Rate of Discount", *Quarterly Journal of Economics*, 81 (1967), pp. 114–15; and Jon Elster, "Marxism, Functionalism and Game Theory", *Theory and Society*, 11, no. 4 (1982), p. 468.

13. David Miller wrongly implies that the indefinite repetition of the game is the key to the supergame solution: see *Market, State and Community* (Oxford: Clarendon Press, 1989), p. 108, n. 19.

14. Tit-for-tat emerges from Axelrod's work *The Evolution of Cooperation* (New York: Basic Books, 1984), as a good representative strategy of conditional cooperation. It carried off the trophy in the tournament he arranged between game theorists for a solution to the Prisoner's Dilemma supergame.

15. Taylor defines temptation differently, as equal to the numerator of t: (a – b). See *Possibility of Cooperation*, p. 116.

16. An alternative to the interpretation of h as a financial discount rate makes it equal to the probability that the game will continue from each round to the next. This interpretation

was introduced by the originator of the supergame solution to the Prisoner's Dilemma, but has tended to be lost in subsequent debates. In the current context, if h is the probability of continuation, the expected length of the game (i.e. the expected duration of the household relationship) is $(1 - h)^{-1} = (1 + k)$ by (8.23). Hence the weighting parameter k is the expected duration of the game beyond round 1. The pioneering article is by Martin Shubik: "Game Theory, Behaviour and Paradox: Three Solutions", *Journal of Conflict Resolution*, 14 (1970), pp. 186–7.

17. This analysis contests Rapoport and Guyer's conclusion about the "force- vulnerable" equilibrium (D, D) in "A Taxonomy of 2 × 2 Games", *General Systems*, 11 (1966).

18. Christopher Lasch is one critic on the left who has taken the former line, for a critique of which see Michèle Barrett and Mary McIntosh, "Narcissism and the Family", *New Left Review*, 135 (1982).

19. A.H. Halsey, "Social Trends since World War II", in Linda McDowell et al., eds., *Divided Nation* (London: Hodder and Stoughton, 1989), p. 16.

PART IV

The Private and the Public Domains

9

Private and Public Goods

9.1 Social Access and Material Constraint

The terms "public" and "private" are among the most primitive, and complex, in the ordinary vocabulary of social description. In the sense intended by the title of this part of the book, the terms designate two separable spheres of social life variously thought to divide institutions, sources of satisfaction, standards of judgment or conventions of feeling and acting. At a first approximation, the private stands for household, family and friends, while the public is a wilderness beginning at the door.[1]

In an alternative, though related, set of meanings prevalent within economic theory, the distinction between the public and the private catches several kinds of variation in the characteristics of goods. Assume to begin with that goods come under particular descriptions and that there exists some set of procedures, rituals or rules specifying the conditions under which people gain social access to a particular good for particular purposes of use. Stipulate next that someone (perhaps a member of some group) has social access of a given type to a given good when and only when they are free to make given-type use of the given good. Here, "freedom" means "lack of appreciable hindrance from other people". "Appreciable' is best left unquantified, except to note that it will be sufficient to delete freedom of access that legal penalties attach to the given use of the given good and probably insufficient that a perfect stranger expresses mild irritation on one occasion at given use of a given good. Those who are free to use a good comprise a public to whom the good is private.[2]

Freedom to use a good is intended to imply that the good exists to use and that there is choice about whether to use the good, but does not require that people have the desire or the will, or perhaps even the power, to use the good.[3] It is also true that someone with freedom to use a good may not use it not because they do not have the desire to use it, but because they fear the consequences of using it, including the consequences derived from other people's reactions to it being used. In this case, it might appear that a person did not have the freedom to use a good because the deterrent effect of other people's (actual or anticipated) reactions is an appreciable hindrance to use. I acknowledge that it is going to be difficult to draw the line between freedom-cancelling hindrances to use and prudential discouragements of free use, but I think the basic distinction must lie between deterrence directed at the fact of use and ancillary harms arising from any of the manifold consequences of use. Of course, it may be that one of the good reasons for directing deterrence at the fact of use is the likely consequence of a particular type of use, but there is still a viable distinction between the two sources of deterrence, and it is this distinction which seems helpful in marking the boundary of what freedom of access entails.

Let us assume, for example, that I have a choice between visiting an interesting art gallery and completing my annual income tax return. I am free to visit the gallery even though an inevitable consequence of my visiting the gallery today will be a further delay in my tax return, which could land me in deep trouble with the Inland Revenue. It may then come about that the government loses so much tax, or incurs so much extra administrative cost, from art lovers failing to file tax returns, that a decree is passed requiring the presentation of a "certificate of completed tax return" at the entrance to all art galleries and museums. Henceforth, it is the fact, and not just the consequence, of uncertified gallery attendance which incurs adverse social reaction. From the moment the decree is passed, but not before, access to the gallery is so much unfree. In this spirit, I take social access to involve a combination of social acceptability of given use of a good with material availability of the same good. For some fine purposes, we can distinguish potential access from access, just as we have distinguished access, which gives potential use, from use.

With these basic considerations in mind, we can elaborate the senses in which, or the dimensions on which, variation regarding social access rules may relate to what is "public" and "private" about goods. It seems that there are at least four analytically and almost practically independent sources of such variation.

There is a first variation in *the type of body which decides what the social access rule shall be*. The most public body would involve maximum equal participation of everyone in the world in the decision about the contents of the social access rule for a given good. The most private body would vest all decision-making power in a single individual. There is some connection of public determination with democracy and private determination with private ownership, but this connection is not by any means straightforward.[5]

The next two dimensions pick out variations in the *content* of social access rules. Any social access rule will contain clauses, first, which specify procedures or requirements for gaining access to a good. Thus, to advertise a price for a good is to lay down access conditions and to specify a group of people with potential access (those who can afford the good at the advertised price). A subset of those with potential access are those who buy the good, thereby satisfying the access conditions (or at least the financial access conditions). The term "consumer" is nicely ambiguous between the set of potential customers and the subset of actual customers, so that the term "consumer society", for example, denotes a society where there are many goods to choose, and people do generally afford several of them, without necessarily being able to buy them all.

On this dimension the general principle will be that *a good is supplied more in the public social mode and less in the private mode, the larger the number of people who are granted (actual or potential) access under the conditions for the time being established.* All other things being equal (such as wealth or income of the relevant population), lowering the price of a good will make it more public, and in the limit, a free good is a public good, on this second dimension of publicness. We note that the first dimension (of public or private control over the character of the access rule) is in general independent of the second (the public or private modes of access under the rule). A despot could place a given good unconditionally at the disposal of all (so ceasing in this respect to be a despot?), or a perfect democracy could vote it to the exclusive use of one.

Alongside the clauses which specify the conditions of access, *an access rule will very likely include clauses which specify conditions of use.* Those who qualify for access by satisfying the conditions of access will generally be allowed access only for particular purposes of use, enjoyment and consumption. These use-clauses set forth the purposes which determine that access is to be of a given type, as the "type" term was introduced into the definition of access written above. If I buy a motor vehicle, for example, I cannot use it freely to drive on land away from the public highway, or to run down pedestrians who stray upon the road. And even upon the highway there are possible legal as well as physical penalties in driving my vehicle into the space currently occupied by your vehicle.

In respect of this third dimension the general principle of ordering from private to public would seem to be that *an access rule to a good gives more private access the fewer the conditions that are attached to the use of the good.*[6] Private access gives greater latitude in use than public – so that, for example, buying a good and being free to destroy it is a more private type of appropriation than hiring it and not being free to destroy it.

Three dimensions of access have been roughed out, and principles of ordering from public to private on each dimension suggested. The questions then arise, first, whether the ordering is complete over all access rules taking the dimensions one at a time, and second whether the qualities of publicness and privateness are correlated on the three dimensions, given a (possibly incomplete) ordering with respect to each dimension.

Consider, then, whether the ordering of access rules on the first dimension – by an index of participation in their choice – is likely to be complete. The answer is fairly clearly "No". Suppose the bodies that could decide on the access rule to a local museum are (i) a representative democracy with a universal franchise, (ii) a direct democracy of those who have visited the museum in the past, or otherwise expressed tangible interest in its existence. Which method of determination – which political system – gives greater aggregate participation and is more "public" as a result? It will not be possible to say, in general, except in the unlikely event that the greater participation of the few can be weighed in general against the lesser participation of the many.

In any case, Arrow's Theorem and related findings suggest that even if we define the ideal limit of a "public" political system as involving "maximum equal say", there is no institutional mechanism (like majority voting, for example) which can implement the ideal and deliver a determinate social decision under all possible preferences for social access rules.[7] If there is no institutional peg at the public end of a spectrum of political systems from the public to the private, it is unlikely that we can fill in all points in between. (The "private" end is easy: dictatorship means that the social access rule will be the one preferred by the dictator.) The point is not that we cannot ever make judgments about whether one political system is more public – it is natural to say, more open – than another. The point is that we cannot expect always to make that judgment.

A similar story is told for the second and third dimensions. On the second dimension, the basic ranking principle is that a more public access rule grants access to a greater number of people. But there are many kinds of condition which can be used to regulate who is allowed access.[8] We may need a great deal of collateral information to decide exactly how many people will gain access as a result of different access rules. And even if we could decide on the relative numbers, the relative numbers might not be the only relevant point. Suppose, for example, that whoever is involved in determining access rules to a museum can decide what the opening hours are, and how much to charge for admission. Each of these options is ranked, and plausibly ranked from public to private, since the lower the charge and the longer the hours, the more people have access, and the more public is the museum, all others things being equal. But things are not always equal because a choice might exist between, say, free five-day opening and low cost seven-day opening. It is not clear what the ranking is of these two options, and clarity would not necessarily be restored by showing, or estimating, whether the one rule or the other was likely to lead to a greater number of admissions to the museum overall: the first option will discriminate against the busy and the second against the poor, so our judgement will tend to be influenced by our evaluation of business against poverty.

On the third dimension – the one concerning purposes or conditions of use – it is easy to see that latitude of purpose does not rank all purposes. There is ranking when one compares a museum in which smoking is allowed to another museum with all the same allowances of behaviour except smoking. The first museum is more like home: you can do what you like, it is freer, and more private – more relaxed. But suppose the first museum now bans jellybeans from the galleries, whereas the second does not. Is the prohibition of smoking more or less of an infringement of personal liberty than the prohibition of jellybeans? Latitude of use does not define a complete ordinal variable.

Let us accept, then, that in some but not all contexts there is a sense of scale from the private to the public in each of the three respects. Consider only those contexts for which the requisite scales exist. The issue at stake in asking whether these scales are correlated, so that privateness on one scale goes with privateness on another, is as follows: suppose that the scores on the three dimensions are perfectly correlated. Then there would in fact be a single scale of the private and public character of goods. A totally private good – or rather, a totally private political economy of goods provision – would presumably involve a dictator giving one person exclusive access to each good, with totally unlimited rights of use, disposal or consumption. At the other end of the scale, totally public political economy would have the whole world voting for free access of everyone to everything under equal, but perhaps limited rights of use, disposal or consumption. Between these extremes would lie in regular order all possible constitutions for systems of providing goods – at least with respect to variations in access rules. And, it might be added, one could use this rank order to generate a ranking of meta-preferences for one kind of political economy rather than another. Political positions would be in various degrees rightward, privately inclined and pro-capitalist or leftward, public-spirited and pro-socialist.

This line of thought has already received one blow: the first and second dimensions of publicness and privateness are uncorrelated. Public control of access rules can go with private modes of access, and vice versa. A democracy could vote to institute capitalism and a dictatorship decree equality.[9] But what about the second and third dimensions? Does more private access imply more liberal conditions of use, because with fewer people there is somehow more room for them to move? Strictly speaking, the answer is again "No". Whenever we can rank access rules by their latitude, or liberality, there will be a rule (the more liberal one) which allows a person all the varieties of use of the less liberal rule, plus some other uses. And it need not be the case that the extra usages allowed under the more liberal rule are usages which significantly affect the access to the good enjoyed by others, should there be public access to the good.

Suppose, for example, that one museum allows silent appreciation and shouting, while another museum allows silent appreciation, shouting and posturing as modes of interacting with the great works on display. The second museum has a more liberal, and thus a more private access rule, but, unless the posturing is truly extravagant, posturing is unlikely to alter the prospects either for quiet appreciation or for boisterous acclamation, so that the gallery can easily accommodate poseurs among its existing clients, and wider latitude of use does not in principle require more private kinds of access.

On the other hand, it is difficult to overlook in the same example the possibility that if shouting is allowed, and it occurs, it will crowd out, or pollute, silent appreciation. There is a negative externality from a particular variety of use, consumption or enjoyment of a good by one person to the enjoyment of another. In these circumstances, there is a correlation of the presumed kind between the degree of openness of access and the degree of restriction as to use. If you and I have our own private gallery, we can shout the house down if we wish, but if we decide to endow a public gallery which we sometimes wish to enjoy in silence, we will do well to write silence into the rules. And a rule which allows silence alone is less liberal than one in which we can shout as well. On making access public, we deprive ourselves of the privilege of shouting we enjoy in private.

It can be seen that if there is a negative externality, a connection between access conditions and use conditions is likely to arise in two ways. First, if there is public control of access, each of us – *qua* controller – has an interest in drawing up the use clauses of a public access rule in such a way as to restrict or eliminate the negative externality that we would suffer *qua* consumer or user of the good. It is plausible that we would vote to impose upon ourselves a rule of silence in museums, or in general vote against nuisance in a public place.[10]

Second, the example of shouting in the museum points to the general circumstances in which my use of any good to which I have access may be blocked or pre-empted in practice by the manner or the fact of your use. This is never a logical consequence of access, as that has been defined above, because access is potential use, and we might all be allowed to shout in the museum without any of us doing so, so that the externality in question might never arise. But self-interested people will certainly avail themselves sometimes of the opportunities for use that their access provides, and whenever they do, they can generate a negative externality for other potential consumers. The paradigm case of pre-emption occurs when the effect of your use of a good is to reduce the quantity or quality of the good that is available for me. In an obvious application of a useful Marxian distinction and an extension of access terminology, it might be said that there is *formal* social access when there is social acceptability with or without material availability but *real* social access only when material availability supplements social acceptability. In these terms, we are formally but not really free to join a congested freeway or we are formally but not really free to enjoy a museum in silence when others shout.[11]

Under what circumstances will negative externalities of this sort arise? The answer will supply the fourth and final dimension of publicness and privateness in goods, as this was introduced to modern economic theory in a classic series of papers published by Paul Samuelson from 1954.[12] Samuelson was not concerned with social access rules, in the sense we have discussed so far. Instead, he concentrated on the material behaviour of goods under given types of use or consumption. He distinguished consumption-variant from consumption-invariant goods and he called them respectively pure private and pure public goods. *Pure private goods* are those whose consumption generates a negative externality because *whatever amount of the good I use, I use up*, and that amount of the good is not available to you, even if you are formally entitled to it under a public social access rule.[13] A *pure public good*, on the other hand, is *used, but never used up*, so that it never generates a negative externality in this way.

Another – and perhaps the only – way that a pure public good can generate an externality is through a mechanism such as jealousy, in which the mere fact that you are enjoying a good plunges me into depression – and this psychological mechanism can obviously operate in addition to the material mechanism in the case of a pure private good.[14]

Having established the fourth dimension in its bare bones, the usual pair of questions arises: is there a complete ordering between the private and the public on this dimension, and how is the position of a good on this dimension related to the position of a good on the previous three dimensions? The first question is answered at greater length in the next section, but the conclusion can be briefly stated in advance: under plausible but not totally general assumptions, there are essentially only two behaviours of goods under consumption. These behaviours are those of

Samuelsonian pure private and pure public goods. From this point of view, the fourth dimension offers a disjoint and exhaustive bipolar classification of goods rather than an ordinal scaling, and we only have to consider these two cases (the situation is a little more complicated than this summary, but not much).

When we come to the relation between the Samuelsonian classification and the previous dimensions of social provision, we hear the deafening sound of Samuelson falling over backwards to make clear that his pure public goods don't have to be provided by the Government.[15] If we accept for a moment that a quietly appreciated museum is a pure public good because the exhibits don't perish from being before our eyes, then sight of the show can be supplied under any of the private or public social arrangements considered thus far. Paul Getty can own the museum as well as the Federal Government, and both or neither can charge admission to get in. *The material character of goods does not ordain the politics of access.* The general significance of this point is nevertheless mitigated by the fact that economically relevant Samuelsonian pure public goods are rather rare birds. Indeed, I think it quite possible that the species is virtually extinct.

Of much greater empirical significance, and theoretical interest, is the relation between Samuelsonian pure private goods and variation on the second and third dimension of social access. It is noteworthy that Samuelson is much less emphatic about the possibility that pure private goods could be provided in a public social mode than he is about the converse possibility discussed above.[16] The fact that it is a pure private good in the Samuelsonian sense did not prevent milk being provided free of charge to all school children in the UK. If it had been otherwise, the practice would not have had to be prevented for older children by the first privatization decision of our celebrated former Prime Minister.

There is, nevertheless, an inherent material problem concerning public modes of social access to pure private goods. For a pure private good existing in finite amount there may be a finite use-constraint: a finite amount of use before the good is used up.[17] Under a given type of use, which implies a given relation between use and some relevant consumption-variant measure of the good, there is a direct inverse relationship between the amount of good that each person can use and the number of people who can use it.

The bearing of this fact on public access rules is twofold. On the one hand, one might say that where the use clauses of an access rule do not specify an amount of use to each user, then the effect of larger numbers of people taking advantage of their access (or the same number of people taking greater advantage of their access) is to delete the real access of any remaining would-be user, because there will not be enough of the good left to go round.

On the other hand, it is possible, and indeed likely where the outcome just envisaged recurs, that the use-conditions of the public access rule will specify certain maximum amounts of use. In this case, the inevitable rationing is built into the rules, and we have recovered a perfect correlation between the second and third dimensions of social access. The more public the rule, in the sense of the number of people who both have and take advantage of access, the more public the use-conditions, in the sense of the smaller quantity of the good they are each able to consume. It follows by the same token that for pure private but not pure public goods, greater privacy of access tends to imply greater privacy of use.

I will take for example the exhibition of the Crown Jewels in the Tower of London. It was said above that a museum was a pure public good, because the exhibits it contains are used for enjoyment without being used up by enjoyment. But this truth is not quite the whole truth, because I cannot contemplate the same object as you from exactly the same angle of vision at the same time. If I am standing behind you, you are blocking my view (just as David West persuaded me against the prevailing wisdom that sunlight could not be an example of a pure public good because I could sit in his shadow on the beach, as much as in the text). Sometimes, this aspect in which a good acts like a pure private good does not intrude upon the access rule, because the good is available in such abundant supply relative to the maximum demand that there will always be "enough and as good" to satisfy all second comers.[18] Ordinarily, visitors to museums are allowed to browse, and view the pieces for as long as people will (though they are not normally encouraged to set up camp, for this incursion would use the museum too privately, for political or residential as well as cultural purposes).

Now although an abundance in supply of a pure private good will considerably ease the constraints on use that may be required in a social access rule, and in this respect an abundant supply of a pure private good imitates the use-unconstraining supply of a pure public good, one should not be confused by this fact about the fundamental difference in the material behaviour of the two types of goods. For the use constraints on a pure private good will tighten as the demand increases, whereas those on a pure public good will not, and this is the point the Tower of London makes.

The problem at the Tower is that up to two million visitors a year must be threaded through a subterranean bank vault to inspect artefacts whose presence ideological stands inversely to their presence temporal.[19] The visitor is guided first around the foothills of British state regalia – the ceremonial swords, the paraphernalia of nobility and the tableware for special feasts – before being led underground to the climax of the show. At the entrance to the vault, the choice is offered between two access routes. There is first of all a swift current of people circulating just outside the armoured glass hexagon containing all the coronation jewels at the centre of the vault. If the speed past the Crown is about one mile an hour, then about fifteen thousand people a day will wait for about an hour and a half to see the jewels for about five seconds each.

Beyond this inner circulation, and just above it on a peripheral circular platform, winds a more leisurely, meandering stream, in which people are allowed to stop, and stare from a distance, and generally take their time. The use conditions are more relaxed, and the throughput correspondingly lower. On these grounds, the outer circle would give the private view, but if this were a genuine privilege, and the choice of stream free, the system would break down, because everyone would opt outwards and the jewel house rapidly silt up. What is lost in the outer circle is another way of being privy to the throne – of being so close to the Crown that you can reach out in imagination through the armoured glass to touch its power. And so people are nicely sorted by their preferences either for slightly distant contemplation or for royal close encounter into two streams which solve the same equation between people and time – between social access rules and material constraint – at slightly different numbers.

Three dimensions of social access and one dimension of material use have been outlined in this section. The first three dimensions concern respectively the procedure for determining what the social access rule shall be; the conditions of access under the rule; and the conditions of use once access is acquired. None of these dimensions generates a complete ordering of access rules. A fourth, dichotomous dimension establishes whether or not the good is consumption-variant. The first dimension is largely uncorrelated with any of the others. The second and third dimensions will tend to be correlated when the good occupies one of its two possible positions on the fourth dimension. In this case, the behaviour of a pure private good under consumption will tend to induce a correlation between wider access and narrower use of access. Here lies the contribution of the dismal science: one would generally like both access conditions and use conditions to be wider, but whenever there is an element in use or consumption of a good which is private in the Samuelsonian sense, there are liable to be material equations in the range of real access rules that can be applied. In these most common circumstances, there may be difficult political decisions for dictator and democrat alike, about how many of which people can make how much use of what.

9.2   The Bipolarity of Consumption Goods

The strict taxonomy

In this section I will sketch, without the detailed argument it deserves, a general taxonomy for the material character of consumption goods. In what now follows, the terms "public" and "private" are understood to refer to the material behaviour of goods and not their mode of social provision.

The taxonomy comes in two versions. The strict taxonomy seems mandated by economic theory. The relaxed taxonomy is more appropriate to applications. It enables us to treat certain goods as if they belonged to a category of the strict taxonomy when strictly they do not.

According to the strict taxonomy, a disjoint and essentially exhaustive classification of consumable goods with respect to any single manner of consumption contains just three categories, namely (i) *pure private goods* – the staple of economic theory; (ii) *pure public goods*; and (iii) *composite goods* (which behave in at least one respect like pure private goods and at least one other respect like pure public goods).

As has been mentioned, the fundamental idea is that pure private goods are consumption-variant and pure public goods are consumption-invariant. The consumption of a pure public good leaves no effect on the good; it is able to change the consumer without itself being changed in the process. The consumption of a pure private good on the other hand affects the good (negatively) as well as the consumer (positively). The good possesses attributes whose satisfaction-generating power deteriorates with use. If it starts out with a definite (and finite) amount or stock of a given attribute, then increasing use will progressively erode this stock until the good may cease to have satisfaction-generating power altogether (i.e. it may cease to be an instance of the good). By convention, this exhaustion point corresponds to zero stock. If the amount of use at which zero stock occurs is finite, then patterns of use are subject to a stock constraint under any conceivable social arrangement. There is only so much of the good to go round.

This bipolar classification into pure public and pure private goods is fairly well-established. Less certain is the status, or existence, of goods living away from Samuelson's "North and South poles".[20] Sometimes it seems to be thought that non-polar goods are those which behave in all respects in some fashion intermediate between pure public and pure private goods. I claim that under assumptions to be stated there is no such intermediate behaviour. With respect to any one of their possibly numerous material attributes there are essentially only two possible behaviours under consumption: those characteristic of pure public goods and pure private goods respectively. But since goods typically have numerous material attributes which are capable of independent variation in the process of consumption, it is possible for a single good to have both pure-private-goods-behaving attributes and pure-public-goods-behaving attributes. In order to represent these possibilities, we require a slightly richer data base than is conventional within economic theory. In particular, we need to allow for a finite number of different (cardinal) measures of the different material attributes of any given good, and a (cardinal) measure of the amount of consumption (or use) of the good which is defined independently of any of the material attributes of the good.

The problem now posed is the behaviour of this large family of attribute-measures with respect to a single measure of consumption. The relationships between these variables reflect the effect of consumption on the good, thereby yielding the required taxonomy of goods. There are two kinds of reason why an independent measure of consumption is required. First, in the case of a consumption-invariant "public" property of a good, variation in the property cannot be used to measure the amount of consumption, because there is an amount of consumption without variation in the property. Second, even in the case of a consumption-variant "private" property of a good, the amount of change in the property (roughly, the amount of the good consumed) is not necessarily the only relevant measure of consumption.

To see this, contrast the eating of oranges with the taking of baths. Suppose I start with a pile of ten oranges. I eat three. How much orange-eating have I done? The answer seems to be: "three oranges' worth of eating", and three oranges is also the amount by which my stock of oranges has shrunk. My utility, in the standard assumption, depends on how many oranges I have just eaten (eventually I may get pretty sick of oranges) but not on the size of my original stock. I would enjoy eating three oranges from a stock of one hundred just the same – unless, I suppose, I was unusual in being an orange collector, who also loved contact with a stock of such enormous size.

Now I take a bath. The bath begins at 8°C above my body temperature. Gradually it cools to 5° above my body temperature because of my presence in the water. I have used up 3° of bath. But my utility depends on the total stock of temperature and not just the change in the level of the stock, because I would not enjoy a bath so much which went from 4° to 1° above my body temperature. Utility does not depend only on the use I make of the bath, if use is measured by the change in temperature. But is the amount of use measured entirely by change in temperature in any case? Suppose I have a supernatural public bath, that gives up its heat to me while not losing any heat itself. Will I stay in that bath forever? Presumably not, because my ardour for a bath will cool just like my taste for oranges, even if the bath itself does not. The utility function for physically possible baths plausibly contains independent entries both for temperature and time spent in the bath. The distinction between the measure of use and the measure of consumption is required to make explicit the distinct sources of satisfaction in a single process of consumption, even of a consumption-variant pure private good.

The discussion motivates a definition of the strict taxonomy which hinges on a proof whose assumptions are as follows:

(1) We posit an irreversible functional relation between any one measure of the stock or state of the good and the amounts of consumption of the good which occur during n discrete *episodes of consumption*. An episode of consumption is an interaction between one consumer and the good on one occasion (n episodes thus include the case of n different consumers on the same or different occasions, or the same consumer on n different occasions, or some combination of consumers and occasions totalling n). The stock function is given by $s = s(q_1, q_2 \ldots, q_n)$ where s is a cardinal measure of the given material attribute of the good and q_1, q_2 etc. are the cardinal amounts of consumption (or use) of the good that occur in the first, second etc. episode of consumption. $q = q_1 + q_2 \ldots q_n$ is the total amount of use or consumption. The stock function is assumed to be continuous and differentiable in each of its arguments. It specifies the amount of the good remaining after consumption (q_1, $q_2 \ldots$, q_n) has taken place. The function is everywhere normalized to zero stock (i.e. stock level $s = 0$ always implies that what remains is no longer an instance of the good).

(2) *Irreversibility* of consumption implies that none of the partial derivatives of the stock function is ever positive. This assumption is designed to exclude the possibility of a local minimum in the stock function. If we hold all of ($q_2 \ldots$, q_n) constant and vary use in the first episode of consumption then a local minimum would correspond to the following circumstances: as q_1 increases, the stock of the good is decreasing until it reaches a minimum at which the good is instantaneously behaving as a consumption-invariant pure public good. Thereafter, the stock of the good is increasing with increasing consumption. In effect, we could produce the good by consuming it beyond a certain point, so it does not seem unreasonable to exclude such bizarre economic behaviour.

(3) The key assumption is now introduced: *episode neutrality*. This assumption says that the way in which a marginal change of use affects the stock of the good is independent of the episode in which the marginal change occurs. Mathematically, this is a very powerful symmetry assumption, since it states that all the partial derivatives of the stock

function are identical functions. The assumption gains some of its justification from something about human nature, namely that people interact with consumable things in the same material fashion. For example, I get whatever orange-eating satisfaction I can derive from three oranges by eating three oranges, and the same goes for you. Adopting the viewpoint of the good, one could say that goods don't have preferences one way or the other for particular people or occasions. People always look the same, and what affects the good is only the amount of use the people make of the good. Episode neutrality is violated where, for example, the effect that time spent in the bath has on the temperature of the bath is different for different bathers because of the bulk of the bathers. In general, episode neutrality abstracts from differential weight, height, clumsiness, wastefulness or accident-propensity of consumers.[21]

Episode neutrality is certainly compatible with some varieties of economy of scale in consumption (as in the case of the temperature of the bath), but there are other varieties which require a more general treatment than is offered here. Consider the differential effects on a car of journeys involving different numbers of passengers. If the measure of total use is passenger-miles, then the effect on the car is presumably less for an extra mile carrying two people on the same occasion than it is for an extra two miles carrying one person one mile each on two separate occasions. The economy of scale in consumption violates episode neutrality: cars prefer occasions which involve larger numbers of persons. The underlying problem in this example is that both mileage and passengers/vehicle are being treated as independently variable measures of use of the vehicle, corresponding to different ways in which the same good can be used. Under any single type of use (constant passengers/vehicle, variable mileage; variable passengers/vehicle, constant mileage) episode neutrality is a reasonable assumption. In this case it doesn't matter which journey adds the extra mile; it doesn't matter who is the extra passenger on every journey – and the preceding analysis applies. I do not generalize the taxonomy to deal with more than one measure of use of a given good. It should finally be stressed that episode neutrality says nothing about interpersonal variation in utility (i.e. the preferences of people for goods rather than goods for people).

The proof begins by observing that

$$ds = \frac{\delta s}{\delta q_1} \cdot dq_1 + \ldots + \frac{\delta s}{\delta q_n} \cdot dq_n \tag{9.1}$$

$$= \frac{\delta s}{\delta q_1} \cdot [dq_1 + \ldots + dq_n] \tag{9.2}$$

$$= \frac{\delta s}{\delta q_1} \cdot dq \tag{9.3}$$

by episode neutrality.

The idea of the proof then asks: what are the stock-conserving patterns of use? Stock-conserving patterns of use imply $ds = 0$. From (9.3), this entails either

$$\frac{\delta s}{\delta q_1} = 0 \tag{9.4}$$

or

$$dq = 0 \tag{9.5}$$

(i) If $\delta s/\delta q_1 = 0$, the good is behaving momentarily as a consumption-invariant pure public good with respect to the first episode of consumption. Moreover, since

$$\frac{\delta s}{\delta q_1} = \frac{\delta s}{\delta q_2} = \ldots = \frac{\delta s}{\delta q_n} \text{ (episode neutrality)} \tag{9.6}$$

all the partial derivatives are zero at this point, and

$$\frac{ds}{dq} = 0 \tag{9.7}$$

so that the good is momentarily consumption-invariant with respect to total use q.

(ii) If $dq = 0$, the good is behaving momentarily as a pure private good. Since

$$dq = dq_1 + dq_2 + \ldots + dq_n = 0 \tag{9.8}$$

the only way to compensate for increased use in one episode is to decrease use by exactly the same aggregate amount in other episodes of consumption.

The proof establishes that under the assumptions of differentiability of the stock function and episode neutrality the behaviour of a consumption good at any point in q-space is bipolar: characteristic either of a pure public good in the Samuelsonian sense, or of a pure private good.

We next extend the discussion to cover regions of q-space. If ds/dq $\neq$ 0 in some region, then ds = 0 implies dq = 0, and the converse follows immediately from (9.3). Hence s = s(q) over this region. Stock level is a function of total use alone (it has one argument instead of the original n arguments). Moreover, it is a decreasing monotonic function of total use in this region (because all derivatives are negative in this region).

If $\delta s/\delta q$ = 0 throughout some region, s is invariant over the region, no matter what the distribution of total use q among the various episodes of consumption.

The overall consumption profile of a good with respect to a given measure of use is now determined by the arrangement of the regions of q-space in which it behaves respectively like a pure public and a pure private good. The irreversibility assumption comes into play, so that the possible profiles are as laid out in Figure 9.1.

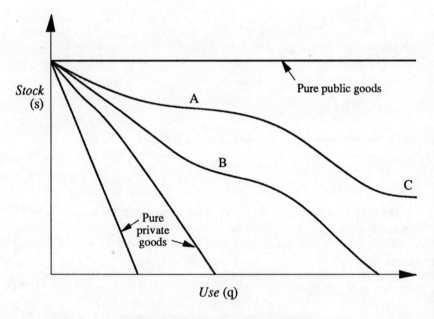

Figure 9.1 Consumption Goods

We see that it is analytically possible for a stock function to have a public goods plateau as at A in the figure, or a point of inflection as at B.

Neither of these possibilities seems very plausible economically. We therefore assume that goods are characterized by either ds/dq = 0 for all q (public goods pattern) or by ds/dq < 0 for all q (private goods pattern).[22] In the latter case, there is a (1 − 1) relation between stock level and total use. We can interpret this relation to imply that in nearly every case where there is a finite level of initial stock there is also a maximum total amount of use possible from the initial stock. Total use is therefore constrained by stock in the manner of a pure private good, even though the use-constraint is not given directly and the stock function need not be linear in total use.

The only exception is where the stock function is asymptotic from above to some value of stock greater than zero (as if the bath were to cool off continuously with use while tending to some plateau of temperature still qualifying as a warm bath).[23] This is indicated at C in Figure 9.1. In this anomalous, entropically unlikely case consumption-variance does not imply a finite use constraint. A good is a pure private good from the taxonomic point of view but behaves like a pure public good with respect to constraint. Overall, the proof establishes that with respect to any single measure of a material attribute of a good (and single measure of the amount of use) the behaviour of consumption goods is indeed bipolar: *either* the good is consumption-invariant *or* consumption-variance is a function of aggregate use. There are no intermediate behaviours. Private goods status nearly always implies use-constraint. Public goods status always implies lack of use-constraint.

We now consider an extended (finite) list of measures of distinct material attributes of the good, say s, s′, s″, and run them through the proof one at a time matched against the same measure of total use, q. The bipolarity property quarantees that the measures fall into two classes: those which measure attributes of the good which behave like pure private goods under consumption and those which measure attributes behaving like pure public goods. The private goods measures are in (1 − 1) correspondence with each other via their (1 − 1) correspondences with total use. We are now in a position to generate the categories of the strict taxonomy by noting the distribution of consumption-variant and consumption- invariant measures, taking account of all economically relevant measures. The strict taxonomy is as follows: A *pure public good* is consumption-invariant under all of its economically relevant measures. A *composite good* is consumption-invariant under *some but not all* of its economically relevant measures. A *pure private good* is consumption-invariant under *none* of its economically relevant measures.

We know that all consumption-variant measures are economically relevant, because consumption-variance is of economic relevance. A consumption-invariant measure is economically relevant when it enters someone's utility function (as a constant under consumption, but not necessarily constant in any other respect).[24]

The relaxed taxonomy

Moving from theory to practice, the question arises how many types of goods there are likely to be in each category of the taxonomy. Observe first that the strict definition of a pure public good is extremely demanding. *The pure public good must be utterly immune to consumption.* This is bound to make such goods rather unusual. This claim is not especially controversial, since the pure public good is widely recognized as an ideal type. The analysis above nevertheless suggests two main ways that goods can fail to attain the status of pure public goods.

First, a good might be genuinely pure public with respect to one explicit measure of its attributes and yet pure private with respect to some other latent measure. For example, live performance may be a pure public good if what is seen and heard is unaffected by the size of the audience. But live performance in a theatre is limited by the capacity of the theatre: a seat occupied by me for the duration of the performance is not available to you. Since goods of nearly all kinds are bounded in time and space, some measure of reception capacity is almost certain to be constrained. (For broadcast radio signals, capacity is finite but very large.) In such cases, a pure public good becomes a composite good on closer inspection for the latent measure of capacity. Here is a case in point:

> Perhaps a classic example of a public good is a lighthouse. If the owner of a shipping firm erects a lighthouse to protect his ships from a treacherous shoal, then the warning that the lighthouse provides is available to all ships passing the shoal. And ignoring congestion of the waterway, as many ships that pass the shoal are warned without any costs beyond those that the builder originally incurred. The lighthouse and its warning are thus a public good.[25]

Note the phrase "ignoring congestion of the waterway". Supposing that the warning signal is a pure public good, there is still a latent measure of signal reception capacity (namely, the ship-capacity of the adjacent waterway) which acts like a pure private good (two ships cannot occupy the same position at the same time). And this is hardly an incidental effect of lighthouse provision, since if the waterway were not prone to congestion by shoals and other land-like objects there would be no need of any lighthouse.

Yet if the lighthouse is less pure a public good than it first appeared, can we be confident about its light? Recall the sunbeam, and its tendency to be absorbed by a neighbour on the beach. Is not the lighthouse beam the same? If I am in a dinghy leeward of a freighter, I just don't receive the signal because the signal is used up by the freighter on the way. But it may be that there is no means by which a signal can be registered that does not in some degree attenuate the signal. This suggests that the only thing about the lighthouse which behaves like a pure public good is the meaning of the signal – the warning in the message as distinct from the medium of the message; the signified as distinct from the signifier.[26]

Second, a good falling short of public purity may do so because an attribute of the good is *almost* consumption-invariant. The foundations of the lighthouse are undermined by waves from passing super-tankers, but not by very much; a shadow falls across the beam, but not for very long. This suggests the definition of the *relaxed taxonomy*: replace "consumption-invariant" with "almost consumption-invariant" in the definitions above. Under the relaxed taxonomy, goods falling just short of pure public status will be allowed to remain pure public goods and other goods will move from pure private to composite and composite to pure public status.

The difficulty, of course, is to know how variant "almost invariant" is supposed to be. The treatment above allows us to attach some meaning to the phrase. The key point is that for any instance of a given type of good, we can compare the relative rates of deterioration of the different measures of the good with respect to a given amount of total use. This is because all the consumption-variant measures are monotonic functions of the same variable (i.e. total use). Here is the obvious procedure: the initial state of a good is given by $(s'_o, s''_o, s'''_o \ldots)$ where s'_o etc. are the stocks of the good with respect to all of its consumption-variant measures. Then there are (not always finite) values of total use q' (s'_o), q'' (s'_o), ... etc. which represent maximum total uses from given stock. We stack the stock measures one behind another according to the tightness of the use-constraint that they impose. Suppose the measures are labelled so that $q' \leq q'' \leq q''' \ldots$ etc.

First examine the case in which finite $q' = q'' = q''' \ldots$, etc. for all economically relevant measures. This is the case in which a pure private good is exhausted simultaneously with respect to all of its measures. The $(1 - 1)$ correspondence among all consumption-variant measures already implies a certain homogeneity in the behaviour of the good under consumption: the good shrinks in step with respect to all of its stock measures. But it is only in the case envisaged that the stock shrinks to a point, and converges uniquely towards non-existence as a good however it is described and measured. I suspect it is one of the intuitions underlying the distinction between pure private and pure public goods that pure private goods only occur at stock levels with this property (for instance, however we describe and measure milk, zero milk with respect to one measure implies zero milk with respect to all measures). In this case, we can take any of the consumption-variant measures of the good as representative of their class.

But the intuition that this property *defines* a pure private good is misjudged, according to the strict taxonomy, since it may be that $q' < q''$ $< q''' < \ldots$ etc. (I ignore the possibility of equalities in this chain of inequalities for expository convenience.) For this sub-category of strict pure private goods, the good encounters a series of use-constraints as total use increases. This occurs first with respect to the attribute measured by s', second the attribute measured by s'' and so on. s' seems the appropriate representative measure, since it offers the most pressing, most privative constraint to use. The amount of the good used up is given by the vector quantity $(s_o', s_o'' - s'' (q'), s_o''' - s''' (q'), \ldots)$ where $s'' (q')$ etc. are the stocks remaining with respect to the less pressing measures at the point when stock runs out with respect to the most pressing measure s'.

This vector helps to clarify another of the senses in which private goods have been distinguished from public goods, related to the ordinary language distinction between consumption and use. A private good is consumed as if by fire, and is destroyed in the process. It is used up whereas a public good is used. But how much is a private good used up? With respect to any single measure, the amount by which the stock decreases is the amount of the good wholly used up, and if this amount is less than the initial stock, then the initial good has been partly used up. But the good has a number of parts in a different sense of "part": those aspects of it distinguished as separate attributes and measured by s', s'' etc. The vector above establishes that when the first part of the strict pure private good is wholly used up, all the remaining parts are in general partly used up. In fact, the ranking of measures by use-constraint enables us to distinguish those attributes of the good that can be treated for the purposes of the relaxed taxonomy as if they were (more or less) subject to "private" consumption from those that are (more or less) subject to "public" use. (A good that is "public" in this sense would behave like fixed capital in the theory of production.)

We are now in a position to resolve the problem of quasi-invariance. Select a finite cut-off point of total use q_c, say, and treat all measures with use-constraint larger than q_c as "almost-invariant". The choice of q_c will vary with application, but it is presumptively large. Then one can reclassify the good from the strict to the relaxed taxonomy. Note first that the anomalous pure private good with asymptotic behaviour and no finite use-constraint will automatically become a relaxed pure public good, thus restoring the handy correlation between being a (relaxed) pure private good and suffering use-constraint. The major tendency will however be for a large number of goods to be transferred from the strict pure private goods category to the relaxed composite goods or the relaxed pure public goods categories (depending on whether $q_c > q'$ or $q_c \leq q'$). The relaxed composite goods category includes goods all of whose material attributes deteriorate with use, but some of whose attributes are considerably more durable than others.[27]

It is true that the translation from the strict to the relaxed taxonomy here depends on the initial state of each instance of each type of good and does not apply to types, but this is surely as it should be. For example, it is a fairly stable feature of cars that their expected mileage before total mechanical failure – which is assumed to be a continuous (probability) function of mileage – is larger than the mileage from a tank of gas. The car will run out of gas before it breaks down. Usually, mechanical soundness acts like a "background" public attribute and gas an "urgent" private attribute of the same vehicle. But if the car is on the point of breakdown, the reverse is true. And this fact is not irrelevant to the kind of action the intending consumer has to take in order to restore, or otherwise produce, the use-value of the whole machine.

The conclusions of the previous sections are as follows:

(i) Under the assumptions of stock continuity, irreversibility and episode neutrality, the behaviour of consumption goods with respect to a single type of use is essentially bipolar. In these circumstances, it is false that "a thing ... not located at the South Pole (is) not logically place(d) at the North Pole".[28]

(ii) From the strict point of view, types of consumption goods fall into three and only three categories. The bipolarity property divides all measures of the distinct attributes of the good into two classes. If the public goods class alone is represented, the good is a pure public good. If the private goods class alone is represented, the good is a pure private good. If both classes are represented, the good is called a composite good. The taxonomic distinction between pure private and pure public goods is correlated with the existence of use-constraint, but not perfectly.

(iii) The relaxed taxonomy treats almost invariant pure private goods attributes as if they were invariant public goods attributes. An almost invariant attribute is one whose initial stock level is exhausted only with large amounts of use, where the meaning of "large" depends on application. The categories of the relaxed taxonomy match those of the strict taxonomy under the relaxed definition of consumption- invariance. The relaxed taxonomy classifies instances of each type of good rather than types of good (though one can expect some uniformity in the reclassi-

SOCIAL DIVISION

fication). The correlation between categories of the taxonomy and the
existence of use-constraint is perfect.

Notes

1. Raymond Williams, in *Keywords* (Glasgow: Fontana, 1976), found a general movement from the root sense of "private" meaning "withdrawn from public life", still evident
in the surviving senses of "deprived" and "privation", towards a revalued emphasis on
" 'independence' and 'intimacy' " and thus the familiar and personal – a change occurring
from around 1550 to 1750. In fact, the "private" is being transformed in company with
linked changes of "family", "individual" and "personal", to achieve a central place in
a cluster of meanings which offer "a record of the legitimation of a bourgeois view of
life: the ultimate generalized privilege, however abstract in practice, of seclusion and protection from others (the public); of lack of accountability to 'them'; and of related gains
in closeness and comfort of these general kinds" (pp. 203–4).
2. For the time being, I treat this division of people between an included public and
an excluded non-public as like a step function: there is a group of people with equal access
and the rest of the world with none.
3. I take access to imply existence on the grounds that to have access to something
that does not exist when you come to use it is not to have much access at all. The further
distinction between real access, which is meant here by "access", and merely formal access,
which does not imply existence, is introduced below. I am slightly uncertain whether having
the power to use something should be included as one of its real access conditions. If
people cannot read, do they have real access to a public library? I think not, but it is
complicating to build conditions into the consumer as well as the consumed, and here
I am concentrating on the latter. On the general close connection between freedom and
its material and cultural conditions, see Richard Norman, *Free and Equal* (Oxford: O.U.P.,
1987), ch. 3.
4. "Distinct from the partitioning of the domain of uses to which a resource may be
put is the decision making process that may be relied on to determine that use"; and "It
is more useful and nearer to the truth to view a social system as relying on techniques,
rules, or customs to resolve conflicts that arise in the use of scarce resources rather than
imagining that societies specify the particular uses to which resources will be put" (A.A.
Alchian and Harold Demsetz, "The Property Rights Paradigm", *Journal of Economic History*, 33 (1973), pp. 16, 18).
5. I have preferred the language of access to that of ownership, in order to avoid the
legalistic connotations of the latter term (on which, see n. 6).
6. "While it is true that the degree of private control is increased when additional
rights of use become privately owned, it is somewhat arbitrary to pass judgment on when
the conversion to private control can be said to change the ownership of the bundle of
rights from public to private". "What is owned are *rights* to *use* resources including one's
body and mind, and these rights are always circumscribed, often by the prohibition of
certain actions": Alchian and Demsetz, pp. 17–18, and see for example, Philip S. James
in *Introduction to English Law* (London: Butterworth, 1979), p. 426: "Ownership is ...
a relative and not an absolute concept. An owner has greater rights than anyone else over
his [sic] property; but these rights are always subject to some restrictions imposed by the
general law of the time and place in which he lives."
In historical perspective, "ownership belongs to a flat legal world in which rights in
land or other forms of wealth are dependent upon no authority except the State" (S.F.C.
Milsom, *Historical Foundations of the Common Law* (London: Butterworth, 1981), p. 100.
Compare: "Behind a typical free market is centuries of patient development of property
rights and other legal arrangements, and an extraordinary standardization of goods and
services and the technology for describing them" (Thomas C. Schelling, *Micromotives and
Macrobehaviour* (New York: W.W. Norton, 1978), p. 29). Modern conceptions of ownership

are exceptionally simple ones, as David Miller also recognizes in *Market, States and Community* (Oxford: Clarendon Press, 1989) pp. 49–52.

7. Each social access rule is an outcome of a decision making process, so that the assumption of unrestricted domain in Arrow's theorem here means a lack of ideological or other constraints on preferences for social access rules.

8. Alchian and Demsetz, p. 21, give an example in which they claim social discrimination was an alternative to price discrimination: "In a Chicago newspaper, the percentage of apartment for rent advertisements specifying that the apartment was for rent only on a 'restricted' basis or only if the renter purchased the furniture rose from a pre-war low of 10 percent to a wartime high of 90 percent during the period of World War II when rent control effectively created queues of prospective renters. Attenuations in the right to offer for sale or purchase at market clearing prices can be expected to give greater advantages to those who possess more appealing racial or personal attributes." This discussion is continued in Section 14.1.

9. This point is pursued in Section 15.2.

10. I deliberately beg certain questions. What each of us supports as a self-interested voter is in fact an access rule giving no one but ourselves the right to be a nuisance: each of us wants a unique shouting privilege. But there is an overwhelming majority (of everybody else to one) against each privilege proposal. So if we only allow for consideration a social access rule which is someone's top preference, and there is a majority voting system, no social decision on access rules will be forthcoming. This distribution of preferences illustrates the problem of circularity, which Arrow's Theorem shows cannot be avoided by any general institutional device.

11. Marx made the distinction between the real and formal subsumption of labour to capital in terms of whether or not the material labour process had been transformed as a result of capital hiring labour-power: see *Capital*, I (Harmondsworth: Penguin, 1976), p. 645. The distinction between formal and real access cuts across the distinction between potential access and access.

12. P.A. Samuelson, "The Pure Theory of Public Expenditure", "Diagrammatic Exposition of a Theory of Public Expenditure" and "Aspects of Public Expenditure Theories", in *Review of Economics and Statistics*, 36 (1954), 37, (1955) and 40 (1958); and "Pure Theory of Public Expenditure and Taxation", in J. Margolis and H. Guitton, eds., *Public Economics* (London: Macmillan, 1969).

13. In associating the idea of an externality with that of a pure private good by definition, I am changing, indeed almost reversing, the common association whereby "public goods" are "those that exhibit *externalities*" (Ordeshook, *Game Theory and Political Theory* (Cambridge: C.U.P., 1986), p. 210). I regard the conventional usage – which is in any case confused between the social and the material dimensions of publicness – as thoroughly ideological, because it suggests that only public goods consumption has implications for other consumers.

14. My physics is not sufficiently comprehensive to know if the psychological mechanism is the only one by which the consumption of a pure public good could generate an externality, but it does seem implausible in the light of various conservation principles that there could be ancillary material consequences of a consumption process which leaves the object of consumption unchanged.

15. "For the (n + 1)th time, let me repeat the warning that a *public good* should not *necessarily* be run by public rather than private enterprise": Samuelson, "Pure Theory of Public Expenditure and Taxation", p. 108, n. 1.

16. "One might even venture the tentative suspicion that any function of government not possessing any trace of the defined public good (and no one of the related earlier described characteristics) ought to be carefully scrutinized to see whether it is truly a legitimate function of government": Samuelson, "Diagrammatic Exposition", p. 356.

17. The reason for the modal expression emerges in the next section.

18. See Section 6.3 for the political relevance of this Lockean proviso.

19. The figure of two million visitors to the Tower is given by Peter Hammond, *Her Majesty's Royal Palace and Fortress of the Tower of London* (London: Department of the Environment, 1987), p. 13.

20. Samuelson, "Diagrammatic Exposition", p. 356.

21. Measures of use might be contrived to take account of such variation, so that these cases are not excluded in principle: episode neutrality requires neutrality only with respect to given measure.

22. I should make clear that this distinction has a heuristic basis, and does not enjoy the logical status of the bipolarity result which applies at each *point* of q-space. I am grateful to my friend Stephen Joseph, of the Department of Mechanical Engineering, University of Sheffield, for bringing home this fact to me, as I am to my brother John Carling of the Department of Applied Mathematics and Statistics, North London Polytechnic for discussion of the foregoing proof.

23. The fact that a bath will cool without a bather makes clear that consumption is not the only source of deterioration in the useful properties of goods, just as production is not their only source of restoration. Natural decay is ubiquitous and natural growth is common, but the private/public goods distinction abstracts from both processes.

24. Samuelson, "Pure Theory", p. 387. I cannot deal here in detail with the inconsistencies in Samuelson's discussion, or the detailed relation of my proposals to the large family of existing public goods concepts, such as divisibility, excludability and rivalness – on which see Michael Taylor, *The Possibility of Cooperation* (Cambridge: C.U.P., 1987), pp. 5–7, and also Michael Taylor, *Community, Anarchy and Liberty* (Cambridge: C.U.P., 1982), pp. 40–5. As far as I am aware, the confusions inaugurated by Samuelson are still current.

25. Ordeshook, *Game Theory and Political Theory*, p. 212.

26. Information is a pure public good excludable only because it requires media of transmission which behave like pure private goods. Cohen has said of a space, distinct from the things contained in the space, that it "can be more or less useful, [so] counts as used. To be sure, unlike material facilities and labour power, it is not used up, and need not be reproduced and serviced. But its absolute reliability seems a poor reason for denying that it is used" (*Karl Marx's Theory of History: A Defence* (Oxford: Clarendon Press, 1978), p. 51). Perhaps meaning and space are the only pure public goods, speaking strictly and materially.

27. If the cut off value, q_c, is set by the maximum total demand in some context of use, then a relaxed private or composite good will be characterized by rivalness in consumption – that is, there will be some pattern of formally available access which is really constrained. This conforms to Taylor's point that rivalness implies divisibility (i.e. strict Samuelsonian privateness) but not vice versa. See Taylor, *The Possibility of Cooperation*, p. 7.

28. Samuelson, "Diagrammatic Exposition", p. 356.

10

Private Households and Public Goods

10.1 Contribution Principles, Ownership Principles and Needs Principles

The taxonomy of consumption goods applies both to goods that are deliberately produced as goods and to goods that are not produced as such. In this chapter, we consider only produced goods, and study in a simple two-person world how the incentives governing the production of goods alter as we vary the social access rules for their consumption.

In particular, we will be concerned with a variable balance of consumption rights between producers and non-producers. When it is the producer who gains an exclusive right of access to what the producer has produced, desert obeys *contribution principles*: the more you put in, the more you can take out. When a non-producer is given access to the product, we are dealing in general either with *ownership principles* or with *needs principles* of distribution.[1] Under the ownership principles of capitalism, for example, the capitalist enjoys exclusive rights of access to the entire product in virtue of the capitalist's ownership of all the non-human factors of production (coupled with the deal the capitalist had made to hire the producer's labour). Under needs principles, people enjoy access to consumption goods in virtue of the needs they have, rather than the contributions they make or the ownerships they enjoy. In circumstances in which a consumption good is a pure public good from the material viewpoint (in either the relaxed or strict senses) then distribution according to need more or less coincides with distribution on demand, or indeed distribution according to want (i.e. free distribution). In such a case, there is plenty to go round for everyone, and each person simply takes as much as they require to satisfy their needs or wants. I will, however, be concerned with consumption goods that are composite or private goods in the sense of the relaxed material taxonomy, and are therefore subject to use-constraint. In those circumstances, distribution according to need entails a rationing of the available consumption good in proportions predetermined by some comparative estimate of individual need. Thus, if needs are deemed equal, everyone will receive an equal share of whatever is available, whereas if needs are unequal, so will be the corresponding shares. It should be emphasized that distribution according to need does not imply that everyone's needs are always satisfied. On the contrary, if consumption goods are scarce, distribution by need will leave everyone dissatisfied.[2] Systems of distribution according to need tend to involve public social access rules (in the sense of the last chapter), but since I there defined public social access in terms of equal access, public access coincides with distribution by need only if needs are deemed equal. In this chapter, I will treat the household as a two-person microcosm of various production systems based on contribution principles, ownership principles and/or needs principles, and I will re-engage the subsistence actors whose simplified utility profiles will enable me to sidestep certain problems such as that raised by the important distinction between needs and wants.[3] I begin by describing the property relations of the exchange model of the household in two different ways.

10.2   An Exchange of Shares

In the exchange model of chapter 7, there are two kinds of goods – household use-values and money – and each of the two actors can produce either kind of good. There are thus four items to distribute: lower earner's money, lower earner's use-values, higher earner's money and higher earner's use-values. Initially, the four items are distributed as private property to their respective producers, on the basis therefore of a pure contribution principle. The actors then bargain with each other to transfer some of what they own to the exclusive jurisdiction of their partner. We know, however, from the calculations of chapter 7 that the only type of exchange it is in the interests of both parties to make is an exchange of the lower-earner's surplus use-values for the higher-earner's surplus cash where "surplus" means in each case a surplus above subsistence. These surpluses are represented by the hatched areas in Figure 10.1, which depicts an exchange of use-values in quantity s against money in quantity m.

Now it will be justly objected that such a model of exchange utterly misdescribes the workings of a household. Household members do not enjoy the sharply delineated private property rights in household goods that are required to operate the average commodity exchange. Indeed,

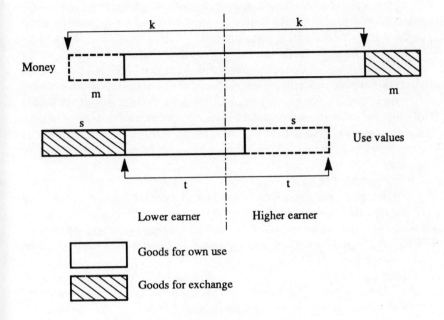

Figure 10.1 Household Exchange

one could say the reverse – that what makes a household private is the public character of the provision it makes for its members. Between 1971 and 1980, UK census practice defined a private household as "a group of people who all live regularly at the [same] address – and who are all catered for, for at least one meal a day, by the same person." By contrast, the "distinguishing feature of a communal [non-private] establishment is some form of communal catering."[4] Notice that under a strict reading a private household will cease to be so when father helps out with the tea. For the 1981 census, the meal criterion for a private household was changed, perhaps in recognition of this problem, and a new criterion was added:

A [private] household is either one person living alone or a group of people (who may or may not be related) living, or staying temporarily at the same address with common housekeeping. Enumerators were told to treat a group of people as a household if there was any regular arrangement to share at least one meal a day, breakfast counting as a meal, or if the occupants shared a living or sitting room.[5]

Sharing has become the order of the day, and that which is to be shared may be a room and not a meal. Any old sharing of meals will do (even breakfast!) but the accommodation that has to be shared is more specific. "A group of people would not be counted as a household solely on the basis of a shared kitchen or bathroom."[6]

We may learn from these official gyrations that the boundaries of a household are not as clear cut as may appear at first sight. All households contain complex and delicate internal gradations of what is deemed "public" and "private" with respect to different individuals and coalitions of individuals, in respect of different goods, spaces, and occasions, within a more general demarcation which serves to identify membership of the household with the set of people who have qualitatively freer access to a range of household goods, spaces, and occasions than is the case for anyone excluded from the set.[7]

We see also that the exchange model of chapter 7 must be adapted to the idea that household members share goods and services. This adaptation is swiftly accomplished, for the exchange agreement of chapter 7 may be looked upon as *an agreement to share money and the fruits of domestic work*.

If an agreement is reached at "m money for s time" then the (k + m) earner is agreeing to share "his" earnings in the ratio m/k and the (t + s) house worker is agreeing to share the fruits of "her" housework in the ratio s/t. These ratios are represented in Figure 10.1 by the relative lengths of the hatched and plain parts of the upper right-hand and lower left-hand bars respectively. The two sharing ratios m/k and s/t (which need not be the same) range from zero (when m or s is zero) to one (when m = k or s = t). These ratios describe different social access rules, and it is natural to regard the household exchange as an *exchange of shares* in *one* aspect of one's partner's work.

In this special two-person world, it is now possible to rank social access rules from the private to the public with respect to any given aspect of the household programme (i.e. either paid work or domestic work). When m/k is zero, for example (and s/t is necessarily zero also), there is no household, and each person is totally privatized in the dual sense that each is totally deprived of access to the resources of the other and that each is totally privileged with respect to the resources of themself. The relevant "public" with equal access is composed of just one person. This privilege in access of the wage earner to "his" money, say, is progressively eroded as m/k increases, until the ratio is one, "his" money is equally divided, the fact that a person happens to be the breadwinner constitutes no privilege within the household regarding bread, and his wage contribution to the welfare of all is totally public – in the new "public" consisting of two people. Social access rules can therefore be ranked from private to public in the two-person world as the sharing ratio moves from zero to one.

We can see in this result an instance of the correlation derived in section 9.1 between wider conditions of access to a good, and narrower use conditions of the good. As the household becomes more public in respect of the fruits, say, of domestic labour, then a non-producer is gaining rights over an increasing proportion of household use-values, and their original "owner" – the producer-for-exchange of the use-values – is losing rights over her output in the same proportion. (She is of course gaining rights in return over some part of her partner's income.)

This point also confirms that the exchange model of chapter 7 applies only to goods that are private (or composite) goods from the standpoint of the material taxonomy. Goods which are public goods from the strict material point of view enjoy a perfect economy of scale in consumption, and this means that while there is not necessarily any economy of scale in the producing of the good, there is in effect an economy of scale in producing that which will satisfy given needs, because any amount of the good able to satisfy one person's needs will be able to satisfy another person's needs without diminution. A similar argument applies to goods which are available in abundant supply, even if they are subject to diminution by use. We are dealing, then, with public and private social access rules to goods which are private goods, materially speaking.

Since the two sharing ratios are not in general equal, it is not possible to characterize the household by a unique degree of privateness or publicness. Instead there is an agreement to be more or less public with respect to (a) the housework of the lower earning partner and (b) the earnings of the higher earning partner. We note also that the housework, if any, of the higher earning partner and the earnings, if any, of the lower earning partner remain thoroughly privatized in this model – they go exclusively to making good the subsistence requirement of their respective "owners", whenever the sharing agreement leaves a body wanting subsistence of either the domestic or the financial variety. This is represented by the fact there there are no hatched areas on the upper left-hand or lower right-hand bars in Figure 10.1.

The whole of the previous analysis now falls into place under the interpretation that the household bargain is about the degree of privatization that shall prevail, and that the bargaining counters are *privatization threats*. We know, for example, that there is a cooperative interest in increased sharing of both money and household goods (i.e. increasing m and s and so increasing both sharing ratios, given that k and t are parameters) until *at least one* of the sharings reaches its most public limit: *either* there will be a breadwinner, access to the breadwinner's money will be equally divided, and all household money will be derived from his work *or* there will be a housewife, access to the housewife's household goods will be equally divided and all household goods will be derived from her work *or* the two sharings will be equally and completely public and the conventional housewife/breadwinner household will exist.[8]

The ultimate privatization threat in this game is the threat of divorce – as modelled by a conditional strategy – but one doesn't have to resort to this threat to recognize the power of similar threats short of divorce. To remove money in my own interest from a joint account; to wash just my car; clean just my room; shop only for myself; iron just my shirts; cook just my meal; label my carton of orange in the fridge; do just my washing up of just my plates, not to mention the deliberate seclusion of my person or my mind: these are all moves which create quite powerful sanctions, though one who tries to use them must take care that their use does not cause a self-defeating loss of confidence in the relationship on the part of the person the sanctions are designed to affect. Carelessness in this respect can bring divorce without intention.

10.3 Short Commons

An equilibrium of public provision

In the previous section, it was argued that the bargaining model of the household could be interpreted as a bargain about the extent to which household access rules should be private or public. We now assume instead that *the rule of distribution is fixed in advance and applies in the same way to both partners*. This means that whenever anything is produced in the household it is divided in the ratio $1:p$ between the producer and the non-producer. Such a rule is the prototype of a *uniform taxation system*. In effect, there is a uniform tax rate of $p/(1 + p)$ on all activities, and if both individuals are producers of the same good, then each individual is both a tax payer and a tax recipient. There is an induced exchange involving part of what I produce given in return for part of what you produce, of a type which in a larger setting characterizes the exchange orchestrated by states.[9] Given the way in which the publicness and privateness of social access rules was defined in the last chapter, we can also say that the rule is totally private if $p = 0$ (corresponding to a tax rate of 0 per cent); totally public if $p = 1$ (corresponding to a tax rate of 50 per cent in a two-person world in which the product is equally shared); and somewhat public if $0 < p \leq 1$. The important point however is that the value of p is not subject to bargaining within the model: the rule of distribution is an invariant household norm. I wish in short to examine the interaction which takes place given the existence of a somewhat public social access rule, when acts that privatize are disallowed.

Formally, we consider a single activity of an unspecified kind (not two specified activities, as in the exchange model). Let the activity cost two individuals amounts t_1 and t_2 to perform (t_1 and t_2 might be time costs, as in the exchange model of the household). Let the individuals have subsistence constraints T_1 and T_2, measured in the same units as t_1 and t_2. Since T_1 is not in general equal to T_2, we envisage for the first and last time in a formal model in this book that individual needs may differ.

To this end, it will be convenient to introduce a parameter n giving the *needs ratio* between the two individuals, defined by

$$T_1 = nT_2 \tag{10.1}$$

where $n \geq 1$. (If there is a needier person, it is the first who is the needier.)

The aggregate benefit $(T_1 + T_2)$ is set equal to the aggregate cost $(t_1 + t_2)$, which implies the simplest possible form of single-sector linear production function.[9] We now study the way in which the benefits T_1 and T_2 can be derived from various inputs of costly effort t_1 and t_2, given a social access rule p, as defined above.

The benefit to the first individual is

$$t_1 / (1 + p) + p\, t_2 / (1 + p) = T_1 \tag{10.2}$$

and to the second

$$t_2 / (1 + p) + p\, t_1 / (1 + p) = T_2 \tag{10.3}$$

The first equation says that the first individual derives benefit $t_1 / (1 + p)$ from their own activity and $p\, t_2 / (1 + p)$ from the activity of the second person; the two contributions totalling T_1. The second equation has a parallel interpretation.

(10.2) and (10.3) are equations in two variables (t_1 and t_2). Straightforward substitution and rearrangement gives:

$$(1 - p)t_1 = (T_1 - p\, T_2) \tag{10.4}$$

$$(1 - p)t_2 = (T_2 - p\, T_1) \tag{10.5}$$

The solution of equations (10.4) and (10.5) has a singularity at $p = 1$. This means that if the social access rule is a totally public one (i.e., contains no element of privateness or, as we might say, privilege in favour of the producer), the solution breaks down, and the values of t_1 and

t_2 become indeterminate. The significance of this singularity is discussed below. For the time being, we assume $p < 1$, and deduce

$$t_1 = (T_1 - p\,T_2)/(1 - p) \tag{10.6}$$

$$t_2 = (T_2 - p\,T_1)/(1 - p) \tag{10.7}$$

(10.6) and (10.7) may be rewritten in terms of the needs ratio n by substitution from (10.1) to give:

$$t_1 = (n - p)\,T_2/(1 - p) \tag{10.8}$$

$$t_2 = (1 - np)\,T_2/(1 - p) \tag{10.9}$$

The equations (10.6) and (10.7) (or (10.8) and (10.9)) specify the unique equilibrium for the provision of the household good, so long as there is at least some element of privateness in its provision. Since

$$(t_1 - t_2) = (1 + p)\,(T_1 - T_2)/(1 - p) \tag{10.10}$$

the person with the higher subsistence constraint will be making the larger contribution, and the gap will increase, as the difference between the constraints grows. If t_2 is to remain non-negative, (10.9) requires $np \leq 1$ (that is, if the needs disparity is too great, the more needy will end up doing all the work, at a given level of publicness of provision). I pause to spell out the workings of this straightforward mechanism for ensuring contributions to the public good, which creates equality of outcome for two equally needy people and unequal outcomes otherwise.

Suppose that in a given household $p = \frac{1}{2}$ and the two members needs differ, because one person eats three meals a day whereas the other eats only two meals a day (we assume this is a needs differential, not a greeds differential). Suppose that the activity to be shared is the washing up, and that each place setting at a meal requires six utensils. Then the couple require thirty utensils to be washed a day, of which eighteen ($=T_1$) are used by the first member and twelve ($=T_2$) are used by the second. If the first member were to perform enough washing up to provide all the utensils for her or his own meals, she or he would have to wash up twenty-seven utensils – taking eighteen for own use and leaving nine clean plates or spoons on the rack for their partner (because $p = \frac{1}{2}$). But nine utensils is not sufficient to meet the entire need of the second household member (whose daily need is twelve clean utensils). The second member then has no alternative but to roll up the sleeves and wash up at least four and a half utensils, in order to supply him or herself with the extra three utensils he or she requires to reach the subsistence constraint of twelve utensils. Yet this action makes available one and a half clean utensils to the first member, who in the event did not have to wash up as many as twenty-seven utensils in order to achieve her or his daily target of eighteen utensils. So the first member reduces her or his washing-up contribution, which induces a further increase in the second person's contribution. It is fairly obvious, and equations (10.5) and (10.6) confirm, that this process always converges, so that, in this example, the respective equilibrium contributions are $t_1 = 24$ and $t_2 = 6$: the first member of the household does four times the washing up of the second.

When necessities are supplied partly in common, we see that the existence of shortage can induce each of us to provide for all – self-interest can be harnessed to an altruistic outcome. This is the essence of the *short commons* model.[10]

Needs versus contributions

Neediness is the force which drives the short commons model, but this does not mean that distribution occurs in proportion to need. Quite the reverse, public provision can throw up new possibilities for the exploitation of the neediest individuals. To investigate this question, we must first spell out the formal implications of our previous discussion of contribution principles and needs principles, and introduce the formal specification of combined needs-contribution principles.

A pure contribution principle will split the output $(t_1 + t_2)$ in the ratio of the contributions to its production, so that the individuals receive t_1 and t_2 respectively. A pure needs principle will on the other hand split the available pool of goods in the ratio of the needs of two individuals, regardless of the origin of the goods. Thus, if goods are available in amount $(t_1 + t_2)$, and the needs ratio is n, the goods will be distributed in amounts $n(t_1 + t_2) / (n + 1)$ and $(t_1 + t_2) / (n + 1)$ respectively to the two individuals.

A combined needs-contribution principle will then allocate part of the output on needs principles and part on contribution principles. Let the needs-allocated proportion of the output be equal to the index j, with the contribution-allocated proportion equal to $(1 - j)$. Then j and n are the parameters of a family of needs-contribution principles, running from pure contribution principles $(j = 0)$ to pure needs principles $(j = 1)$.

Under any such principle, the contributions t_1 and t_2 must satisfy

$$(1 - j)t_1 + jn (t_1 + t_2)/(n + 1) = T_1 = nT_2 \qquad (10.11)$$

$$(1 - j)t_2 + j (t_1 + t_2)/(n + 1) = T_2 \qquad (10.12)$$

at a subsistence equilibrium for the respective individuals, where the first
term on the l.h.s. gives the return from contributions in each case, and
the second the reward to needs. Rearrangement yields

$$[(n + 1) - j] t_1 + jnt_2 = (n + 1) T_1 = n(n + 1)T_2 \qquad (10.13)$$

$$[(n + 1) - jn] t_2 + jt_1 = (n + 1)T_2 \qquad (10.14)$$

It is readily seen that (10.13) and (10.14) offer a more general version
of the basic short commons equations (10.2) and (10.3). The difference
is that (10.2) and (10.3) impose a uniform tax rate on the contributions
of the two individuals, whereas in (10.13) and (10.14) the tax rates may
differ, because the coefficient of t_1 in (10.13) is not in general equal to
the coefficient of t_2 in (10.14). Equations (10.13) and (10.14) thus offer
a prototype of *a graduated or redistributive taxation system*. Yet this is
still a model of public provision, implemented by a short commons mechanism which this time observes the ethical judgements enshrined in a given
needs-contribution principle (that is, the balance between the respective
ethical demands of needs and contributions registered by a particular
choice of value for j).
   A singularity in the equations (10.13) and (10.14) occurs at $j = 1$.
Thus, the short commons allocation mechanism breaks down for pure
needs principles – an eventuality considered below. If $j < 1$, we see by
inspection that

$$t_1 = T_1 = nT_2 \qquad (10.15)$$

$$t_2 = T_2 \qquad (10.16)$$

is a solution to (10.13) and (10.14). And since the solution to the equations
is unique, (10.15) and (10.16) must give that solution. It follows that
*combined needs-contribution principles always imply that contributions are
equal to needs at equilibrium*. The equilibrium turns out to be quite insensitive to the particular value chosen for j. The reason is that if two individuals are making contributions T_1 and T_2, then they receive respectively
T_1 and T_2 whether the operative criterion of distribution relies on relative
contributions (in the ratio $T_1 : T_2$) or relative needs (in the same ratio
$T_1 : T_2$). The argument leading to (10.15) and (10.16) proves that the same
point holds good for any rule of distribution involving a linear combination of needs criteria with contributions criteria.
   To underline the surprise inherent in this result, compare solutions
(10.15) and (10.16) to the solutions (10.8) and (10.9) of the previous section. The solutions are equivalent if and only if

$$(n - p)/(1 - p)\, T_2 = nT_2$$

or

$$p(n - 1) = 0 \qquad\qquad\qquad (10.17)$$

so that equivalence implies either $p = 0$ or $n = 1$.

(i) $p = 0$ If $p = 0$, there is no public element in the distribution rule whatever and yet the equilibrium is identical to that obtained from any needs-contribution principle: the application of a needs-contribution principle leads to the same outcome as that obtained via privatization, and a zero tax rate.

(ii) $n = 1$ If $n = 1$, the needs of the two individuals are the same, and any choice of p will implement some needs-contribution principle. Comparison of (10.13) with (10.1) for $n = 1$ shows that

$$p/(1 + p) = j/2 \qquad\qquad\qquad (10.18)$$

so that the uniform tax rate in the equivalent short commons model is equal to half the index value j of the needs-contribution principle it implements. But the outcome is egalitarian regardless of which value of p is chosen, and hence which needs-contribution principle is being implemented.

Yet (10.17) also implies that if neither $p = 0$ nor $n = 1$, a uniform tax rate does *not* implement a needs-contribution principle. In fact, the existence of a uniform tax rate (which corresponds to the existence of a uniform degree of publicness in the social access rule to each producer's output) always makes things worse for the more needy of two people with different needs, compared with what the more needy person would receive under any needs-contribution principle (which we have shown includes privatization as a special case). To see this, we calculate from (10.9) that if $n > 1$,

$$(1 - np)\, T_2 / (1 - p) < T_2 \qquad\qquad\qquad (10.19)$$

The l.h.s. of this expression gives the contribution of the less needy person at the equilibrium of a uniform taxation system. The r.h.s. gives the equilibrium contribution according to needs-contribution principles. There is then a systematic tendency for uniform public access under a short commons mechanism to imply the disadvantage of the neediest element in society. We must call this *needs exploitation*, where the counterfactual standard is supplied by needs-contribution principles, embodied in the solutions (10.15) and (10.16).

Although needs-contribution principles implemented by graduated taxation thus imply a more egalitarian outcome than a regime of uniform tax rates levied without regard to differential need, combined needs-contribution principles may still be criticized for being insufficiently egalitarian. In particular, they do not guarantee equal welfare. If, for example, the two individuals whose demand for clean pots is respectively eighteen and twelve are equally satisfied when they have respectively eighteen and twelve clean pots to consume, then the person who has to wash up eighteen rather than twelve pots has the lower welfare of the two individuals because of the unequal contribution to the production of clean pots. Welfare egalitarianism demands that each wash up fifteen pots and this is evidently incompatible with needs-contribution principles (whose application leads to inegalitarian results, according to (10.15) and (10.16)). In so far as Marx's commitment to public modes of provision is inspired by welfare egalitarianism, the results of this section suggest that needs-contribution principles of the type formalized by (10.11) and (10.12) are insufficiently radical, when needs differ. In fact, the overall conclusion with respect to welfare is that *if needs are equal, any needs-contribution principle implements equal welfare, whereas if needs are different, no needs-contribution principle implements equal welfare.*[11]

Since this conclusion applies only when the short commons mechanism converges to a determinate equilibrium, it does not extend to the case we have discovered when $p = 1$ (which leads to a singularity in equations (10.4) and (10.5)) or the case when $j = 1$ (which leads to a singularity in equations (10.13) and (10.14)). If either $p = 1$ or $j = 1$, the respective sets of equations each reduce to

$$t_1 + t_2 = T_1 + T_2 \tag{10.20}$$

which is indeterminate in t_1 and t_2. Thus, if distribution occurs either (i) without an element of privateness in the social access rule or (ii) without an element of reward to contribution, t_1 and t_2 must be determined by some mechanism other than short commons. We will investigate in the next chapter what other mechanism is liable to be called into play when the social access arrangement becomes a wholly public one.

Notes

1. I do not claim that these three types span the universe of possible distribution principles.

2. This is because every person will have the same proportion of their needs satisfied, which will be less than 100 per cent if consumption goods are scarce.

3. See Philippe Van Parijs, "In Defence of Abundance", in Robert Ware and Kai Neilson, eds., "Analysing Marxism", *Canadian Journal of Philosophy*, Supplementary Volume 15 (1989), for concepts of abundance (and therefore scarcity) defined in terms of wants rather than needs.

4. J. Atkinson, *A Handbook for Interviewers* (London: HMSO, 1977), p. 182.

5. *Census 1981: Definitions, Great Britain* (CEN 81 DEF, HMSO), pp. 6/7.

6. Atkinson, p. 182.

7. "One couple lived separately, but still regularly ate and slept together and the man gave the woman money for his keep. Another couple lived together, for lack of any alternative accommodation, but a court order forbade the woman to prepare food for the man, and forbade the man to enter the woman's bedroom. Should either of these two couples be defined as a 'household'? The answer is important not only for the purposes of enumeration, but also in deciding to whom social security benefits should be paid": Jan Pahl, "The allocation of money within the household" in Michael Freeman, ed., *The State, the Law and the Family* (London: Tavistock, 1984), p. 39. For a telling historical example see Leonore Davidoff, "The Role of Gender in the First Industrial Nation", in Crompton and Mann, eds., *Gender and Stratification* (Cambridge: Polity Press, 1986), pp. 199–200.

8. The ratio of the sharing ratios is a measure of the extent to which earnings are more (or less) publicly provided than housework. This ratio is $(m/k) / (s/t) = (m/s) / (k/t)$. So, as m/s decreases, say, the houseworker's position is deteriorating at the same time as "her" contribution is becoming more public. The two sharing ratios are equal, with the household having a univocal "degree of privatization" only if $(m/s) = (k/t)$. The only possible occurrence of this case in a Pareto-optimal household under the exchange model is if the parameters are such that a conventional household is formable, with $m = k$ and $s = t$. In that case, the degree of privatization is zero. In other words, we have the slightly surprising result that the degrees of privatization of the two types of work are equal only if they are both zero. We also remark that the most public of households in this model has the most extreme division of labour. (This is not the case with the models of the next chapter.)

9. In particular, there is no surplus production net of labour costs.

10. Brian Barry has suggested an example in which there is imperfect thermal insulation between adjoining flats in the same building, and the heat losses from each flat make each occupant contribute to the warmth of every other occupant. If heating needs differ, so that for example I can survive at low temperatures, maybe I won't have to turn on my own heating, because what seeps through the walls will satisfy all my needs. In this way, I may enjoy a free ride on my neighbour's heating bill.

11. John Roemer discusses needs exploitation in very general terms in *A General Theory of Exploitation and Class* (Cambridge, Mass.: Harvard University Press, 1982), pp. 279–83. His remark that "a distribution in which needs exploitation is absent is one in which the needy receive more income than the needless" suggests that his ethical standard is indeed welfarist. Although the results of this section imply that needs-contribution principles do not in fact implement welfarism when individuals differ, I do not pursue these issues any further in this book.

PART V

Gender Division

=========== 11 ===========

Chicken, Gender, Class

11.1 Provision by Need and Distribution by Chicken

"Good heavens" – or words to that effect – "we can't have run out of milk *again*. I don't know how many times I've told those blessed children *not to take the last milk from the fridge*. Why don't you pop round to the shop for a pint while I make the coffee?"

"Oh, leave it."

"Don't you want any coffee then?"

"I'm not bothered really; I'll have a cup if you're making one."

"Oh well, I suppose I'll have to go round to the shop for the blessed milk, as per blessed usual."

"OK. Oh, while you're there, could you get me a packet of cigarettes."

Read as an essay in distribution, the first speech proposes a division of labour, which the second refuses to take up. The third appeals to the needs mechanism and is again adroitly blocked. The fifth acknowledges defeat but avoids retaliation. The sixth completes a triumph by revealing a weakness.

In such cases, it is not usually open to a person to supply some determinate fraction of their partner's need for milk, coffee or cigarettes. So the shortness of the partner's supply will not induce a reciprocal response which converges to the short commons equilibrium. Failing this option, both parties will conspire to define the situation as a situation that distributes according to need, even as they engage in a fitful struggle about who is going to supply what is being supplied according to need.

Take in this spirit a single household task – "housework" or "earning" or "washing up" or "shopping" or "taking the kids to school today" or "cleaning the toilet". The options are (i) to contribute to the doing of the task (call this "C"); (ii) not to contribute to the task (call this "D"). Assume that contributions are burdensome and distribution occurs according to need. For the sake of definiteness and continuity with the previous discussion, assume this means that contributions t_1 and t_2 are made by two individuals, with the fruits of these contributions distributed according to needs T_1 and T_2. Then

$$t_1 + t_2 = T_1 + T_2 \qquad\qquad (11.1)/(10.20)$$

where

$$0 \le t_1, t_2 \le T_1 + T_2$$

For any values of t_1 and t_2 satisfying (11.1) rewards are invariant, because differential contributions are not differentially rewarded. So each of us has an interest in our personal contribution to the production of the reward fund being as small as possible, and the contribution of our partner being as large as possible. This implies that among values of t_1 and t_2 which satisfy (11.1), the first person will always prefer $t_1 = 0$ to any positive t_1, with similar preferences over t_2 for the second person. The strict ordinal preferences for all patterns of contribution which satisfy (11.1) are then in descending order, with the usual notation, and ordinal symmetry between the two players:

> (D, C)   a
> (C, C)   b
> (C, D)   d

To complete the payoff structure, a new piece of information is required. What happens if no-one makes a contribution? Evidently, nothing is produced, and so (11.1) cannot be satisfied for positive T_1, T_2. The question, then, is how bad it is going to be if nothing is produced. This option has not had to be quantified in any of the previous models, since the welfare comparisons have occurred among outcomes all of which met the given subsistence constraints (for example, the comparison between a joint household and individual living arrangements in the exchange model).[1]

We can assume in the present case that the default option (D, D) is not better than the cooperative outcome (C, C). If the good is not worth having even if both partners contribute to its production, it is unlikely that it will be provided at all: it is beyond the reach of the household. So (D, D) is not in the first place or second place of the ordinal preference scale. The question remains whether it is in third place or fourth place. The answer depends on *whether or not there is an incentive to provide for the needs of everyone, even if you are the only person making a contribu-tion.* If the seriousness of the individual need being unmet is outweighed by the total cost of the contribution necessary to ensure that everyone's needs are met, then (D, D) is in third place, preferred to (C, D). Roughly, this means that the need is less pressing – or relatively so, given the cost of providing for everyone's need. If, on the other hand, the seriousness of the need being unmet outweighs the cost, then (D, D) is in fourth place.[2] Unmet needs of this variety give the worst possible outcome. They create a disaster; too horrible to contemplate.

There are accordingly two cases to consider.

(a) *The case of lesser need*: (D, D) > (C, D)

(D, D) is in third place and the payoff structure yields a Prisoner's Dilemma:

(C, D) a
(C, C) b
(D, D) c
(C, D) d

Not much will be said of this case, which has been analysed in general terms at length above. The application to this context is as follows. In a one-shot game, lesser needs will be left unsatisfied among non-coopera-tive players, but not among sufficiently cooperative players. In the super-game, the needs may be met by rational cooperation (i.e. mutual contributions). It may be the case that cooperation will be sustained with an unequal pair of contributions ($t_1 \neq t_2$; $t_1 + t_2 = T_1 + T_2$) despite the existence of the exploitation which unequal contributions may well imply. Unlike the previous models, we cannot tell in advance who is going to be the exploiter, should exploitation occur. In particular, it is not necessarily the actor with the superior external bargaining position who is inevitably (as in chapter 7) the exploiter, because the bargaining positions are here exactly the same. Nor will it be the case (as in section 10.2) that one person is forced to make a larger contribution because of their higher need, since the inegalitarian equilibrium of section 10.2 depends on a connection between the making of contributions and the satisfaction of needs that has here been broken. The domestic outcome is therefore unpredictable.

We may distinguish at this point between the core and the periphery of household provision – or perhaps it should be called the skeleton and the flesh – in terms of the respective provisions for greater and lesser needs. Households may vary in the extent to which and the areas in which they overcome the Prisoner's Dilemma associated with provision for lesser needs. Thriving households no doubt manage to resolve this problem for a wide range of goods and facilities. Yet all households must manage to create a skeleton, whose anatomy we are about to dissect. Skeletal provision will in practice include (clean) clothes to wear, a (leak-proof) roof over the head, (edible) meals on the table and (surviving) children in a warm room, subject to some marginal variation by culture, class and region.[3]

(b) *The case of greater need*: $(C, D) > (D, D)$

The payoff (D, D) is now in fourth place and the payoff structure becomes:

(D, C) a
(C, C) b
(C, D) d
(D, D) c

The outcome (D, C) implies contributions $(0, T_1 + T_2)$ by the first and second individuals to the public good: the second individual provides everything; (C, D) implies contributions $(T_1 + T_2, 0)$: the first individual provides everything; (D, D) implies contributions $(0, 0)$ and (C, C) implies contributions $((t_1, t_2): t_1 + t_2 = T_1 + T_2; t_1, t_2 > 0)$. The given preference ordering evidently applies for all pairs of positive values (t_1, t_2). It defines the two-person binary-choice symmetrical game known for good reason as Chicken. The payoff structure of Chicken differs from that of the Prisoner's Dilemma simply in the transposition of the third and fourth ranked payoffs. Taylor and Ward have summed up Chicken thus: "There is a minimum amount of work which must be done: *either individual alone can do it all*, but each prefers the other to do all the work. The consequences of *nobody* doing the work are so disastrous that either of them would do the work if the other did not."[4]

Recall that in the Prisoner's Dilemma, there is a dominant strategy (D in the present context) and a single non-cooperative equilibrium (D, D) which is Pareto-inferior to the outcome (C, C). I concluded in section 8.2 that there is never a real dilemma of individual decision-making in the Prisoner's Dilemma, and that individual decision-making would sometimes lead to cooperative behaviour, granted what I called cooperative beliefs.

It is otherwise with Chicken. First, there is no dominant strategy. If my opponent is playing C, I should play D. If she is playing D, I should play C. Second, there is an equilibrium (or rather a pair of equilibria) in which *either* first player plays D, second player plays C *or* first player plays C, second player plays D. (The reader can check that neither player has an incentive to change their strategy in either of these cases, given the strategy of their opponent.) Both of these equilibria are Pareto-optimal, as is the non-equilibrium cooperative outcome (C, C).

The characteristics of these equilibria are of great theoretical interest. Notice initially that the equilibria are at the extremes of the distribution of possible contributions: either one person does all the work or the other person does all the work. If it is an axiom of rational-choice theory that a social situation will end up at an equilibrium, then *distribution according to need in the two-person game will generate extreme inequality, where needs are great.*

It is easy to see why this occurs. The extent of their needs creates such a pressure on each player to satisfy their own needs (and thereby the needs of the other player, when distribution goes according to need) that each player risks being trapped at a highly inegalitarian outcome. With lesser needs the pressure is not so great; the mutual vulnerability is less severe and the risk of inequality recedes. Players can afford to adopt more of a "take it or leave it" attitude to their lesser needs, with the consequence in the corresponding one-shot Prisoner's Dilemma that all non-cooperative players do leave it, and the lesser needs remain unmet. The outcome of the one-shot Prisoner's Dilemma is the non-provision of the public good, though there is equality in its non-provision; the outcome of Chicken is the provision of the public good, with gross inequality of contributions to its provision.

Sometimes it is said that the Prisoner's Dilemma is about the free rider problem. This is not really true. There are no free riders in the Prisoner's Dilemma, nor any prospect of them. No one in their right non-cooperative mind is going to begin, or remain cooperating, let alone get trapped in unilateral cooperation.[5] In Chicken, on the other hand, the equilibrium *consists in* unilateral cooperation, with one person almost inevitably free-riding on the efforts of the other. The maldistribution is at least as serious as anything considered in the previous chapter.[6] Within the confines of the model, things are as bad as they could be.

If the Chicken equilibrium conforms to Roemer's general conception of exploitation, the explanation for its occurrence differs significantly from the cases considered thus far. In Roemer's scheme of things, exploitation always arises from some inequality of resource distribution or initial situation. The evidence for the required causal effect of the initial inequality is that when the initial inequality is eliminated, the outcome is no longer unequal, and exploitation disappears. We have followed the same approach in the exchange model of households (based on external wage inequality) and in the models of short commons (based on needs inequa-

lity). When wages or needs were respectively equalized, outcomes converged. For exploitation to exist in these cases, there had to be some
cardinal asymmetry of the payoff structure (which is consistent with ordinal symmetry, in many cases).

In Chicken, on the other hand, exploitation can exist even when there
is perfect cardinal symmetry of the payoff structure – when, for example,
the outcome (C, C) is the equal contribution outcome, and needs are
identical, so that $T_1 = T_2$. The game can be perfectly egalitarian, in the
sense that each player is placed indistinguishably with respect to the other
player at the outset, and yet the outcome is highly inegalitarian. There
are no initial handicaps, and indeed nothing to distinguish the competitors, and yet there is a clear winner and a clear loser. Evidently, it is
impossible to regard the outcome as a consequence of unequal initial
positions, when initial positions are the same.

In Roemer's scheme, we are comparing equilibrium outcomes between
two different games: a game with unequal resource distribution versus
a game with equal resource distribution. In Chicken, we are comparing
two outcomes within a single (let us say cardinally) symmetric game:
an equilibrium outcome in which the first player plays D, say, and the
second player plays C, versus a non-equilibrium outcome in which both
players play C. The counterfactual levelling is not a levelling of resources
or constraints. It is a levelling of the only inequality in sight: the fact
that the choices of the two players have differed despite their equal circumstances.

But this brings us to a deeper question: why is it, or how is it that
one person plays D, say, and the other person plays C, when they are
identically placed, equally rational individuals facing a perfectly symmetrical decision structure? The point is that there are *two* equilibria in two-
person Chicken, although the two equilibria are of the same type. Rational-choice theory is supposed to tell us that one of these equilibria will
occur, but it certainly can't decide which. In particular, *no process of
strategic reasoning can lead one player to a non-cooperative strategy choice
that differs from the strategy choice made by an identically placed, equally
rational opponent.* I invite a reader sceptical of this conclusion to begin
by imagining the kind of reasoning a fairly sophisticated Chicken player
might adopt.

A fairly sophisticated Chicken player will think: my crude, unsophisticated opponent will be very frightened of the disastrous (D, D) outcome,
so he will play C to avoid it. (Perhaps he will be so innocent that he
will adopt the maximin strategy he has just read about in an introductory
text on Game Theory.) But if he plays C, then I can play D with impunity,
and I am bound to win. On the other hand, an *extremely* sophisticated
Chicken player will say: my opponent is *fairly* sophisticated, and will

go through the previous process of reasoning. She will play D. So I am forced to play C and I cannot help losing. The extremely sophisticated player has thus come round to the same conclusion as the unsophisticated player, and both disagree with the fairly sophisticated player. But why stop there? Presumably an *extraordinarily* sophisticated player will think their opponent is *extremely* sophisticated, and so the extraordinarily sophisticated player will come to the same conclusion as the merely fairly sophisticated player: play D.

Each player is evidently involved in an infinite regress of argument which recommends different strategies at alternating steps of the argument: C, then D, then C, then D ... It is arbitrary where this chain of reasoning might stop, and indeed one cannot even come to any of the provisional conclusions which constitute the links of the chain without assuming an inequality – namely a difference in the level of sophistication of the two players.

This suggests the most general form of the argument for the indeterminacy of Chicken. Assume that there is some process of reasoning, call it R_1, which leads me to be confident that my opponent will choose one of the two strategies – it doesn't matter which, but say for the sake of argument the strategy C. Then I will certainly play D. But now there is a second process of reasoning, call it R_2, consisting of R_1 plus the new clause anticipating the inevitable response any player will make to R_1. But if R_2 applied to my opponent instead of myself, it would lead me to be confident that my opponent would choose the strategy D rather than the strategy C. In that case, I would respond with C instead of D.

By induction, there is a series of processes of reasoning $(R_1, R_2, R_3 ...)$ which fall into two subsets. The set of reasonings $(R_1, R_3, R_5 ...)$ – call them the odd reasonings – tells me to play D. The complementary set of even reasonings $(R_2, R_4, R_6 ...)$ tells me to play C. Since the behavioural consequences of reasonings belonging to the same subset are the same, each person is faced in effect with a binary choice: do I behave according to even reasons or odd reasons?

Notice that players facing this problem are not just very sophisticated at Chicken; they approach the game with a different order of sophistication, because they are so self-controlled that they can monitor how sophisticated they are going to be. Yet these meta-players will find their choice no easier than the crudest of players in the lower level game, for it is clear that the decision in favour of odd or even reasons reproduces the original decision structure regarding the strategies D and C. If I reason oddly while my opponent reasons evenly, the outcome will be (D, C), with the converse equilibrium (C, D) for the converse distribution of reasoning. If we both reason oddly, the outcome will be (D, D) and if we both reason evenly, (C, C). The Chicken payoff structure has a property of closure under orders of sophistication in its players.[7]

To reach an equilibrium, meta-players must attribute reasoning to their opponent which they do not accept for themselves. The set of reasonings is either (odd, even) or (even, odd). But this inconsistency is not the worst of it in Chicken. It is obvious what to do if I know what my opponent is doing, or can reconstruct what my opponent is thinking (recall that R_1 is *any* process of reasoning to a determinate strategy choice). But my opponent doesn't know what to do or to think unless I tell him what I am doing or thinking. In the absence of this information, it is simply impossible to work out in advance what to do in Chicken, and so impossible to predict the outcome. But having the information depends on working out in advance what to do in Chicken, and being able therefore to predict the outcome (whereas in the Prisoner's Dilemma, the existence of a dominant strategy makes the outcome all too predictable). Even though we know that there are non-cooperative equilibria in the game, it is impossible to know how they can be reached, within the set framework of non-cooperative rational-choice theory, strictly conceived.

It follows that if there is a process of reasoning which leads to equilibrium, it must contain agent-specific considerations, able to count as reasons for one actor without becoming thereby reasons for the other actor. Such a lack of generalizability would evidently block the reversion between the points of view of the two actors which is basic to the line of argument just given.

It is perhaps significant that the most relevant class of agent-specific considerations is a class of *identity* considerations. Thus, it might be believed by both actors that a D-player is playing D because the D-player, being a tough guy, is not the sort of person who could be expected to play C. If the second player is a tender person, unlikely to play D, then the reasons why the members of a tough and tender duo are acting respectively tough and tender could not be reasons for them acting respectively tender and tough. But it is an open question whether such identity considerations ever really give reasons for actions, rather than giving explanations for actions. It is probably a sound instinct that tells us that agent-specific considerations do not count as proper grounds for choices we wish to construe as rational.

What is required to reach an equilibrium in Chicken is a kind of tie-breaking device. This cannot be just a conventional device (in David Lewis's sense that it is apparently conventional to adopt it). Lewisist conventions break ties when there is no fundamental conflict of interest – when, for example, we have to decide whether to drive on the left or the right of the road, and it does not matter greatly which decision is made, so long as everyone abides by whatever decision is made.[8]

This is not the case with Chicken, for it matters a good deal to me whether or not I am the one who is going to end up doing all the housework. Hence the tragic aspect of the game. It is reasonable to represent the tough-minded player determined to play D as the oppressor, because his toughness has deprived his opponent of the possibility of the egalitarian cooperative outcome (C, C). This act of oppression victimizes the opponent, because it makes exploitation the best remaining option: it forces the victim to play C.

But what motive has the oppressor for abandoning his oppression? We know that whenever there is an exploitative equilibrium, the exploiter has an interest in the status quo. However, we hope that an exploiter might more readily accept an egalitarian outcome out of a sense of justice if egalitarianism would stick. The trouble with Chicken is then its bi-stable, flip-flop property: equality won't stick. If the oppressor goes soft and plays C, he will end up the victim of a new oppression. So both players might struggle to oppress mainly for fear of otherwise becoming a victim. What one wants to do is break out of the cycle of oppression and victimization. But Chicken keeps the circle closed. Chicken is deeper and more fraught with paradox than the Prisoner's Dilemma. It raises fundamental doubts about the comprehensiveness of the rational-choice approach and is altogether the most intriguing of the symmetrical two-person binary-choice games.[9]

11.2   Three Ways Out of Chicken

Confidence in Chicken

At this point, something of a theoretical impasse has been reached: how is Chicken solved?

It is worth exploring briefly two ideas that worked quite well for the Prisoner's Dilemma: the confidence condition on the beliefs held by actors regarding mutual causation, and the supergame solution. The two ideas are considered in turn.

Formally speaking, the confidence condition for the Chicken Game is given by the same expression as that for the Prisoner's Dilemma. The cooperative strategy (C) will be chosen if and only if

$$p(b - d) + q(a - c) > (a - d) \qquad\qquad (11.2)/(8.4)$$

where $p = \text{pr}[C/C]$, $q = \text{pr}[D/D]$ and $a > b > d > c$.

It is easy to see that if there is perfect confidence, comprising perfect trust in a cooperative response to a cooperative move, and perfect fear of a non-cooperative response to a non-cooperative move (so that p = q = 1), then (11.2) is always satisfied and cooperation will prevail. Indeed, there is some sense in Chicken that fear is better founded than in the Prisoner's Dilemma, since what one has to fear from retaliation is worse – the outcome (D, D) is now the worst-ranked, awful outcome because payoff c is now lower than payoff d. The difficulty is that the very awfulness of this possibility may make the threat to play D – which is implicit in both the confidence and supergame solutions to both the Prisoner's Dilemma and Chicken – a less plausible threat in the case of Chicken than it is in the case of the Prisoner's Dilemma. I pursue this issue when the supergame solution is discussed in the next section.

Here I consider the difference made by the changed payoff structure to condition (11.2) as it applies to non-cooperative players, for whom by definition

$$p + q = 1 \tag{11.3}$$

In such a non-cooperative world, condition (11.2) reduces to

$$p\,(a - b) + (1 - p)\,(c - d) < 0 \tag{11.4}$$

In the case of the Prisoner's Dilemma, this condition is always false, a result shown in section 8.2 to be equivalent to the fact that the non-cooperative strategy choice (D) is a dominant strategy.

In Chicken, on the other hand, the fact that $d > c$ (instead of $c > d$) makes it inevitable that values of p exist $(0 < p < 1)$ which satisfy (11.4). In fact, the paradox in Chicken arises because the line

$$p\,(b - d) + q\,(a - c) = (a - d) \tag{11.5}$$

intersects the line $p + q = 1$ in the range $(0 < p, q < 1)$, as shown in Figure 11.1 This means that the decision of non-cooperative players to play either C or D depends on their estimate of the unconditional probability of their opponent playing C or D.

A non-cooperative Chicken player will thus play C if and only if

$$p < (d - c)\,/\,[(a - b) + (d - c)] \tag{11.6}$$

where p is the probability that the opponent will cooperate (play C). It follows that each person will "cooperate" (i.e. play C) only if they think it rather *unlikely* that their opposite number will operate in the same way. (This is why it is not clear it is apt to call C the "cooperative"

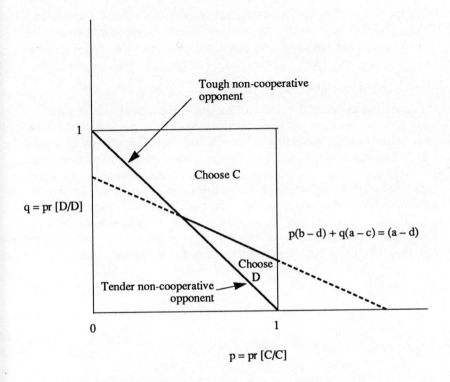

Figure 11.1 Confidence in Chicken

strategy in Chicken.) Now it is true that two non-cooperative Chicken players could contrive to both play C (because both had p-relative beliefs which conformed to (11.6)), but in such a case they would each act believing it to be rather likely that their opposite number was going to act in a way that their opposite number was not in fact going to act. Condition (11.6) says in other words that a person will play tender only if they think their opponent is tough, and both are tender only if each believes wrongly that the other is tough.

We can have cognitive consistency only if there is a (Tough, Tender) couple, wherein Tender believes correctly that Tough's probability of playing C satisfies (11.6) and Tough believes correctly that Tender's probability of playing C does not satisfy (11.6). And in that case there will also be a behavioural equilibrium of a highly inegalitarian kind, in which Tough plays D and exploits Tender, who plays C.

This result conforms with the conclusion of the previous section: that

no process of reasoning in advance can lead a person to choose C or
D, unless identity considerations – or other agent-relative ascriptions –
are invoked which treat the two players as distinct in qualities amounting
to toughness and tenderness, as quantified by (11.6).

The Chicken supergame

The second putative solution to Chicken is the supergame. If there are
conditional, punitive strategies in the long-term game, can they reduce
the attractions of free-riding sufficiently to make a community of mutual
cooperation a rational alternative to a stable system of exploitation?

Assume as in section 8.3 that the two strategies available in the supergame are T and D, where T is the tit-for-tat strategy and D involves
unconditional non-cooperation. The calculations of payoffs for the
Chicken supergame are then identical to those of the Prisoner's Dilemma
supergame. The crucial condition which transforms the payoff structure
so that free-riding becomes an unattractive option is once again:

$$h > (a - b)/(a - c) \tag{11.7}$$

or

$$h > t \tag{11.8}$$

where t is the temptation to defect in the one-shot Chicken game. Condition (11.8) is directly analogous to condition (8.24), under which the
Prisoner's Dilemma was resolved by transforming its associated supergame into an assurance game. With Chicken, the transformation is even
more impressive. If condition (11.8) holds, then the tit-for-tat strategy
(T) dominates unconditional non-cooperation (D), (T, T) is the only equilibrium in the supergame, and this outcome gives both players their top
preference.[10] Under these circumstances, the public good will be produced
from the first week for evermore.

The achievement of this equilibrium of the Chicken supergame is even
smoother than in the case of the assurance game. In the assurance game,
there were two equilibria (mutual cooperation and mutual non-cooperation) and an additional argument had to be given that two players
would manage to reach the better of the two equilibria – the cooperative
one. Sufficiently far-sighted Chicken supergame players don't need to
think twice before choosing their only equilibrium strategy. In effect,
mutual non-cooperation is so unattractive that it is not worth considering.
But the same thing that makes mutual non-cooperation so unattractive
also makes it more likely that condition (11.8) will be true, and so makes

symmetrical mutual cooperation more likely an equilibrium outcome than asymmetrical first week exploitation. If we assume that the payoffs a and b are fixed, as between a Prisoner's Dilemma and its Chicken counter-part, then a variation in c (the payoff from mutual non-cooperation in the elementary game) is equivalent to the distinction between a lesser need (generating an elementary Prisoner's Dilemma) and a greater need (generating an elementary Chicken). The effect, plausibly enough, is that as needs become greater the temptation to defect from their collective provision is reduced: (a – b) will be constant, and (a – c) will increase, leading to a decrease in the temptation index on the right hand side of (11.7). And so it is more likely that a given level of farsightedness will satisfy (11.7) if the game is Chicken than if it is a Prisoner's Dilemma. If disaster looms larger, one need not look so far to see it coming.

Everything to date points to the greater likelihood of achieving mutual cooperation in two-person Chicken, because the seriousness of failing to cooperate so concentrates the players' minds. But this very seriousness introduces a fundamental reservation to this rather optimistic picture. The effect of provision according to need alone is to link the fulfilment of my needs indissolubly with yours. But this means that any punishment I try to inflict on you will rebound on me. If you know that I will hurt so much, are you going to believe that I seriously intend to go for weeks without food, or weeks without washing up or weeks without tending to the baby or weeks without responding to the demands of an elderly relative? And if you don't believe in the threat implicit in my conditional strategy, because you don't believe I will cut off my own nose to spite my face, then you may be inclined to sweat it out, to wait for me to crack week-by-week, on the assumption that the consequences of no-one cracking even for a single week are so bad that it will not occur. Yet if we cannot afford to play the supergame, and we both know it, we are back looking for another way to settle the indeterminacy of the one-shot game.

11.3   Gender Socialization and Strategic Pre-commitment

In the work which has made explicit the connection between Chicken and public goods provision, Michael Taylor and Hugh Ward have consis-tently stressed the role of a particular type of initial inequality in the resolution of the game. Where there is *differential pre-commitment* to the two strategies, and in particular where a first person persuades himself and his opponent that he will hang tough and play D, the second person will be forced to accept defeat by playing C.[11] The first person has success-fully psyched out his victim, who qualifies as "Chicken" in the scenario which gives its title to the game. I propose a variation on this theme as another way round Chicken. The proposal is that *differential socialization by gender resolves the household game of Chicken.*

Let us go back to the washing up. If we are too revolted to eat from filthy plates, then clean plates are a basic need, and ultimately each of us will be prepared to wash up plates for everybody under a needs distribution principle (provided the household is not too large). If the Chicken supergame solution is ruled out, then neither of us will volunteer to share the washing up. As the dirty dishes begin to pile up round the sink, our sense of hygiene is being taxed. Perhaps your threshold for squalor is marginally lower than mine. You can take the sight of seven or eight dirty plates, but seventeen or eighteen make you sick. You can't stand it any longer. You crack first, and do all the washing up. For all you know, and perhaps for all I know, my threshold was one tea-spoon higher than yours, so that if you had held off just a moment longer, I would have been the one to crack. But as things stand, you are marginally more vulnerable than me to the accumulating pressure to do the washing up, and this margin makes all the difference. It seems highly plausible that such a margin is created by that network of differential expectations we call *socialization into gender difference.* For example, it has often been remarked that women are more anxious to maintain a clean and tidy house because they have internalized higher standards of domestic order and because visitors will blame whatever woman is in sight and not whatever man for chaos, dirt and mess. The internal impulse and the external code point in the same direction.

A feature of our proposal is that it does not attach enormous weight to gender socialization. In its abstract realization, the Chicken game is balanced on a knife edge, and very small influences – in fact, infinitesimal ones – will tip the balance. Yet we know that once the balance is tipped, the rational-choice mechanism will ensure the most extreme inequality of outcome in the one-shot game. Perhaps we might think of the rational-choice mechanism as responsible for an *amplification of socialization.* People are led by marginal differences of initial socialization into patterns of behaviour which leave them trapped, with the wish perhaps but no incentive to escape.

This process of amplification also has significance across the generations. No child will know what a close-run thing it was that mother did the washing up. The child will only see that mothers seem to do the washing up. When the child is later poised at the same knife edge as its mother, the message will tip the girl child one way and the boy child another, with the result that the grandchildren will receive the same clear message from their parents that their parents received from the grandparents.

I now offer some qualification and elaboration of these basic ideas.

First, the household game is a Chicken game largely because of the inviolability of the norm of distribution according to need. Although it is no doubt part of socialization into caring ways that this norm be maintained, all kinds of strategies of privatization (or perhaps short commons) which violate this norm remain available to those who suffer by the inegalitarian outcome of Chicken. We shall shortly be reflecting on the aptness of the various models.

Second, the scope of the norm and its associated Chicken game is limited by the extent of the household: indeed, falling under the scope of the norm defines membership of the household. It follows, and is a matter of observation, that when no women are around, men will eventually take on household chores. Here is an account from a man named Adrian of his experience sharing a flat with six other men.[12]

> At first I lived out of tins and dinners for one. Then I thought this is revolting, there can't be much to this cooking business. I made a few mistakes, like mixing peas with scrambled egg – the most revolting colour, and it didn't taste too good either. And I used to save the blood to make gravy. I thought it was having the heat wrong that always made it curdle. I had to learn to cook. We took turns to make a roast at weekends. If you didn't do it properly, you were told in no uncertain terms.

In his course of cookery Adrian started with the Chicken and ended with the beef. (There may be differential socialization in such cases among men, so that the "softer" men will end up doing all the housework, and in this way take up the feminine role.)

Third, even where the pairing process brings together cross-sex partners for the Chicken game, these partners will have attended different "socialization depots" in their families of origin. While it is generally true that "the home training of the two sexes will differ, beginning to orient the girl to taking a domestic supportive role, and the boy to a more widely based competitive one", it does not follow that the standards of domestic routine, or the strength of the impulse to care, are in every particular higher in every woman than in every man.[13] What matters for the household outcome are not the relative mean values of these variables in each gender group, but the particular values of the players self-selected for each game. A woman's standards can be higher than her brother's and lower than her husband's. So a husband can crack before his wife, who would crack before her brother.

Fourth, whether or not socialization of the household pair has taken its accustomed course, the solution of the Chicken game is not always

entirely predictable. What may happen is the replacement of the original
contest by skirmishes of pre-commitment, in which prior socialization
figures more as resource and less as foregone conclusion. Here is a case
where accustomed standards of domestic order are reversed, and yet the
outcome is unpredicted by Chicken:

> I'm not in charge of the house – my husband is – but I am in charge of the
> chores. He fusses at me about getting things done. He's more tidy than I am,
> neat and precise. He expects me to come up to his standards but won't do
> it himself. He nags at me to get up and do things. He sees it as my job.[14]

Or accustomed standards may be in place, and the outcome again be
unpredicted by Chicken:

> "If I do clean, I tend to skip over things, whereas Pat will actually rip things
> apart, get underneath beds. Neither of us likes doing it, we've always shared.
> I think if Pat had spoiled me, given me one inch I would have been in there
> like a shot but she actually made it clear – I just cooked this meal, if you
> don't wash up, Tony, it can sit there for a week till it gets fungus on it. Just
> to get through your life you have to do certain things and they're chores,
> so we share it, which is very different to my background."

Tony's wife Pat never *played* at housework as a child. She was forced to do
it for real, from the age of eight. As an adult, therefore, she readily rebelled
against it, allowing the cleaning threshold to drop to the point at which Tony
began to notice:

> "This is the type of house that when I was a boy, my mother would whisper,
> afterwards, it wasn't very clean, was it? And although that doesn't bother me,
> when the hand-basin starts to get scummed I think well, that's not on, Tony.
> It's nice to be a little bit in control of the entropy in this house."[15]

Fifth, although the game theory of pre-commitment is not fully developed, there are recognizable tactics to deploy.[16] References to these tactics
litter accounts of domestic interaction. Among men, a useful stance is
contrived insensitivity to domestic chaos. Whether it is a consequence of
strategic impression management or a genuine result of ingraining from
early life, the stance will make it appear that what are basic needs for
a partner are lesser needs for oneself. In this case, there will be the appearance of an asymmetrical payoff structure: Prisoner's Dilemma payoffs
will be playing Chicken payoffs, and contriving Prisoner's Dilemma
payoffs is a way of committing oneself to a dominant strategy of non-
cooperation in the short term, knowing that a Chicken-playing partner
will be induced to make a positive response.

Here are some reports of pre-commitment, the first five from men, and the last three from women:

(i) I come in sometimes and the place is a complete mess and I just sit amongst it. Other times I blow my top and get the children to clear everything, everywhere.

(ii) It doesn't bother me whether the house is clean and tidy. Sometimes, though, I get annoyed if it's a mass of Lego and Action Men just where I want to sit down.

(iii) Helen does all the decorating, wall plugging, drilling. It's not that I can't do it, but I make out that I can't.

(iv) I do the shopping. I don't mind, I don't like it, but I do it. With Cathy working up in the city, there's nowhere for her to do any shopping. I do a lot of it when I'm working ... I can do it [ironing], but I don't like it. I do muck a few things up, my wife's blouses and things like that. I used to stick a hot iron on them and that's goodbye to them.

(v) Ideally, everything should be shared but there are certain areas where I don't do as much, to do with keeping things ideally clean. I am prepared to leave things.

(vi) He doesn't do much. I get irritated at him at times. He's unaware that there are things to do. ... He'd leave the paper on the couch but now he picks it up. He does this for a month, forgets, and then I have to remind him.

(vii) He tries to be helpful. He tries. He's a brilliant and successful lawyer. It's incredible how he smiles after he sponges off the table and there are still crumbs all over.

(viii) The housework is my job, my responsibility. My husband does none. I frequently feel I have two jobs, especially at end of term. I work so hard and then come home and have to start again. I begin to resent the demands put on me. I toyed with the idea of working part-time but I knew that I wouldn't be satisfied with that. My husband helping is not an option. There are times when he's sitting watching the telly and I'm out there in the kitchen and a bit frustrated about it all, but I don't do much about it.[17]

Sixth, the Chicken analysis is not designed to account for the overall division of labour in the household. In principle it could be applied separately to each of the component activities of a household, and the result would be that one person would do all the cooking, one person all the earning, one all the child care and so on, without the one person in each case having to be the same person in every case. Men may be differentially socialized to break first in respect of some tasks and responsibilities, while women are socialized to break first in respect of others. If there is a pattern to these differential breakings, it seems to relate back to the distinction between the public and the private, in several of its senses.

If we take as a first approximation the division between the private world of the household and the entire public world outside, and if the household needs come under the broad headings of the external and the internal (the needs provided respectively from the market and from the home), then Chicken played against a backdrop of conventional socialization will allocate all earning to the breadwinning husband and all domestic labour to the house-occupying wife.

At a second approximation, however, there appears to be a scaling among the private household tasks, which propels men, whenever they feel propelled, towards the more public of these tasks, in two senses of public: towards the "show" tasks that are visible from outside the house and towards intermittent tasks of maintenance on goods that are public goods according to the relaxed material taxonomy – those capital items which form the material fabric of the home. In this respect, the findings of a very thorough recent study of the division of household labour are almost too good to be true. Sarah Berk found that 335 US wives reported that their husbands took primary responsibility for particular household tasks in the following proportion of cases: household repairs (38 per cent), taking out garbage/trash (36 per cent), doing yard work (31 per cent), mowing lawn (20 per cent), painting (13 per cent), car maintenance (13 per cent), cleaning floor (11 per cent), washing dishes (8 per cent), washing windows/storm windows (7 per cent), shovelling snow (6 per cent), child care (6 per cent), preparing meals, cooking, baking (6 per cent).[18]

The existence of work reserved for men in the public domain and on the outskirts of the private domain should suggest a woman's counter to the man's insensitivity to domestic chaos: *contrived incompetence in engineering*. Thus Jill, who had married Adrian upon his return from the odyssey in blood and eggs and gravy:

> If I get a screwdriver out, to take off the bathroom cabinet, I say in mock indignation, I shouldn't be doing this, this is a man's job. And the same when Adrian's ironing, he grimaces and says I hope nobody turns up and sees me! We joke about this role business, don't we?[19]

Yet the role business may be quite serious, when men take responsibility for the most masculine of tasks about the house in less than forty per cent of cases.

Seventh, if we take the uncertainty surrounding the partition of the household into Chicken games along with the indeterminacy surrounding the outcome of each constitutent game, it is difficult to predict what the overall distribution of household burdens is going to be. It is certainly possible in theory for a man to end up with the worst of the deal. But there is, I think, this much sting in the tail of the Chicken. Suppose it is not an uncommon experience that "our first meal together she cooked and I washed up, and this is how we carried on" and true that this kind of pattern radiates outwards from the kitchen.[20] Then it may also become true quite rapidly that bankable skills, experience or knowledge in the public domain will accrue to the man, and that the overall bargaining power of the woman will suffer more from the lack of these skills and openings in public than the bargaining power of the man will suffer from his incompetence in private.

A Chicken game resolved in one way at one stage of a relationship may help to create that differential access to a public domain (and hence differential access to the major resources that the society can provide) which, at a later stage of the relationship, implies the exploitation of the woman. Chicken might help to explain the bounding assumptions of the chapter 7 exchange model. By that stage, economic arguments against a rearrangement can be pressed in the male cause, and "women are separated from one another by the stake they acquire in the very organization which divides them."[21]

11.4   The Double Face of Class

The exchange model and the Chicken model of the household extend the application of rational choice from the public to the private domain. What implications do these models have for the theory of social class? In chapter 4, I introduced Elster's synoptic proposal for

a general definition of classes, in terms of endowments and behaviour. The endowments include tangible property, intangible skills and more subtle cultural traits. The behaviour is defined in such economic terms as working vs not working, selling vs buying labour-power, lending vs borrowing capital, renting vs hiring land, giving vs receiving commands in the management of corporate property. *A class is a group of people who by virtue of what they possess are compelled to engage in the same activities if they want to make the best use of their endowments.*[22]

I now argue that one who accepts this analytical Marxist approach to social class is bound to regard the household division of labour as a *bona fide* class phenomenon.

Take the exchange model first. Here there are two behaviours "defined in economic terms": earning behaviour versus housework behaviour.[23] The differential endowment is differential earning-power, which is intangible, like skill (indeed it might be a consequence of differential skill) but is distinctly unsubtle – differential earning-power would be difficult to exclude from any general catalogue of resource endowments of the type Elster has in mind. The exchange model then claims that by virtue of the differential endowment in earning capacity, rational-choice people wanting to optimize the use of their endowments will be compelled to engage more in the "same activity" of earning or more in the "same activity" of housework, depending as their earning endowment is greater or less than their domestic partner's.

The corresponding roles of breadwinner and houseworker are on this account unmistakably social class roles, and there must be at least one person in any Pareto-optimal household who is exclusively occupied with one of these roles (no symmetrical household is Pareto-optimal). Moreover, there is a Class Exploitation Correspondence Principle: the houseworker is always the exploited one. This means that there is not just a social difference but a social division, a clash of interests implied in the performance of distinctive activities.

It follows that wherever the domestic element in the subsistence constraint is recognized to exist (and of course it always *does* exist), reference must be made to two components of a person's class position. First, there is the public face of social class, in the familiar Marxist typology of bourgeois and proletarian, as expanded by Roemer and expounded by Elster and Wright. Second, there is the private face of social class, which depends on the person's relation to the provision of household goods. The private face bears three principal expressions: those of the houseworker, the breadwinner and the domestic equivalent of the petty bourgeois – the self-sufficient single adult person catering for their non-market subsistence requirements in the double privacy of a household that is secluded from the world and unique to themselves. Indeed, the exchange model says that a "class divided" household containing two persons will form because it is preferable for both parties to an autarkic, "petty bourgeois" existence, and this logic is identical to the logic of capitalist class formation in the Roemer models of chapters 4 and 5.

It follows from the addition of the private to the public face of social class that the class status of a proletarian is altered, depending on whether the person is or is not their own houseperson. It is no longer possible to entertain the simplifying assumption almost invariably made by Marx in his discussions of the value of labour-power: that domestic labour does not exist, that the proletarian therefore meets all subsistence needs on the market, and lives in a take-away paradise.[24]

In chapter 7, we emphasized, following Jane Humphries, that the proletarian couple exist in a conspiracy against the world to withdraw their lower-earning member from the labour market.[25] But it is possible to recognize another conspiracy; the higher earning proletarian is passing on some of the exploitation he (say he) inevitably suffers at the hands of the capitalist to his domestic partner. And there is no logical class limit to this process. It can be shown that in a simple three-person world (whose full description lies beyond our current scope) this proletarian can exploit his domestic partner so much as to outweigh his exploitation by the capitalist – thereby becoming a net exploiter overall.[26]

This result implies that it is in general impossible to read off the exploitation status of a proletarian from the public employment data considered by itself. This lends considerable weight to the idea that class position is inseparable from private domestic role, and that the public and the private should be yoked together in the definition of social class.

The exchange model of households is gender-blind; it would predict exactly the same division of roles in a high/low earning lesbian or gay household, for example.[27] On the other hand, it may be that the cause of the differential endowment of earning power was, directly or indirectly, discrimination by that cultural trait whose subtlety has often placed it beyond Jon Elster's ken: social recognition as a member of one sex rather than another. In this case, a person owes a certain fundamental aspect of their class position to gender. It is the uneven distribution of the gender resource which, given unequal treatment by gender in the labour market, stands at the back of the earning differential which causes the class polarization in the private domain. If this process were universal, and exclusively responsible for earning differentials, then the household classes would be gender-classes, and the overall class structure would be a gendered whole.

The application of Elster's definition to the Chicken model is in one sense equally direct and in other senses more ambiguous than the application to the exchange model. There is only one activity in the Chicken model, but at the equilibrium one person is engaged in the activity and one is not, so that the two parties fall under the scope of Elster's polarity between "working" and "not working". Once again, the distributive outcome at the equilibrium exhibits the full paraphernalia of an exploitative class division. Indeed, the free-riding idler looks much more like your friendly local capitalist than the exploiting-but-working breadwinner in the exchange model. One cannot, it seems to me, accept (something like) the case against capitalism made out in part II above, and assert that the Chicken equilibrium involves no class division.[28]

The doubts, and the interest, begin to creep in when the indeterminacy of Chicken is considered. What the Chicken model establishes is essentially the existence of a *system of class roles*; it cannot determine who is going to fill which role. This is the only case in which I can make sense of the Althusserian picture of the social structure, according to which there seems to be a supra-individual mechanism creating a series of empty places into which individuals are subsequently impressed. In Chicken, the empty places are labelled "oppressor" and "victim", and gender ideology acts to interpellate individuals into them.[29]

The problem for Elster is that the indeterminacy of Chicken threatens the connection between endowments and behaviour which he wishes to make essential to the definition of class. There are two counter-examples to consider: (i) the Chicken model backed by gender socialization (the gender-Chicken model), and (ii) the unadulterated Chicken model.

It looks as if the gender-Chicken model can be accommodated within Elster's existing general definition, because gender identity can act once again as the resource whose unequal distribution causes the difference in behaviour and hence welfare at the equilibrium of Chicken. Indeed, the relation between gender and class is more immediate and direct than in the exchange model, where the effect of gender was mediated through the labour market. The social positions at the equilibrium of the gender-Chicken model are unambiguously gender-classes – that is, antagonistic class positions caused by gender difference – and gender identity must for this purpose be considered alongside the more conventionally "economic" endowments in Elster's definitional list, as one of his "more subtle cultural traits".

Although this argument might appear to vindicate Elster's definition, I do not think it eliminates the general problem posed by Chicken for the theory of social class, for the following three reasons, given in order of increasing generality.

First, although the gender-Chicken model can be made consistent with the letter of Elster's general definition, I doubt that the gender differential is operating in the spirit of that definition, which emphasizes the bargaining power actors possess through their holdings of assets. If Chicken is resolved because gender socialization causes a person to crack a millisecond before their partner, and therefore end up with all the work, then it is less that one has used one's endowment, and more that one's endowment has used you.

Second, it is very doubtful that the gender-Chicken model applies to every household, and equally doubtful that Chicken applies only to households (further evidence in support of these claims is adduced in the next chapter for households, and chapters 14 and 16 for ethnic groups and socialist economies). In many applications, there may not exist a plausible unequally-distributed resource, such as gender identity in the case of the gender-Chicken model of the household, to give Elster's general definition the helping hand it needs against the indeterminacy of Chicken.

Third, the deepest problem is in any event the conceptual problem, not the empirical problem. We can arrange for perfect symmetry between actors in respect of resources, identity, past history – whatever you like – and we still have to face the fact that there is a *difference of behaviour* at equilibrium *without difference of endowments*. I have argued that this problem is intrinsically connected to a failure of the rational-choice paradigm. It is just not obvious, going into such a perfectly symmetrical Chicken game, what it would be "to make the best use of... endowments", because best use depends in an irreducible way not on the respective endowments of the players, but the respective uses that the players make of their respective endowments.

If we have already decided that the inequality at a Chicken equilibrium is a class inequality, then this third point establishes a case in which a class inequality is caused by unequal behaviour, not unequal endowments, and it must be false that unequal endowments are necessary to class difference. Elster's definition must therefore be changed in a way which makes it possible to have class division even when all resources are equally distributed. But I have already concluded, also in chapter 4, that behavioural difference is insufficient for class difference. A proposal which embraces the discussion of both chapters is the following *general Marxian definition of class: Class position is about the range of options a person has as a result of the distribution of social access to forces of production. A class division exists between two agents whose welfare differs systematically at an equilibrium of social interaction, as a result of differential possession of forces of production, differential behaviour with respect to the production process or both.*

It will be recalled that another feature of the chapter 4 discussion was its structuralist disposition, expressed in the preference for resource difference over behavioural difference as a criterion of class division. Has our present move back towards behaviouralism undone the incipient structuralism of the earlier conclusion? The answer will depend on how one defines the "structure".

If "structure" is identified with the *distribution of resources*, then the fact that resource difference is no longer deemed necessary for class difference clearly contradicts structuralism (class difference can arise in Chicken between agents who are identically placed in the structure, in the resource-regarding definition of structure).

But I would rather draw a different conclusion from this case, namely that *behaviour can be structural*. The relevant point about Chicken is that a variation in my partner's behaviour is entirely responsible for the variation in what constitutes the optimum use of my resources.[30] This view is fully consistent with another idea of structure – *structure as constraint* – but it does play havoc with received notions of the distinction between structure and action. For it implies that structure and action are not disjoint. The same behaviour can count as both; your action is part of my structure. And this means that there is not just one social structure, but as many social structures as there are individuals in a society:

one structure from the distinctive viewpoint of each individual. What constrains each individual is thus a combination of what every individual possesses and what every *other* individual *does*. The game theoretic concept of equilibrium then corresponds to a certain meshing of everyone's social structures: no actor has any incentive to act differently at equilibrium, which means that there is no tendency to structural alteration.

I conclude on an ambitiously structuralist note, hoping to have shown in the process that no theoretical breakwater can exist, from the analytical Marxist standpoint, between the public domain of capitalist economy and the private domain of household labour.

Notes

1. Insufficiency has been quantified implicitly, because the disutility of working times t_1 and t_2 must be assumed less than the disutility of failing to satisfy the earning and housework constraints k and t in the formulation of inequalities (7.1), (7.2) and all their sequels. I have tried to keep utility functions out of the picture as far as possible.

2. The distinction is closely related to Olson's distinction between a latent and a privileged group in the n-person context. An individual is privileged in Olson's sense with respect to more serious needs, because there is an individual incentive to meet the need. The existence of this incentive does not imply that the individual will act according to the incentive, as we will see. Olson's seminal contribution is discussed in Russell Hardin, *Collective Action* (Baltimore: Johns Hopkins University Press, 1982), ch. 3. Hardin introduces the needs-related concept of the step-good on p. 51.

3. In their study of *Poor Britain* (London: George, Allen and Unwin, 1985), Joanna Mack and Stewart Lansley report the results of a survey to determine whether there was a public consensus on what constituted "necessities". There was a striking unanimity about such items as heating (97 per cent of respondents), freedom from damp (96 per cent) and three meals a day for children (82 per cent). Consumer durables ran interestingly from warm waterproof coat (87 per cent) to two pairs of all weather shoes (78 per cent), refrigerator (77 per cent), toys (71 per cent), carpets (70 per cent), washing machine (67 per cent), child's bicycle (57 per cent), television (51 per cent), telephone (43 per cent), dressing gown (38 per cent) and car (22 per cent) (p. 54). The influence of the British climate is apparent.

4. Michael Taylor and Hugh Ward, "Chickens, Whales and Lumpy Goods: Alternative Models of Public Goods Provision", *Political Studies*, XXX, no. 3 (1982), p. 352.

5. On the mistaken association between free-riding and the Prisoner's Dilemma, Taylor and Ward note: "It is only in Chicken-like structures that the phenomenon of free-riding – in the sense of not contributing while others contribute – can be adequately understood" (Taylor and Ward, "Chickens, Whales and Lumpy Goods", p. 354).

6. It was noticed in the previous section that the needs inequality might happen to be such as to yield an equilibrium at which the less needy person was making a zero contribution. This type of outcome is exceptional in the short commons model. With Chicken, it is inevitable.

7. Chicken players are in chronic violation of the "axiom of symmetry" Elster uses to define strategic rationality and according to which "the agent acts in an environment of other actors, none of whom can be assumed to be less rational or sophisticated than he is himself" (*Explaining Technical Change* (Cambridge: C.U.P., 1983), p. 76.

8. "Conventions are solutions to *coordination problems*. The most clear cut case of a coordination problem ... is the situation facing the players in a *game of pure coordination*. This is a game, having two or more proper coordination equilibria, and in which the players' interests coincide, so that their payoffs at each outcome are equal": Michael Taylor, *The*

Possibility of Cooperation (Cambridge: C.U.P., 1987), p. 156 (original emphases) describing David Lewis, *Convention* (Cambridge, Mass.: Harvard University Press, 1969).

9. I became clear about the oppressor-victim tangle in conversation with Libby Wattis, to whom I am grateful for several insights.

10. The Chicken supergame was first analysed by Hugh Ward in *Behavioural Models of Bargaining*, University of Essex, Ph.D., 1979 and the results summarized in Taylor and Ward, "Chickens, Whales and Lumpy Goods", pp. 366–7.

11. The existence of an incentive to make such a commitment is chosen by Taylor and Ward as the defining characteristic of the N-person generalization of Chicken: see "Chickens, Whales and Lumpy Goods", p. 355, and see also Taylor, *The Possibility of Cooperation*, p. 93. The problem of identifying the generalizations of two-person games such as Prisoner's Dilemma, the assurance game and Chicken in the N-person context is tackled in "Symmetry and Social Division", *Behavioral Science*, 34, no. 3 (1989), p. 167.

12. Mary Ingham, *Men* (London: Century Publishing, 1984), p. 58.

13. Erving Goffman, "The Arrangement between the Sexes", in Mary Jo Deegan and Michael Hill, eds., *Women and Symbolic Interaction* (Boston: Allen and Unwin, 1987), p. 62.

14. "Mrs. Paton", quoted in Susan McRae, *Cross-Class Families* (Oxford: Clarendon Press, 1986), p. 136.

15. Ingham, p. 61.

16. Hugh Ward has shown that in the Chicken supergame for more than two players with a viable cooperative coalition of size at least two, making too tough an impression on opponents can frighten them away from cooperation, to the detriment of all. This important mechanism of mutual restraint is clearly inoperative if the cooperative coalition is of size one, as is the case in two-person Chicken. In this respect, as in others, the Chicken problem may be at its worst in the two-person context, and this may help to explain some of the peculiarities of domestic politics. See Hugh Ward, "The Risks of a Reputation for Toughness", *British Journal of Political Science*, 17 (1987).

17. The reports are from: (i), (ii) unidentified; (iii) "Frank, a former travelling salesman who seemed to have abdicated all responsibility for his home other than as somewhere to eat and sleep"; (iv) Ken "a central heating engineer ... more than competent around the house because his wife works full time and has a physical disability" (all from Ingham, *Men*, pp. 47–59); (v) "Simon (28, unemployed, single)" from Yvette Walczak, *He and She* (London: Routledge, 1988), p. 103; (vi), (vii) unidentified, from Sarah Fenstermaker Berk, *The Gender Factory* (New York: Plenum Press, 1985), p. 206; (viii) "Mrs Mason" from McRae, p. 136.

18. Berk, *The Gender Factory*, Table 3.4, p. 70.

19. Ingham, p. 52.

20. "Ralph (50s, teacher, divorced) who appears to have strong moral principles in a number of areas, such as advocating nuclear disarmament and equality in all spheres": Walczak, pp. 104–5.

21. Goffman, p. 57.

22. Jon Elster, "Three challenges to class", in John Roemer, ed., *Analytical Marxism* (Cambridge: C.U.P., 1986), p. 147. This represents an interesting amendment of the virtually identical definition in *Making Sense of Marx* (Cambridge: C.U.P., 1985) (hereafter *MSM*), pp. 330–31. The earlier, *MSM* definition has "the behaviours include" rather than "the behaviour is defined in such economic terms as" and adds: "These enumerations [of behaviours] are intended as exhaustive." In *Rational Choice* (Oxford: Basil Blackwell, 1986), pp. 17–22, Elster shows himself well aware of the issues raised in this section, but I am not sure he is aware how much they upset his conception of social class.

23. The *MSM* definition would exclude housework by fiat; the later definition, cited in the text, is more easy going, and lets it in (see previous note).

24. Marx departs from his usual assumption in a passage beginning: "The value of labour-power was determined, not only by the labour-time necessary to maintain the individual adult worker, but also by that necessary to maintain his family. Machinery, by throwing every member of that family onto the labour-market, spreads the value of the man's labour-power over his whole family. It thus depreciates it" (*Capital*, I (Harmondsworth: Penguin,

1976), p. 518). The problem is that the final inference is false: a change in the numbers or identities of the wage earners in a given family will not change the amount of labour embodied in the goods required to meet the subsistence constraint either of the whole family or of any of its members considered separately. There will be an influence of the family working pattern on the total amount of labour the family has to perform in the capitalist work-place to meet this constraint only if there are relationships between the real wage rates of different family members and the patterns of labour market participation of different family members.

25. Jane Humphries, "Class struggle and the working-class family" *Cambridge Journal of Economics* 1, no. 3 (1977).

26. In the three-person world a single-sector corn economy of real productivity P is attached to the exchange model of households. The condition for the capitalist profitability of the economy is $P > w_2 > w_1$, where w_1 and w_2 are the woman and man's real wage rates. Depending on the actual household that is formed, it is possible for the woman to be the only exploited person if the parameter values are such that

$$(w_2 - w_1) / (P - w_2) \geq \text{Max} [k/t, w_1]. (1/P)$$

Speaking roughly, this means that the man is more likely to be able to completely offload his exploitation by the capitalist on to his domestic partner, the closer he is to the capitalist (as measured by $(P - w_2)$, related to the rate of capitalist exploitation of the man) and the further he is from his partner (as measured by the wage differential $(w_2 - w_1)$).

27. I have not discovered any studies of this issue, although I note that the Kinsey organization concluded its investigation of the Bay Area lesbian and gay communities in the 1970s with a typology of sexual styles that relies somewhat on the household arrangements of its subjects. Both women and men were categorized as Close-coupled, Open-coupled, Functional, Dysfunctional and Asexual, in which the second and third categories tended to "cruising" and the fourth and fifth to sexual and social isolation. There is unfortunately no data on the internal household arrangements of the couples. See Alan P. Bell and Martin S. Weinberg, *Homosexualities* (New York: Simon and Schuster, 1978).

28. I thus dispute that Philippe Van Parijs' hypothetical predicament is equitable: "If my wife's standards of tidiness at home are much lower than mine, I may end up doing (in my own interest) all the tidying up," before her threshold of tolerance is reached. She will derive some benefit from my activity, but not because of any resource she controls. Hence, no power and no exploitation." See "Exploitation and the libertarian challenge", in Reeve, ed., *Modern Theories of Exploitation* (London: Sage, 1987), p. 114.

29. I emphasize that it is the peculiar character of the Chicken payoff structure which is responsible for this result. It is not a general feature of rational-choice models, nor even of rational-choice models with multiple equilibria, as is shown by the case of the split-role equilibria discussed in chapter 4, which exhibit different behaviours yet equal welfare and so, in my view, identical class positions of all actors at every equilibrium.

30. Which I take of my two available options in Chicken depends entirely on which option my partner takes, whereas in the Prisoner's Dilemma, for example, my choice of (non-cooperative) action does not depend at all on what my partner does.

The Difference Gender Makes

12.1 Gender and Stratification

In this chapter I wish to test the exchange model and the gender-Chicken model, which are respectively a model in pure economics and a model which blends economics with sociology.

One apparently promising area for an empirical test is the evidence accumulated from a series of increasingly sophisticated and comprehensive household time-budget studies (especially from North America). Is there evidence of overload? The answer is a qualified Yes. Women do tend to work (or have historically tended to work) longer hours overall than men, taking account of paid and domestic work.[1]

This body of evidence does not, however, serve the testing purpose very well, because the two models broadly speaking predict the same thing: the thing that broadly speaking happens. It is the major prediction of the exchange model that there will be a woman's overload. The Chicken model does not in itself predict the overall distribution of effort, because it only predicts the outcome separately for each department in the total household game. But if we add to the Chicken model a departmental organization in which women's socialization will trigger their effort first in the more private departments, whereas men's socialization will trigger theirs first in the more public departments, we are likely to end up with an overall distribution of effort similar to that which seems to be observed. If anything the Chicken model outperforms the exchange model, because it accounts for an anomalous part of the evidence: when the household task exists in just two departments (public earning and private housework) and the housework task is relatively light, the man's load tends to exceed the woman's.

A more decisive test will involve cases in which the predictions of the two models diverge significantly. The general circumstance in which this occurs is when the *direction of the correlation between wage and gender assumed hitherto in the exchange model is reversed*. The exchange model predicts that if the woman has a higher wage, and preferential access to the public world, then there will be an utterly painless role reversal. The houseworker will be the househusband. The Chicken model makes no such prediction, because it emphasizes the "stickiness" of the gender roles in each of the departmental contests that together comprise the household game.

The usual correlation between gender and pay will tend to be reversed when male unemployment occurs, especially in the context depressingly familiar in Eighties Britain of mass redundancy rather than individual misfortune. The effect will be a sudden collapse in, and perhaps a virtual elimination of, the man's local earning power. If the couple do not respond to the thoughtful cycling invitation once issued by one of Mrs Thatcher's favourite Ministers, because the couple are less inclined to be part of the capitalist process which flings people hither and thither across the face of the globe than Ministers are inclined to applaud the same process from comfortable positions immune from its effects, then the woman's earning power might become predominant. Leonard and Speakman's summary of the British research into the effects of unemployment does not much confirm the exchange model:

> [The] studies ... which have looked at the effects of redundancy, agree that unemployed husbands certainly do not take over the housework from their wives, enabling the women to try for jobs (except occasionally in households where there are no children). Quite the reverse. Men's unemployment often actually increases their wives' work load, through the need to "shop around" and "make do and mend" on a much reduced budget, and through the need for wives to be present in the home, e.g. to cook a meal at midday, and for women friends not to be around when the husband is at home, thereby restricting women's day-time freedom of movement and association.[2]

A less traumatic case occurs when the background, qualifications or work experience of the woman give her a niche in the world of occupations superior to that of her domestic partner. Thanks to a fine study by Susan McRae, something rather more detailed can be said of the case known to mainstream sociology as the "cross-class family".[3] McRae's study arose in the context of a debate among stratification theorists which in many respects runs parallel to the debate between orthodox Marxism and heterodox feminism. Indeed, the tone and substance of the orthodox defence by some senior stratifiers so reminds one of the tone and substance of the equivalent defence of Marxism as to suggest that the issue is more one of gender than of social class.[4]

As it presented itself, however, the stratification debate centred on the question of whether gender "makes a difference" – a difference, that is, in terms of what concerns stratification theorists.[5] John Goldthorpe offered a hostage to fortune by remarking that "it is always congenial to find one's critics at odds among themselves", for Goldthorpe and David Lockwood have characterized the concerns of stratification theory in two quite different ways, leading them to defend what they respectively take to be orthodox stratification theory in quite different ways against its heterodox opponents.[6]

For Lockwood, the primary aim of stratification theory is to delineate the major collective actors in the social formation; specifically, to determine "the extent to which class or status systems are the predominant modes of social action at the societal level."[7] In order for gender to qualify as such a "predominant mode", it would apparently be necessary for organized groups of women to meet organized groups of men in pitched battle to settle the interests which divide them. Now if we permit Lockwood his neglect of the suffrage movement, on the curious ground that it was too successful (unlike, one presumes, the social democratic movement, which remains a predominant mode of social action because its aspirations are so infrequently fulfilled), then it is true that gender conflict seldom develops into that kind of pitched battle.[8] It is indeed rare for the women on the two sides of a societal level conflict between status groups or classes to join forces across the status or class divide against their menfolk: "outside the pages of *Lysistrata*, the war between the sexes does not eventuate in society-wide 'class struggle.'"[9] One good reason for this is that societal level collective action typically mobilizes networks of households, and a good reason for mobilizing households to sustain widespread collective action is that since existing households have already solved one problem of collective action for their members they are well placed to resolve other problems of the same kind.

Lockwood, in his description of status groups, contends that "some degree of endogamy and commensality is what marks one status group from another." Commensality leads to the existence of separate households and endogamy constitutes part of the principle of cohesion for the set of distinct households whose interrelationship in turn constitutes the status group.[10] Both description and explanation have been developed much further for the class action of peasants and proletarians in the work of Samuel Popkin, Michael Taylor, Craig Calhoun and others. Class collective action, just as much as status group collective action, mobilizes communities of households. And however much supra-communal, sectional or national political organization is required to coordinate and direct the mobilization in order to secure its macropolitical goals, the national movement will fail unless it is grafted on to strong local organiza-

tion, which is at its strongest when the reciprocal practices defining the
existence of the basic unit – the household – extend outwards in a network
of reciprocal ties between households.[11] This is the lesson superpowers
seem to have to learn again and again; it is unfortunate that so many
die in the teaching.

On this account, societal level collective action is likely to occur when
household organization is strong. And although it is not inevitably the
case, we have given many reasons why strong household organization
will be unequal household organization, from the gender point of view.
It follows, and is an observation conspicuously absent from the literature
on either status groups or social classes, that when mobilization of either
status groups or social classes takes place, it is very likely to be *a mobilization of gendered groups*. I do not mean by this that when the ostensible
goals of the collective action are phrased in terms of class or status interests
and values, the actual interests and values are undisclosed, or psychoana-
lytically repressed, gender interests and values. (I do not discount the
possibility. The correlation between gender and organization makes it
entirely plausible, but it would be hard to prove, and my present case
does not depend on it.)

I mean that the collective mobilization in pursuit of the (let us grant)
lucid class or status interests and values tends to reproduce the forms
of social division of the units mobilized. Since the predominant units
of local organization are divided along gender lines, so is the resultant
collective action. In particular, the split tends to be reproduced, within
the forms of political organization and action, between the public and
the private domains – and with this, the public and private roles of men
and women.

To understand this is not in itself to argue conclusively that the forms
of mobilization for collective action are determined in part by gender
or – a stronger claim – are mobilizations of gender difference. Lockwood
in effect claims that if, say, work and family life and union office and
picket-line duty and police activity were organized in a way exhibiting
no correlation with or reference to gender difference, then the collective
action would go on more or less exactly as before. I have no idea whether
this is true, but I am pretty certain that neither Lockwood nor anyone
else can know if it is true either, because collective actions in which women
and men have been engaged equally in the workshop, in the front line
and upon the home front are about as rare as the events narrated in
the *Lysistrata*.

Lockwood does courteously allow that gender relations may "partake
of some kind of ubiquitous, class- or status-oriented interaction at the
situational, as opposed to the societal, level" where they enjoy "so to
speak, ... 'subterranean' importance".[12] An uncharitable reader might

take the meaning of this passage to be that feminist concerns are perfectly acceptable, so long as they are kept in their place: a place that is lower ("subterranean") and on a smaller scale ("situational" not "societal"), a place, in fact, that is intimate and private, more like home and less for publication. In these restricted spaces we find genuine status interactions, but they are "more commonly" "dyadic", "involving a particular man and a particular woman, and not groups of men and women".[13] It seems that a million dyadic social interactions will never add up to a single phenomenon of macroscopic social significance. As he soars thus, far above the landscape of ordinary social life, can David Lockwood spot John Goldthorpe stumbling about in the undergrowth beneath? For while Lockwood says that gender difference does not make a difference to stratification theory because although it does makes a difference microscopically to "the documentation of ... inequality of opportunities and outcomes", it does not make a difference macroscopically to collective action, and only macroscopic collective action makes a real difference to stratification theory, John Goldthorpe says, *au contraire*, that the "primary concern" of stratification theory is "with certain social relationships in which individuals and groups are daily involved and which are believed to exert a pervasive influence on their lives" and that gender does not make a difference to stratification theory because – despite what Lockwood concedes microscopically – gender does not exert the most pervasive influence on our microscopic daily lives.[14] It requires, on the face of it, considerable sociological imagination to reach the last conclusion, but Goldthorpe shows us how it may be done.

The argument goes as follows. If one restricts the reach of stratification theory to the extra-familial public domain, then (an elegant twist) precisely *because* of the inequality within the family emphasized by feminism, the life-chances of all family members are most heavily conditioned by the position within the public domain of that member with the strongest link to the public domain. Since it is a matter of fact, emphasized with much regret by feminists, but regrettable because it is a fact, that men generally tend to have the strongest link to the public domain, it follows that it is for the time being legitimate to allocate the class position of the whole household, including women members of the household, according to the public class position of the major male wage-earner. It is, one might say, because gender makes a difference that gender makes no difference.[15]

I believe this would be a defensible procedure for stratification theory, defined as Goldthorpe prefers, if all the following provisos were true. Firstly, the procedure would have to be applied consistently, so that the class position of everyone in the household would be determined by the woman's occupation, if the woman had a superior occupation. (Strictly speaking, a "cross-class family" could never exist under Goldthorpe's procedure.) Secondly, the hierarchy of occupations would have not to be drawn up to favour (i.e. place higher) the kind of jobs men tend to have, just because men tend to have those kinds of job. Gender must make no difference to the classification, in other words, since otherwise what appears to be a gender-neutral class distinction is in fact a class non-neutral gender distinction. And thirdly, it would have to be justified to construe a person's overall life chances as determined almost exclusively by life chances in the public domain and hardly at all by life chances in the private domain.

I think the first proviso can be and generally has been met.[16] It is very difficult to know whether the second proviso has been met, because meeting it would require in effect that the stratification theorist was able to judge the status component of the occupational classification without regard to the typical genders of the occupants of the occupations. It is not just that the stratification theorist must guard against the kind of bias that would place doctors higher than nurses in the scale, if it were the case that society at large gave higher income and status to nurses than doctors.[17] Stratification theorists must be supremely confident (as for example Lockwood is) that the status and income which they correctly observe society giving preferentially to doctors over nurses is not given because doctors have historically tended to be men and nurses women; in this particular case for reasons which at least *prima facie* seem to betray the gendered character of claims to knowledge as well as social practices.[18]

The third proviso is I think rarely fulfilled. It seems as arbitrary and one-sided for stratification theorists to restrict their scope of attention to life chances in the public domain as it was said to be for analytical Marxists to restrict their admissible economic endowments and behaviours to the same domain. Sylvia Walby is surely correct that "the lack of incorporation into class analysis of the structured positions associated with this domestic division of labour ... is the major flaw of the conventional approach".[19]

Once the private domain is open for business, we can appeal to Susan McRae to see if gender makes a difference. For if one's life chances in the matter of balancing the public working life with the private domestic life are not the same for a woman whose life chances in the public domain place her in the position of the average working man, then it *is* gender that has made the difference. And this is, I believe, the general conclusion of McRae's fascinating study.

12.2   Cross-Class Families

The term "cross-class family" is a considerable misnomer. It should apply
to any family of which it is true that at least two members fall into different
classes (on some given scale of social class). In particular, it should apply
to cases in which the husband's occupation places him in a higher class
than his wife and to cases in which the wife's occupation places her in
a higher class than her husband. It is an indication of the bias to be
found even in the technical literature of sociology that the term is applied
only in the second set of circumstances and never in the first. But I shall
resist the temptation to use alternative descriptions, and relapse under
this modest protest back into the standard usage.[20]

Cross-class couples in which the wife's occupation is unambiguously
superior to her husband's are thin on the ground, and McRae took considerable pains to locate a sample of just thirty such couples.[21] Partly
because the class scales used by McRae depended on status and conditions
elements as well as pay elements, and partly because of the correlation
between women's gender and low pay which persists throughout the class
scale, it was not true of every couple in the sample that the wife's pay
was higher than her husband's, despite the considerable disparity between
the wife's and husband's class positions. In fact, "half of the wives earn
higher incomes than their husbands, half do not."[22] From collateral evidence in the book it is possible to construct a list of eleven couples in
which the wife's earning power is unambiguously higher than her husband's.[23] The exchange model can therefore be tested more loosely in
the sample of thirty couples and more strictly in the sub-sample of eleven.[24]
But this problem is perhaps not as serious as it might appear, for the
simple reason that the exchange model performs almost equally poorly
in both sample and sub-sample.

Recall that the exchange model makes a straightforward prediction:
the lower-earning husband will always take on a preponderance of the
domestic work. What is actually the case? In the 1980s, only one couple
out of eleven showed anything that might plausibly be regarded as a
reversal of the normal roles (and there are no other candidates in the
remainder of the full sample, either).

Mrs Stone is an architect and Mr Stone is described as a downwardly
mobile graduate who has had a succession of manual jobs before training
to be a carpenter. Mr Stone is unique in the sample and rare in the
world in staying at home to look after two pre-school children. He states:
"My wife refuses to be dependent upon anyone. It was clear when we
married that, if I wanted children, I'd have to be prepared to stay at
home and care for them. And I was – I am."[25]

Apart from the Stones, there are only two couples in the sub-sample of eleven (and only six in the sample of thirty) in which *husbands take some share in the overall responsibility for domestic work*. Of these two cases, the Roberts are a young couple in their twenties without children and the Abbots a couple, likewise child-free, in their early fifties. Mrs Roberts is a librarian and Mr Roberts a motor mechanic. Although it is said that Mr Roberts might emulate Mr Stone in a future child-care role, domestic work is at the moment equally divided in the Roberts' household, despite the fact that Mr Roberts is currently unemployed. Mrs Roberts says:

> We do [the housework] at weekends really. Not much gets done during the week except Tom usually tidies up. We tend to see it as putting in a certain amount of work rather than who does what. Sort of trading jobs. Like: I'll spend the morning doing this, if you spend the morning doing that. I think so long as you're both putting the same amount of effort in, one of you isn't sitting there with their feet up while the other works, it's okay. It works out in the end.[26]

If Mrs Roberts is defining an abstract egalitarian norm ("certain amount of work rather than who does what"), the Abbots' domestic life exemplifies a rather different response: a partial reversal of the usual correlation between gender and the type of domestic work exclusively performed by the respective partners. Largely as a result of the pressure of Mrs Abbot's work as a Head Teacher, Mr Abbot has come to shop, cater, cook and iron, whereas Mrs Abbot launders, hoovers and cleans. But she still takes on this considerable amount of domestic work in addition to her homework from school of up to two hours per evening, while earning twice as much as her husband, who is a foreman at a saw-mill.[27]

These three couples are all those in the sub-sample of eleven who conform to the most "advanced" stereotype in the study. This stereotype requires sharing of responsibility for housework, linked with "an agreed family ideology of equality which allows for family income from both spouses, permits occupational primacy for either spouse, and dispenses with competition between spouses."[28] In such families, according to McRae, a unifying egalitarian norm governs the disposition of family members in both the public and the private spheres.

There is, however, an important distinction insufficiently clarified by McRae about where and how the shared egalitarian values make their impact. On the one hand there is the possibility of a *substantive egalitarian norm*, of the kind outlined in its domestic branch by Mrs Roberts, which imposes equal participation on the two partners in both paid and domestic work. (This is, of course, the norm whose operation would give rise to the "symmetrical family" that Wilmott and Young believed was becoming the predominant type.) On the other hand, we may have something closer to what McRae defines as a "family ideology of equality" which strictly speaking is more like a norm of *gender neutrality*, than of gender equality.

It is true that under McRae's definition there is prior equality, in the sense that no presumption exists that the man's job is going to be the more important job just because it is the man who has the job. But such equality of esteem, if I can put it like that, is quite compatible with – and may indeed facilitate – one person's job being or becoming more important as a result of all the contingencies of life apart from the gender organization of the household. In these circumstances the norm of neutrality invites an unequal not an equal outcome. There is economic pressure to divide involvements unequally between the public and private spheres, and, if the exchange model is apt, there will be an unequal distribution of effort overall.[29]

Thus Mrs Roberts, for example, is probably doing much more housework under a substantive norm of equal participation than she would do if the norm of neutrality were in force and she cashed in on her superior occupational position in the self-interested way the exchange model demands. Although McRae is surely correct to characterize both the Roberts and the Abbots families as being unusually ready to acknowledge to all and sundry that it is the wife who has the superior occupational position, it is not so clear that the Roberts and the Abbots have carried through the implication of this acknowledgement in the domestic environment – namely, that the husband make a larger contribution than the wife at home. It is this latter acknowledgement – which is, I suspect, the most difficult for a man to make – that uniquely distinguishes Mr and Mrs Stone.[30]

The attitudes in this area of the four remaining ideologically advanced couples are not easy to discern, largely because the attitudes themselves have not yet faced the test. In these cases, the wife has potentially higher earnings and general occupational position but employment at the moment is roughly balanced between husband and wife. In these circumstances, both the norm of neutrality (joined with the exchange model) and the norm of substantive domestic equality would predict the roughly equal outcome in the home that seems to take place. It is difficult to know, in particular, whether the husband, if pushed, would tolerate a reversal of his normal role.

One way in which this problem may be side-stepped is illustrated by the Merediths, who seem to represent the type of the deliberately child-free, public-oriented, career-minded couple in their mid-thirties, and whose method of domestic allocation is instructive for us all:

The housework isn't organized. We both tend to leave it until we can't stand

it any more. We do so much else we don't have time to fuss about it. I always
feel I ought to do more. My wife tends to do more cooking than I do.

We do it as and when we can. It's shared out and it tends to be a blitz. We
get fits of cleaning and luckily usually at the same time, although he tends
to do more cleaning than I do. I don't feel it's *my* responsibility to keep the
house clean, or to get food on the table.[31]

One sees the Merediths as two exceptionally gifted players who would
always win a household game of Chicken played against anyone other
than their spouse; yet in meeting their match they have turned what others
would regard as a domestic disaster – the "generally low level of household
cleanliness" observed by McRae – into a joint personal triumph. For,
in the battle between expectations and performance which surely lies at
the root of much marital discord, two people may come closer together
either by increasing performance or by decreasing expectations, and in
terms of keeping the peace it is always wise to attribute a norm-exceeding
performance to a partner which one never claims for oneself.

This lesson is brought home as we move beyond the "advanced" couples
in McRae's example. What characterizes the remaining couples is a much
more rigid normative distinction between the public and the private
domains, accompanied often by normative disagreements of a rather fundamental kind: systematic mismatching of partner's perceived performance with expectations of partner's performance in the minds of one or
both partners, and resultant zones either of tense silence and deliberate
unconcern, or of flaring interpersonal conflict – in short, a bit of a mess.[32]

The distinguishing feature of all the non-advanced couples is that,
regardless of several different forms of agreement or disagreement about
the fact and meaning of the superior public position of the wife, there
is explicit or tacit acceptance of the wife's sole responsibility for the private
domain.

It is at once clear that Chicken is liable to come into its own under
such a regime, because the normative disjunction – the heightened sense
of boundary – between the public and the private domains establishes
the separate compartments in which Chicken may be played.

Indeed, Chicken may have a more fundamental role in this application
because something of the Chicken psychology may be implicated in the
normative process which creates the compartments. I have in mind the
question of what it is to take responsibility for something, or – not quite
the same thing – what it is to be given, or left with, the responsibility
for something. To have responsibility for something is to expect to be
the person, and/or to be expected to be the person, who will do something
about something. In circumstances in which the relevant somethings have
a public service dimension (i.e. there are public benefits or positive externa-

lities of the something I do in order to discharge the responsibility for something I have), then having responsibility – or, in a significant variation of expression, "bearing" or "carrying" responsibility just like the burden a responsibility is – is very close to giving a generalized pre-commitment to the choice of unilateral cooperation in a Chicken game. Notice in support of this contention that when something goes wrong, and people are shifting about for someone else to blame, the response of the apparently responsible person is rarely that whoever was responsible was not in fact required to act before anyone else, to forestall the calamity: the response is more commonly that the apparently responsible person was not the really responsible person.

Now it is true that the implications of being the responsible person vary from context to context. In public life, the burden of responsibility largely consists in the burden of deciding who else is going to shoulder the burden of action.[33] Thus, when a responsible government minister proclaims that the government is absolutely going to do something about something, what the minister usually means is that the minister is absolutely going to get somebody else to do something about something. This practice has been extended to a fine art by the Conservatives in Britain, whose impression of continuous activity consists so much in the activity of getting people other than ministers to do things, that the ministry seems absolved of the responsibility for any of the consequences of what these other people might be doing, or, more frequently – in a range which covers industrial and infrastructural investment, scientific research, health provision and community care – what these other people might not be doing. In this way the claims of the public and the private are being rearranged in the public mind.

In private life, this separation between management and execution is not so often *de rigueur*, although something like it does exist. McRae isolates three different responses in the cross-class households in which the wife retains overall responsibility for domestic order, namely "husband refusal to participate in domestic work; husband willingness to help out with such chores; wife unwilling to allow husband participation".[34] In the case of the helping husband (nine out of twenty-three in the "non-advanced" section of the sample), there is a distinction between management and execution, so that when the managing wife breaks first, breaking may take the form of ministerial direction to her husband. Here there is, so to speak, Chicken at the level of management, but a more egalitarian distribution of the actual work than the Chicken model would predict. (It remains rare beyond the classes who are able to employ others for domestic service that the boss gives up all work herself.)[35]

In the majority of cases, management and execution remain united in one person, and the burden of responsibility implies the sole responsibi-

lity for action by the wife. In four cases, this responsibility is accepted
with reluctance; it is given, or left, rather than taken. "Husband refusal"
is a description of the husband's attempt to pre-commit himself to non-
cooperation, and the outcome of success for this strategy is the highly
inegalitarian equilibrium predicted by Chicken. Thus Mrs Harvey, a 36-
year-old head librarian earning £5,000 a year more than her 41-year-old
engineer husband, remarks:

> I tend to get snappy. Especially on weekends if I've got all the housework
> to do and I've had a really hard week. Then I get resentful. I think: why
> is he down at the pub and here I am pushing the hoover around. I hardly
> ever see him at weekends ... so sometimes I get resentful. I feel very much
> that I have to do two jobs.[36]

If helping husbands conform to Chicken at the level of management,
and refusing husbands at the level of execution too, the final response
of the "wife-in-control" involves a quite different way to play the game.
Here there is such an aggressive pre-commitment of the wife to the cooperative strategy in both management and execution, and of therefore
becoming the victim from the distributive point of view, that the husband
hardly gets a chance not to be the exploiter. One such wife comments:

> It is too much, I get very tired. But a lot of it is my own fault. I'll be honest,
> I keep the work to myself. I've spoiled them [husband and children]. I find
> it quicker and easier, without a lot of arguments, to do it myself. And that's
> how it's gone. And it's wrong – I pay. But then, no one could do it the way
> I wanted it done. I'm very houseproud. It's my own fault. And if they do
> do it, I have to sort of bite my tongue and leave it for a day or two and
> then do it all over again.[37]

Is Mrs Jason being irrational? Her testimony makes clear how difficult
it may be to break the mould, and how much effort she would have
to make to retrain her family. But she is also aware of having to retrain
herself. As things stand, she seems to know as well as anyone that what
she is doing is damaging to her own interests in several respects. But
even if it is irrational, her response to the Chicken situation is readily
understandable, and explicable partly as an attempt to maintain something of her conventional self-image as a wife and mother, intensified
if anything by the somewhat counter-conventional nature of her public
employment. The superwoman response, in other words, might be an
attempt to compensate for the partial role reversal in the public world
with an exaggerated role performance at home. It is certainly very striking
that one third of the wives in the full sample display this response: it

would be very interesting to know whether this is a higher proportion than in non cross-class families.[38]

Summing up, we can say that the predictions of the exchange model are borne out in one case (perhaps 1½ cases) out of eleven (also equal to one or 1½ out of thirty), the Chicken model in three cases out of eleven (four out of thirty), and the superwoman role model in five out of eleven (ten out of thirty).[39]

Overall, this is good evidence that gender makes a difference, although it is still not quite clear how the difference is made. One would like to know what accounts for the diversity observed in the response of these couples to a similar set of social and economic pressures. McRae investigates whether the occupational-class histories of the husband and wife before and after the marriage affect the norms governing or the outcomes pertaining to paid and domestic work, but the results of the investigation are inconclusive. Neither is there any obvious correlation between the various responses to the wife's occupational role and the various internal household norms: superwomen and refusing husbands appear among couples who are able to agree that the wife's occupation is superior and among the riven couples containing disgruntled wives or truculent husbands.[40] It does not look from this evidence as if the Chicken response of the refusing husband is, for example, a special consequence of resentment directed at his wife.[41]

In so far as the theory developed in this book can illuminate the causes of differential response to the cross-class reality, it will suggest, first, that gender socialization rather than class background is the place to look. It may matter more what the tolerance thresholds were to various shortcomings of the domestic scene, and what degrees of toughness and tenderness were inculcated in the daughters and the sons, than it matters whether the homes of origin were working-class or middle-class. Second, it may be difficult to make systematic causal prediction because it *should* be difficult to do so. If the Chicken game captures anything of the reality of household interaction – as it seems to do, both formally and colloquially – then it will amplify, and therefore make causally significant, what would otherwise be statistical "noise" created by small differences in social backgrounds and/or the gender related personalities of the husband and wife.

Three points nevertheless emerge clearly:

(i) The economic pressures described schematically in the exchange model very rarely translate themselves directly into changed behaviour, if the traditional gender roles are exerting a pressure in the opposite direction. This is a way of saying that the gender pressure is real, or in other words, that gender ideology is relatively autonomous.

(ii) Women's gender ideology tends to prevent women taking full economic advantage of men, when women are in an economic position to
do so. Quite often, it seems to result in the self-sacrificial (or is it self-
preservative?) attempt to combine the role of career woman with the
role of faultless wife and mother.

(iii) Men's gender ideology can sometimes tolerate domestic equality,
but in the current state of play it rarely embraces domestic role reversal,
even where the economic pressures foretell reversal. We may be moving
some way towards an ideology of gender equality; we have a long way
to go towards an ideology of gender neutrality.

12.3   Domestic Economy and Gender Ideology

These findings might incline us to go overboard on the sociological side:
to discount economics and attribute most of the explanation of social
change to changing perceptions of the gender roles. I think this would
be a mistake. It is fairly obvious that Engels was over-optimistic, to put
it mildly, when he delivered himself of the opinion that "since large-scale
industry has transferred the woman from the house to the labour market
and the factory and makes her, often enough, the breadwinner of the
family, the last remnants of male domination in the proletarian home
have lost all foundation."[42] But Engels' line of thought may not be entirely
beside the point.

Recall that in the large majority of households, the economic argument
(of husband's higher earning-power and generally greater clout in the
public domain) still supports the ideological argument (that woman's
place is in the home).[43] Now it may be that in many cases the social
change is being led by ideology. In particular, it may be the woman's
rejection of the ideological argument, under the direct or indirect influence
of feminism, that has led to a change in the economic reality. Women
have determined not to stay at home and have fought for a place in
the public domain which would conform to their new expectation of themselves.[44] In McRae's study, there is however more evidence of the converse
type of dissonance between reality and ideology, which finds the new
economic reality pitted against the old ideological form, and the ideology
putting up a stubborn resistance. Yet this finding in favour of ideology
does not rule out the possibility that ideology – in this case gender ideology
– is explained by economics.

Recall the type of functional explanation discussed in part I. In this
type of explanation, something is explicable only when it enjoys relative
autonomy from that which explains it. It follows that the proof of relative
autonomy is part of the explanation of that which enjoys the autonomy.

It is because gender ideology has the independent efficacy that McRae's study documents so well that it could act as a superstructure to economic arrangements conforming to the ideology. The suspicion is, in other words, that conceptions of gender difference (of the appropriate places of women and men) have been aligned in the past with economic reality precisely because that alignment shores up the economic reality. If gender ideology was not so efficacious, it would not have the required shoring effect.

Yet we have also learnt from Elster's grim warnings that such functional intuitions must be backed by plausible elaborations. In the present case we might claim, for example, that the economic realities of marriage are changing as a result of factors external to gender ideology, and that McRae's study casts light on the confusions of a transitional period during which a new ideology is in the making, catching up with the new economic reality. We can even glimpse the general mechanism at work: the reduction of cognitive dissonance, such that the gender perception is brought closer to the economic reality.[45] The problem, of course, is that dissonance can be reduced either by changing the perception of gender (the "progressive" move) or by acting to change the economic reality (the "conservative" move). Among McRae's subjects, those characterized by normative agreement on either "equality" or "female superiority" (ten couples in all) exhibit the progressive tendency (either in the public and private domains, or the public domain alone), whereas four couples exhibit conservative agreement on "male domination" and the rest are often slightly or seriously confused.

Now whether the progressives, the conservatives or the merely confused will win the day depends, on this account of explanation, upon whether or not there is the kind of unstoppable economic pressure, independent of gender ideology, which is bound to throw up more and more cross-class (or perhaps egalitarian) couples. (This parallels the historical materialist problem of whether an unstoppable tendency exists for the forces of production to develop.) Will the likes of the Stones become more typical, because the likes of the Ungers will find it impossible to keep the lid forever on the new economic reality?

It is very difficult to tell, but one fact may be sufficiently momentous to lend the development of relations between the sexes a general bias towards the Stones. The point is something like this: it is because Mrs Stone is in a position to choose whether or not she will have children that she is in a position first to become an architect without sacrificing her private, sexual life and subsequently to require of any husband that he look after the children, should he want children. As Mary O'Brien has emphasized, a materialist account of twentieth-century relations between the sexes must start from the introduction of artificial birth control.[46] This is a change in reproductive technique or – straining the language of analogy to some kind of limit – an enhancement in the level of development of the forces of reproduction which makes gender equality an historical possibility for the first time. It is, *pace* Engels and Marx, not the fact that women enter the labour market that is crucial, but the terms under which they enter. And these terms may be set in the sphere of reproduction and not production.

The role of the rational-choice exchange model in such an explanation is not, *pace* Elster, the role of microfoundation for household interaction, in which role its performance is lamentable. Much more impressive is the diagnosis it yields of the historical pressures on the household division of labour, as recounted in 7.2. And, if there is a tendency towards equality arising from developments in reproduction, the rational-choice model would take on an explanatory role sandwiched between a history of reproductive technique which ultimately causes a wage differential by gender and a gender ideology which ratifies the differential.[47]

But even supposing this general account is true, there is a long road between the potentiality and the actuality of gender equality, for the change in reproductive technique must first enable a change in the balance of economic power, and the changing balance of economic power must then find a reflection in a changed ideology of gender relations and changed feelings of gender identity. Before all these novelties have become domesticated it is hard being superwoman when you cannot find a superman.

Notes

1. Three studies based on North American data collected between 1965 and 1971 showed employed wives' overloads ranging from 1.3 to 2.4 hours per day. Two of the studies showed an overload for the husbands of not employed wives, the overload being 0.8 hours in one case and 1.8 in the other. The last study makes particularly clear how insensitive a husband's hours were to increasing demands on the household represented by a wife's paid work and children. The fact that this insensitivity exists tends to favour the Chicken model. According to Chicken, when a new task is added to the household, the whole work load will go to one person. And in the case of two paid jobs, there will be no "rebalancing" of contributions of the kind that the exchange model predicts. See Martin Meissner, et al., "No Exit for Wives"; *Canadian Review of Sociology and Anthropology*, 12, no. 4 (1975), Figures 2 and 4, and the other studies summarized in Pleck, *Working Wives/Working Husbands* (Beverly Hills: Sage, 1985), Table 2.1, p. 30. Pleck's surveys in the late 1970s confirmed this pattern, with unemployed wives' underload being 2.0 hours and the overload of employed wives rising from 1.2 hours with no children to 2.7 for older children and 3.5 hours for younger children. Husbands' participation in the household seemed to have increased, and to be more responsive to overall household demands. This suggests perhaps that Chicken is giving way to the exchange model, except that greater flexibility regarding male housework leads to symmetrical households, which the exchange model rules out on account of their sub-optimality! See Pleck, pp. 47–51. On methodological issues, see especially Sarah Fenstermaker Berk and Anthony Shik, "Contributions to Household

Labor: Comparing Wives' and Husbands' Reports", in Sarah Fenstermaker Berk, *Women and Household Labor* (Beverly Hills: Sage, 1980).

2. Diane Leonard and Mary Anne Speakman, "Women in the Family: Companions or Caretakers?" in Veronica Beechey and Elizabeth Whitelegg, eds., *Women in Britain Today* (Milton Keynes: Open University Press, 1986), pp. 33–4. The most recent study, mentioned as showing role reversal, is Lydia D. Morris, "Renegotiation of the Domestic Division of Labour in the Context of Male Redundancy", in Howard Newby et al., eds., *Restructuring Capital* (London: Macmillan, 1985). But Morris comments that "although the couple [with the most amenable man in a sample of 40 redundant Welsh steelworkers] perceived the situation as a 'role-swap' [albeit one expected to be temporary] the woman in effect continued to run the house, with minimal assistance from her husband" (p. 231). See also Christopher C. Harris and Lydia D. Morris, "Households, Labour Markets and the Position of Women", in Crompton and Mann, eds., *Gender and Stratification* (Cambridge: Polity Press, 1986).

3. Susan McRae, *Cross-Class Families* (Oxford: Clarendon Press, 1986).

4. The criticism was directed at the work of analytical Marxists in "Rational Choice Marxism", pp. 211–12, and acknowledged by Jerry Cohen in *History, Labour and Freedom* (Oxford: O.U.P., 1989), p. 141, n. 12. For a comparable sexual solecism in non-Marxist class theory, see Frank Parkin, *Marxism and Class Theory* (London: Tavistock, 1979), p. 34; and for an exemplary response to the intellectual politics of gender, see Erving Goffman, "The Arrangement between the Sexes" in Mary Jo Deegan and Michael Hill, eds., *Women and Symbolic Interaction* (Boston: Allen and Unwin, 1987), p. 51.

5. See Anthony Heath and Nicky Britten, "Women's Jobs Do Make a Difference, Reply to Goldthorpe", *Sociology*, 18, no. 4 (1984).

6. J. Goldthorpe, "Women and Class Analysis: A Reply to the Replies", *Sociology*, 18, no. 4 (1984), p. 491. The only party to the debate who remarks the glaring discrepancy between Goldthorpe and Lockwood seems to be Nicky Hart, "Gender and the Rise and Fall of Class Politics", *New Left Review*, 175 (1989), p. 20.

7. D. Lockwood, "Class, Status and Gender", in *Gender and Stratification*, pp. 11–12.

8. "In this century, the struggle for enfranchisement of women has provided the only significant example of mass mobilization of this kind, and once this single status interest was achieved the movement collapsed": Lockwood, p. 16.

9. Lockwood, p. 15.

10. Lockwood, p. 15.

11. On the importance of pre-existing community to revolutionary mobilization, see the contributions to Part 1 of Michael Taylor, ed., *Rationality and Revolution* (Cambridge: C.U.P., 1988). In "Radicalism of tradition and the question of class struggle", Craig Calhoun remarks of early working-class radicals that "the chances of their movement's being socially revolutionary were in direct proportion to its relative social strength, not its ideological clarity. Such strength was to be found most of all in local communities, least in national organization" (p. 139). For similar argument in relation to the late mediaeval peasantry, see T.H. Aston and C.H.E. Philpin, eds., *The Brenner Debate* (Cambridge: C.U.P., 1985), pp. 40–43, 279, and for general theoretical reflection, Mike Taylor, "Structure, Culture and Action in the Explanation of Social Change", *Politics and Society*, 17, no. 2 (1989).

12. Lockwood, p. 15.

13. Lockwood, p. 20. I think this statement would be true only if one ignored the status dynamics of most forms of popular entertainment, which frequently enact gender difference in a collective setting. As for the significance of popular music, it is worth recalling John Lennon's alleged remark about the relative popularity of Jesus and the Beatles.

14. John Goldthorpe, "Women and Class Analysis: In Defence of the Conventional View", *Sociology*, 17, no. 4 (1983) p. 467.

15. "When Giddens, in a passage that is frequently cited with disapproval in 'feminist' critiques, argues that even those women who are found in paid employment 'are largely peripheral to the class system', it is important to note – though critics have often failed to do so – that this argument derives directly from a premiss which feminists would presumably not wish to deny: namely that within western capitalist societies 'women still have to await their liberation from the family' ... The family is the unit of stratification primarily because only certain family members, predominantly males, have as a result of their labour

market participation, what might be termed a directly determined position within the class structure ... it follows ... that a whole range of life-chances which vary with class have their impact on women to a large extent via their husband's position" (Goldthorpe, p. 468).

16. Robert Erikson's DOMINANCE index is, for example, one that classifies a household by its predominant rather than its male wage earner, and will automatically assign the "cross-class" household to the class position of the woman wage earner. See "Men, Women and Families", *Sociology*, 18, no. 4 (1984).

17. Somewhat ironically, the major bias of this kind has apparently lain in the upgrading of some categories of women's routine non-manual work (especially shop assistance, sales and clerical work), on the grounds that it is non-manual, and therefore above manual work, when in fact the pay and conditions are often worse than male manual work, for reasons that may or may not be connected with the fact that it is typically women's work. See Angela Dale, Nigel Gilbert and Sara Arber, "Integrating Women into Class Theory" *Sociology*, 19, no. 3 (1985).

18. The debate on the cross-class marriage "serve[s] simply to bring into prominence the fact that it is the position of an occupation within some hierarchy of authority that is decisive for its status and not the sex of the person who happens to be in it. This does not mean that the sex (or any other ascriptive property) of the incumbents of these positions has no status implications whatsoever, but merely that these effects are marginal in the sense that they do not disturb the familiar rank order of broad occupational strata" (Lockwood, p. 21). Michael Mann reads the same evidence very differently: "Women in the economy now form a number of quasi-class fractions. In each main case they occupy a 'buffer zone' between the men of their own class grouping and the men of the next class grouping down the hierarchy ... this looks uncommonly like a systematic role for women in what many regard as the core of stratification – the economy and the occupational division of labour. Gender is no longer segregated from the rest of stratification: its segregating mechanisms have become a central mechanism of economic stratification" ("A Crisis in Stratification Theory?", in *Gender and Stratification*, p. 45). Mann accepts that the conventional view is appropriate for pre-modern societies, before the patriarchal pyramid became stepped like a conifer tree.

19. Sylvia Walby, "Gender, Class and Stratification", in Crompton and Mann, eds, *Gender and Stratification*, p. 27. Walby proposes that "while housewives and husbands are classes, women and men are status groups ... many women also have a class position deriving from their participation in waged labour. Thus many women have a dual class position" (p. 36). This is in the spirit of the conclusion of the previous chapter, reading "breadwinner" for "husband" and "houseworker" for "housewife", allowing that whenever a houseworker has a dual class position, so does "her" breadwinner.

20. What is standardly called a cross-class family should perhaps be called a converse cross-class family, or a cross-cross-class family, and if its members were angry a cross cross-cross-class family.

21. There is a considerable overlap in many of the elements of pay and conditions between lower non-manual jobs in the official census class 3NM and the higher manual jobs in class 3M. The overlap is compounded in its application to this case because many of the "women's jobs" in 3NM have worse pay and conditions than "men's jobs" in the same class (see note 17 above). It follows that in order to find a group of women whose occupations are unambiguously superior to their husbands, it is necessary in general to go some way into the semi-professional census class 2 for the women's jobs, and exclude also the highest stratum of men's manual jobs. On this basis, it is probable that fewer than five per cent of dual-earning couples in Britain are cross-class, since less than ten per cent of manual working husbands in dual-earner couples have wives with occupations in Census Classes 1 and 2, according to the 1971 Census. See McRae, pp. 12–13 and p. 17, no. 5. Data relevant to the same calculation for the 1981 Census is in Ivan Reid, *Social Class Differences in Britain*, 3rd Edition (Glasgow: Fontana, 1989), Table 7.7, p. 235.

22. McRae, p. 95. An additional reason for the relatively small number of wives with higher earning power is that only twenty-one of the thirty couples entered the strict sampling frame described in note 21, and McRae relaxed the definition of cross-class slightly to include e.g. senior clerical staff. See McRae, pp. 26–8.

23. The couples are: Abbot, Allan, Barnes, Creighton, Harvey, Henley, James, Parker, Paton, Roberts, Stone. Not all the earning differentials are quantified, but those that are range from a factor of two (Abbot, Creighton) to an amount of *c.* £1,500 a year (James, Parker).

24. It is also possible to construct a list of couples in which the wife's earnings are lower than or roughly equal to the husband's: Ashcroft (=), Fielding (p), Henderson, Jason (c), Leonard (c), Light (=), Mason, Meredith (p), Smith (p), Thompson (c) and Unger (c), where (=) denotes equal incomes, (p) potentially higher earning wives at an early career stage and (c) a "conservative" group of couples with normative agreement on male superiority (i.e. agreement on the primacy of the man's lower status job). Earnings information is not given for the remaining eight couples in the sample of thirty.

25. McRae, p. 82.

26. McRae, p. 130.

27. McRae, p. 133.

28. McRae, p. 97. I have given the Abbots honorary membership of McRae's advanced category containing the Fielding, Meredith, Roberts, Smith and Stone families because the Abbots share housework, and are not classified elsewhere by McRae.

29. A good description of gender neutrality is given by McRae on p. 120: "In a world without specific beliefs about the correct, or expected, behaviour of husbands and wives, which family member makes the most money or is most committed to a career would not matter; decisions about work involvement, promotions, or moving home and family would be made without reference to the sex of the person facing such decisions." But this does *not* imply that these decisions will be made according to a norm of strict equality. The false inference is apparent in the following passage: "We see that egalitarian divisions of domestic labour do occur among cross-class families ... behind such sharing of roles is a relinquishment of traditional gender roles ... [some of these couples] enjoy freedom from traditional ideas about which family member should be the primary earner; enjoy freedom from ideas of male supremacy financially and occupationally ... Their normative solidarity ... prevents an unequal division of domestic labour. In these families performance of household work is frequently a matter arranged with a high degree of flexibility between husband and wife: whoever is best able or most willing undertakes the work needing to be done" (pp. 133–4). The point is that if normative solidarity consists in a norm of gender neutrality, then far from preventing inequality, the norm will invite an unequal division of labour. Flexibility will not lead to a haphazard distribution of work, but to a systematic tendency for the non-primary earner to be the primary houseworker, in violation of a norm of substantive equality.

30. It is not even absolutely clear that this attitude distinguishes the Stones: "Mr. Stone, at home with responsibility for two small children, does a major portion of the domestic work during the day while his wife is at work. When Mrs. Stone returns home, and at weekends, she participates more fully in the household chores." (McRae, p. 142).

31. McRae, p. 129. The Merediths do have a residual division of labour of the expected kind, "Mrs. Meredith taking sole responsibility for only laundry and ironing, Mr. Meredith for gardening and households repairs." And it is also noteworthy that the Merediths are pursuing balanced dual careers largely because Mrs. Meredith has accepted her husband's preference not to have children (p. 98).

32. Membership of the advanced group of seven couples with a unified egalitarian norm and fewer marital difficulties is very highly correlated with the possession of more generalized leftish political opinions: a welcome case of Labour working.

33. The separation of conception from execution, of which the separation of management from execution is one fundamental aspect, was made the point of entry for a famous critique of the capitalist labour process by Harry Braverman, *Labor and Monopoly Capital* (New York: Monthly Review Press, 1974).

34. McRae, p. 134.

35. But compare what Mr. Paton, as the non-working household boss, says in the passage quoted in note 14 to chapter 11.

36. McRae, p. 136, and see Mrs. Mason's remarks quoted in note 17 to chapter 11.

37. McRae, p. 137.

38. The role compensation theory is advanced tentatively by McRae, pp. 139–41. There is nothing to distinguish the ten wives who share the compensatory response "with respect to age, stage in the family life-cycle, ages and number of children ... patterns of participation in paid labour", earnings relative to husband or the normative category of the marriage with respect to the wife's paid work. "It seems an inadequate answer at best to say, simply, it is their socialization. And yet, in many respects, that is all we are left with."

39. The various models, and the couples exemplifying them, are: Exchange model, Stone plus half a point to Abbot; Chicken model, Creighton, Harvey, Paton and Henderson; Superwoman model, Allan, Barnes, Henley, James, Parker; Ashcroft, Jason, Leonard, Light, Unger (the first group in each list refers to the sub-sample of eleven couples).

40. Refusing husbands do not appear in the couples who agree that the husband's job is primary, presumably because the wife's agreement to take responsibility for housework is part and parcel of the deal.

41. The Parkers are an interesting case of wife-in-control ("I do it, I'm in charge: he's quite hopeless, really") in which Mr Parker's pre-commitment takes the form of absence from the home in order to work all hours of day and night on a smallholding to supplement his earnings from farm labouring and bring his income within £1,500 of the income of his teaching wife. Since the economic return from the smallholding is a marginal one, it seems that status-saving, irrational conduct is not confined to the women in the sample (pp. 139, 111).

42. Engels, *The Origin of the Family, Private Property and the State*, discussed by Veronica Beechey, *Unequal Work* (London: Verso, 1987), p. 42. Beechey cites *Capital* I to similar effect.

43. The fact that large numbers of households contain "same-class" families does not invalidate this point, given the tendency for men's jobs to be paid higher than women's jobs at the same level of Census classification.

44. A case in point is Mrs Stone, reported as "the only woman in the study with explicitly stated feminist views" (McRae, p. 82).

45. See Elster, *Making Sense of Marx* (Cambridge: C.U.P., 1985), pp. 466 ff. for a discussion of cognitive dissonance as a "hot" theory of attitude formation. Elster offers this theory as an *alternative* to functional explanation of widely-held beliefs. I am entertaining the possibility that cognitive dissonance might be *part of* a functional explanation of widely-held beliefs.

46. See Mary O'Brien, *The Politics of Reproduction* (London: Routledge and Kegan Paul, 1981). O'Brien's central emphasis, which is in many respects "orthodox" and technologically determinist in the way it applies historical materialism to gender relations, sits rather oddly with the Hegelian approach to Marx's methodology to be found in the same work. For an extended discussion of O'Brien, see especially Jeff Hearn, *Gender of Oppression* (Brighton: Wheatsheaf Books, 1987), pp. 77–89.

47. Such a role would of course be analogous to the role taken by Brenner's ideal types of feudal and capitalist production relations in the Marxist theory of history.

PART VI

Ethnic Division

13

Ethnic and Racial Affiliation

13.1 Two Questions for Social Theory

Reliable placement of a person in an ethnic or racial group seems to require at least:

(i) The existence of a system of ethnic or racial classification in the mind(s) of the person(s) doing the placing.

(ii) The existence in the same mind(s) of systematic ways of recognizing a particular individual as appropriately assigned to a particular ethnic or racial category. This will typically involve the collection of clues from the social background, life experience, physical appearance or fundamental beliefs of a particular individual, which act as signifiers for whatever is signified by placement in a given category.

Recognition as a member of some ethnic or racial group commonly has two kinds of significance. It has implications for a person's sense of self, and for a person's social fate, through processes of discrimination.[1]

It is then possible to distinguish two main questions for social theory in the field of ethnic and racial relations: what are the patterns of affiliation to a group, or within a set of groups, once the groups have been formed? and what are the causes of the formation of a group or set of groups?

A major contribution to the answers to these two questions has been given in Michael Banton's *Racial and Ethnic Competition*.[2] Banton is important to the current study because the name he gives his grand theory is the Rational Choice Theory of Racial and Ethnic Relations.[3] Although it will require a certain forensic endeavour to establish the point, I believe that Banton is advancing two rather different rational-choice theories, concerned respectively with the question of ethnic group affiliation and the question of ethnic group formation. The elucidation of these two theories is the main purpose of this and the following chapter.

13.2   Racial and Ethnic Identification

Boundaries and their crossings

Banton begins with the theoretical idea, or rather the metaphor, of an ethnic or racial boundary, and uses it to introduce a typology:

> Racial and ethnic groups can be differentiated along two dimensions reflecting the hardness of their boundaries and the relative privileges of membership. A hard boundary is one that is difficult to cross; usually it will be a question of someone's wanting to cross the boundary in order to become a member, but groups that are hard to join are often hard to leave. The significance of race is that it can be used to draw a very hard boundary and it is usually difficult for a person of inappropriate characteristics either to join or leave a racial category. The greater the privileges of membership, the more incentive there will be for people to seek to join.[4]

The result of permutating hardness and softness of the boundary with high and low privileges of membership is the fourfold typology reproduced in Figure 13.1.

Now any typology will simplify social reality – that is the point of introducing a typology – but it is arguable that in this case Banton's simplification has been a little too rigorous. It will certainly be necessary to adopt the additional distinction, suggested in Banton's text but omitted from his table, between the difficulty of leaving and the difficulty of entering any particular ethnic or racial group. Distinct sources of difficulty in leaving a group include the difficulty of giving up any identification one has made with the group, and the difficulties arising from the reactions of those remaining in the group and of those outside the group to the news that one is abandoning the group. Distinct sources of difficulty in entering a group include the difficulty of taking on a new identification with a group, which is never a simple act of will and is at best an indirect consequence of other acts of will (of what David West calls *formative commitments*); and the difficulties arising from the reactions of members of the group or of those outside it to the fact that one is joining it.[5] The result of splitting the hardness dimension into two is the more elaborate typology of Figure 13.2.

The taxonomy of Figure 13.2 is intended to apply to every ethnic or racial group, although I note that position in the taxonomy may depend on which category of member, or particularly of non-member, the taxo-

		Privilege	
		– low	+ high
Boundary	+ hard	1 incapsulating	3 excluding
	– soft	2 numerical	4 incorporating

Source: Banton, *Racial and Ethnic Competition*, Fig 5, p. 125.

Figure 13.1 Banton's Typology of Ethnic and Racial Groups

nomist has in mind. Thus if it is true that it is hard for non-members to become Amish because "to be born to Old Order Amish parents is virtually the only way in which a person can become a member of that group", it is presumably also true that one almost inevitably becomes Amish if one has just been born to Old Order Amish parents.[6] And if, as I imagine is the case, it is quite difficult to cease to be Amish because of the self-contained nature of Amish life, then the Amish example is spread between the easy to enter/hard to leave, and hard to enter/hard to leave boxes in Figure 13.2 depending whether the person to whom the classification applies has been born to Old Order Amish parents.

An example of easy to enter/easy to leave and hard to enter/easy to leave might have been supplied by a study of the Maltese in London in the 1950s and 1960s: "because some individuals convicted for organiz- ing vice rackets were believed to be Maltese and had attracted persistent and extensive press publicity, many Maltese in London did not like to

| | Difficulty for non-members to enter group | |
	hard	easy
Difficulty for members to leave group	hard	h/h	e/h
	easy	h/e	e/e

Figure 13.2 Banton Enlarged:
Groups Defined by Two Dimensions of Boundary Hardness

identify themselves or to congregate with other Maltese."[7] In the absence of any social contacts among the members of the group, it would be easy to fade out from membership, even if one had previously gone to enormous lengths to become eligible for Maltese status, rather than simply being born to Maltese parents.

Further illustration of the taxonomy is provided by consideration of saints, graduates and pedestrians. The sainthood must be among the hardest of groups to join, partly because no-one is recognized for membership until some time after death, but also because I suppose it is a sure way to disqualify oneself from membership to act as if one believed one was a member while one was alive. (I am not sure whether it is easy to act in a manner which will qualify as saintly if one is a saint, or whether saintliness implies a victory in a difficult struggle over one's unsaintliness.) In any case, once the identity of a saint is acquired, it is rather difficult, though not quite impossible, to exchange for another.[8] The pantheon of saints is hard to enter and hard to leave.

Being a graduate is like being a saint in that an honours student is rarely dishonoured. A late revelation of plagiarism does not establish that a graduate has ceased to be, in the way that a divorce ends a marriage, but rather that graduation was never consummated. Being a graduate is unlike being a saint in the greater ease of doing, and especially the greater certainty of knowing, what has to be done in order to become a graduate. Graduatehood is (comparatively) easy to enter and hard to leave.

In contrast to saints and graduates, pedestrians form a fellowship easy to join (by walking beside a road) and easy to leave (by stepping inside a building). Neither pedestrians nor onlookers are liable to object much to a person assuming and discarding pedestrian status. It might, indeed, be thought an abuse of language to say that "being a pedestrian" confers membership of a social group in addition to describing a set of walking actions. I think the description does qualify as status-laden, because being a pedestrian seems to confer special rights of way and responsibilities to respect the rights of way of others. So the e/e entry in Figure 13.2 does describe a distinctive kind of social group.

These examples are intended to confirm that it is not only ethnic and racial groups whose types are distinguished by the characteristics used in Banton's typology. It follows that no criterion has yet been established in virtue of which a group counts as an ethnic or racial group rather than a religious, educational, perambulatory or some other kind of social group. This issue is raised again in section 14.3.

Privilege and assimilation

Banton's first dimension of types of ethnic group (which we have just expanded to two dimensions) essentially covers the *ability* of people to migrate between ethnic identities. His second dimension covers the *desirability* of their doing so. "Privilege" creates incentives either to leave or to join various groups. According to a long-run rational-choice theory of ethnic and racial identity, individuals will in the long run respond to these incentives by seeking to migrate between identities.[9] Given a structure of incentives to act (described in terms of privilege) and penalties of acting (described in terms of constraints or barriers), the theory generates a straightforward pair of predictions:

(i) People will only and always want to leave relatively low privilege groups, and they will tend to do so when the group is easy to leave.

(ii) People will only and always want to join relatively high privilege groups, and they will tend to do so when the group is easy to enter.

The effect of adding such a motivational scheme to the boundary taxonomy of ethnic and racial groups is to make some of the boundary crossings envisaged in the taxonomy redundant. Since no-one will want to leave a group perceived internally as a high status group, it is scarcely relevant how difficult the outbound crossing of its boundary would be. (Indeed, it is very unlikely that anyone will *know* how difficult it would be: how long would it have taken the US to impose emigration controls, if all its athletes, authors, ballet stars and rock musicians had started defecting to the East?)

Conversely, since no-one will want to enter a group perceived externally as a low status group, the hardness quotient of the incoming boundary of such a group will never be tested, and perhaps never known.[10] The two boundaries made salient by the rational-choice assumption are the incoming boundary of a group defined externally as a high status group and the outgoing boundary of a group defined internally as a low status group.

What happens next depends on the relation of each ethnic or racial group to the environment created by the existence of other ethnic or racial groups. Suppose, then, that there are just two groups, group A and group B. Suppose next that every member of each group makes the same evaluation of the respective groups, and that this evaluation is comparative and ranked. Every member of group A either thinks group A is "better" than group B or that group B is "better" than group A. These thoughts constitute group A's perception of the privilege relation between group A and group B. The thought is shared by everyone in group A, and sharing this thought may help to define membership of group A. Obviously, members of group B may have different thoughts of their own, although they too all have to believe either that group B is "better" than group A or that group A is "better" than group B. Assume next that the boundary between the groups is indeed a line and not a crevasse: the only alternatives are to leave group A by joining group B and vice versa.

Given all these assumptions, only four kinds of relationship are possible between the two groups.

(i) *Incapsulating relationship*   Group A members believe group B is better than group A, so they want to leave group A, but they are unable to do so, because group A is difficult to leave (it has a high outgoing boundary).

(ii) *Excluding relationship*   Group A members believe group B is better than group A, so they want to leave group A, and are able to leave because group A is easy to leave (it has a low outgoing boundary). However, the intending migrants cannot migrate because group B is hard to enter (it has a high incoming boundary).

The distinction between incapsulation and exclusion can, of course, be a fine one. In the circumstances envisaged here, when the only alternative to staying in group A is to join group B, anything that makes it more difficult to join group B (i.e. makes group B more exclusive) *ipso facto* makes it more difficult to leave group A, and so makes group A more incapsulative. Nevertheless, whenever the alternatives are more numerous, so that the relation between leaving group A and entering group B is no longer a logical one, the distinction between incapsulation and exclusion becomes apparent. In particular, separate actions can now be directed towards preventing or discouraging people from leaving group A and preventing or discouraging people from joining group B. Although it is not logically necessary, it is likely that these distinct actions will find distinct actors acting them. It will be the remaining members of group A who will tend to exert the pressure against insiders leaving group A (i.e. against betrayal of the group, even where, or especially where, the group shares a belief in its own low status), whereas it is likely to be members of group B who exert the pressure to keep outsiders out of group B (to keep the group "pure").

Banton gives two rather different illustrations of the intimate relationship between exclusion and incapsulation. In the North American New World, and especially the southern United States, a particularly vicious and prolonged exclusion by people defining themselves as white of people they defined as black led to the development of a countervailing black identity that was to some degree incapsulatory. Exclusion led to incapsulation.[11] A contrasting case is that of America's Polish Jews. In the narrow circumstances of their Polish environment, the Jewish identity did not have to be defended very explicitly, because any Jew who attempted to break out would immediately confront the wall built by the Poles around the ghetto. But in the comparatively wide-open environment of New York City, the Polish Jewish community had to expend much greater effort to discourage its less orthodox members from leaving the community. In this case, the lack of exclusion apparently led to incapsulation.[12]

(iii) *Incorporating relationship*   Group A members believe group B is better than group A, so they want to leave group A. They are able to leave group A because its outgoing boundary is low and are able to enter group B because group B's incoming boundary is also low. Ethnic migration occurs. Erstwhile members of group A are assimilated into group B. Observe that groups involved in either incapsulating or excluding relationships will always preserve their existing memberships. It is only when one group is incorporating another that movement of members takes place.

The wide-awake reader will have noticed that the three group relationships just described bear the same names as three of the categories in Banton's four-fold taxonomy of groups. This is no coincidence: Banton misdescribes his taxonomy as a taxonomy of ethnic and racial groups, whereas it is really a taxonomy of ethnic and racial group *relations*. In order for a group to be incapsulating, rather than incapsulative, there have to be people trying to leave who are being prevented from leaving, and this will only occur if there is another group (or in general another destination or alternative) in comparison with which current membership of the group is perceived to carry low prestige.

It follows that Banton's taxonomy is not only a taxonomy, in the sense of a merely analytical classificatory device; the categories of the supposed taxonomy embody the theoretical predictions of a type of rational-choice theory of ethnic affiliation. This theory is envisaged in many places in Banton's account and is absolutely in the spirit of his general approach but is never quite isolated for what it is.

The fourth category in the taxonomy is in poorer shape. Banton calls the fourth type of group "numerical", and the fact that it does not enjoy a present participle in its title gives the game away: something is awry. On the one hand, this group might be the kind of group A whose membership is being incorporated into group B. As Henri Tajfel has described the process, the kind of assimilation "which would present no particular problems [of psychological adjustment] to the assimilating individuals is when there are no constraints to social mobility imposed by either of the two groups involved. But whenever this happens (as has been the case, for example, for some immigrant ethnic groups in the United States), the minority ceases to exist as such, sooner or later."[13] Using the appropriate participle to describe such a minority would presumably make it a non-existing group, whose numerical strength is rapidly approaching zero. In any event, this type of "numerical" group is the partner group, unnoticed by the original taxonomy, in an "incorporating" relationship with an "incorporating" group. On the other hand, the "numerical" group might be the unnoticed partner group of an "excluding" relationship with an "excluding" group. On these construals of what Banton intends by the term "numerical group", the group always has a low opinion of itself and a low exit perimeter, and so it either disappears, if it faces an incorporating group with a low entry threshhold, or is subject to the permanent frustration of exclusion from the group with a high entry threshhold.

But I think Banton intends something else as well as, or instead of, the preceding two interpretations of the term "numerical group". In a third interpretation, it is rather that the "numerical" group does not exist as a group because it only exists in numbers. In particular, there is a collection of individuals who are alike in being exposed to the low opinion of a "majority" group which excludes them. The excluded set of individuals is a kind of pre-group, subject to an invidious process of which its members have not fully taken stock: "persons allocated to [the 'numerical'] box 2 do not constitute a group and are better referred to as a minority."[14] Perhaps members of the minority are aware of being excluded in various social contexts but are not yet aware of the extent to which they are suffering exclusion because of the hostile opinion that the excluding group has conceived against them.[15]

There are several ways in which such a "numerical" set of individuals could react either individually or collectively to a growing awareness of their common situation. Which reaction – or combination of reactions – occurs will determine how, or whether, the pre-group is moulded into a fully fledged ethnic entity by the action of external forces.

If Tajfel is right to assume "both on the basis of common experience and of an endless stream of psychological studies, that it is a fairly general human characteristic to try to achieve or preserve one's self-respect and the respect of others; that it is important for most of us to have and keep as much of a positive self-image as we can manage to scrape together; and that having to live with a contemptuous view of oneself, coming from inside or from other people, constitutes a serious psychological problem", then all members of a "numerical" "minority" group will wish to avoid, evade, mitigate or challenge the systematically low evaluation to which they are subject.[16]

Assimilation (or attempted assimilation) of an individual from such a minority group into the majority group counts as a way of evading the aversive stereotype applying to the individual in a manner consistent with accepting the stereotype as it might apply to those the individual is leaving behind. It is a strategy with characteristic pitfalls and problems of psychological adjustment.[17] A less individualistic reaction is piecemeal or wholesale removal from the aversive situation, such as probably lies behind the higher Catholic than Protestant emigration rate from Northern Ireland or the collective flight of religious sects from persecution. Or the minority group might turn in upon itself at the same geographical location and begin to elaborate alternative institutions which could ground a sense of self insulated from the surrounding hostility: "when [the minority] group happens to have its own strongly integrated norms, traditions, values and functions, a 'negative' self-image elicited in comparison with other groups need not by any means become the central focus of an individual's identity. This is why one can remain happy and contented inside a ghetto, as long as this ghetto has not become socially disintegrated."[18]

If the minority is strong and/or confident enough, it may come out of the ghetto fighting, more like a fledgling nation, and compete for material rewards without feeling the need to sacrifice its sense of self. This attitude, sometimes called "'accommodation' or 'social competition' consist[s in] the minority's attempts to retain their own identity and separateness while at the same time becoming more like the majority in their opportunities of achieving goals and marks of respect which are generally valued by the society at large."[19]

With this reaction, we have in a sense come full circle, at least from the psychological point of view. We began by imagining a "numerical" group subject to an invidious stereotype, but progressively liberating itself from the stereotypical self-image. This revaluation movement breaks the social consensus which previously cast the minority group in an unfavourable light, and leads to a new situation which exemplifies the fourth and last type of general relationship among ethnic and racial groups.

Counter-valuation and coexistence

Contemplate the English and the French. The French may consider it a privilege to be French, and quite fail to understand how anyone could want to be English, while the English for their part consider it a privilege to be English, being unable to comprehend who on earth would want to be French – the fact that the French apparently want to be like the French offering conclusive evidence to the English of French lack of discernment, and final proof of their inferior social condition.

I will call two groups like this *coexisting groups*. Under coexistence, group A must believe that group A is better than group B, and group B must return the compliment, by thinking that group B is better than group A. Graham McFarlane found, for example, in his study of four rather different Northern Irish rural communities, not all marked by sectarian violence, that

Protestants willingly contrasted their industriousness, cleanliness, loyalty to the crown, democratic ethics and freedom of religious expression with Catholic laziness, scruffiness, treachery, clannishness, high reproductive drives and priest domination. Catholics, for their part, spoke of Protestant bigotry, narrow-mindedness, illogical clannishness, discrimination, individualism, and moneycentredness contrasting this with their own toleration, openness, community spirit and interest in "culture" and the finer things in life.[20]

Banton has said likewise of the relations between Travellers and their environing society:

> Gaje [non-Gypsy] hostility and condescension, and the mutual incomprehension of the two groups, have helped the Gypsies remain distinct, but even more important have been Gypsy beliefs about pollution. Surveying the refuse left on a recently occupied roadside site, non-Gypsies not surprisingly conclude that Gypsies are dirty. But Gypsies want to keep their distance from gaje because they believe them to be dangerously unclean.[21]

The idea of coexistence is intended to denote both tension and stability. There is tension, because the mutual perceptions of the two groups are incompatible, and competition is liable to erupt about whose evaluation of the relationship between the two groups is the most apt. But there is also stability, because no-one will wish to desert their own group to join the other. It does not matter what are the properties of the boundaries of either of the two groups in either direction, because all boundaries have fallen into disuse. Ethnic and racial identification has established preferences which preserve the distribution of ethnic and racial identity without subsequent social or political action: the system is self-sustaining, so long as socialization remains intact.

The omission of this possibility of coexistence from Banton's formal catalogue is a serious one, both taxonomically and practically. Taxonomically, coexisting groups complete the quartet of relationships which might obtain between a pair of groups, under the descriptive and theoretical assumptions introduced above. An essentially complete set of combinations of perception of privilege with hardness of boundary is given in Figure 13.3, which thus offers a synthesis of Figure 13.1 with Figure 13.2.[22]

The reason this fourth case is so significant is that under certain assumptions about human perception and motivation which might be variously interpreted as pessimistic or realistic, it turns out that coexistence, though in many respects undesirable, may nevertheless be about the best arrangement for ethnic and racial relations we can reasonably expect to get.

I deny that it is necessary to psychic health to have a fully formed sense of ethnic or racial identity – indeed, the catastrophic history of twentieth-century ethnic conflict suggests that the stronger the identity, the less healthy it is – but I also think it unwise to assume that the perceptions and attachments which make for ethnic identification will ever cease to operate. We are stuck, therefore, with the choice between four logical possibilities: incorporation, incapsulation, exclusion and coexistence.

Privilege relation	Group A boundary configuration	Group B boundary configuration	Group A type	Group B type
Ideological consensus (– +)	(*/h)	(*/*)	incapsulating	-
	(*/e)	(h/*)	excluded ('numerical'?)	excluding
	(*/e)	(e/*)	incorporated ('numerical'?)	incorporating
Ideological dissensus (– –)	(e/e)	(e/e)	incorporated/ incorporating (circulating)	incorporated/ incorporating (circulating)
	(*/h)	(*/h)	incapsulating	incapsulating
	(h/*)	(h/*)	excluding	excluding
(+ +)	(*/*)	(*/*)	coexisting	coexisting

In the 'Privilege' column, (– +) means that group A has a low opinion of itself in relation to group B, and group B has a high opinion of itself in relation to group A and similarly for the other entries in the column.

In 'Boundary Configuration' columns 'h' and 'e' refer to hardness and easiness of entering the group (first place in bracket) and leaving the group (second place in bracket). The '*' symbol means that the corresponding boundary crossing is irrelevant to the type of the group: '*' stands for 'h or e'.

Figure 13.3 Banton Retrieved: Four Types of Intergroup Relations

If it were either possible or desirable to establish one of the erstwhile local identities as the model for the whole world (in the way that I have heard it said of the sociologist Talcott Parsons that his cultural value of "universalism" covers all that is particular to the United States), then there might be eventual incorporation of the whole human population into a single global identity. But this would be an identity to end all identities, since the dialectic of incorporation works to eliminate the social evidence for the differential perceptions that motivate incorporation. So it is not clear that a universal identity would satisfy whatever needs or perceptions are now satisfied by the existence of more partial attachments, and we have conceded that such needs or perceptions are likely to recur. Indeed, the more remote and larger-scale the body into which incorporation is taking place, the more scope and prospect there seems to be for the reemergence of local foci for identities of an ethnic kind.[23]

On the other hand, if the long-term solutions involved incapsulation and/or exclusion rather than incorporation, then local attachments would be retained, but the outcome would not be very satisfactory, since both solutions imply the existence of potentially large numbers of people with a low sense of self-esteem, vainly banging on the door either to leave one group, or to join another. Among the four group interrelationships appearing at this level of abstraction, *coexistence is the only arrangement consistent with the psychological well-being of all members of a society split between ethnic or racial groups*. So if one accepts that ethnic or racial difference is likely to persist, perhaps because the human or social conditions which promote the creation of ethnic or racial difference are unlikely to disappear, coexistence looks like the best of a bad job. But because coexistence is tense, it is fraught, since the possibility always remains that the incipient hatred the in-group feels against the out-group can be mobilized, in a whole-hearted attempt to inflict for real the ethnic damage which may well be lurking in ethnic imagination.

If it is utopian to believe that ethnic difference will ever be eradicated, it must be an urgent task of realism to discover what the conditions are which turn ethnic difference into ethnic bloody conflict, and then try at all costs to avoid them.

Notes

1. P. Weinreich, "Psychodynamics of Personal and Social Identity", in A. Jacobson-Widding, ed., *Identity* (Stockholm: Almqvist and Wiksell International, 1983), p. 162.

2. Michael Banton, *Racial and Ethnic Competition* (Cambridge: C.U.P., 1983) (hereafter *REC*).

3. The impact of Banton's theory on contemporary sociology is discussed in Michael Lyon, "Banton's contribution to racial studies in Britain: an overview", in *Ethnic and Racial Studies* 8, no. 4, October 1985 Special Issue "Rational Choice Revisited: A Critique of Michael Banton's *Racial and Ethnic Competition*". Note especially the ill-tempered exchanges between Banton and John Rex in the same volume.

4. *REC*, p. 125.

5. David West, *Authenticity and Empowerment* (Hemel Hempstead: Harvester Wheatsheaf, 1990).

6. *REC*, p. 129.

7. *REC*, p. 129, referring to Geoff Dench, *Maltese in London* (London: Routledge and Kegan Paul, 1975).

8. I am indebted to personal correspondence with Mary Cooper for the case of the Guglielamites, twelfth-century followers of St Guglielma who were deemed heretical after declaring that the saint was the incarnation of the Holy Spirit. Before the proclamation of sainthood became systematized by the fourteenth century, "it seems to have been the case that if [a candidate for sainthood] had a cult they were a saint unless they did something

to upset the ecclesiastical hierarchy in which case they became a heretic." See also Derek Baker, ed., *Medieval Woman* (Oxford: Basil Blackwell, 1978).

9. Perhaps in this case a person takes steps – such as literal migration – which will affect the ethnic affiliations of their immediate descendants rather than the person himself or herself. The long-run identity theory was introduced in connection with the market exchange dilemma of chapter 8.

10. "If no one else wants to join the group, perhaps because it does not control any valued resources, then its exclusiveness will have few consequences for outsiders. Yet if a group is in a privileged position the nature of the boundary has important consequences for non-members": *REC*, p. 126.

11. *REC*, pp. 131–5, 195–6, 207, 265–72.

12. *REC*, pp. 131, 163.

13. Henri Tajfel, *The Social Psychology of Minorities*, Minority Rights Group Report no. 38 (London: M.R.G., 1978), p. 14; and *REC*, p. 151: "Conformist groups are likely to be numerical minorities gradually losing their distinctive characteristics."

14. *REC*, p. 130.

15. "Initially, therefore, the excluded individuals form an involuntary minority and are a social category rather than a self-conscious group": *REC*, p. 129, and see also the discussion of revaluation movements on pp. 195–202.

16. Tajfel, p. 9.

17. Tajfel, p. 15.

18. Tajfel, p. 13.

19. Tajfel. p. 16.

20. See Graham McFarlane, "'It's not as simple as that': the expression of the Catholic and Protestant boundary in Northern Irish rural communities", in Anthony P. Cohen, ed., *Symbolizing Boundaries* (Manchester: Manchester University Press, 1986), pp. 92–3.

21. *REC*, p. 159.

22. One new entry in Figure 13.3 deserves brief comment partly because of its curiosity value. In what I have called a Circulating Group relationship, both groups have a *low* opinion of themselves, so members of group A, say, will want to join group B whereupon, if they assimilate group B norms, they will want to return to group A, and the process starts again: the grass is always greener on the other side. Perhaps this is part of the process by which two groups merge into one, or it might be part of the experience of the disappointed migrant, or rather the disappointed children of the migrant, who come to yearn for the old country after being brought up in the new. For this reaction among Europeans in America and Pakistanis in Britain, see *REC*, pp. 150, 315.

23. This paragraph was written before the unravelling of the Communist regimes in Europe began in earnest in 1989, but I will not pretend to have anticipated the rapidity of that process, just as I do not pretend to guess its outcome. David Miller contributes a level-headed discussion of national allegiances in *Market, State and Community* (Oxford: Clarendon Press, 1989), pp. 237–45.

14

Ethnic Formation

14.1 Precedence, Dispersion and Discrimination

Membership of an ethnic or racial group can have psychological consequences, but it can also affect the prospects of enjoying a whole range of material goods, social positions and social occasions. These effects are achieved in general either by influencing a person's tastes, and thus what a person *wants* to do, or by influencing how the person is received by others, and thus what a person is *able* to do, given that those others in some way control the means by which the person can do what the person wants to do.

These mechanisms come into play in particular when there is some scarcity of goods, positions or occasions – that is, when a good is not a pure public good in the relaxed material taxonomy of section 9.2. In these circumstances, the possibility of ethnic and/or racial *competition* takes its place alongside all the other mechanisms for allocating scarce goods or positions (goods for which demand exceeds supply). Common to all these mechanisms is a precedence system for selecting those persons who will in fact acquire the good or position from among all those who would like to acquire it. Precedence usually works by raising a social barrier to acquisition whose height serves to distinguish the successful from the unsuccessful applicants for the given material good or social position.

An auction, and therefore a competitive market, institutes this kind of precedence system, where the height of the barrier is given by the monetary cost, or price, of the good. But so does a queue (a line-up in the USA) which erects a barrier of waiting time; and so does every system of formal and informal qualification for a position or a benefit, including all competitions, sports and contests, in which the role of the contest is to establish who is qualifed to win, and even perhaps all lotteries and other devices of random selection, in which the relevant qualification is to have drawn the lucky number.[1]

In the case of the market, the queue, and any of the kinds of credential it is possible to gain by costly effort, the precedence system works by deterrence. Only those potential consumers acquire the good who remain willing to acquire it, given what it is now necessary to undergo: precedence is enjoyed by those prepared to bear the highest cost. Yet this introduces a dispersion element – those who do not enjoy precedence are precisely those who prefer to go elsewhere, given the cost. And those who have dispersed because the cost of acquisition has become too high find themselves in company with those who dispersed in the first place because their tastes were different – those who would not have wanted to acquire the given good or social position though it had been handed to them free upon a platter. I conclude that precedence is inevitable whenever scarcity exists (as it almost inevitably does) and that the commonly available allocation mechanisms all involve some combination of precedence mechanisms with dispersion mechanisms.

Now what I have called precedence I might have called discrimination, on the grounds that the several allocation systems all discriminate in their several ways between the successful and unsuccessful customers among the whole group of people who would want a given good if it were freely available. But I have resisted this usage, because I have reserved the term discrimination for a specific category of precedence: *unjustified* precedence.

I believe the semantics conforms with the coming linguistic norm. It may still be permissible to say that the task of the police is to discriminate between wrong-doers and law-abiding citizens, or that the task of coroners is to discriminate the quick from the dead. If any evaluation is registered by the use of such expressions, it is positive. These are justified cases of unequal treatment, and hence precedence.

But often, and increasingly, discrimination means *unjust* unequal treatment. Once one has nowadays proved a case of discrimination, it is not necessary to go on to prove that the discrimination was of the unjust variety. In this usage discrimination implies oppression; it describes an unjust exclusion from something which others are allowed.[2] This changing emphasis has no doubt been brought about partly because of the close association of the term with its racial and sexual exemplars. Thus, the term "racial discrimination" might have started life meaning something like "a process of distinguishing between people (that is, a process of discrimination) which would have been acceptable if it had not occurred on racialist lines (that is, if it had not been *racial* discrimination)". But now the term discrimination has absorbed so much obloquy that it is no longer available for use in its neutral connotations.

The effect of membership of particular ethnic or racial (or gender) groups is thus either to change a person's tastes, in which case the members of different groups are liable to disperse freely in pursuit of their different preferences, or to subject the members of one group to unequal treatment of an unjustified kind with respect to the acquisition of goods and/or social positions which are allocated preferentially to members of other ethnic or racial (or gender) groups.[3] This constitutes discriminatory practice, whose main variants I next outline.

In the first variant, membership of a particular group is a dominant qualification of access to a given good or position. Certain access routes are labelled "Slegs Blankes" or "Men Only". The criterion is exclusive. It acts lexically so that it is never outweighed by other personal characteristics. The only way in which a person from a disadvantaged group can become "qualified" is by changing their identity, which is in general extremely difficult and costly, or even almost impossible if the criteria are racial or sexual.

In the second variant, membership of a particular group is a qualification for access to a given good or position, but it is not a dominant qualification. This means that the personal criterion is one among several relevant criteria. Members of a group disadvantaged by the personal criterion are less likely to be regarded as qualified, though they are not excluded completely. This, very roughly, is the system of racial classification imposed by Southern Europeans in South America, according to Banton, compared with the exclusive, Apartheid regimes which were imposed by Northern Europeans in Africa, North America and Asia.

Banton takes the contrast between Brazil and the United States as symptomatic:

> Imagine that when one person meets another he [sic] obtains an impression about the other's education and wealth, that he makes a judgement about him from his mode of dress and his complexion, and that he gives the other marks out of 10 in respect of each of these. Imagine that in Brazil the other man is a dark-skinned lawyer, he might score 9 on education, 6 on wealth, 8 on costume and 1 on complexion, an average of 6; he would rank above a fair-complexioned bank clerk who scored 5, 3, 4 and 8 on the four scales. In the United States a similar pattern of assessing people usually obtains within white groups and within black groups but in many situations of contact between whites and blacks the decision about whether the other person is white or black is separate and distinct from the appraisal of status within the category in question. The Brazilian pattern is that of a continuous scale of social status; in the United States there have been two categories which usually have not been allowed to overlap.[4]

Adopting the numbers from Banton's example, there might be a qualification threshold for access to some good in Brazil of six points average, which the Brazilian lawyer would meet and the bank clerk not, so that at least some members of the disadvantaged group to which the lawyer belongs would gain access to the relevant social good. The unfairness to the lawyer, and to all members of the lawyer's ethnic group, consists in the fact that in order to gain a given qualification level, members of that group have to perform that much better on all the non-ethnic criteria than members of the privileged group – on average greater than six on education, wealth and costume – in order to score six overall. If the ethnic bias were eliminated, the proportions of the two groups attaining a given precedence level would adjust in favour of the disadvantaged group.

In the third variant, membership of a particular group is a qualification – even a dominant qualification – but it is said not to be such a qualification. This case tends to occur when the social reality is considerably less enlightened than the official gloss would have it: the case, that is, of contemporary Britain. The problem in a sense arises from the prevalence of precedence. The effect of official disapproval is to deem some forms of precedence not-OK. But since not-OK forms of precedence are bound to exist in the context of other forms of precedence which remain OK, it becomes possible to disguise instances of not-OK precedence by claiming that they are actually instances of OK precedence. The technique is to displace the ethnic or other non-OK grounds, which are in fact operating but are not publicly acceptable, onto bogus grounds which are not in fact operative but would be publicly acceptable.

The difficulty in proving the existence of this case is evidently that one must be very confident of the premiss (that precedence has occurred on non-OK grounds) before making the inference that the OK grounds being offered are being offered bogusly. A useful research technique in these circumstances is to make parallel applications to positions from fictitious persons matched, or randomly allocated, on all the relevant OK variables – education, nationality, experience, language, etc. – who differ purposely on the non-OK variable under scrutiny (ethnicity, gender, perhaps age, etc.). One can then infer which criteria are truly operative from the differential fate of the applications. In particular, one can sometimes catch the discriminator red-handed in the surreptitious displacement of the grounds which caused the exclusion of the disadvantaged applicant.

I reproduce in Figure 14.1 a particularly telling instance from an important study carried out by Political and Economic Planning (PEP) in the 1970s.[5]

The ethnic discrimination against the fictional Mrs. Mirza which has

---

12th February 1974

Dear Mrs. Mirza,

Thank you very much for your letter of the 9th February replying to our advertisement in The Manchester Evening News for a Secretary.

Unfortunately, we have a policy in the office not to employ married women as we unfortunately had a bad experience recently.

I am sorry that I am unable to help you in this instance.

Yours sincerely,

12th February 1974

Dear Mrs. Hayes,

Position of Secretary

Thank you very much for your letter of the 8th February applying for the position of Secretary.

Perhaps you would be kind enough to telephone the office as soon as ever possible to arrange a mutually convenient time for you to come in to see us.

I look forward to hearing from you.

Yours sincerely,

Source: D.J. Smith, *Racial Disadvantage in Britain* (Harmondsworth: Penguin, 1977), p. 124

Figure 14.1 A Case of Discrimination

beyond reasonable doubt motivated the differential response to these two applications has been displaced into discrimination by gender and marital status: "we have a policy in the office not to employ married women." It is just a little unfortunate for the author that the bogus grounds offered in the letter do not seem to be much more acceptable than the real grounds which the bogus grounds were designed to conceal. Protestations of innocence to charges of racial discrimination are not well served by pleas of guilty to sexual discrimination.

The details of this case aside, the overall findings of the PEP report were very disturbing: discrimination against black applicants for unskilled manual jobs occurred in at least 37 per cent of cases, and for skilled manual jobs the figure was 20 per cent. The research also made clear that the situation was worse than many black people realized. Since individuals were not in a position to judge whether a refusal was valid or whether it was a disguised form of racism, discriminators would often be given the benefit of the doubt.[6]

It has been the hope of reformers that the effect of legislation such as the Race Relations Acts in Britain will have been to change attitudes by sending out clear signals of what is acceptable behaviour. Michael Dummet has argued that: "just as English people with 'liberal' attitudes to race quickly become racist after migrating to South Africa, so no English people now living in independent Ghana or Nigeria manifest, even in the company of other English people, the least trace of racial prejudice. All that you need, to overcome racial prejudice, is a social climate in which it does not pay and earns public disapproval; it will then rapidly vanish without residue."[7]

The PEP research implies that the process of attitude change is more complex than this hopeful prediction allows. This is borne out by the fact that the position did not improve markedly from the 1970s to the 1980s, according to a more recent report from the Policy Studies Institute (PSI).[8] There need not be a continuous process of convergence of relatively backward attitudes in the population at large towards a more progressive governmental norm. There is even the possibility in principle that the situation might stabilize with a permanently hypocritical distance established between the overt and the covert practice – as exists already with sexual relations. When we speak of the long-run rational-choice theory of identity, we may be speaking of a very long run indeed.

In the interim, the hypocrisy generated by the distance between the official and actual reality is liable to breed cynicism about the aims of an anti-racist policy, and black people would be right not to trust the refusals they might receive from whites in respect of employment, housing and so on. Yet some of those refusals might be genuine, in which case we are dealing with a converse situation in which – a fourth variant – *membership of a particular group is not a qualification – not even one qualification among others – but it appears to be such a qualification.*

This could arise in any circumstances in which a member of a generally disadvantaged category falls foul of a precedence system which is in fact using OK criteria of precedence. But perhaps it is most serious whenever *group membership is correlated with an OK criterion.* Then evidence will tend to exist of the kind one would expect to see if discrimination were occurring, even though discrimination is not occurring.

Language and age are cases in point. If facility in English is an OK criterion for a job, and recent immigrants to England have not learnt the language, then they would be differentially excluded on OK grounds. Similarly, since the black population in Britain is considerably, though decreasingly, younger than the white population, age precedence would work against the black population at higher age levels (proportionally speaking) and in favour of the black population at lower age levels, without any discrimination taking place.[9]

The effect of possible correlations of these kinds is to make it more difficult to infer the existence of discrimination from the proportions in which various groups are represented in different occupations, types of housing, and so on. Disproportional representation is at best *prima facie* evidence of discrimination, not conclusive proof. (It is true also that *proportional* representation of a social group in an occupational category etc. is at best *prima facie* evidence of *lack* of discrimination.)

Thus, if one observes that there are very few black people, or women, in high managerial positions, one's suspicions are immediately aroused. But the suspicion in terms of global proportions must be tested using PEP-style research into local interactions, for the global pattern might be caused by the operation of OK factors at local level. Such would be the judgement of a PEP experiment which failed to reach an appropriate level of statistical significance in a social context in which OK factors were correlated with membership of ethnic and gender groups.

This possibility bears on two concepts much referred to in the field: *indirect discrimination* and *statistical discrimination*. I deal with these topics under the current heading and the next.

According to the 1976 UK Race Relations Act a person discriminated *indirectly* against another if "he [sic] applied to [an]other a requirement or condition ... (i) which is such that the proportion of persons of the same racial group as that other who can comply with it is considerably smaller ... and (ii) which he cannot show to be justifiable ... and (iii) which is to the detriment of that other."[10]

Now if the definition of indirect discrimination were given by the first clause alone, the Act would outlaw any precedence system using variables of precedence which were correlated with (racial or ethnic) group membership. This would be a most exacting policy, because it would probably outlaw, for example, language and age (and hence experience) as possible qualifications for jobs. This is presumably why the second clause is introduced into the definition of indirect discrimination: the precedence system in operation does not offend against the law if it is justifiable independently of any entanglement it may have with ethnic or racial division. Yet this does not quite settle the issue of indirect discrimination. For it is possible to take two distinct attitudes to the use of an independently defensible criterion in a context in which it is correlated with a non-OK criterion.

In some cases, precedence by language or age, say, might be permitted, albeit that the use of the criterion has the side effect of differentially excluding members of one particular racial, or ethnic (or gender) group. In other cases, it might be held that the relationship an otherwise OK variable has with a non-OK variable in some particular context turns the previously OK variable into a not-OK variable. This was the line taken by the British Appeal Tribunal in the case of Price v. The Civil Service Commission. It was decided that the upper age limit of 28 years for applicants for Executive Officers to the Civil Service discriminated indirectly against women, despite the fact that there is presumably nothing offensive about the use of age-limits *per se*.[11]

In the fifth variant membership of a particular group is not in itself a qualification, but group membership is deliberately used as a surrogate for a second, correlated criterion which is a qualification. We saw in the case of indirect discrimination that the use of an otherwise OK variable could have non-OK side effects; in the present case of *statistical discrimination* an otherwise non-OK variable is used rather in the role of *'understudy'* to an OK variable.[12]

We have come across an example of statistical discrimination already, in the reply to Mrs. Mirza. Recall that the author of the letter had displaced the racial discrimination, which he presumably knew to be unjustifiable, onto gender discrimination, which he then tried to justify rather lamely by saying that "we unfortunately had a bad experience recently." Insofar as the author could be said to have had a train of thought, it might have run thus: it is quite legitimate for employers to seek employees who will not give them bad experiences. We had a bad experience with a married woman recently. It is accordingly quite justified for us to avoid married women in future in order to avoid bad experiences in future.

Statistical discrimination will tend to appear in circumstances in which some desired characteristic of a person is inherently, or practically, difficult to observe or predict, such as reliability, productivity, conscientiousness and so on. Since the characteristic is difficult to get at directly, the discriminator believes it can be got at through group membership, given the discriminator's belief in the correlation between observable group membership and the unobservable characteristic.

The difference between this case and all the previous cases (called categorical by Banton) lies in the motive of the discriminator.[13] The categorical discriminator directs animus against a particular group. The statistical discriminator by contrast uses group membership as a technical device to establish other kinds of precedence. The corresponding policy question is: is it ever OK to use an otherwise non-OK variable as a surrogate for an OK variable?

Although this is a delicate question, to which there may be no blanket answer, the general presumption must be against the practice, for a number of reasons.

First, the practice would undoubtedly create a loophole, by allowing precedence to occur as a special case on criteria which would usually be condemned as discriminatory.

Second, the adoption of the practice would tend to generate complacency, and relax investigation into better ways of measuring the putative OK variable. If the employer assumes that all married women (and no other group?) create a bad employment experience, the employer is unlikely to seek more refined ways of discovering which individuals among all their potential employees are likely to create bad experiences.

Third, statistical discrimination does involve an injustice, although not always an injustice against a disadvantaged group considered as a whole. Those who suffer by statistical discrimination are the individual members of the disadvantaged group whose ranking on the OK variable is higher than would be predicted from the correlation between group membership and the OK variable. Those who gain are, conversely, the members of the advantaged group whose ranking on the OK variable is lower than would be predicted from the correlation. The effect of statistical discrimination against married women would be, for example, to replace some number of reliable married women by unreliable unmarried men.

A theoretically subtle possibility of this kind is reported from the US.[14] The Scholastic Aptitude Test is apparently a more accurate predictor of college grades among white than among black students (the variance of the residual term of the regression is lower for white than black students). This means that greater uncertainty surrounds the black than the white student with the same test score. Supposing that the test score were being used in some recruitment drive as a surrogate for the eventual college grade, then a risk averse employer would discriminate statistically against the black student. This would occur even if the average scores of the black group and white group of students were identical. The person who has suffered here is the gifted black student, and the student has suffered *from* the differential diagnostic capacity of the Scholastic Aptitude Test.

We can see moreover from this example how the use of statistical discrimination is liable to produce self-fulfilling prophecies. The reason black students are tested less accurately than white may well be that the test depends on a range of cultural reference more familiar among white than black students. This bias need be neither blatant nor deliberate. It just reflects the fact that the test is probably designed by white teachers who select examples more familiar to themselves. But as a result of the fact that the test isn't as good a diagnostic instrument for black students as it is for white students, white students will tend to get the jobs, including the job of setting the Scholastic Aptitude Test. So the exclusion is self-perpetuating.

Another example of a self-fulfilling prophecy is the use of the notorious "Sus" laws by the Metropolitan Police in London in the 1970s and early 1980s. The police might well have argued that "more blacks were arrested for the attempted theft of purses because more blacks attempted to steal purses."[15] Given the alleged correlation between colour and crime, one can hear the officer claiming that it was an intelligent piece of detective work, and not an act of discrimination, to use colour as a surrogate variable for criminal intent. The problem with the police argument, though, is that evidence for the correlation is derived in large measure from the differential proportion of blacks among those arrested – a result in part, of the belief of the police that such a correlation existed. Their resort to colour discrimination made it more difficult for the police to do what they are supposed to do – namely, discriminate on the basis of the intention to commit theft.

In sum, then, there are several good reasons against permitting the practice of statistical discrimination, including the lack of justice that certainly accompanies a less than perfect statistical correlation.[16] In that case, statistical discrimination fails to meet the legal bill of health, and Banton is right to conclude that "the legal definition of indirect discrimination will cover statistical discrimination."[17]

14.2   The Economics of Discrimination

The explanation of discrimination has long posed a problem for economic analysis. For there is a broad argument that the competitive logic of the market should banish discrimination. Suppose, for example, that I, a white, refuse to sell my house to you, the highest bidder, a black. Or suppose that I, a man, refuse to employ you, the lowest bidder, a woman. In either case I am cutting off my nose to spite my face. I am foregoing the best deal, and the market ultimately punishes non-maximizers by driving them out of business. In the long run, market forces should work against discriminatory practices.[18]

Yet the empirical record of market societies does not bear out this argument. We have seen that gender segregation is a chronic feature of capitalist work places, and it is not obvious, to put it mildly, that the development of capitalism is bound up with a relaxation of racial, ethnic and national conflict.[19] To explain these facts must be to explain why it is that the logic of competitive markets does not apply in these cases, even though they occur in the context of competitive market activity. In the language of precedence, we must explain the occurrence of a composite system of allocation which mixes market forms of (price) precedence with non-market forms of discriminatory precedence by race, gender and other variables of personal identity.

Economic theories of discrimination attempt to explain the non-market (non-competitive) element of the overall precedence scheme in terms borrowed from the standard rational-choice analysis of competitive market precedence. This is not on the face of it a promising avenue for research, and one has to admire those who have made the attempt to pursue it.

In a pioneering journey in this field, Gary Becker assimilated discriminatory precedence to market precedence via the concept of a taste for discrimination.[20] The existence of the taste places a monetary premium on discriminatory practices, so that actors are prepared to pay to indulge their taste for discrimination. A white employer, for example, will be happy to pay higher wages to whites out of a racist sense of loyalty to his group. Although this theory can explain the existence of a discriminatory wage by reference to the employer's preference, it does not explain why the employer has this preference. And because the preference is costly, and strictly irrelevant to the technical conditions of production, the discriminatory employer should be driven out of business by a competitor who learns to overcome racist prejudice and no longer pays the premium. Becker's theory is vulnerable, in other words, to the broad argument in favour of the progressive tendency of market forces.

Roemer traces the explanation of discrimination to the unsavoury tastes of the workforce rather than the unsavoury tastes of management. The existence of working-class racism (and/or sexism) makes the labour force vulnerable to manipulation by a management which is able to divide and rule. Sectional antipathies weaken the bargaining power and therefore depress the wages of a mixed workforce, compared with a workforce composed of either kind of worker alone. There may also be differential depression of the wages of the two groups, so that one group in a mixed workforce is paid more than the other.

In these circumstances employers employ as few of the higher paid group as possible (because they are more costly to employ) but as many as is necessary to foment the antipathy which reduces the bargaining power of the mixed workforce. A few members of the higher paid group are introduced, or tolerated, by management as a virus to destroy healthy union organization. The upshot is an equilibrium of lowered wages for all, consistent with a wage differential in favour of a privileged few distinguished by some social marker such as colour or sex.[21]

There are two main problems with Roemer's analysis. First, it is not obvious that employers are in a position to control the ethnic (or gender)

composition of the workforce in the required way, because the composition is to a certain degree dependent on employee choice as well as
employer strategy. Thomas Schelling has investigated the phenomenon
of "tipping", which is usually associated with residential neighbourhoods,
but would apply within a labour force as well. In general, there will
be differential degrees of prejudice and aversion on the two sides of a
social division and this can lead to the following unstable situation. Suppose a member of one group takes a job (or a house) usually occupied
by a member of another group. Then the most prejudiced person in the
"indigenous" group might leave, to be replaced by a second member
of the incoming group. This further changes the balance of occupancy
between the two groups, prompting the second most prejudiced person
in the original group to defect. The process could trigger a chain reaction
which results in a complete evacuation of the original group.[22] In Roemer's
model, the newly-homogeneous group would then recover its bargaining
power and restore its higher wage. Thus the workings of prejudice could
frustrate the attempt of the employer to use prejudice to divide and rule.

This insight is consistent with a more conservative and less Machiavel-
lian employer strategy than the one posited by Roemer. Employers will
be frightened to disturb what they perceive to be the ethnic (or gender)
balance of a section of their labour force, precisely because it might lead
to the tipping phenomenon, and instability of the labour supply. Thus
they err on the side of caution, and assume a greater degree of prejudice
in their existing workforce than in fact exists. They give precedence to
workers of the traditional sort, and only seek out workers of other groups
when their existing supply dries up. Far from seeking deliberately to mix
up the labour force, they strive to keep it homogeneous.[23]

Even if this objection is set aside, Roemer's analysis is subject to the
main criticism adduced against Becker. Each theorist has traced discriminatory outcomes to discriminatory preferences which themselves cry out
for explanation. And since the weight of the explanation falls on the
peculiar character of the preferences, rather than the predictable behaviour given the preferences, neither economic model has carried us far
towards what we most want to know.[24]

A third theory arises less from a specific economic model than from
a sociological generalization about contemporary capitalism. This dual
labour market theory holds that industrial and commercial organizations
can be boarded nowadays at just two points. The lower port of entry
is used by steerage passengers. There is a competitive labour market for
all hands below deck, pay is low, work uncertain, skills in short supply
and technology backward.

The higher port of entry is marked "cabin class". Passengers here are
insulated from the full rigour of market forces by their higher pay, greater

security of employment, better skills and formal qualifications, and the symbiosis which exists between them and the officers on the bridge. The cabin class is needed, so it is said, to design and run the sophisticated equipment that keeps the ship afloat. Their specialized, and sometimes localized, expertise make these people hard to replace. They advance by internal promotion up the career ladders within each firm and do not have to subject themselves to the vicissitudes of open labour market competition.

This dual character of the capitalist labour supply is explained, it is said, by the contradictory pressures facing capitalist enterprises. Enterprises must retain their full capacity to produce goods and services while remaining responsive to the fluctuations in the market for their goods and services. The first imperative would require the company to keep on all competent personnel no matter what; the second would require it to make nimble adjustments in the size of its organization according to the state of demand. These opposing pressures can be reconciled by surrounding the primary core of well-paid, essential staff by a secondary penumbra of casualized employees.[25] The essential staff carry the blueprint of production in their collective head and it is put into effect by a phalanx of interchangeable proletarians on a scale which varies according to the precise state of the market.

This conception is not, of course, a novel one. Booth noted long ago that it was the regularity of earnings as well as the level of earnings which mattered for the delineation of strata in the labour force. The dual labour market is really a version of the labour aristocracy theory, which arose in the period of Booth's researches. It was mentioned by Engels and furthered by Lenin in his well-known connection of imperialism with social reformism, and it has more recently been the subject of painstaking historical investigation by John Foster and Robert Gray, among others. The idea of the industrial reserve army is in any case vintage Marx.[26] The valuable new emphasis, introduced by Piore and his fellow dual theorists, is on the extent to which the split between primary and secondary labour markets coincides with other forms of social division: the reserve army comprises disproportionate numbers of members of ethnic minorities, women and young people.[27]

However, the theory as proposed is subject to the criticism that it drastically oversimplifies the experience of employment. At the very least, one would have to introduce four separate ports of entry to the capitalist unit of production. The conception of the secondary labour force will arguably cover all unskilled, unorganized labour. But even in its grossest outline the upper port of entry surely contains at least three separate doors – each leading to a different level of the organization. The first is for the skilled and/or unionized manual workers. The second is for the formally qualified non-manual technical and professional employees. The third is marked Private Property – we must not forget that the son and heir can enter the company for the first time at the level of the Board.

If there are thus more strata in the organization than the dual theory allows, there is perhaps less differentiation between the strata than the dual theory requires. It is not impossible to move from a secondary to a primary position, and not the case that the employment conditions in the several parts of the labour force are utterly at variance one with another. In the main Western countries, labour market polarization occurs, according to Robin Blackburn and Michael Mann, only where immigrant labour is deprived of citizenship and suffers inferior formal rights in addition to adverse social status: "In all these cases, the immigrants are naturally at the mercy of their employer ... This is a dual labour market with a vengeance, separating the working class into free and semi-free legal statuses reminiscent of feudalism rather than capitalism."[28] Otherwise, there is a more nuanced relationship between competitive processes, qualifications of the technical and formal kind, the systems of precedence which give the organization its fundamental structure, defensive counter-organization by trade or profession, and processes of discrimination by ethnicity, gender and age. The dual labour theorists usefully draw attention to one aspect, or tendency, of modern capitalist organization, without providing thereby a comprehensive explanation of the forms of segregation they describe. Neither have the more strictly economic theories of Becker or Roemer taken us very far.

The great merit of Banton's work is to set out boldly on the hazardous quest for a genuinely general theory of ethnic formation.[29] I proceed to discuss his theory in order of its three basic propositions.

14.3   Banton's Theory of Ethnic Formation

Proposition one

1. Individuals utilize physical and cultural differences in order to create groups and categories by the processes of inclusion and exclusion.[30]

Whenever an individual discriminates, the individual is choosing to make use of physical or cultural differences for social purposes. The use is inclusive when the individual discriminates in favour of another person and exclusive when the individual discriminates against the other person. Banton's first proposition can be read as summarizing all the processes of affiliation and discrimination discussed thus far.

However, I don't think this is all that Banton intends. It is true that any act of discrimination helps to perpetuate the system of perceptions on which other acts of discrimination feed, so that all acts of discrimination in one sense "create groups and categories". But such perpetuation of existing distinctions is usually termed the "reproduction" of groups and categories. I believe that what Banton intends is that individuals utilize differences in order to create groups and categories *de novo*, where none existed before. The question then arises whether individuals are ever in a position to "create groups and categories" in this more ambitious sense.

Recall that the theory is intended to be governed by rational-choice motivational assumptions: "individuals act so as to obtain maximum net advantage."[31] Recall also that systems of discrimination systematically benefit one group at the expense of another. Then an individual white person might say to herself or himself: "Well, supposing there were a system of discrimination in my favour, I would definitely be better off." Yet the existence of the incentive does not give such a person the power to bring the system into being. The advantage contemplated by our hypothetical discriminator does not arise in the comparison of the payoffs from two actions that the discriminator might perform. It arises almost regardless of the person's actions from the person's comparative positions in two social systems: one of which is free of and the other disfigured by discriminatory forms of social precedence.

A *general* explanation for the existence of the latter type of system (including the differential perceptions and preferences which sustain its discriminatory arrangements) would have to propose that: *groups and categories whose membership depends on perceptions of physical and cultural difference will be found to exist when and because it is in the interests of the members of such groups and categories that such groups and categories exist.* The explanation is not in the standard format of a rational-choice explanation, and deliberately so. It is deliberately reminiscent of a functional explanation. It says that the groups which we observe having formed will be the groups which it would have been in their members' interests to have formed. When this alternative construction of Banton's first proposition is set alongside its original, it becomes apparent that Banton may be confusing a theory which depends on the notion of maximum net advantage with a theory which depends on a rational-choice conception of human action.[32]

I am emboldened in this view by the conclusion of Part I above, where the puzzle had a similar abstract structure. It would have been to the advantage of society as a whole that capitalism superseded feudalism, because capitalism's development of the forces of production would eventually lead to a higher average standard of living. This comparative advantage of capitalism over feudalism can figure in an explanation of why capitalism superseded feudalism, without any individual, or coalition of

individuals, ever being in a position to act in the light of that prospective
advantage in order to bring capitalism into being. It is not obvious from
Banton's first proposition that his theory does indeed enunciate a rational-
choice account of its chosen topic.

Proposition two

Baynton's second proposition reads:

> 2. Ethnic groups result from inclusive and racial categories from exclusive
> processes.[33]

This second proposition is corollary to the first: it amplifies a point about
inclusive and exclusive processes by connecting them respectively with
ethnic groups and racial categories. There is, however, a considerable
ambiguity about the kind of connection Banton has in mind. To sharpen
this point, I will reformulate the second proposition in two versions,
one of which serves to define what is an ethnic and what a racial group,
and the second of which puts forward an empirical generalization about
independently-defined ethnic and racial groups.

The *definitional version* proposes that any group whose identity arises
from *inclusive* social processes is an *ethnic* group; any group whose identity
arises from *exclusive* social processes is a *racial* group. The *empirical
version* proposes that *ethnic* groups tend to set most store by *inclusive*
practices of boundary maintenance; *racial* groups tend to set most store
by *exclusive* practices of boundary maintenance.

Banton's wording leans strongly in the first, definitional direction, since
the respective groups are said to "result from" the respective processes.
This is unfortunate, since the definitional version encounters severe taxonomic difficulties. The main problem is that the respective processes of
exclusion and inclusion are always associated to some extent with each
other. We considered in chapter 13 the case of the Polish Jewish community
before and after its migration to New York. This community, let us agree,
suffered exclusion in Warsaw at the hands of the gentile Poles, but had
to contrive inclusion in New York to preserve itself from being incorporated without remainder into its new American surroundings. Yet the gentile Poles were to a degree creating an inclusive group of gentile Poles
in the process of excluding the Polish Jews; and the Jewish community
in New York was implicitly excluding non-Jewish New Yorkers by the
inclusive measures it took.

It is often very difficult to disentangle whether a given act or pattern
of segregation is governed by exclusive motives which have inclusive side-
effects or by inclusive motives which have exclusive side-effects.[34] If it

is the most common pattern that two groups are simultaneously inclusive of their own members and exclusive of members of other groups, then most groups will count as simultaneously ethnic and racial, depending upon whether they are seen from the "inside" or the "outside". This likelihood, which Banton concedes at one point, rather defeats any taxonomic purpose of the second proposition.[35]

It follows that this second proposition is more plausibly regarded as an empirical generalization than as an attempt to distinguish racial from ethnic groups.[36] Yet to assess the proposition in this empirical version we must first establish what are the criteria of ethnicity and race, independent of processes of inclusion and exclusion. Banton has implicitly given us the answer: ethnicity depends on perceptions of cultural difference, whereas race depends on perceptions of physical difference.

In elaboration of this distinction, I would say that what makes a group an ethnic group is that the members of it believe a story of their common descent, whereas members of a racial group believe a biological story of their common descent.[37] (This ruling implies that racial groups are strictly speaking a sub-type of ethnic groups, although I have usually used the two terms disjointly. It also – thankfully – relieves me of the obligation to judge the validity of the beliefs held by typical ethnic and racial groups about their common descent.[38])

With this distinction in hand, we can return to the case of the Polish Jewish community. It may well be true that the gentile Poles defined the Jews in racial terms in Warsaw, whereas the Jews defined themselves in ethnic terms in New York. Thus the switch in emphasis from exclusive to inclusive processes of boundary maintenance coincided with a switch in the operative criterion of group membership from a racial to an ethnic criterion.

And perhaps this is a part of a more general historical pattern. The great excluders have been the whites, who have excluded the blacks on a racial basis; the great includers have been the nationalists, who have often conceived their fellowship culturally – according to Benedict Anderson's mixed spatial metaphor, "a deep, horizontal comradeship".[39]

Yet an intriguing historical correlation is not in itself a proposition in any theory. As part of Banton's theory, and in view of earlier commentary on its first proposition, the explanatory claim would have to be that *whenever it would be in the interests of a group to form by exclusive processes, the group will form using criteria of physical difference rather than cultural difference for the purposes of exclusion because it is more apt to use criteria of physical than cultural difference for such exclusive purposes in such circumstances.* (A comparable statement would apply to the converse connection between inclusive processes and cultural criteria of inclusion.)

To state the claim in this form is to show how difficult it would be to establish, and to emphasize that no grounds have been given why it might be true. Indeed, there are some ferocious historical counter-examples. The notion of the Aryan race was designed to include Aryans as well as exclude non-Aryans; Christendom as a cultural entity excluded Islam as well as including Christianity (and *vice versa* for Islam in relation to Christianity). Under this construction of his second proposition, Banton is attempting one of the most ambitious feats in all social science: to explain a variation in the meaningful content of a certain type of symbolic system by the variable social function that it serves.[40] If the proposition fails to be convincing, this is as much as anything else an index of how much it would take to become convinced of such an ambitious proposition.

Proposition three

The nub of Banton's theory is a third proposition, read in conjunction with his first:

> 3. When groups interact, processes of change affect their boundaries in ways determined by the form and intensity of competition; and, in particular, when people compete as individuals this tends to dissolve the boundaries that define the groups, whereas when they compete as groups this reinforces those boundaries.[41]

The third proposition spells out the processes by which groups either establish themselves or fail to do so: group competition secures the group-like character of the group; individual competition erodes it. An initial problem is that the statement elides two distinct ways of contrasting "group competition" with "individual competition". On the one hand, "group competition" might mean "competition among individual persons which is affected by the group memberships of the individuals concerned." In this construal, "group competition" denotes a society which legitimizes group *discrimination* in the individual allocation of jobs, housing and so on (in the sense of section 14.1 above.) A society in which individual competition prevailed would be, by contrast, a society free of discrimination.

On the other hand, the term "group competition" might refer to the fact that social rewards are sought by collective (political) action, whereas "individual competition" would imply that rewards are sought by individual action. I remarked in the commentary on Banton's first proposition that individuals are unlikely ever to be in a position to choose the form of society in which they live. So they do not in general face the choice of whether or not their society shall be free of discrimination. But given the existence of a society which either is or is not already discriminatory (and thus in which either group or individual competition prevails, according to the first interpretation of the term "group competition"), individuals certainly can choose whether or not to engage in collective action designed to change or to preserve the existing character of their society.

Thus if we assume that the society is *discriminatory* already, collective action ("group competition" under the second interpretation of the term) would be designed either to uphold the existing pattern of discrimination, or to overthrow it. Group action designed to uphold an existing pattern of discrimination on behalf of its beneficiaries thus has "group goals" whereas group action designed to overthrow the pattern will typically have the goal of creating a society in which people compete only as individuals (irrespective of their erstwhile group attachments). Thus group action can have group goals or individualistic goals. If the society is *non-discriminatory* already, collective action might conversely either encourage or discourage the installation of a new regime of discrimination as a "group goal" of some would-be privileged group.

The alternative to collective actions of any of the aforementioned types is to do nothing politically, which implies that the status quo will carry on, and individuals will compete in whatever way the existing society imposes: as group members in a discriminatory society and as individuals in a non-discriminatory society.

The question of whether there is a rational-choice model of racial and ethnic competition thus comes down to the question of whether there is a rational-choice model of the decision to engage in collective action with a view to installing a regime of a type from which the individual will derive a benefit (relative to some other type of regime). Such a model will compare the costs of participation in a collective action with the benefits should the collective action prove successful.

Banton comes closest to this conception of what his theory is about when he writes that

a rational choice theory of racial and ethnic relations must concern itself ... with the establishment and maintenance of monopoly as a social form.... A monopoly pattern in racial relations can be maintained only when members of the privileged group can be persuaded that their individual interests point in the same direction as that in which they believe their collective interests to lie.[42]

The first and apparently insurmountable difficulty faced by such a theory is that, as all game theorists agree, collective action will hardly ever occur, because it involves an N-person Prisoner's Dilemma: the benefits of installing a new regime favourable to their group will go to all group members, but the costs of installing the regime will be borne only by those who take part in the collective action, so all hang back, and the collective action never gets off the ground.

I have already given notice, in the discussion of the confidence game in chapter 8, that I regard the difficulty presented by the N-person Prisoner's Dilemma as surmountable. And I have up my sleeve (in chapter 17) the Curious Incident of the Vanishing Police. These police inhabit a political superstructure which ensures perfect compliance of rational actors with the demand that they take their share in the costs of a collective action. Since all actors comply with the demand, no police force need exist to ensure compliance with the demand. It follows that ethnic groups (or any other social constellation facing a similar problem of social order) can be treated as if they were collective actors, who can costlessly enforce participation in their joint action.

The conclusion of chapter 17 is nevertheless subject to a caveat which should be borne in mind here. The argument of the vanishing police claims that groups can always in principle overcome their collective action problem; it says nothing about the circumstances in which, or the path by which, specific groups actually do so. In particular, argument does not allow one to predict that any group which has an interest in collective action will organize itself to pursue the given interest.[43]

Granted this caveat, I proceed on the assumption that ethnic and racial competition pits two perfectly-formed collective actors against one another. Call the actors i and j, with numerical sizes i and j in a total population of N individuals, so that

$$i + j = N \qquad\qquad (14.1)$$

Because i and j are collective actors, they can, unlike single individuals, pursue the goal of installing or overthrowing social systems. In particular, they can pursue the goal of instituting a monopoly on behalf of their own members, or overthrowing a monopoly established by their opponents.[44]

What groups might want to monopolize in this way is any aggregate, divisible social benefit, say, U. Assume that if it were spread out evenly to everyone, this benefit would give each member of society an amount, u, where

$$Nu = U \qquad\qquad (14.2)$$

Then we say that group j monopolizes the benefit if it divides the benefit equally among its members, completely excluding members of group i. What members of group j would gain by their group membership is their

individual share of the amount that would otherwise have been spread
among group i, but is now added to the spoils of group j. Thus the
prospective benefit of j-group membership is

$$iu/j \qquad\qquad\qquad\qquad\qquad\qquad (14.3)$$

Members of group i would on the other hand get nothing if group
j successfully installed a group-j monopoly, so that the penalty of i-group
membership would be

$$u \qquad\qquad\qquad\qquad\qquad\qquad (14.4)$$

(14.3) and (14.4) establish the interests of the respective groups in a
monopoly regime and an egalitarian regime respectively.[45] Now assume
that a contest develops between the two groups to install and/or defend
whichever social regime it most prefers. This contest is conditioned by
the amount the two sides stand to gain or lose under the two social
regimes (as given by (14.3) and (14.4)) and therefore by the amount of
effort the two sides are prepared to invest in the political campaign. The
costs of participation and the benefits of success are thus brought into
the same frame of reference, which is what we require of a rational-choice
theory inspired by Banton's approach.[46]
We assume therefore that each side has solved its internal problem
of social order. There is a vanishing i-police to ensure compliance with
the egalitarian politics of the i-side; there is a vanishing j-police to ensure
compliance with the monopolistic politics of the j-side. Compliance takes
the form of a tax (s) imposed equally on each member of the i-side and
a tax (t) imposed on each member of the j-side. The respective tax levels
are set by collective decision on each side, and the tax is wholly used
to finance sanctions against the other side. Tax rates s = 0 or t = 0
correspond to circumstances in which one of the sides has either failed
completely to get its collective act together or decided collectively not
to engage in collective activity. The sanctions directed by the advantaged
group (j) against the disadvantaged group (i) are designed to uphold or
establish their monopoly position; the sanctions flying in the other direction are designed to undermine or resist the monopoly position of the
advantaged group. Members of both groups suffer twice over, from the
taxes they pay to support their own war effort and from the sanctions
imposed on them by their opponents. These just are the double costs
of war.
The limit to the collective war effort is set by the costs and benefits
to the *individual* members of each side. It is not going to be worthwhile
for any j to spend more to uphold a monopoly than the given j gains

from the existence of the monopoly (the incentive iu/j established by
(14.3)). Conversely, it is not going to be worthwhile for any i to pay
more to prevent a monopoly than the given i loses by the existence of
a monopoly (the incentive u established by (14.4)).

Formally, the model of interaction is as follows. Suppose that group
i converts its tax revenue into sanctions against group j at a rate y. In
effect, y is the parameter of a *linear military function*, which specifies
how much deterrent against the opposing group is delivered by each unit
of military resource.[47] Then each member of group j suffers a military
sanction isy/j. Suppose conversely that group j converts its tax revenue
into sanctions against group i with the same efficiency – at the rate y.[48]
Then group j members will act to sustain their monopoly position so
long as

$$iu/j - t - isy/j > 0 \qquad (14.5)$$

And group i members will be prepared to sustain the egalitarian regime
so long as

$$u - s - jty/i > 0 \qquad (14.6)$$

Inequalities (14.5) and (14.6) divide the strategy space (s, t) into four
regions, depending on which combination of the two inequalities is
satisfied:

(i) (14.5) is satisfied, but not (14.6). In this case, the j group – the monopolists – can sustain their sanctions from the prospective benefits of monopoly, despite their opponents' war effort. The i group – the egalitarians
– would on the other hand be better off if there were no struggle between
the groups (s = 0, t = 0), even if the consequence of the cessation of
struggle would be the perpetuation of an adverse monopoly which gave
them nothing. I take it that these conditions describe *the victory of the
monopolists by their defeat of the egalitarians*, and imply the stability of
the monopoly formation.

(ii) (14.6) is satisfied, but not (14.5). This is the converse of the previous
case. By similiar reasoning, I take it to describe *the victory of the egalitarians by their defeat of the monopolists*, and the corresponding stability
of the egalitarian formation.

In the remaining cases, the issue of the struggle is still in doubt:

(iii) Both (14.5) and (14.6) are satisfied. Here both sides are able to
keep up the fight; the relative costs make it worthwhile to start or continue

the war. There are various possibilities for attributing payoffs in this case, in view of the uncertainty of the outcome. For the sake of sharpness, I will assume that *neither side receives any of the prospective social benefit of the struggle while the struggle is in progress*. Thus both payoffs are negative, reflecting the fact that political action is an investment with known penalties but precarious payoffs.[49]

(iv) Neither (14.5) nor (14.6) is satisfied. This is close to Marx's "common ruin of the contending classes."[50] Each side is so heavily taxed for war and suffers so much from military action that both would do better to give up and go home. I assume again that neither side receives the prospective social benefit while the conflict is on, even though the two sides are in the process of fighting each other to a standstill. Trench warfare might be an appropriate name for this sector of the strategy space.

The overall payoff structure thus contains four sectors: Victory (M)/Defeat (E); Open Warfare; Victory (E)/Defeat (M); and Trench Warfare (where M and E denote the monopolists and egalitarians respectively). The sectors are separated by lines in (s, t) space along which the political incentives to war and peace are evenly balanced, so that (14.5) and (14.6) become equations rather than inequalities. These are called *surrender lines*. The arrangement of these lines and their corresponding sectors is displayed in Figure 14.2, (which is drawn up also under the "non-backfire condition" that $y > 1$).[51]

I argued in chapter 7 that any such payoff structure can be interpreted either parametrically or strategically. From the parametric point of view, we fix an opponent's strategy, which is treated as part of the environment, and optimize with respect to that strategy. Consider in this light the optimization problem of the egalitarian popular front. If the given strategy of the monopolistic opponent is sufficiently low in Figure 14.2, then the egalitarian forces can win by increasing their military effort until the monopolist's limit of struggle is reached (as is depicted by the line A–B on the figure). At that point the monopolistic j-group surrender. If the j-group's strategy is on the other hand sufficiently high, then escalating egalitarian military effort will be self-defeating, because the forces of resistance will exhaust themselves (along a line C–D) before they exhaust their j-opponent. The watershed strategy between "low" and "high" is the value of t at the intersection of the two surrender lines $t = [iu/j(1 + y)]$.

An analogous argument applies to the parametric behaviour of the j-opponent against an i-group whose strategy is taken as fixed: j's raising of the stakes can lead to j's victory or to self-defeat, depending on the

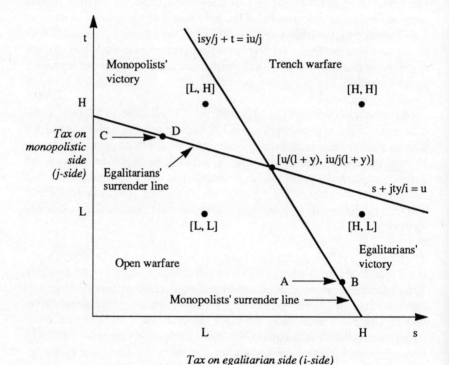

Tax on egalitarian side (i-side)

Figure 14.2 Ethnic Formation

level of the i-strategy against which j competes. The watershed i-strategy is given by s = u/(1 + y).[52]

Here is an historical application of parametric analysis. Suppose that there is an invading group in some territory intent on monopolizing the resources of the territory. Suppose that this group is small numerically with respect to the indigenous population, relatively well organized and relatively well-armed. The first point gives each member of the group a large incentive to sustain monopoly, the second gives the group the capacity for collective action in pursuit of monopoly and the third enables it to install monopoly with relative ease (y is assumed to be large). Initially, the indigenous population is neither organized to defend itself, nor capable of doing so with the same ruthless efficiency as the invaders. These facts conspire to impose s = 0 for the indigenous population. Given that the indigenous population lack the capacity for immediate collective resistance, the invaders choose a level of taxation given by iu/jy, which generates a sanction u, and this is sufficient to deter any action designed to overthrow the invaders' regime of monopoly. For any such attempt would involve costs which would outweigh the prospective benefit from overthrowing the monopoly.

If, as we have assumed, i is much larger than j, and also y is large, so that y is approximately equal to i/j, then u is approximately equal to iu/jy, which is in turn much less than iu/j. Hence the costs to the invader of maintaining the monopoly regime are low in relation to the invaders' gains from the monopoly regime, and the regime is stable, because resistance is counter-productive. These conditions are intended to approximate those of *white settler colonialism*, showing how difficult it may be to topple a regime established by surprise attack on an unsuspecting population.

If we suppose, on the other hand, that an egalitarian regime is already established, the disadvantage lies with the potential monopolist. For if the egalitarians maintain a tax level of u/y, which is low in relation to their social gain u (if y is much larger than 1), then any attempt by a monopolist to establish a discriminatory regime will be counter-productive. Perhaps this helps to explain Ernest Gellner's point that nationalists have been remarkably unsuccessful, in that there are so many fewer national states than there are potential nationalities.[53]

These applications address the problem of group formation, but they also illuminate the problem of affiliation. Once a monopoly is established, there will be an incentive to join the j-group. But if every member of the i-group manages to pass as a member of the j-group, the advantages of j-group membership will be lost. Thus we can expect that the defence of the monopoly will consist partly in the maintenance of exclusive j-group boundaries. If the monopoly is broken, however, the incentive towards joining the putative j-group disappears. The j-group characteristic (colour, religion, historical origin or whatever) will therefore remain latent, in the sense that members of the group have less motive to assert their identity. The j-group remains a "numerical" group within an i-group population at an equal welfare level. It follows that either the monopoly condition of society or the egalitarian condition of society is consistent with the long-run rational-choice theory of identity.

In the preceding *parametric* applications, we have taken an opponent's strategy as given. In the *strategic* perspective, collective actors will choose a level of war effort taking account of their opponent's responses.

In the present model, the actors face a choice from within a continuum of tax rates. To concentrate on the strategic interaction, we reduce this choice to a binary decision: a war effort being mounted, are the taxes imposed to be high or low (where the values of high and low depend on the watershed values calculated before: high above the watershed, low below)? If a collective actor chooses a low war effort, it can never win, and if it chooses a high war effort, it can never lose. But neither is it bound to lose by choosing low, nor bound to win by choosing high: either strategy risks an outcome of continued conflict in either the open warfare or the trench warfare mode. If we focus only on strategies which give each side a chance of outright victory (pairs such as the (H,L) pairs depicted in figure 14.2), the players are involved in a game with ordinal symmetry whose payoffs are ranked as follows:

>   (H, L)   Victory
>
>   (L, L)   Open warfare
>
>   (L, H)   Defeat
>
>   (H, H)   Trench warfare

This payoff structure is our old friend Chicken, and we know now what that means.[54] The victory of either side is a stable equilibrium, and yet there are in general no rational grounds on which collective actors can decide whether to go for victory (by choosing a high war effort) or risk the possibility of defeat against an aggressive oponent (by choosing low). It follows that it is very difficult to predict what distribution of ethnic discrimination and the lack of it will be observed, even if one is prepared to swallow all the assumptions which have been made in order to formalize Banton's theory. The rational-choice approach has led to a theory of ethnic and racial competition which is radically indeterminate.

14.4   Historisis

This conclusion is inconclusive, but we may learn something from its very inconclusiveness. In the foregoing model, two collective actors were locked in struggle over the installation of a monopolistic social system which would benefit the members of one group at the expense of the members of the other. We have taken for granted the existence of an internally oriented *police function* within each collective actor, and considered the possibilities of a politically-inspired and externally-oriented *military action*, conditioned by the prospective gains and losses from monopoly, the character of the coercive technology and the relative sizes of the groups. It has been shown that either of the two possible outcomes (monopolistic or non-monopolistic) is a stable equilibrium, both in the sense of rational political action and in the sense of the incentives to affiliate to the various groups, and therefore, in particular, to maintain the relative sizes and identities of the two groups.

This result reinforces a view that the task of theory in general, and rational-choice theory in particular, is to investigate the equilibrium properties of social systems. And if it is true of any complex social system that it has multiple equilibria, then it becomes the task of historical analysis to investigate why it is that one rather than another of the equilibrium states is the one which is observed to obtain in the real world.

This point bears on some seminal, though relatively underdeveloped, reflections of John Roemer. He has construed a "reasonably general materialist history" (reasonably!) as involving the combined analysis of a "preference formation process" and a "solution process".[55] These two processes correspond respectively to the formation of human subjects with given wants and desires, and the achievement of a social equilibrium, given human subjects with specified wants and desires. (This distinction is reflected in the respective topics of the two chapters in this part of the present book: ethnic affiliation deals with the formation of differential preferences; ethnic competition with the equilibrium possibilities of ethnic group existence.) Roemer proposes a cogent taxonomy of received theoretical schools according to the partial emphases they apply either to the preference formation process or to the solution process, and goes on to outline a combined understanding of the two processes: "individuals are formed by society, and these individuals react rationally to their environments to produce tomorrow's environment, which in turn produces individuals who think somewhat differently from before, and react in their environment to bring about yet a new equilibrium."[56]

History in this view becomes a kind of concatenation of preference formation with equilibrium strategy choice in a way which allows for a fairly strict, if complex, determinism over historical time. The conclusion of this chapter implies a slightly different view. What Roemer calls the preference formation process is here included as part of what he calls the solution process, because a long-run rational-choice theory of identity was shown to be consistent with either of the equilibrium outcomes. Thus there are two states of the system – monopoly or equality – either of which could in principle persist for ever. Yet the solution process is unable to decide between them, which is why we have appealed for adjudication to historical analysis. The theory allows only a small number of discrete equilibrium states (like the possible directions of magnetism in a metal). It seems appropriate to coin the term *historisis* for this phenomenon.[57]

This, at any rate, is the lesson of Chicken as it applies in this chapter to collective action in pursuit of ethnic ends, where the given historical configuration of the two collective actors arguably assumes the role of pre-commitment in the Chicken game. One might say, to take liberties with a famous saying, that it is *only* if "circumstances [are] directly encountered, given and transmitted from the past" that rational actors are in any position to make a history of their own.[58] For unless each collective actor infers from past history what the other actor is liable to do, neither actor can work out what to do themselves.

Notes

1. Elster has concerned himself with random allocation systems in Part II of *Solomonic Judgements* (Cambridge: C.U.P., 1989).
2. But oppression need not imply discrimination: see note 21 to chapter 6.
3. Not all unequal treatment on gender grounds is unjust unequal treatment, as witness segregated toilet facilities. Nor, in my view, is unequal ethnic treatment always discriminatory: does one have an equal right to attend a church, temple, chapel, synagogue or mosque regardless of whether one shares the faith? I think by contrast that occasions of justified unequal treatment on racial grounds are very closely circumscribed. The only cases are perhaps (i) for certain closely-defined purposes of dramatic representation or reconstruction and (ii) where employment and/or services are offered on a selective basis as a response to an existing pattern of racial disadvantage, as is allowed, for example, under Section 5 of the 1976 Race Relations Act.
4. Michael Banton, *Racial and Ethnic Competititon* (Cambridge: C.U.P., 1983) (hereafter *REC*), p. 29.
5. David J. Smith, *Racial Disadvantage in Britain* (Harmondsworth: Penguin, 1977), p. 124.
6. Smith, Table A34. These are minimum figures of discrimination by skin colour, because of the way the research design controlled for factors such as xenophobia by including a Greek actor in the actor tests. See also pp. 129–32 for the underestimation of the extent of discrimination by minority group members.
7. Michael Dummett, *Immigration: Where the Debate goes Wrong* (London: Action Group on Immigration and Nationality, 1978), p. 5.
8. "It is clear that racialism and direct racial discrimination continue to have a powerful impact on the lives of black people": Colin Brown, *Black and White Britain* (Aldershot: Gower, 1985), p. 318.
9. Runnymede Trust and the Radical Statistics Race Group, *Britain's Black Population* (London: Heinemann Educational Books, 1980), Figure 1.6; *Social Trends 18*, (London: H.M.S.O., 1988), Table 1.7. For a discussion of the relevance of this point to the situation in Northern Ireland, see Rosemary Harris, *Prejudice and Tolerance in Ulster* (Manchester: Manchester University Press, 1972), pp. 214–15, and Jonathan Kelley and Ian McAllister, "The Genesis of Conflict: Religion and Status Attainment in Ulster, 1968", *Sociology*, 18, no. 2 (1984).
10. Michael Banton, "Categorical and Statistical Discrimination", *Ethnic and Racial Studies*, no. 3 (1983) (hereafter "Discrimination"), pp. 279–80.
11. Banton, "Discrimination", p. 280.
12. The theory behind statistical discrimination was developed in the early 1970s by Kenneth Arrow and Edmund Phelphs, and the term was probably first used by Michael Piore in 1970. See Banton "Discrimination", p. 282, n. 2 and Mats Lundahl and Eskil Wodensjo, *Unequal Treatment* (Beckenham: Croom Helm, 1984), p. 43 and p. 78, n. 121.
13. Banton, "Discrimination", pp. 270–71.
14. Lundahl and Wodensjo, p. 44, citing Dennis Aigner and Glen Cain, "Statistical Theories of Discrimination in Labor Markets", *Industrial and Labor Relations Review*, 30, no. 2 (1977).
15. Banton, "Discrimination", p. 277, paraphrasing Clare Denuth, "*Sus*" (London: Runnymede Trust, 1978).

16. Lack of justice might also accompany a perfect correlation, since although two perfectly correlated variables will pick out exactly the same groups of individuals, the same individuals will still have been picked out for the wrong reasons if they have been picked out using the wrong variable. And since justice probably requires that the right people are not only picked out, but picked out for the right reasons, statistical discrimination would still be unjust, even if the statistical correlation of the "right" and "wrong" variables were perfect.

17. Banton, "Discrmination", p. 281.

18. Roemer, "Divide and Conquer", *Bell Journal of Economics*, 10, No. 2 (1979), p. 695; Michael Hechter et. al., "A Theory of Ethnic Collective Action", *International Migration Review*, 16 (1982), p. 414.

19. On gender, see Sylvia Walby, *Gender Segregation at Work* (Milton Keynes: Open University Press, 1988), and on ethnicity, the references cited by Hechter et. al., p. 414 (among other sources). I once heard Roger Scruton argue that capitalism must be a peaceful system because it is based on free market exchange rather than coercive economic relations. This sounds fine, until one bears in mind the concomitant development of slavery, colonialism, the concentration camp, World Wars I and II, genocide . . .

20. Gary Becker, *The Economics of Discrimination* (Chicago: University of Chicago Press, 1971).

21. The existence of a wage differential is not essential to the argument, because the employer could keep down the wages of both groups in the workforce to an equal extent. I am also not quite sure why Roemer calls his theory a "Marxian" theory of wage discrimination when it is the workers whom he blames for it. This is an accolade that Marx could well do without.

22. Thomas C. Schelling, "Dynamic Models of Segregation", *Journal of Mathematical Sociology*, 1 (1971) and *Micromotives and Macrobehaviour*, ch. 4

23. "Employers often deliberately resist such concentration, fearing trouble from their existing workers if they allow numbers to creep past ten to fifteen percent": R.M. Blackburn and Michael Mann, "The Role of Immigrant Labour", in Peter Braham et al., eds., *Discrimination and Disadvantage in Employment* (London: Harper and Row, 1981), p. 83. In the example of the Bradford worsted trade, it certainly seems to have been labour shortage "closely associated with new capital investment" which explained the recruitment of Asian workers. It was even enshrined in agreements with the textile unions still in force in the late 1970s that employers should not recruit foreign labour – either European Volunteer Workers after the war of Asians later on – unless "no suitable British labour [was] available". See B.G. Cohen, "The Employment of Immigrants", in Braham, ed., p. 113 and pp. 117–21; and Ralph Fevre, "Racial discrimination and competition in British trade unions", in *Ethnic and Racial Studies*, 8, no. 4 (1985), p. 564. But this does not mean that divide and rule never occurs, for example in the instances cited by Roemer, "Divide and Conquer", n. 1 and perhaps in the South African gold mines conflict of the 1920s discussed in *REC*, pp. 223–6.

24. Roemer is explicit on p. 704 that his is a "*partial* equilibrium analysis" (my emphasis). An analogous application is suggested by John H. Whyte in "How is the boundary maintained between the two communities in Northern Ireland?", *Ethnic and Racial Studies*, 9, no. 2 (1986), p. 223.

25. "The most promising theory roots [labour market] dualism in the flux and uncertainty that inheres in all economic activity": Michael J. Piore, *Birds of Passage* (Cambridge: C.U.P., 1979), p. 36. See pp. 35–43 for an exposition of the theory condensed in the text here.

26. For Booth, see Keating, ed., *Into Unknown England* (Glasgow: Fontana, 1976) p. 113; Lenin, *Imperialism* (Peking: Foreign Languages Press, 1965); John Foster, *Class Struggle and the Industrial Revolution* (London: Weidenfeld and Nicolson, 1974); Robert Gray, *The Aristocracy of Labour in Nineteenth-century Britain* (London: Macmillan, 1981) and *Capital*, I (Harmondsworth: Penguin, 1976), ch. 25.

27. Piore, ch. 4.

28. Blackburn and Mann, in Braham, ed., p. 81.

29. Many of the essays in the 1985 *Ethnic and Racial Studies* symposium on Banton are disappointing because they do not on the whole rise to the challenge of this generality.

30. *REC*, p. 104.

31. *REC*, p. 104.

32. See *REC*, p. 224 for the contention that "explanations are deductive; something is explained when it is shown to conform to general laws."

33. *REC*, p. 104.

34. In his "Mixed motives and the processes of rationalization", *Ethnic and Racial Studies*, 8, no. 4 (1985), p. 535, Banton seems to argue for the position that the question of motivation is beyond the scope of sociological inquiry, strictly conceived. This would make it odd for him to define types of group by the motivations of their boundary maintenance procedures, as he appears to be doing in his Proposition Two.

35. "The same collection of individuals can be both a racial and an ethnic minority": *REC*, p. 135.

36. Banton hints at this interpretation when he writes: "There is an inclusive, group-forming process. Those groups which are characterized as ethnic *exemplify* the process" (*REC*, p. 106 – my emphasis).

37. On the related question of national identity, compare the views of three writers: "[Shared nationality] is not a matter of the objective characteristics that [a people] possess, but of their shared beliefs: a belief that each belongs together with the rest; that this association is neither transitory nor merely instrumental but stems from a long history of living together which (it is hoped and expected) will continue into the future . . ."; "Nations require ethnic cores if they are to survive. If they lack one, they must 're-invent' one. That means discovering a suitable and convincing past which can be reconstructed and re-presented to members and outsiders"; and "All that I can find to say is that a nation exists when a significant number of people in a community consider themselves to form a nation, or behave as if they formed one". The writers are David Miller, *Market, State and Community* (Oxford: Clarendon Press, 1989), p. 238; Anthony D. Smith, *The Ethnic Origins of Nations* (Oxford: Basil Blackwell, 1986), p. 212; and Hugh Seton-Watson, *Nations and States* (Cambridge: C.U.P., 1977), p. 5.

38. That biological criteria are unlikely ever to give rise to a disjoint classification into racial groups is apparent from asking the question: am I the same race as my mother, or my father?

39. Benedict Anderson, *Imagined Communities* (London: Verso, 1983), p. 16.

40. A claim of comparable difficulty is discussed by Cohen when he considers the possibility (contrary to Weber's account) that Protestant doctrines evolved in a way which adapted them to capitalist social relations. See "Restricted and Inclusive Historical Materialism" in E. Ullmann-Margalit, ed., *The Prism of Science* (Dordrecht: D. Reidel, 1986), pp. 67–8.

41. *REC*, p. 104.

42. *REC*, p. 119.

43. See Hechter et al., p. 413 on this fallacy of "structural theorists": but I am not certain that the allegedly microfoundational theory of the Hechter team avoids the same fallacy. I note in particular that their formalization of the incentive for an individual to embark on collective action (see p. 419) contains a variable p defined as the actor's "estimate of the probability of successful collective action". Now I think that if the Hechter theory were to be genuinely individualistic, p would have to refer instead to the probability that the actor's contribution to the collective action would make the difference between collective failure and collective success. In general, this probability p is very small in a large collective, except if actors are using conditional strategies of the type discussed in section 16.4. This is precisely what gives rise to the free-rider problem which Hechter's theory allegedly overcomes. My proposed solution of the free-rider problem in chapter 17 relies not on the probability of the success of the collective action but on the certainty of suffering sanctions for not taking part in the collective action.

44. The model can apply more generally, and is not restricted to ethnic competition. The monopoly might, for example, consist in a monopoly of private property in some productive resource, so that i and j might be the Friday and Crusoe of Part II, and our discussion would concern the stabilization of capitalist relations of production.

45. An alternative model might involve a competition to establish an exclusive monopoly

of one or other of two groups, each at the expense of the other. I have chosen to concentrate on the struggle between a racist and a non-racist system rather than the struggle between two opposing racisms.

46. This approach bears some resemblance to John Roemer's treatment of the contest between Lenin and the Czar in "Rationalizing Revolutionary Ideology" (Michael Taylor, ed., *Rationality and Revolution* (Cambridge: C.U.P., 1988), but it differs from it for reasons given in note 49 below.

47. Linearity is no doubt an unrealistic assumption, but no more so here than in the usual production models of Part II.

48. This assumption could easily be varied to take account of variable military prowess.

49. In "Rationalizing Revolutionary Ideology", Roemer associates particular probabilities of collective success with each combination of the incomes and penalties of his model (equivalent to the monopoly rewards and taxes in my model). My guess is that this formal difference is responsible for some of the difference in the predictions of the two models, which are in any case addressed to somewhat different questions.

50. K. Marx and F. Engels, *Manifesto of the Communist Party* (Moscow: Progress Publishers, 1953), p. 41.

51. This is one of the problems with military technology; it is possible to do a lot more damage with a gun than it costs to fire a gun, or even to make it and fire it.

52. Much of the excitement of any real contest derives of course from the fact that the precise position of these watersheds is unknown to the participants, but the perfect information assumption is no more and no less unrealistic here than it is when applied within standard economic theory.

53. Gellner points out that the rough number of 200 different states in the world is much smaller than the rough number of 8000 different languages (Ernest Gellner, *Nations and Nationalism* (Oxford: Basil Blackwell, 1983), p. 44).

54. Chicken keeps rearing its head not through some fowl preference of the author, but because it is paradigmatic: the prototype in the two-person case for any inegalitarian equilibrium in the N-person symmetric binary-choice game. See "Symmetry and Social Division", *Behavioral Science*, 34, no. 3 (1989), Section 7, and Section 16.2 below.

55. John Roemer, "'Rational choice' Marxism", in John Roemer, ed., *Analytical Marxism* (Cambridge: C.U.P., 1986), p. 196.

56. "'Rational choice' Marxism"; p. 196.

57. I do not claim that this is an original way of conceiving the relation between theory and history. Although it departs from Roemer's formulation in "'Rational choice' Marxism", it conforms with his position in "History's effect on the distribution of income", *Social Science Information*, 26, no. 2 (1987) in which the word "hysterisis" appears on p. 44. Elster has also remarked that "if there are multiple equilibria, accident and history might provide the explanation" (*Nuts and Bolts for the Social Sciences* (Cambridge: C.U.P., 1989), p. 158).

58. K. Marx, *The Eighteenth Brumaire of Louis Bonaparte* (Moscow: Progress Publishers, 1934), p. 10.

PART VII

Socialism and Social Division

== 15 ==

Communism and Socialism

15.1 Communism

Karl Marx before the Gates of Eden

What Marx said about the transition to communism is consistent with the following thought: beyond the opposition between the social and the material lies the fully social individual.[1]

The most important instance of the opposition between the material and social is that between the material forces of production and the social relations of production, discussed at length in Part I. This opposition leads to technological development, with its attendant phenomena of class struggle and political revolution. In so far as they are implicated in the causes of this process, whole systems of thought and whole institutional orders, such as the state, are subsumed under the same contradiction between the material and the social. But Marx is quite happy to expand the scope of the contrast to include the opposition between the country and the city, the existence of separate nationalities, and other phenomena of very broad historical significance.[2]

When reading Marx in the light of this persistent contrast, it is easy to miss the fact that the opposition between the material and social exists in company with a third pole of his thought, namely the individual. This acts as a kind of latent counterpoint to the interaction of the social with the material.

The connection between the individual on the one hand and the social-cum-material on the other is effected largely through the theory of alienation. This holds that powers belonging properly to individuals become vested in an external entity constituted in the opposition between the material and the social, and this entity returns to oppress the individuals upon whose alienated powers it feeds. This entity is a terrifying monster that assumes a multitude of poisonous forms – religions, of course, and the cherished "illusions of the epoch", but also the division of labour, state, family, property, money, social class and history – everything in fact that Marx spends his life discussing.[3]

Now Marx never denies that these various processes and forms of social organization are conducted by real individuals, or that individuals are deeply implicated in their functioning. In his Preface to the First Edition of *Capital*, he wrote.

> I do not by any means depict the capitalist and the landowner in rosy colours. But individuals are dealt with here only in so far as they are the personifications of economic categories, the bearers of particular class-relations and interests. My standpoint, from which the development of the economic formation of society is perceived as a process of natural history, can less than any other make the individual responsible for relations whose creature he remains, socially speaking, however much he may subjectively raise himself above them.[4]

I think Marx means here exactly what he says: the effect of capital – the whole system of political economy he is about to analyse – is to divide individuals into two. There is a socio-material complex, or better, Komplex (which I shall call hereafter by the cruel letter K), within which capitalism, or better, Kapitalism, lies. K is Mordor, Babylon, the Castle. People relate to this fundamentally alien construction only in so far as they take roles within it: K enters their soul. Individuals are part of K, true, but K has become a part of them, and the really objectionable fact is the second not the first. What seems to be wrong with taking roles in the socio-material complex K, according to Marx, is first that the roles are beyond the control of the individual who assumes the role, and secondly that they are *deformative*: they lead to a one-sided development, or over-specialization of the individual.

Capitalism is particularly bad in this respect because it represents the highest development of the contradiction between the individual and society. (This is only to be expected – name any contradiction, and you will discover that capitalism has the most profound version of it). Marx even hazards that "the division between the personal and the class individual, the accidental nature of the conditions of life for the individual, appears only with the emergence of class, which is itself a product of the bourgeoisie".[5]

Whether or not the problem of personal bifurcation is peculiar to the modern era, the tension has become chronic in the modern world between the spectacular development of human powers in general – expressed by the enormous development of K – and the stunted growth of human individuals in particular.[6] One-sidedness is endemic, whether it appears in the monotony of detail labour in the capitalist process of production, or the Benthamite attempt to reduce all social thinking to the single standpoint of utility – to perceptions congenial to the circumstances of one class alone.[7]

In his analysis of the material/social complex K, with its technologically determined inter-relationships of roles and ideas, Marx is a thoroughgoing structuralist, sociologically speaking. Individuals are not "responsible for relations whose creature [they] remain". Individuals-in-themselves have fled the scene, in favour of the roles individuals are required to fill. But those who misguidedly regard Marx on this evidence as a structuralist thinker overlook one vital feature of his attitude to what he studies: *for Marx, the fact that a structuralist analysis is applicable to K is precisely what is wrong with K.*

Slightly more directly: Marx counterposes to K and all its works an alternative vision of life under which individuals recoup all the powers vested in alienated form in K and exercise those powers freely for themselves. Marx's abiding theoretical passions are a hatred for K and a love of what transcends it. In a society the other side of K, one-sidedness of individual development is finally overcome, and "the free development of each is the condition for the free development of all."[8] It is as if humankind sloughs off the straitjacket imposed by K, and enters into its true kingdom. As Marx puts it in his enigmatic Tenth Thesis on Feuerbach: "The standpoint of the old materialism is civil society; the standpoint of the new is human society, or social humanity."[9]

It is often said that Marx did not have an articulated vision of communism, partly out of a prudential motive: he did not wish to predict future developments he could not foresee. This seems pretty unlikely to me. Marx is not notable for his caution as a thinker, nor did he eschew large forward-looking claims. In fact, the larger the claim, the more he tended to like it. Here he is on communism in the *German Ideology*:[10]

> Communism differs from all previous movements in that it overturns the basis of all earlier relations of production and intercourse and for the first time consciously treats all natural premises as the creatures of hitherto existing men, strips them of their natural character and subjugates them to the power of the united individuals. Its organisation is, therefore, essentially economic, the material production of the conditions of this unity; it turns existing conditions into conditions of unity. The reality, which communism is creating, is precisely the true basis for rendering it impossible that anything should exist independently of individuals, insofar as reality is only a product of the preceding intercourse of individuals themselves.[10]

There is no false modesty on behalf of the future in this passage. But note also the content of the vision it displays. The relation between individuals and their conditions is reversed, compared to the prologue of *Capital*. The same word is used, but in exactly opposite application. In K, individuals are "creatures" of their social and material conditions, but in communism, social-material conditions are the "creatures" of the individuals. Everything issues from, and returns to, some truly individual personality: nothing "should exist independently of individuals". This is a striking formulation for the thinker whose chief fault is allegedly a neglect of the individual.

The point cannot be emphasized too strongly: *Marx's vision creates an individualist's Utopia.* Heaven on earth occurs when human beings come into their own for the first time in history, in the free exercise of all their manifold powers and possibilities. For then,

> the liberation of each single individual will be accomplished in the measure in which history becomes transformed into world history ... it is clear that the real intellectual wealth of the individual depends entirely on the wealth of his real connections. Only then will the separate individuals be liberated from the various national and local barriers, be brought into practical connection with the material and intellectual production of the whole world and be put in a position to acquire the capacity to enjoy this all-sided production of the whole earth (the creations of man). *All round* dependence, this natural form of the *world-historical* co-operation of individuals, will be transformed by this communist revolution into the control and conscious mastery of these powers, which, born of the action of men on one another, have till now overawed and governed men as powers completely alien to them. [11]

The powers in the alien complex that "have till now overawed and governed men" derive from individuals; they are "born of the action of men on one another", but the emancipation of individuals from the complex is at once a victory over material conditions, and over the whole social realm as an external power which coerces the individual. We know too, given Marx's materialism, that the key premise of such an emancipation is material emancipation, and indeed he goes on to write that

> this development of the productive forces (which itself implies the actual empirical existence of men in their world-historical, instead of local, being) is an absolutely necessary practical premise because without it *want* is merely made general and with destitution the struggle for necessities and all the old filthy business would necessarily be reproduced. [12]

Freed from the socio-material complex, and the "illusory community life" induced by the socio-material complex in the form of state, family or tribe, individuals can express their individuality in a fully social form, under which the individual interest no longer competes with the general interest.[13]

Cohen is right to say of the true community life implicitly counterposed here to its illusory predecessor that "the liberated association of individuals is less a new social structure than freedom from social structure."[14] But I think it is less satisfactory to characterize the liberation – as Cohen does – as a "liberation of the content". In his reading, which I usually follow, the form-content metaphor describes the relation of the social to the material: the material is the content, and the social is the form taken by the material content. Now Cohen points out that Marx sometimes uses the term "human" to denote the "bare human": the natural individual outside social relationships, with various biological appetites and needs. In this sense, the "human" belongs to Marx's material vocabulary, where she or he exists in contrast with the social, or, as we might say, socialized individual.[15]

Liberation of such a human being would indeed be liberation of the content – of the person freed to follow his or her natural inclinations. But I am certain that Marx did not hold this Romantic view.[16] I note the stress he lays on the cultural range of the communist individual, the sense of humankind now standing on the shoulders of all previous generations, the striking phrases from the Tenth Thesis – "human society, or social humanity". These phrases conjoin key terms of the social and material vocabularies. Communism is not the liberation of the material individual from the social individual: it is the synthesis of the two. Under this synthesis, the form-content couplet is suppressed by the joint activity of newly integrated human beings, who are able in one and the same movement to dispense with social form and impose themselves on material content. Communism "strips [natural premises] of their natural character and subjugates them to the power of the united individuals."[17] It follows that "in communist society, where nobody has one exclusive sphere of activity but each can become accomplished in any branch he wishes, society regulates the general production and thus makes it possible for me to do one thing today and another tomorrow, to hunt in the morning, fish in the afternoon, rear cattle in the evening, criticize after dinner, just as I have a mind, without ever becoming hunter, fisherman, herdsman or critic."[18]

Are these heady visions from the *German Ideology* of 1845–6 merely adolescent outpourings, youthful solecisms from Marx before he settled down to the serious business of K-theory, and wore himself out writing *Capital*? I think not, for an identical visionary landscape is lit in a bolt of lightning delivered thirty years later, when Marx was as mature as he ever would become:

In a higher phase of communist society, after the enslaving subordination of
the individual to the division of labour and with it also the antithesis between
mental and physical labour, has vanished; after labour has become not only
a means of life but itself life's prime want; after the productive forces have
also increased with the all-round development of the individual and all the
springs of co-operative wealth flow more abundantly – only then can the narrow
horizon of bourgeois right be crossed in its entirety and society inscribe on
its banners: From each according to ability, to each according to need.[19]

The vision unfolds line by line: "the enslaving subordination of the individual to the division of labour" is not only a recapitulation of the Babylon
evoked in *German Ideology*; it is a full-dress rehearsal using the same
portmanteau term.[20] In order to overcome this Babylon the productive
forces must have increased, and this increase moves in step with the progress of human individuals. It is not just that higher productivity releases
humankind from material cares so that they may pursue higher aims;
higher productivity is one expression of greater "all round" human
powers. Given these powers, the "springs of co-operative wealth" start
up spontaneously from a million independent centres, and merge into
a great confluence of shared resourcefulness, from which individuals can
refresh themselves at will: "from each according to ability, to each according to need".

If society is able to write such words on its banners only when the
narrow horizon of bourgeois right has been crossed, it follows that what
society intends by the words cannot be a new schedule of bourgeois rights.
It cannot be that each of us is *entitled* to what she needs or *obliged* to
produce according to ability. The formula does not constitute a new *rule*
of distribution – some ultimate variant of a needs-contribution principle.
It is instead a *description* of what altered individuals will do in altered
circumstances, when the social and the individual interest are no longer
at loggerheads, and individuals who are free produce according to ability,
because this is just what free individuals want to do.

And, given the enormous productivity of productive activity, distribution can occur on demand. It is true that, if one stopped to make the
calculation, those with high ability and low needs would be contributing
more to the stock of co-operative wealth, which would be consumed
disproportionately by those with low ability and high needs. But we are
not here considering short commons. Those with high ability do not suffer
a burden as a result of greater labour, because "labour has become life's
prime want". To impose equality would be to decrease everyone's welfare,
and restrict self-expression, under circumstances in which no-one's freedom needs to be infringed. Any attempt at social control would be a
gratuitous act. We are here beyond roles, and norms, and calculations

of equality. In this higher phase of communism, the vicious complex K is finally laid to rest. Communism is true individuality, and, for that very reason, true community.

Jon Elster's icy blast

Marx on communism is a sauna bath of feverish imagining. What better corrective than a roll in the snow and an application of birch twigs from Professor Elster?[21]

Elster objects to the assumptions Marx makes about both individuals and their social conditions. According to Elster, the ideal of all-round development is an impossible dream, because if you try to be really good at more than one or two things, you end up being pretty hopeless at nearly everything. It is also a welcome side-effect of the oppressive social structures against which Marx inveighs that they protect us all against our lack of talent. One who tries hard and still fails under capitalism can always blame the system, whereas under communism there will be no-one else to carry the can. In communism, we stand before ourselves naked and abashed, like Protestants before their Maker. "Could it be an important consequence of human finitude," asks Elster, "that our failures would be unendurable if we had only ourselves to blame for them?"[22]

Also, there are more conceptions of the good life than Marx is eager to allow. Karl's communist is a very busy body, who can do anything she pleases, as long as it engages her deepest creative impulses. There is plenty of time in Marx's Utopia for being a concert pianist or a brain surgeon, less time for catching the late movie on TV.[23] Suppose in any case that each of us is preoccupied with creating our unique personal monument to the human spirit. Who will be left free to appreciate the great works we have made?

If Marx's view of fundamental human motivation is intolerably energetic, his projection of future social conditions is absurdly unrealistic. Resources will always be scarce in relation to the demands we make upon them; the individual interest can never chime completely with the general interest, nor will the burdens of labour ever be removed.[24] There will be pain, conflict and frustration of a systematic sort under any conceivable disposition of the social world. Marx

conceived of communism as a society of individual producers in spontaneous co-ordination, much as the cells in a body work together for the common good, each of them reflecting the whole from its point of view. No such society will ever exist; to believe it will is to court disaster. Although Marx stood for an *ethical* individualism in his approach to communism, he did not see that the actual organisation must also take into account the possibilities and limitations of individuals. Had he done so – as we today must do – he might have set his goals lower and made it possible to approximate even his undiluted goals to a greater degree.[25]

If Marx had enjoyed the benefit of Professor Elster's lecture, he might indeed "have set his goals lower". Yet I cannot help feeling that if Marx had thus trimmed his sails, he would not have been Marx, and we would not be in a position today to inject that common sense into Marx's vision which Elster instructs us all to do.

15.2   Socialism

Democracy and equality

Before he took off for the land of cockayne, Marx described in the *Critique of the Gotha Programme* a lower phase of communist society. This account, briefly analysed in section 6.2, is the closest Marx got to a definition of socialism.[26] Robert Van der Veen and Philippe Van Parijs have recently paraphrased this definition as invoking "a society in which workers collectively own the means of production and in which therefore they collectively decide what these should be used for and how the resulting product should be distributed, namely according to the principle 'to each according to his labour'."[27]

Following Erik Olin Wright, I will call this the VP definition of socialism, leaving for later comment the question of how faithful VP socialism actually is to the conception outlined in *The Critique of the Gotha Programme*.[28] The core idea of VP socialism is evidently, and reasonably, the idea of collective ownership. But the ambiguity in the idea is easily revealed by asking what happens if the workers collectively decide that the resulting product should be distributed according to some principle entirely different from "to each according to labour". The VP definition runs together at least three distinct conceptions of what collective ownership might entail: collective management of resources; collective decision on the principles that are to govern the management and allocation of resources; and a specific rule for the allocation of consumption goods amongst the members of the relevant collective, such as "to each according to labour".[29]

In very broad outline, the first two aspects of collective ownership appeal to democratic values and the third appeals to egalitarian values, so that the tensions in the definition of socialist collective ownership are tensions within and between these two sets of values.

An emphasis on the democratic side of the equation is prominent in the work of Wright. In his view, socialism actually consists in an increasingly democratic control over the productive forces, exercised by workers through political systems which keep any specialized stratum of managers or technocrats on a suitably short leash.

In this conceptualization of socialism, a socialist society is essentially a kind of non-bureaucratic technocracy. Experts control their own skills or knowledge within production, and by virtue of such control are able to appropriate some of the surplus from production. However, because of the democratization of organisation assets, the actual making of planning decisions would not be under the direct control of experts but would be made through some kind of democratic procedure (this is in effect what democratization of organisation-assets means: equalizing control over the planning and co-ordination of social production).[30]

Two points are in order, the first of which relates to a technical issue in contemporary class theory. Wright's term "organisation assets" does not denote, as one might think, the material and social assets possessed by a given organization. The term refers instead to Wright's idea that *organization is itself an asset*. It follows, as Wright says, that democratizing the economy is equivalent to equalizing control over organization, just as the egalitarian redistribution of money would be equivalent to equalizing free market access to forces of production. This allows Wright to bring management under the scope of John Roemer's theory of class, and incidentally blurs the distinction between – or perhaps triumphantly synthesizes – exploitation-centred and domination-centred theories of social class.[31] It also tends to make democratic values into a branch (the political branch) of egalitarian values. We may hope that this elision of the political with the economic will not unduly confuse the discussion.

The second point is that Wright does not specify in any detail what he means by democratization of power within each organization. He seems to have in mind the collective management of resources, probably via a fairly direct democracy ("the actual making of planning decisions would not be under the direct control of experts"). Now a direct democracy is not feasible for an enterprise employing more than a rather small number of people: I would put the number at somewhere between 25 and 100, but it is in any case less than 1000. And even though one can imagine pyramiding arrangements which might allow a very large company to count as an indirect economic democracy (as one presumably allows very large nation-states sometimes to count as indirect political democracies), the virtues claimed for workers' control are bound to be attenuated as the number of steps in the pyramid increases, and the real centres of power once again recede beyond the workers' ken.

These considerations suggest that collective ownership in a large society must involve, at best, *a revisable democratic decision about the general form of the exclusive property rights with which smaller productive units are to be endowed.* What public ownership means in practice is public control over the content of private ownership. The property rights given to each productive unit will typically define (i) the boundaries of the relevant ownership unit (for instance, who has a vote in the management election); (ii) the kinds of transactions which the productive unit can undertake as it deploys its material and social assets; and (iii) the relative proportions and destinations of the income streams generated by the disposition of the assets.

In terms of the three dimensions of collective ownership isolated above, there would be collective decision at the national or international level about the principles which are to govern the actual management of resources in the productive unit. It is then easy to generate a possible contradiction between collectivization in the sense of democratically-achieved management principles and collectivization in the sense of democratic management.

Imagine, for example, that an international referendum is held which specifies that any group of adults can constitute themselves an ownership unit, under one of two possible *management laws*, which the referendum is to decide between. On the ballot paper are

Management law one: There must be direct democracy in the management of each ownership unit.

Management law two: Each ownership unit must decide by direct democracy what its management law will be.

The first law decentralizes management, whereas the second decentralizes managerial sovereignty, and there is a good deal of difference between the two cases. Suppose, for example, that the world passes the second law. Then workers in a particular unit might decide that they did not want responsibility for management, so they could give specialist managers control over the operation of the plant, and they could even bind themselves Ulysses-fashion against the temptation to resume managerial control by selling all the voting rights in the assets of the company as shares on the open market.

Suppose, again, that some large group of approximately two hundred million people constitute themselves one of the ownership units, and call themselves, naturally enough, us. (They are also a proud people, so they usually write us thus: US.) This particular electorate is now free, under international management law two, to decide what its internal management arrangements will be. This US electorate is, we suppose, well versed in political philosophy. It has digested its John Rawls and its Adam Smith, but is unimpressed by its John Roemer. It believes that justice is served when social arrangements conduce to maximize the welfare of the least advantaged members of society. It believes moreover that despite the great inequalities it is known to breed, capitalism meets the Rawlsian test better than any other system. Then the US electorate votes recurrently to sustain capitalist social relations, with unfettered private property rights and no limit on the potential development of social inequality.

These stories are intended to show that in a world governed by management law two, which has deliberately decentralized economic sovereignty, a whole variety of different ownership institutions might be expected to develop, including some fairly standard capitalist ones. Does such a world implement democratization of the forces of production more or less fully than another world which passes the first law, thereby imposing democratically a uniform workers' democracy within each productive unit?

The basic point is that to define socialism by the democratic character of its economic institutions is to define it procedurally. And once socialism is defined procedurally, it would be impossible to quarrel with the outcome of any socialistically-sound decision procedure, even if the outcome looked extremely unsocialist according to other understandings of what socialism entails. So if it is accepted that unbridled capitalism might result from the passage of a management law like law two above, and that no socialist can support unbridled capitalism, it follows that no socialist can adopt a purely procedural definition of socialism. *Socialists have an irreducible commitment to equality, independent of any commitment they might also have to democracy.* (If Wright's conceptual assimilation of democracy to equality is accepted, the conclusion reads: socialists have an irreducible commitment to economic equality, independent of any commitment they might also have to political equality.)

This suggests that the alternative to a procedural definition of socialism, such as Wright's, is a *substantive* definition, which specifies the content of the social access rules for consumption units – that is, the content of the rules by which individuals (or households) regulate their exchange with society vis-à-vis consumption goods.[32] We have seen Van der Veen and Van Parijs recommend the principle "to each according to labour" and commend it as the distributive principle of Marx's *Gotha Programme* socialism. Their formulation is slightly misleading. As I argued in 6.3, Marx advanced a rather primitive version of a combined needs-contribution principle, not the pure contribution principle attributed to him by Van der Veen and Van Parijs. I suggested that the most plausible rationale for the needs-contribution principle was Marx's commitment to welfare egalitarianism. And it is true (by the results of 10.3) that in a world of equally needy, equally able persons, the application of any combined needs-contribution principle (or a pure contribution principle) will lead to an equal welfare outcome. It would then be plausible to define socialism as *a society of equal welfare with respect to the production and consumption of scarce goods.* Given the way that differential welfare was made a necessary condition of class division by the definition of 11.3, we arrive at a compact statement of the substantive definition: *socialism requires a classless society.*

A yet more general substantive definition of socialism, which I am happy to endorse, extends the notion of welfare equality to cover any social division. In that case socialism would be defined substantively as: *a society without social division.*

I will proceed with these definitions because I am mainly concerned in this book with just such a world of equally needy, equally able actors, but I wish to state a problem concerning the general applicability of the definitions which I am frankly unable to resolve. It was also shown in 10.3 that if needs and/or abilities differ then needs-contribution principles working via the short commons mechanism will *not* implement equal welfare. If the generically socialist social access rules thus fail to conform with their most plausible ethical foundation, one is left with a formidable problem of how, precisely, to define socialist distributive principles among unequal individuals.

Marx grappled with this problem in the passages of his *Critique of the Gotha Programme* preceding the disclaimer that "to avoid all these defects [in the proposed socialist distribution principle], right instead of being equal would have to be unequal." Yet Marx nowhere specified exactly how the rights should be made unequal in order to overcome the "defects" in his original disjunctive needs-contribution proposal. And recent work on the theoretical and normative problems in this field has hardly yielded conclusive results. I must therefore rest content with the thought that while the implication of the socialist's indispensable commitment to equality is clear enough in a social world composed of equal individuals, it is otherwise the subject of continuing debate.[33]

Given that equality (of some kind) is indispensable to socialism, we come to another question: is democracy dispensable? I entertained above the possibility that a class-ridden capitalist society might emerge from a procedure of indirect economic democracy (that is, from collective ownership, in one sense of the term). I now consider the opposite possibility, which is – or at least was – all too real, historically speaking: an egalitarian distribution of assets, and consequent welfare, is imposed undemocratically. Lack of democracy exists either in the polity, in the form of one-party rule, or economically, in the form of bureaucratic central planning, and lack of workers' control in the productive unit. Do we consider such a society socialist, despite its lack of democracy? The answer turns on two considerations.

First, it might be argued that centralized control leads to new social divisions, in that those who have control of the disposition of forces of production use that control to enhance their access to consumption goods (and welfare more generally). There is exploitation by state and party officials of the lack of political leverage possessed by the lay public. It is fairly clear that to the extent that the regime is thus corrupt (according to the egalitarian standard we set the regime, and that it ought to set itself), the regime is not a socialist regime, because socialism requires the absence of such social class division. There is no conflict of values in this judgement, because lack of democracy has caused inequality, and the regime stands condemned on both counts.

More difficult is the case in which the party officials are models of Spartan virtue. The regime is spotless in its egalitarian distribution of consumption goods, educational opportunities and the like, all administered by a selfless priesthood of public service. I note that the effect of Wright's conceptualization of organization assets is to prejudge this question against the selfless priesthood. Wright's motive is a worthy one: to deny the title socialism to Stalinist regimes (even uncorrupted ones).[34] His method has been to assimilate political power to the more normal varieties of economic resource, so that the distinction between leaders and led (or managers and workers, officials and lay public), is in itself a social division – and a class division, in so far as it entails differential control over forces of production. The judgement is that having an equal say in the use of a resource is as valuable as having an equal income from the use of the resource. It corresponds to the idea that welfare derives from process as well as outcome or, equivalently, that alienation harms as well as exploitation. Because on this view democracy is a form of equality, the overall socialist commitment to equality entails a commitment to democracy.

Whether or not Wright's judgement is accepted is ultimately a matter of personal values, but it is worth saying that it would be very odd for a Marxist to refuse it. For although, as we have seen, Marx's vision of communism was never intended to apply to any historical situation in which talk of rights, or equality, was appropriate, the value that informs his vision is almost solely one of self-determination. It is doubtful, moreover, that the seal which separates the realm of freedom from the realm of necessity is so impervious that what is the primary value in the first realm enjoys no resonance in the second. So I think a Marxian socialist above all others should deny the adjective socialist to a society that derides the value of democracy either in its state or its economy.[35]

Yet isn't this a recipe for prevarication? If the socialist is defined as a person with indispensable commitments to both democracy and equality, what happens when they clash?

The first point is that socialists are not alone in avowing values which
may come into conflict. A liberal democrat is much more a contradiction
in terms than a democratic socialist. For any distinctive liberal (by which
I mean a libertarian) the limits of democracy are set by inalienable rights,
and an inalienable right does not mean a right revocable by a two-thirds
majority of the Congress. Distinctively liberal liberals can therefore be
democrats only in so far as the democracy decides issues that are unimpor-
tant to them as liberals.

This point is as true of right-wing libertarians, whose mission in life
has been to protect private property rights against the incursions of democracy, as it is of left-wing libertarians, like Hillel Steiner, whose aim has
been to develop a levelling argument within a liberal framework.[36] For
the upshot of Steiner's several attempts to limit the rights of private appropriation could not be an increase in the latitude of Parliamentary powers
to determine rights. If, for example, the appropriators of natural resources
owe compensation to the rest of us for the use of the Earth we all own
jointly as a natural right, the legislature has a bounden duty to impose
the necessary taxation, just as it would have the bounden duty to resist
such taxation to the death, were private owners held to enjoy a legitimate
right of exclusive appropriation of the same resources.

The democratic credentials of democratic socialists do not emerge too
badly from this comparison. There is another point which may count
in their favour. The socialist facing a genuine quandary of values, torn
between democracy and equality, may not be very much torn in the two
cases most pressing to decide, namely Western capitalism and Eastern
state (non)socialism.

I have perhaps been rather generous to capitalism in imagining that
it could have come about as a result of a democratic procedure, thereby
qualifying as a species of collective ownership (in one meaning of the
latter term). Democratic elections in the West clearly do not have the
character of an open referendum on property rights. A Western election
is no disinterested collective enquiry into the best arrangements for society
conducted by an electorate of judicious persons sheltered behind a Rawlsian veil of ignorance regarding their prospective standings in the post-
election society. So the fact that capitalist societies can be political democracies, inestimably valuable though that is, does not imply that their
private property arrangements have been democratically achieved.

When we turn to consider the content of capitalist property arrangements rather than the manner of their achievement, Western capitalism
as a whole is evidently so undemocratic in its property rights, and so
unequal in its distribution of resources, that no socialist will have difficulty
criticizing it in both respects.[37] It is no coincidence that Mrs Thatcher
in office was both very undemocratic and highly inegalitarian. Britain

and the USA for two would have to go a very long way towards democracy, which would probably lead to considerably greater equality, before
a choice would ever be forced between the two values.

Eastern state (non)socialism on the other hand has been so undemocratic (and hence unsocialist) that it can afford to become much more democratic, even if that means that it may become somewhat less equal (which
is not altogether obvious: democratization may arguably lead to greater
equality in some respects – of political power and access to resources
– as well as fostering greater inequality in other respects, above all by
the introduction of market mechanisms).

Socialism, in sum, can be said to exist either within a democratic society
or within an undivided society. These definitions of socialism, and their
corresponding political aspirations, do not always coincide. But neither
do they always compete. And such problems are inherent in any programme which treats neither democracy nor equality as a dispensable
luxury.

Basic wealth and basic income

If a socialist society is defined (in one of its two major aspects) as a
society without social division, what would be necessary to achieve it?
The answer will depend on the type of social division one wishes to remedy,
and what its causes are.

John Roemer's work suggests that in market societies inequalities in
wealth lead to class divisions and associated welfare differentials. The
remedy for this form of division is plainly the equalization of wealth.
Yet this might not imply a complete equalization of wealth. In section
6.4, I advanced what I regarded as the bedrock case against capitalism.
The case seemed especially strong because all the criticisms one could
make of capitalism converged within it. According to the bedrock case,
the really objectionable feature of free-market capitalism is that the propertyless classes depend for their access to the means of life on an unequal
contract of labour exchange with the propertied classes. Even a right-wing
libertarian ought to condemn this state of affairs, because the labour
contract is coerced, and hence unjust, by the standard libertarian criterion
of justice in transfer.

Now this kernel of capitalist exploitation would be removed by giving
the propertyless an amount of property (or income) sufficient to meet
their subsistence requirements, thus ending their dependence on the
wealthy for access to the means of life. The amount required to achieve
this result would be a wealth $w = 1$ in the model of chapter 4. And
we also know from chapter 4 that this need not entail a complete equalization of wealth in the society. Under the step-shape preferences of the

subsistence model, no-one will want to work longer than the subsistence minimum, and if everyone has enough wealth to gain subsistence from self-employment, no-one will become a wage-labourer, and there may be a great deal of unused wealth in the hands of wealthy would-be capitalists.

Yet it may be unrealistic to expect that large sums of money will be lying in shoe boxes under the beds of frustrated capitalists, because it will be unrealistic to expect preferences for work to behave strictly like step-functions. Perhaps labour is still a burden, but income has independent appeal, so people are willing to work a little more to bring home extra pay, employing in the process more of the available social capital. This is where Roemer's accumulation models enter the picture. If we skate lightly over the counter-example discussed in 5.4, the normal social correlations apply in the accumulation models: the wealthy employ the poor, who work longer hours than the wealthy. It follows that if the relative preferences for labour and income vary in the same way for everyone in the society, then the wealthy enjoy higher welfare than the poor at a competitive equilibrium.[38] A welfare egalitarian would require a complete equalization of wealth in the society of accumulators, more thorough than might be required to meet the bedrock case against capitalism in the society of subsistence actors.

Now it is difficult to determine whether the more radical or the less radical programme would command greater popular support, if people decided their views simply on the basis of whether they would lose or gain resources from the redistribution, all other things being equal. It all depends on the existing distribution of resources, although the fact that in actually existing capitalist societies distributions are highly skewed tends to suggest that a numerical majority would gain from a radical redistribution (provided it could be costlessly accomplished, of course).

The less radical redistribution nevertheless has stronger arguments in its favour. The idea of a basic guarantee of livelihood has powerful moral appeal, and the idea that the proletariat is unfairly compelled to accept an unequal burden is clearest in the bedrock case, and its associated subsistence model of capitalism. In life above the breadline, there is greater opportunity for choice, and arguably more responsibility for outcomes.[39]

I will therefore concentrate in what follows on the less radical forms of redistribution designed to meet the bedrock case. Given that the market mechanism is used to distribute final consumption goods, there are two ways to implement a subsistence standard: either by giving a lump-sum grant of wealth which would be sufficient to generate a subsistence income, or by paying a subsistence income directly.

The lump-sum approach would give everyone a wealth $w = 1$ at the age of, say, eighteen. As a good rational actor in one of Roemer's subsistence models, the young person will invest all their new found wealth in their own small business. This is a rather appealingly Thatcherite form of anti-Thatcherism. The proposal sounds great for the spirit of enterprise and yet it will lead to the immediate demise of capitalism, because the labour market will dry up forthwith.

Yet we might have to reckon in practice with extra-rational conduct. Suppose that the young person blows all his (say his) capital on a brand new car, which he neglects to insure, and piles up on his first motorway trip, incurring extensive third party liabilities and an expensive stay in hospital. Who picks up the tab? Has he blown his once-in-a-lifetime chance of personal independence – so tough? Or do the rest of us still retain some responsibility to make good the damage he has done?[39]

The alternative to basic wealth is basic income, which comes in two versions: conditional and unconditional. The conditional version is familiar from Western welfare systems, where subsistence income is conditional on lack of wage earnings or other means of support, or on past labour contributions (via unemployment insurance schemes). The alternative is the idea of an unconditional basic income: a periodic payment to every person in the society regardless of any other circumstances. I will call this Basic Income, with capital letters. The idea was mooted by Bertrand Russell and G.D.H. Cole between the wars, was revived among Claimants Unions and publicized by Bill Jordan in the early 1970s, and has generated a great deal of discussion in the 1980s since Robert Van der Veen and Philippe Van Parijs proposed that unconditional Basic Income might constitute a "capitalist road to communism".[40]

Proponents of the scheme claim many advantages for it: it would eliminate the poverty traps which seem to arise under any system of conditional assistance payments; it would end at a stroke the stigmatization of welfare claimants; it would make redundant overnight nearly the whole baroqueracy of social security; it would restore work incentives to the poor and make it much easier to introduce the new patterns of flexible retraining and work sharing that the post-modern economy of the twenty-first century will demand.

I restrict myself to a comment on the idea that this scheme, whatever its other merits, constitutes a "capitalist road to communism". I comment first on the capitalist nature of the road and then on the communist nature of its destination. In a vigorous rejoinder to Van der Veen and Van Parijs, Wright complains that the introduction of a Basic Income scheme is likely to affect capitalist property rights to such an extent that the hypothetical society of the transition could not be plausibly represented as a capitalist society.[41] The reason is that Basic Income is an incredibly expensive scheme, and capitalists are not going to hang around to be taxed to the extent necessary to finance the scheme. So great restrictions would have to be imposed on the mobility of capital – unless, of course, the scheme was introduced world-wide: in which case capital would no doubt migrate to Mars.

I am sure Wright is correct on this point, but I am not sure his argument is especially an argument against the Basic Income scheme. Redistribution of money on a scale necessary to meet even the bedrock case against capitalism is an expensive business, however it is achieved, and it will always involve readjustments of property rights which the propertied classes will resist rather fiercely. His argument is an argument for the difficulty of any wholesale redistribution of resources in an egalitarian direction.

A more direct argument that Basic Income is not obviously a capitalist measure is that the effect of a sufficiently generous Basic Income is precisely to eliminate bedrock capitalist exploitation. Faced with a society of Basic Income recipients, capitalists' bargaining position is weakened, because they are less likely to be able to fill the awful jobs they offer at awful rates of pay. Unconditional Basic Income appears to achieve this result more smoothly than conditional welfare schemes, precisely because it eliminates the punitive, disincentive effect of the conditional scheme. People in a Basic Income society do not appear to be faced with Hobson's choice: either a job they don't want or the stigma of claimant status. Indeed, it would be a good anti-capitalist argument in favour of Basic Income that it eliminated the worst form of capitalist exploitation in a non-divisive fashion.[42] From the capitalist point of view, Basic Income adds insult to injury: profits taxed to high heaven so that the poor can have free hand-outs which make them reluctant to work for us anymore. I should coco!

So if Basic Income does not in any obvious sense place us on a capitalist road, does the Basic Income path nevertheless lead in the direction of communism?

The argument that it does depends on the contentions that (i) Basic Income distributes according to need, and (ii) a communist society is a society based on the principle of distribution according to need. It is then held to follow that a society approaches nearer to communism the higher the level of Basic Income it provides. As we increase the level of the Basic Income that is paid, a greater proportion of output is distributed along communist lines, and eventually everything goes as Marx would have wished.

Unfortunately, both contentions are false: the first for straightforward empirical reasons, and the second in the light of Marx's conception of communism.

In the various political discussions, Basic Income has usually meant an equal payment to all adults.[43] Many of the virtues of the benefit, such as its simplicity and absence of administrative intrusiveness, depend on this characteristic. Yet an equal payment is a payment according to need only if needs are equal (if the ideal is actually equal welfare from the benefit, we probably have to specify equal ability as well). Basic Income satisfies a pure needs principle only under highly restrictive assumptions – in a group A world, in the language of chapter 6. And any serious attempt to take account of differential needs or abilities administratively will plunge us back into the bureaucratic nightmare that Basic Income was specifically designed to avoid.[44]

Secondly, communism in Marx's view is *not* a society based on the principle of distribution according to need, because it is not a society based on any principle of distribution. Communism occurs under social conditions which make the very idea of distributive principles superfluous. These include the conditions that productivity is virtually infinite and that labour is not burdensome. In such a context, the question about the transition to communism is not whether the introduction now of Basic Income delivers a quantum of communism on account, but what effect the current introduction of Basic Income would have on the creation of the conditions under which communism eventually becomes possible. This is, of course, to pose the orthodox historical materialist question whether one needs a distinct socialist phase sandwiched between capitalism and communism, in order to develop the forces of production beyond what is possible under capitalism, before one arrives at what is allegedly necessary for communism.

I shall not dwell on this question, except for two remarks. First, as Elster points out, Marx seems to have believed that socialism was required in this force-enhancing role, without giving any argument as to why it was suited to the job. What we need for the theory of the transition to communism is something analogous to Brenner's Axiom in the theory of the transition to capitalism – and we don't have it.[45] Second, there exist fairly respectable general arguments both that a Basic Income scheme does and that it does not foster the development of the forces of production.[46] So it is a fairly open question what Basic Income would do to productivity, and hence the prospects for communism, if one accepts the orthodox premise that very high productivity is a precondition of communism.

I am not altogether depressed on behalf of Van der Veen and Van Parijs by these conclusions. The fact that Basic Income is uncapitalist rather inclines me to support it and I am not so persuaded by the orthodox picture of the transition to communism that I would be disturbed to learn that Basic Income worked against the transition in its orthodox construal, if Basic Income did indeed work in that direction.

What does worry me, as much as it worries Elster, is something else.[47]

Practical Basic Income schemes attempt to introduce one of the most appealing features of communism – distribution according to need – in circumstances of finite productivity and painful labour which were never intended by Marx to exist within a communist society. The problem I will address in chapter 16 is this: Basic Income is a gigantic system of free lunch. And if everyone gets a free lunch, who makes the lunch?

Basic attitudes

However it is achieved, and whatever its pitfalls, the redistribution of money as Basic Wealth or Basic Income is designed to alleviate the class divisions caused by market mechanisms. What about the forms of social division which exist outside the market-place?

It was shown in chapter 7 that class-like phenomena of household division arise from unequal wages, and that such a household division of labour becomes an aspect of gender division when, as is empirically the case, the wage differential is correlated with gender.

Two remedies can be imagined for this state of affairs: either break the correlation between differential pay and differential gender, or equalize pay. Now the equalization of pay entails the lapsing of the correlation between gender and pay, but it is worth considering them as distinct options. Suppose then that pay differentials exist, uncorrelated with gender. The effect will be to eliminate the gendered aspect of the household division, but not the household division. Thus, if the distributions of pay of all prospective domestic partners are identical, the partner selection process is random, women and men are separately identifiable and there is no sexual bias in partner selection, we shall find four types of (two-person) household existing in equal numbers. There will be 25 per cent woman-woman households and 25 per cent man-man households, in all of which the lower paid female or male partner is exploited. The remaining 50 per cent of households will be cross-sex, with the woman being the exploited partner in half of them, and the man the exploited partner in the remaining half. Overall, then, half the women will be exploited, and half the men, and half of the exploiters will be women and half men.

Presumably this set of arrangements would remain objectionable on socialist grounds, since it would give little comfort to an exploited woman that she had an exploiting twin sister living somewhere up the road. It therefore looks as if pay would need to be equalized, which would bring in its wake the suppression of the correlation between gender and pay. The best way to eliminate (this aspect of) gender division is therefore to eliminate the class-like basis of household division.

This appears at first sight to tell in favour of class politics, as against gender politics, but I do not think it does, for two main reasons. First, we saw in chapter 12 that the exchange model of households, on which the foregoing discussion depends, did not perform well when it faced the competition of gender ideology. It follows that wage equalization is unlikely to be sufficient in practice to eliminate an unequal division of household labour. Second, the wage differential is at best the proximate cause of household division, even if the exchange model told the whole story within the household. It is very likely that in order to reduce the wage differential between women and men, many kinds of discrimination would have to be curtailed. And the abolition of discrimination entails a change in the ideological construction of sex. This will be especially necessary, too, if the household is modelled on the Chicken game instead of the exchange game. The perceptual inequalities associated with the resolution of Chicken are particularly recalcitrant because of the tie-break property of the convergence to equilibrium in that game: very small differences in ideological conditioning have very dramatic distributive effects.

All these considerations suggest that in the matter of gender division, one has to work directly on gender ideology. (Who could seriously expect any other conclusion?) What corresponds in this case to the equalization of Basic Wealth or Basic Income is the equalization of basic *attitudes*. This would have the effect of eliminating discrimination, and thence the gendered forms of class division which stem from discriminatory practices. And what I have said of gender division is intended to apply, *mutatis mutandis*, to ethnic division.

Yet can one assimilate the case of attitudes to the case of wealth and income in this casual fashion? Are not attitudes subjective – a matter of opinion – where wealth and income depend on the objective constraints of cash-in-hand? I argue that the required analogy between the politics of personal identity and the politics of private property follows from the facts that *neither identity nor currency is a material asset*.

Since I imagine that the reader will readily accept the claim of unmateriality in relation to identity, I will need to defend the idea that *money* is not a material asset. There are of course some usages of "material", such as are implied in the complaint that we live in a materialist society, which make money the most material asset there is. But we are engaged at the moment not so much in moaning about the cultural depravity of late capitalism as in developing a general materialist account of social division compatible with historical materialism in the sense used by Marx, as elucidated by Cohen. And in that sense of "material", it is perfectly sensible to say that money is not a material asset, because money is not a force of production. It is not something "*used* by producing agents to produce products", even though it may take its place alongside the mobilization of conscience and the threat of the lash as a very effective means "of motivating producers" – to extend some remarks of Cohen on the exclusion of laws, morals and government from the process of production materially conceived.[48]

In a central passage of the first volume of *Capital*, Marx argued likewise that money was money only in so far as it was disqualified by its nature from being a force of production:

> The universal equivalent form is a form of value in general. It can therefore be assumed by any commodity. On the other hand, a commodity is only to be found in the unversal equivalent form if, and in so far as, it is excluded from the ranks of all other commodities, as being their equivalent. Only when the exclusion becomes finally restricted to a specific kind of commodity does the uniform relative form of value of the world of commodities attain objective fixedness and general social validity.[49]

Shorn of its Hegelian excrescences, this paragraph says that the mechanism of market prices exists (in the shape of the "uniform relative form of value") only when a certain commodity is withdrawn from ordinary contact with production and consumption in order to act exclusively as the measure of exchange for all other commodities (thereby assuming "the universal equivalent form", alias the money form). It follows that money has use value only in virtue of the social form taken by commodity relations (via its role in a network of exchange), but is not, in itself, useful for any productive purpose.[50] And this is precisely to say, in our terminology, that money is a *social* asset; but money is not a *material* asset.

In terms of the distinction between the social and the material, both money and identity stand wholly on the social side, even though the tokens of money and of identity may enjoy a corporeal existence. Thus, to have money is to present the signs which signify socially acceptable claims on resources in a market society; and to have an identity is to present the appearance which signifies differential claims on resources in a society which legitimizes discriminatory practices. According to this argument, it is no more and no less easy *a priori*, nor is it any less a political task, to change the signifying routines of personal identity than to change the signifying routines of the cash nexus. Hard currency and personal reception rely alike on soft perception.

This argument establishes, I claim, that the position of individuals with respect to gender, ethnicity or age is not different *in principle* from their position with respect to money. Position on any of these dimensions inserts a person into a social structure (the complex K, if you will) whose objectivity with respect to each individual resides in the way the given individual is perceived by every other individual. And I have generally favoured a structural definition of a person's social position over a behavioural definition – that is, I have favoured the idea that each person's position depends on what the other people think and do, not what the person thinks and does themself.

In the current context, a structural predisposition leads one to endorse Elster's view on social class: Rockefeller would not cease to be a capitalist simply by ceasing to behave as most capitalists do.[51] The same structural ruling would also imply that men do not cease to be men or white people cease to be white simply by abjuring the behaviour available to them. For their position in the social structure depends on how others would treat them differentially if the hypothetical man or white person sought advantageous treatment, not on whether the hypothetical person seeks such treatment. So far, there is a good analogy between the politics of property and the politics of personal identity. In either case it is the system that must be changed, not the individual's behaviour, given the system.

But how can the system be changed? In the case of money, I also endorsed Elster's view that Rockefeller would cease to be a capitalist after he had given away his money, because he had then relinquished his ability to act like a capitalist, should he ever want to. Now, strictly speaking, Rockefeller has not changed the system by his generous donation, only his position within the system: perhaps his gift was split between Andrew Carnegie and J. Pierpont Morgan. Yet if all capitalists give to the poor, or are constrained to do so, we have undoubtedly changed the capitalist system: we have instituted Basic Wealth or Basic Income.

Can we do something similar with personal identity? What would it mean to say that a man had given away his identity as a man, or a white person donated their whiteness? The analogy has pretty clearly broken down. To repudiate an identity from which one gains unfairly at the expense of others is not to hand something over for others to collect. It is rather to help bring it about that the identity no longer counts in the way it did before. It should become literally meaningless, in an increasing array of social contexts, that a person exhibits the attributes which formerly assigned his or her place in a certain individuous system of gender grouping or ethnic categorization. It looks as if the appropriate basic attitude to have is one that takes no attitude at all. To redistribute attitudes is to dissolve them, or make the previous attitudes irrelevant, not to parcel them out to everyone in equal quantities. What is analogous to the elimination of discriminatory attitudes is not the redistribution of money but the abolition of money.

If this is true, it follows that the elimination of gender division or ethnic division is likely to require a more profound process of adjustment than the elimination of class division within a market society (which is

SOCIAL DIVISION

not in any way to belittle the difficulty of the latter reform). I think, probably naively, that I can just about imagine what it might be like to live in a non-sexist, non-racist society. There are even several powerful principles in the culture which already beckon in the right direction: the ideas of equal prior respect, innocence before guilt, and equality before the law, for instance.

Yet it is impossible to overestimate the factors pulling in the opposite direction. I have commented above on the tendency of meaning to crystallize around stories of physical or personal difference. Even if the prejudicial beliefs are fairy-tale castles built upon sand, they are typically difficult to shift because of their resilience against falsifying evidence. This is part of what Ernest Cashmore means by "the logic of racism".[52]

We seem to understand very little about the social and cognitive processes which lead to the crystallization of prejudicial attitudes, and thus about what would promote decrystallization. We can nevertheless expect that it is going to be very difficult to unlearn a whole vocabulary of social perception, when all the triggers of the old perceptions – the physical and personal cues – remain present to the eyes. The elimination of sexism and racism are attainable goals, no doubt, but they are each far away, and desperately difficult to achieve. We are not even in a position to write a new book: the text will be open at the same page, from which must be read quite different social meanings.

Notes

1. I am grateful to Graham Macdonald for discussion which led me to add the words "fully social" to my first version of this thought.
2. Marx, *The German Ideology* (London: Lawrence and Wishart, 1970) (hereafter *GI*), pp. 52–57, 68.
3. *GI*, p. 57.
4. *Capital*, I (Harmondsworth: Penguin, 1976), p. 92.
5. *GI*, p. 84 – cited also by Elster, "Three challenges to class", in John Roemer, ed., *Analytical Marxism* (Cambridge: C.U.P., 1986), p. 148, as evidence for the different point that Marx sometimes restricted the application of the class concept to the bourgeois era.
6. "Marx ... thought that the growth of productive power of humanity proceeded in tandem with confinement of the creative capacity of most humans": G. A. Cohen, "Reconsidering Historical Materialism", in *History, Labour and Freedom* (Oxford: O.U.P., 1989), p. 150; and see also Elster, *Making Sense of Marx* (Cambridge: C.U.P., 1985) (hereafter *MSM*), pp. 73, 515.
7. This argument is given in *GI*, p. 113, but its apparently devasting consequence for the attempt to construct a rational-choice Marxism is considerably softened by the discussion immediately following, from which Marx concludes that up to a certain point, the utilitarian analysis of "the exploitation relations of separate classes ... was able to base itself on definite social facts" (p. 114). It is in any case very difficult to construe the main mathematical model underlying *Capital*, I as anything but a rational-choice model, as I have tried to show in "Value and Strategy", *Science and Society*, XLVIII, no. 2 (1984). If utility is out, so is *Capital*, Volume I.

8. Marx and Engels, *The Communist Manifesto* (Moscow: Progress Publishers, 1953), p. 76.

9. Cited in an Appendix of *GI* at p. 123.

10. *GI*, p. 86.

11. *GI*, p. 55.

12. *GI*, p. 56.

13. "In a real community the individuals obtain their freedom in and through their association": *GI*, p. 83.

14. G.A. Cohen, *Karl Marx's Theory of History: A Defence* (Oxford: Clarendon Press, 1978) (hereafter *KMTH*), p. 131.

15. As in "the productive activity of human beings in general ... in its bare natural existence, independent of society, removed from all societies [is] an expression and confirmation of life which the still non-social man in general has in common with the one who is in any way social": *Capital*, III, cited in *KMTH*, p. 99. Compare "other terms of [Marx's] material vocabulary are 'human', 'simple' and 'real', while 'historical' and 'economic' consort with 'social'": p. 98.

16. I am not certain Cohen does either, for the view is deduced from the conjunction of Cohen's view of the social-material vocabulary as it sometimes applies to human beings in Marx with Cohen's undialectical description of communism as the "*conquest of form by matter*" (*KMTH*, p. 129, original emphasis). See also "Reconsidering Historical Materialism", p. 141. But Cohen also says in *KMTH*, p. 99, that "material production does not occur in history except enveloped in a social form, for 'non-social man' if he ever existed, disappeared when history began." The question is whether he reappears when history ends. (I am grateful at this point to John Dunn, whose work brought the last quotation to my notice.)

17. *GI*, p. 86.

18. *GI*, p. 54.

19. Marx, *Critique of the Gotha Programme* (Peking: Foreign Languages Press, 1976), p. 17.

20. "Division of labour" is the term under which *The German Ideology* subsumes all the particular divisions of class, state, nation, town and country, family, tribe and community (see especially *GI*, "Private Property and Communism" pp. 52–7). There is thus some licence in Marx for using the term "social division" in the general sense of this book.

21. "No one could deny the Utopian strand in Marx's thinking, but I for one am loath to attribute to him a view that could only be described as a pure expression of the pleasure principle": *MSM*, p. 453. Compare, however, the moving testimonial to Marx on p. 521.

22. *MSM*, p. 233, and compare p. 525.

23. *MSM*, p. 523.

24. *MSM*, pp. 231–2, 453, 526. See also Alec Nove, *The Economics of Feasible Socialism* (London: George Allen and Unwin, 1983), pp. 15–20 and Nove's remark that "abundance is a chimera. So, therefore, is full communism." ("'A Capitalist Road to Communism': A Comment", *Theory and Society*, 15 (1987), p. 674).

25. *MSM*, p. 527.

26. "Le pays de cocayne" is from Nove, "'A Capitalist Road to Communism': A Comment", p. 677.

27. Robert J. Van der Veen and Philippe Van Parijs, "A Capitalist Road to Communism", *Theory and Society*, 15 (1987), p. 636.

28. Erik Olin Wright, "Why Something Like Socialism is Necessary for the Transition to Something Like Communism", *Theory and Society*, 15 (1987), p. 657.

29. Philippe Van Parijs has objected, and I accept, that the link word "namely" in the VP definition is not meant to extend the logical scope of its preceding "therefore", which "therefore" does not therefore cover the last clause of the definition. This does not affect the most important point, namely, that the definition offers a good example of the way several distinct conceptions of socialism are often rolled into one.

30. Erik Olin Wright, *Classes* (London: Verso, 1985), p. 85.

31. Wright's *Classes*, chs. 2 and 3, records his conversion to the Roemer scheme of class analysis: a change of heart which had somewhat traumatic ramifications for at least

one international research project which was in the process of using Wright's famous original scheme of "contradictory class locations". See Gordon Marshall et al., *Social Class in Modern Britain* (London: Unwin Hyman, 1988), p. 31.

32. A parallel is intended with procedural versus substantive definitions of justice: on which see David Miller, *Market, State and Community* (Oxford: Clarendon Press, 1989), ch. 2.

33. The issues I am therefore trying to side-step are those raised by Ronald Dworkin, "What is Equality? Part 1: Equality of Welfare"; "Part 2: Equality of Resources", in *Philosophy and Public Affairs*, 10 (1981); Amartya Sen, "Equality of What?", in S. McMurrin, ed., *The Tanner Lectures on Human Values, 1* (Cambridge: C.U.P., 1980); and John Baker, *Arguing for Equality* (London: Verso, 1987), in so far as all these discussions involve unequal individuals. Philippe Van Parijs tells me that the same expedient motivates Rawls' distinction between natural and social primary goods: I, too, am concerned almost exclusively with social primary goods.

34. This part of the chapter was originally drafted in August 1989, and I have left the text untouched by the extraordinary events of that autumn. I will say, however, that by December it would have been even more difficult to envisage the existence of an uncorrupted Stalinist regime.

35. Recent treatments of this issue include Frank Cunningham, *Democratic Theory and Socialism* (Cambridge: C.U.P., 1987); Bryan Gould, *Socialism and Freedom* (London: Macmillan, 1985); Keith Graham, *The Battle of Democracy* (Brighton: Wheatsheaf, 1986); John Keane, *Public Life and Late Capitalism* (Cambridge: C.U.P., 1985); Andrew Levine, *Arguing for Socialism* (London: Verso, 1988); Michael Rustin, *For a Pluralist Socialism* (London: Verso, 1985) and Raymond Williams, *Democracy and Parliament* (London: Socialist Society, 1982).

36. Hillel Steiner, "The natural right to the means of production", *Philosophical Quarterly*, 27 (1977); "Land, Liberty and the early Herbert Spencer", *History of Political Thought*, 3 (1982); "Three Just Taxes", in Philippe Van Parijs, ed., *Arguing for Basic Income* (London: Verso, 1992).

37. The best Scandinavian practice may escape this overall judgement.

38. I take this to be the implication of Roemer, *Value, Exploitation and Class* (Chur: Harwood Academic Publishers, 1986), pp. 45–50.

39. Cohen, Roemer and John Baker have been occupied with the responsibility issue in unpublished work, and this is also a central theme of Miller, ch. 1.

40. G.D.H. Cole, *The Next Ten Years in British Social and Economic Policy* (London: Macmillan, 1929); Bill Jordan, *Paupers* (London: Routledge and Kegan Paul, 1973) and *The State* (Oxford: Basil Blackwell, 1985); Philippe Van Parijs, "On the Ethical Foundations of Basic Income", in Philippe Van Parijs, ed., *Arguing for Basic Income* and publications of BIEN including Anne Glenda Miller, ed., *Basic Income* (Antwerp: BIEN, 1988). As well as the original article by Van der Veen and Van Parijs cited in note 27 above, see "Universal Grants versus Socialism: Reply to Six Critics", *Theory and Society*, 15 (1987).

41. Wright, "Why Something Like Socialism is Necessary for the Transition to Something Like Communism", p. 662–3.

42. I question the non-divisiveness of the proposal in chapter 17.

43. The disabled are exempt from this rule, and entitled to an extra allowance, in all the proposals known to Philippe Van Parijs. See "Basic Income: A Terminological Note", in Miller, *Basic Income*, p. 5.

44. This point was made forcefully by Brian Barry at the 1989 Louvain Conference of the Basic Income European Network.

45. *MSM* p. 452 and "The Theory of Combined and Uneven Development: A Critique", in *Analytical Marxism*.

46. Basic Income might foster the development of the forces of production because of its effect on wages at the lower end of the wage scale, leading to a capitalist investment bias. It might not foster the development because of its inroads into investment funds, and capitalist incentives more generally. I owe the first point, though not this application of it, to a participant in the Louvain conference.

47. Jon Elster, "Comment on Van der Veen and Van Parijs", *Theory and Society*, 15 (1987).

48. *KMTH*, p. 32.

49. *Capital*, I, p. 162.

50. For further discussion, see my "Forms of Value and the Logic of Capital", *Science and Society*, L, no. 1 (1986).

51. Elster, "Three Challenges to Class", in *Analytical Marxism*, p. 144, and see section 4.4 above.

52. Ernest Cashmore, *The Logic of Racism* (London: Allen and Unwin, 1987), and see also Rosemary Harris, *Prejudice and Tolerance in Ulster* (Manchester: Manchester University Press, 1972), p. 154.

===================== 16 =====================

Symmetry and Social Division

16.1 Equal Resource Socialism

Socialism involves a commitment to both democracy and equality, and there is tension between these two commitments. But there is another tension within the commitment to equality, between a commitment to equality of resources and a commitment to equality of final welfare. This chapter examines the second tension.

Suppose that society is simplified to such an extent that each of its N members is equal in abilities and needs, and each faces a choice between just two courses of action, stylized (as in chapter 8) as cooperate [C] or defect [D]. The N members choose either C or D, and what each member receives in return from her choice depends on the entire configuration of choices made by all. Society therefore splits itself into (at most) two sets: the set of C-choosers (size c) and the set of D-choosers (size d), where

$$c + d = N \tag{16.1}$$

Under what conditions do we consider that resources are equally distributed in such a society?

Let us proceed by suggestive elimination. Suppose the choices C and D stand for "invest wealth" and "do not invest wealth" respectively. Then the returns (in money) from investing wealth at a competitive interest rate are equal if and only if the wealth levels of two investing individuals are equal. An equal wealth society therefore appears to make the payoff from the choice of C independent of which individual it is that is making the choice. Now suppose that C represents "work for an hour" and D "do no work at all". Then the returns in money terms from the cooperative action are equal for two individuals if and only if their wage rates are the same. Or suppose, again, that men get greater credit than women for doing exactly the same housework or childcare, so that a person's identity makes a difference to their returns from effort. An equal identity society, like an equal wealth or an equal wage society, appears to be a society that imposes a certain anonymity on the relationship between actions and benefits: it may matter what you do, but it does not matter who you are. The essence of unequal wealth, earning power or social identity is captured, by contrast, in the fact that different individuals with the same abilities and needs nevertheless receive different rewards from the same generic actions.

The formal counterpart of the anonymity condition in the relation between actions and benefits is that the payoff structure of the appropriate game exhibits *cardinal symmetry*. This means that the payoff from interaction depends only on (i) which coalition a player is in and (ii) how large the coalition is. Thus, there exist two functions

$$f(c): c = 1, \ldots N \tag{16.2}$$

$$g(d): d = 1, \ldots N \tag{16.3}$$

giving the payoffs respectively received by a C-player in a C-coalition of size c and a D-player in a D-coalition of size d.[1] At any given partition of the society, with $c + d = N$, the values of the payoffs to members of the two social coalitions are f(c) and g $(N - c)$ respectively.

(16.2) and (16.3) are the data of the *general N-person symmetric binary-choice game*. No further conditions are imposed on the functions f and g, such that, for example, they are monotonic in c and d (which would imply that payoffs either always increase or always decrease with coalition size).

Under the interpretation of this game given above, we can study the properties of the N-person binary-choice society with equal resource distribution by studying the properties of this game. In particular, we are interested in the *equilibrium* properties of the game, because equilibria in the game will correspond with stable configurations of the corresponding egalitarian societies (under rational-choice assumptions of human motivation). I submit that this is an appropriate test-bed for the study of the kind of socialism which might occur after all the resource redistributions discussed in the previous chapter have somehow taken place, yet well before the onset of anything resembling Marxian communist abundance.

16.2 Class in a Classless Society

We define an equilibrium in the given symmetric game by the following
conditions: (i) C-players have a (positive) incentive not to desert the C-
coalition, and (ii) D-players have a (positive) incentive not to desert the
D-coalition.[2]

These conditions are observed when the current payoffs from coalition
membership exceed the payoffs the players would obtain from switching
their allegiance to the opposite coalition. Consider in this light a member
of the C-coalition, of size c. This individual compares their current payoff,
f(c), to the payoff obtainable from membership of the D-coalition of
size $(N - c + 1)$ - namely, $g(N - c + 1)$. (The reason the comparison
is with a D-coalition of size $(N - c + 1)$ is that the D-coalition increases
from size $(N - c)$ to size $(N - c + 1)$ after the putative defection of
the C-player from C to D.) It follows that the C-player will remain a
C-player if and only if

$$f(c) > g(N - c + 1) \tag{16.4}$$

The equivalent comparisons made by the complementary D-player in
a D-coalition of size $(N - c)$ involve the payoff in a prospective C-coalition
of size $(c + 1)$. Hence a D-player will stay put in a coalition of size
$(N - c)$ if and only if

$$g(N - c) > f(c + 1) \tag{16.5}$$

I now introduce a change of notation, whose purpose will soon become
apparent. Define a new function g' by

$$g'(c) = g(N - c + 1): c = 1, \ldots N \tag{16.6}$$

Then the conditions (16.4) and (16.5) can be rewritten as

$$f(c) > g'(c) \tag{16.7}$$

$$g'(c + 1) > f(c + 1) \tag{16.8}$$

Recall that these conditions refer to the stability of the C and D coalitions respectively. The change of notation has enabled us to express this
stability in terms of the relative values of the functions f and g' at given
coordinates c and $(c + 1)$. If function f exceeds function g' at point
c, the C- coalition is stable; otherwise the C-coalition starts losing members
to D and the coordinate c (which measures the size of the C-coalition)

decreases in size. Conversely, if function g′ exceeds function f at point (c + 1), the D-coalition is stable; otherwise the D-coalition starts to unravel, and c increases.

This suggests that there are only three possible opportunities of equilibria in the symmetrical game, of only two possible *kinds*.[3]

(i) The D-coalition unwinds completely, by losing members until none are left. There is an egalitarian equilibrium in which all members of society choose C and each receives the payoff f(N).

(ii) The C-coalition unwinds completely, by losing members until none are left. There is an egalitarian equilibrium in which all members of society choose D and each receives the payoff g′(1) = g(N). These two equilibria are called *boundary* equilibria, since they occur at either of the two extremes of coalition size (c = N or d = N).

(iii) There is a value c: $1 \le c < N$ for which both conditions (16.7) and (16.8) are satisfied. C-coalition of size c is stable, with payoffs to each of its members f(c); D-coalition of size (N − c) is also stable, with payoffs to each of its members g′(c + 1) = g(N − c). Because both the C and D coalitions are stable, and each is non-empty, the game is said to be at an *internal* equilibrium − that is, at an equilibrium away from one of the boundaries of the interval (1, N) on the c-axis.

We note that an internal equilibrium may be visualized conveniently in terms of the intersection of the functions f and g′. Thus, if we regard f and g′ as continuous functions of real-valued coalition size, (16.7) and (16.8) can be satisfied only in the vicinity of an intersection at which a "falling" f function crosses over a "rising" g′ function. But such an equilibrium need not be an egalitarian equilibrium for the society as a whole, since it is not true, in general, that

$$f(c) = g'(c + 1) \qquad\qquad (16.9)$$

The significance of this fact can be brought out in two ways. I reiterate first a point made in Section 11.3: the variation in welfare of the members of the two coalitions at such an internal configuration has been brought about entirely by differential behaviour, not differential resources (which are equal by hypothesis). Yet this is an equilibrium, in which each person's behaviour is constrained by every other person's behaviour. This shows that behaviour can have "structural" importance.

Second, the argument of the previous chapter has been that resource equalization is necessary in order to end social division. The conclusion of this section is that even such a radical social reorganization is, in general, insufficient to satisfy the aims of egalitarians. It is possible in theory to have socialism, in the sense of resource equalization, and social division, in the sense of a systematic inequality of welfare at an equilibrium of rational-choice interaction (even if actors are also equal in needs and abilities). Putting the matter in the most provocative language, it is possible to have class in a classless society.

Whether this abstract possibility is a likely contingency in practice is the subject of the next two sections. The brief answer, unfortunately, is Yes.

16.3 Basic Wealth versus Basic Income

We define different varieties of socialist economy by making assumptions about technology and property relations from which the payoff functions f and g' are deduced.

(i) *Binary choice assumption* Each person has the choice of working (C) or not working (D) for a unit time – an hour, say, or a week.

(ii) *Technological assumptions* Each person is equally able, so the personal cost of working is the same for all workers – one unit, say – and the output of the labour process is the same for all workers – an amount x, say, measured on the same scale as the scale of labour costs. Since this amount is constant, there is, in effect, a linear technology in the society. If c members decide to work, the total social output is cx.

(iii) *Property relations assumptions* We investigate two models, corresponding to the two rules of distribution at the extreme ends of the spectrum of needs-contribution principles. Under a *pure contribution rule*, each worker receives the entire product of his or her work (equivalently: each worker receives an equal share of the total output, and non-workers receive nothing). Each worker therefore receives a quantity x, conditional on their work. Under a *pure needs rule*, each member of society receives an equal share of the total output. Everyone therefore receives cx/N, unconditionally. (This is, of course, a needs rule only under the assumption we have made that everyone in the society is equally needy.)

The functions f and g' are derived as follows. Under the pure contribution principle each worker receives an amount of goods x, which cost her or him one unit to produce (on the same scale used to measure x). So the net benefit from working is $(x - 1)$. If we normalize the functions so that the combination of not working and receiving nothing has zero utility, the functions are

$$g'(c) = 0 \tag{16.10}$$

$$f(c) = (x - 1) \tag{16.11}$$

We notice that both these functions are constants, so that, in economist's jargon, there are no externalities, or mutual effects of the separate decisions of the members of society to work or not to work.[4] The decision each faces is also a remarkably simple one. If $x < 1$, no-one works; whereas if $x > 1$, everyone works. I assume therefore that $x > 1$, which is the counterpart in this model of the idea familiar from Part II that the society can generate a surplus, or in other words is capable of producing an output net of labour costs.[5] The functions $f(c)$ and $g'(c)$ are exhibited in Figure. 16.1 for $x > 1$, with the equilibrium shown on the right hand boundary of the figure. Because this is a boundary equilibrium, with everyone cooperating, it is necessarily egalitarian – everyone enjoys the same payoff equal to $(x - 1)$.

An obvious way to implement this equilibrium is to give everyone in the society an equal share of the wealth of society under private property arrangements. They would then trade on their own account to gain an equal return $(x - 1)$ from self-employment. It is thus clear that a form of egalitarian popular capitalism is actually consistent with the distributive rule of VP socialism: "to each according to contribution". Basic wealth is, one might say, the capitalist road to socialism. Or, if this were rejected on the dynamic grounds that it would soon lead in practice to inequalities of property ownership, and thus capitalist exploitation, the pure contributions principle could be implemented by a wage of $(x - 1)$, such as might correspond with Lassallean "undiminished proceeds of labour".[6] At the present level of abstraction, basic wealth is indistinguishable from a big wage.

The alternative is to try and introduce the "communist" rule of distribution – "to each according to need" – in a situation in which, by hypothesis, labour is a burden – because it has a (unit) cost – and the technology is not cornucopious (because x is finite). This is the Basic Income alternative to basic wealth. When distribution of such a Basic Income is unconditional, each person receives the benefit cx/N, but the workers alone suffer the costs of working. Hence

$$g'(c) = g(N - c + 1) = (c - 1) x/N \tag{16.12}$$

$$f(c) = (cx/N - 1) \tag{16.13}$$

These functions define the Basic Income Game (hereafter BIG, for short).

Each of these functions is linear increasing in c, with the same coefficient

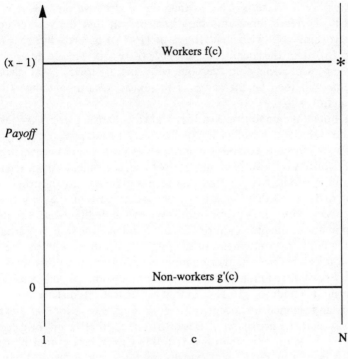

Number of workers in the society

* Boundary equilibrium

Figure 16.1 The Basic Wealth or Big Wage Game

(x/N). We know, therefore, that they cannot intersect in the open interval
(1, N): the equilibria must be at one of the boundaries c = 1, or c =
N. But which boundary? Everyone will work (choose C) in this crypto-
communist society if and only if

$$f(c) > g'(c) \qquad\qquad (16.14)$$

which reduces to the condition

$$x/N > 1 \qquad\qquad (16.15)$$

The interpretation of this condition is as follows. A member of society inevitably incurs a cost of one unit by working. But if the member does not work, the social product is reduced by an amount x, of which the given worker's share is 1/N, so that the worker would lose x/N. This quantity therefore represents the direct benefit that the worker derives from working. If this benefit (l.h.s. of (16.15)) exceeds the cost (r.h.s. of (16.15)) then the member of society will work. This logic applies to all members of society, so everyone will work if (16.15) is satisfied. The outcome will then be the same as the Basic Wealth outcome (if c = N, then f(c) = f(N) = (x − 1)).

We note that condition (16.15) is always satisfied for x = infinity. In other words, it is sufficient for a society to adopt a needs principle without ill effects that labour is infinitely productive, however large the society. Since x is the ratio of output to cost an equivalent way of interpreting infinite productivity is that labour has zero cost, or in other words ceases to be a burden. This is an important part of the way towards labour becoming "life's prime want". We conclude that Marx's economic intuition about the preconditions for communism was sound: it does look as if the level of development of the forces of production has to be fairly astronomical before unaided communist property relations work properly. For if x is finite, there will always be some N sufficiently large to invalidate condition (16.15).[7] In that case, the needs distribution principle has undermined the incentive to work. One way to look at this result is to say that the provision of Basic Income requires a uniform tax rate of (N − 1)/N on contributions. It follows that distribution according to need in a large public will lead to tax rates tending to 100 per cent, (since (N − 1)/N goes to 100 per cent as N goes to infinity) and this will eventually destroy the incentive to work in any economy of finite productivity. If this point has been reached, and x/N < 1, then

$$g'(c) > f(c) \text{ for all } c \tag{16.16}$$

In this case, the equilibrium shifts abruptly from the right hand to the left hand boundary as depicted in figure 16.2: no-one works, the economy collapses, and everyone receives the egalitarian payoff $g'(1) = 0$. Yet everyone would be better off if they all worked, receiving as before the (positive) payoff (x − 1). This result yields, of course, a Prisoner's Dilemma in the particular N-person form which has been studied extensively in the literature of public goods provision.[8]

The solutions to this problem implicit in the foregoing discussion are either to privatize property rights, and redistribute money as wealth rather than income, or to pay a wage which consumes the whole surplus product in order to restore the incentive structure. But we are not forced to go to these lengths, because, as we have seen in chapter 8, there may be

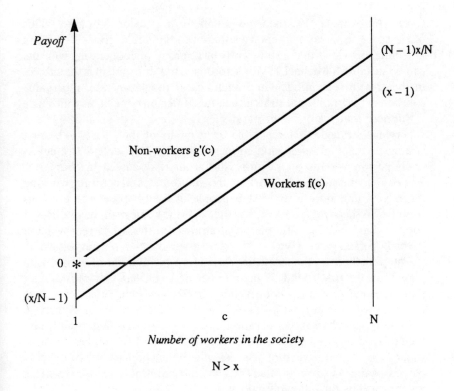

Figure 16.2 BIG: The Basic Income Game

rational-choice solutions to Prisoner's Dilemmas. We might be able to retain distribution according to need, and yet overcome its disincentive effects, if we can generalize the earlier solutions from the two-person to the N-person case. It transpires that this generalization can be achieved, but the price to be paid is one that should prove unacceptable to an egalitarian.

16.4 Taylor on Public Goods

The possibility of cooperation

In the BIG society of figure 16.2, the function f(c) intersects the horizontal axis at the point $c = N/x$, where $1 < N/x < N$. This implies that there is some level of cooperative working in the society which will leave the working cooperators better off than they would be if cooperation had failed completely, and no-one worked. (If the number of workers in the society (c) exceeds N/x, then the payoff f(c) is greater than zero.) This offers scope for a rational-choice solution to the public goods Prisoner's Dilemma, provided that a sufficiently large group of cooperating workers can be sustained. Michael Taylor's approach to this problem is the subject of the present section.[9] The approach adapts the two-person supergame solution with conditional strategies to the N-person context, as follows.

Suppose that the discount parameter is h ($0 < h < 1$), and that two supergame strategies are available to members of the society. The first strategy is unconditional non-cooperation (D). The second strategy is an N-person variant of the tit-for-tat strategy discussed in chapter 8. The strategy says: begin by working the first round, and continue working the next round only if at least n people in total worked the previous round. Call this strategy T_n. Notice that T_1 is the strategy of unconditional cooperation, and T_2 is the tit-for-tat strategy in the two-person version of the N-person game. (We can therefore assume $n > 1$ in what follows.)

The payoffs from the strategies depend on the number of people who play T_n in the first round. If the number of T_n players (say c) is greater than or equal to n, then cooperation is sustained indefinitely by a core group of workers at least as large as n. But if the number of T_n players is initially less than n, cooperation collapses after the first round, and society reverts to its wholly uncooperating state. This implies that the supergame payoff structure for the wholly uncooperative strategy D played against a given strategy T_n has a discontinuity at $c = n$. This is confirmed by the following calculations:

(i) $c < n$. D-players receive basic income cx/N the first week, and nothing thereafter. T_n players receive the same income stream, but suffer unit disutility from the first week's working. So the payoffs functions are

$$g'(c) = (c - 1)x/N \qquad (16.17)$$

$$f(c) = cx/N - 1 \qquad (16.18)$$

These expressions are, of course, identical with the expressions for the one-shot game ((16.12) and (16.13)) because the game has essentially terminated at the end of round one.

(ii) $c > n$. In this case, a different picture emerges, because there has been sufficient cooperation in the first round to sustain cooperation over all subsequent rounds. Basic Income is therefore sustained indefinitely, subject to discounting by factors 1, h, h^2 etc. in successive rounds of the game. Payoffs are those given by (16.17) and (16.18), grossed up over the infinite duration of the game by a factor $1 + h + h^2 + \ldots = 1/(1 - h)$. Hence

$$g'(c) = (c - 1)x/N\,(1 - h) \tag{16.19}$$

and

$$f(c) = [cx/N - 1]/(1 - h) \tag{16.20}$$

For $c > n$, the functions therefore remain linear in c, but with an increased gradient, reflecting the fact that the cooperative payoff has now been sustained into an indefinite future.

(iii) $c = n$. If $c = n$, cooperation is just sustained, so that the payoff to T_n players (from (16.20)) is

$$f(n) = [nx/N - 1]/(1 - h) \tag{16.21}$$

The defection of any one member of the coalition will however cause cooperation to collapse completely, so that each member of the T_n-coalition compares payoff f(n) with the payoff which would occur if that member switched to strategy D and the whole society reverted to non-cooperation after round one. From (16.17), this payoff is

$$g'(n) = (n - 1)\,x/N \tag{16.22}$$

We know from previous results that the function g' is greater than the function f in the two ranges $[1 \le c < n]$ and $[n < c \le N]$ covered by the two pairs of equations [(16.17), (16.18)] and [(16.19), (16.20)] respectively. But this is not necessarily the case at the discontinuity $c = n$. Since the elementary game has cardinal symmetry, and the same set of supergame strategies is available to all players, we know that the supergame has cardinal symmetry also. We can therefore apply the general results of section 16.1. In particular, we can apply the equilibrium conditions (16.7) and (16.8) at the point $c = n$. We know from (16.19) and (16.20) that $g'(n + 1) > f(n + 1)$. So there is an equilibrium at the discontinuity if and only if

$$f(n) > g'(n) \tag{16.23}$$

Substitution from (16.21) and (16.22) gives

$$[(nx/N) - 1]/(1 - h) > (n - 1)x/N$$

which reduces to

$$h > [N/x - 1]/(n - 1) \tag{16.24}$$

Condition (16.24) says that there is an equilibrium at the C-coalition of size c = n if and only if the discount parameter is sufficiently high, as quantified by (16.24). Observe first that the r.h.s. of (16.24) is always positive, since n > 1 and N/x > 1. But it is also required that h < 1, so (16.24) can only be satisfied if the r.h.s. of (16.24) is less than one. This occurs when

$$n > N/x \tag{16.25}$$

This result confirms the argument at the start of this section: the only prospects for a rational-choice solution to the Basic Income supergame occur with a sufficiently large coalition of conditional cooperators. We now know that the conditional strategy they use must be conditional upon the cooperation of a sufficiently large number of people. But we can then conclude that so long as this condition (16.25) is met, there will be values of the discount parameter h which imply an equilibrium solution to the Basic Income supergame for each of the conditional strategies T_n as n varies in the range $N/x \le n \le N$. I depict such an equilibrium solution of the supergame in figure 16.3, in which the characteristic discontinuity of the payoff structure is called, painfully, a greenstick discontinuity. The reader can verify that the payoff structure drawn close to c = n satisfies the equilibrium conditions (16.7) and (16.8).

To interpret the figure, notice that the upper and lower stretches of the payoff structure each display the Prisoner's Dilemma effect. Thus, above the coordinate c = n the coalition of workers is unravelling, with the value of c decreasing (moving leftwards on the figure). But the coalition does not unwind completely, because it encounters the greenstick discontinuity. At the coordinate c = n, the remaining n cooperators look over the precipice (from payoff f(n) down to the payoff g'(n)) and decide to stay where they are. (It is only at c = n that f(c) > g'(c) rather than g'(c) > f(c).) Thus, the game has an internal equilibrium at c = n.

This in a nutshell is Taylor's solution to the problem of cooperation, as it applies to a binary-choice society with a linear technology that pays Basic Income unconditionally to all its members.

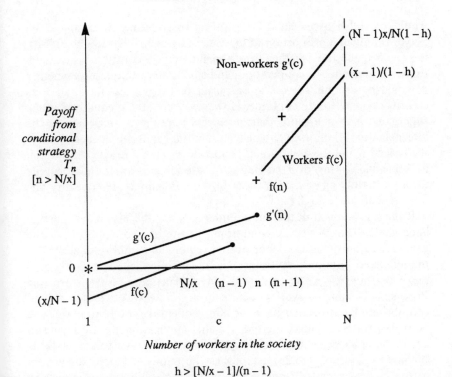

$$h > [N/x - 1]/(n - 1)$$

* Boundary equilibrium   + Internal equilibrium

Figure 16.3 The Greenstick Equilibrium

The greenstick equilibrium

The greenstick equilibrium has arisen as a solution to an N-person Prisoner's Dilemma analogous to the two-person solution discussed in chapter 8.

It is very like the confidence solution in the following respect. We saw in chapter 8 that a solution to the two-person Prisoner's Dilemma could occur if players attributed causal efficacy to their own strategies. But this is exactly what occurs here too: if just n players are playing the conditional strategy T_n it is true of each player that they cause all the remaining $(n - 1)$ cooperating players to continue cooperating after round one. Each T_n playing action is a necessary condition, and the n T_n actions taken together are jointly sufficient conditions for the continuation of cooperation.

If more than n players are playing the strategy T_n, we have a case of overdetermination, in which any cooperative sub-coalition of size n would be sufficient to cause cooperation to continue. Since any given player is only in a proportion of these causally-equivalent sub-coalitions, it is an open question whether any given individual is contributing causally to the maintenance of cooperation, and so it is an open question whether it would be rational for the given player to believe that he or she was causing cooperation to continue. However, there are no equilibria in the supergame in which more than n players play the strategy T_n. At the internal equilibrium itself the beliefs in mutual causal influence are correctly held by all the conditional cooperators. They form a group which is rather like a ring of n playing cards stood upon their ends, leaning inwards slightly against each other in mutual support: remove any one card, and all the rest fall flat.[10]

If the solution is thus like the confidence game, it is also like the assurance game. The greenstick equilibrium is one of two equilibria in the game, since universal non-cooperation retains its equilibrium status (at the left hand boundary of Figure 16.3). The effect of introducing conditional strategies in the context of the supergame is to transform the Prisoner's Dilemma payoff structure in a way which creates a second equilibrium, Pareto- superior to the non-cooperative equilibrium we have been desperately trying to avoid. (In this application we are trying to avoid the collapse of the socialist economy under the weight of Basic Income.) Condition (16.25) establishes the requisite Pareto-superiority in the N-person case. If enough people can be induced to cooperate, it is in each person's interest that cooperation occur.

But now we come to a decided difference between the two-person and N-person solutions. In the two-person case, both players would act to bring about the cooperative equilibrium preferred by all (rather than act to bring about another equilibrium which no-one preferred). This is what turned one-shot confidence behaviour into supergame assurance behaviour in the two-person case according to the analysis of section 8.3.

Yet we cannot apply the same analysis to the N-person case. In the N-person case, any coalition of n people can act to bring about the preferable equilibrium. If n < N, there are a (large) number of such coalitions (in fact $_nC_N$ of such coalitions). This corresponds to the fact that although there is one greenstick equilibrium depicted in Figure 16.3, there are in fact $_nC_N$ copies of the equilibrium derived from the $_nC_N$ ways we can select a coalition of n conditional cooperators (in this case, conditional workers) from the total population of size N.

The question then arises whether individuals are indifferent about whether or not they are counted among the workers. The answer, of course, is that they care about it a good deal, since the workers are the ones who do all the work and no-one likes to work. At the greenstick equilibrium, there is an inequality, since the non-workers receive

$$g'(n + 1) = nx/N(1 - h) \qquad (16.26)$$

whereas the workers receive

$$f(n) = [(nx/N) - 1]/(1 - h) \qquad (16.27)$$

These two equilibrium values are represented by the crosses at the discontinuity of the payoff structure in Figure 16.3. The difference between the payoffs is, of course, equal to the unit burden of work performed by the workers during each round of production, grossed up into an indefinite future. The equilibrium is an example of the abstract possibility raised in section 16.2 of *symmetry and social division*. What attitude do we take to this inequality?

I think the answer is fairly clear – we cannot approve it. Recall the grounds on which capitalism was roundly condemned in section 6.3. It was wrong that as a result of their differential property ownership, able-bodied capitalists were able to avoid their fair share of unpleasant work. Here, the able-bodied non-workers have been able to avoid work just by their behaviour (playing strategy D instead of strategy T_n). As a result they are permanent free-riders on the backs of the cooperating workers, just as capitalists were free riding permanently on the proletariat. The greenstick equilibrium involves a genuine class division, which seems inherent in the Basic Income game. What Roemer says of his models, that "exploitation ... is essentially equivalent to initial inequality of assets", is not true of this model, and thus not true in general.[11]

But there is worse to come, from the point of view of Taylorian solutions to public goods provision. We know in the case of capitalism who is going to be an exploiting free-rider – the person with the greater amount of property. In the current case we have a different situation in which (i) everyone prefers there to be a class-divided society than that the economy collapses (this is the element analagous to the assurance supergame solution of the two-person Prisoner's Dilemma), but also (ii) everyone prefers not to be a member of the working class at the class-divided equilibrium.

We have, of course, met this second element before, in chapters 11 and 14. It is the Chicken problem, and (ii) describes a Chicken competition to avoid being a member of the working class in our proto-communist society. Yet we know from the analysis of section 11.1 that a Chicken game is rationally insoluble. There is no basis in a symmetrical Chicken game for deciding who is going to be a worker, and therefore which of the $_nC_N$ copies of the greenstick equilibrium is going to be the outcome of the Basic Income game.[12] I register a pessimistic interim conclusion: rational-choice solutions to the Basic Income predicament are, firstly, indeterminate, and secondly, unacceptable to egalitarians, since they almost inevitably involve a class division of a sufficiently large society between the workers and a free-riding leisured class.

I will argue as a finale that the resolution of these difficulties delivers us out of the theory of rational choice into the arms of sociology.

Notes

1. Note that the functions f(c) and g(d) in this chapter are equivalent to the functions g(r) and f(l) respectively in "Symmetry and Social Division" *Behavioral Science*, 34, No. 3 (1989). The option here labelled "Cooperative" was there labelled "Right".

2. This is the concept called "strong equilibrium" in "Symmetry and Social Division", where weaker concepts are also discussed, involving non-negative instead of strictly positive incentives for actors to remain at equilibrium.

3. These contentions are established in "Symmetry and Social Division", pp. 163–7.

4. Though there are material externalities in the consumption of the goods once produced. See chapter 9, note 13.

5. There is an analogy with the condition $(a + b) < 1$ discussed in section 6.1.

6. See section 6.2.

7. This is the formal reason why I think it is mistaken to try and rescue Marx's vision of communism from its dependence on a concept of abundance, as Normal Geras attempts to do in "The Controversy about Marx and Justice", in Callinicos, ed., *Marxist Theory* (Oxford: O.U.P., 1989), pp. 261–5. Geras is no doubt right to say that communism could not be expected to satisfy someone's need to wander undisturbed in an area as large as Australia. But this misses the point. The expansion which threatens the viability of communism is not the expansion of each individual's need, but the expansion of the number of individuals whose more moderate needs must be satisfied. When I grow corn in my small corner of communist Australia, I am also growing corn for every other Australian (because distribution is *per capita*). There are so many Australians that this will not be worth my while for the tiny proportional return I get from my own efforts, unless the productivity of my agricultural labour is truly colossal. This is the problem of households (see chapter 11) writ large, because communism makes Australia into one giant household. For further discussion, see Philippe Van Parijs, "In Defence of Abundance" in Robert Ware and Kai Neilsen, eds., "Analysing Marxism", *Canadian Journal of Philosophy*, Supplementary Volume 15 (1989).

8. Michael Taylor, *Anarchy and Cooperation* (London: John Wiley, 1976); Russell Hardin, *Collective Action* (Baltimore: Johns Hopkins Press, 1982).

9. His most recent treatment is in *The Possibility of Cooperation* (Cambridge: C.U.P., 1987), which is an updated version of *Anarchy and Cooperation*.

10. I would have called this a "Ring of Confidence", before being told by Chris Carling that the phrase is indelibly associated with a certain brand of toothpaste.

11. Roemer, "Should Marxists be interested in exploitation?", in John Roemer, ed., *Analytical Marxism* (Cambridge: C.U.P., 1986), p. 274. Roemer uses the term "socialist exploitation" to describe inequalities based on skill differentials, whereas the term would seem to be more appropriately applied to the inequality at the Taylor equilibrium – which is more intimately connected with characteristically socialist property relations. I note also that the social division at the Taylor equilibrium is a counter-example both to Roemer's claim (see *Quarterly Journal of Economics*, 1986) that "Equality of Resources implies Equality of Welfare" and to Elster's general definition of classes – a point Elster unwittingly concedes in his comment on the Basic Income scheme that "it is unfair for able-bodied people to live off the labor of others. Most workers would correctly in my opinion, see

the proposal as a recipe for exploitation of the industrious by the lazy". See "Comment on Van der Veen and Van Parijs", *Theory and Society*, 15 (1981), p. 719.

12. The argument of section 11.1 would simply be reworked, with each actor thinking of the reasons why fewer or more than $(n - 1)$ other actors would play the strategy T_n, and applying the same reasoning by parity to each of the other $(N - 1)$ actors.

The Problem of Social Order

17.1 Two Solutions of the Basic Income Game

Gotha programme socialism

Perhaps the overall title of this chapter is a little grandiose. I will offer two solutions to the Basic Income Game. Yet this is just one instance of the general problem posed by the N-person Prisoner's Dilemma, and that game is commonly thought to capture the essence of the problem of social order. Hence the solution to the smaller problem may illuminate the larger problem, as the main title claims.

The proposed solutions rest on two ideas: first, that because the cooperative outcome of an N-person Prisoner's Dilemma is Pareto-superior to the non-cooperative equilibrium, there are large potential gains from co-operation gains which can be used in part to finance the social systems which will ensure the maintenance of cooperation; and second, that it is possible to meet the theoretical requirements for a functional explanation of the existence of the social systems which act to maintain cooperation. The social systems exist, to wit, in virtue of the function they have of maintaining cooperation. I spell out the implications of these ideas for the Basic Income Game (BIG).

The existing elements of BIG are (i) a technological system (a linear relation of burdensome work input to useful output); (ii) an economic system (a rule of equal proportional distribution equivalent to distribution according to need among equally needy individuals); and to these elements we now add (iii) a political system.

The sole function of the political system is to ensure compliance with the work ethic. It does this by creating differential incentives between the "working" and "not working" alternatives in the underlying economic model so that free-riding ceases to be an attractive option. These are either selective incentives to work, or selective disincentives to not working.

Recalling our earlier commentary on the application of communist forms of distribution in non-communist circumstances, the political system may be viewed as the element in society which enforces contribution according to ability, when distribution occurs according to need. The discussion of this chapter is thus relevant to the Marxian idea of the withering away of the state.

The effect of the existence of any such political system is to alter the property relations of the "underlying" economic system, since the political system will surely enjoy an impact only to the extent that it succeeds in changing the economic payoff structures. We are really considering a composite system of political economy, in which we separate the economy from the polity for analytical convenience.

The two different solutions I will be offering possess an "economic" and a "political" flavour respectively. The economically oriented solution is best envisaged as operating through selective incentives to work, tantamount to the introduction of wage payments for work in our Basic Income society. The politically oriented solution is envisaged rather as the institution of a system of sanctions against not working, whose cost is borne by the people who work. The analytical distinction between these two solutions is a rather slim one (since any incentive to work *ipso facto* creates a disincentive to not working, and *vice versa*). But a rough correspondence is intended between the two types of solution and fundamental varieties of social organization. The market offers a solution via the carrot: the state or community offers one through the stick. I discuss the two solutions in turn, beginning with the wage payment solution.

We have seen that the difference in welfare between the workers and the free-riding non-workers at any outcome of BIG is equal to unity: workers are worse off by the unit cost of working. So a wage of unity will just compensate workers for working. But each worker produces an amount x, where $x > 1$, so a surplus of amount $(x - 1)$ exists after compensatory wages are paid. Let this surplus be distributed equally as Basic Income to everyone in the society. (Before, it was the gross product, rather than this net product, which was distributed as Basic Income.)

This proposal seems an appropriate way to implement "Gotha Programme socialism", in so far as the rationale for the latter is equal welfare, because the welfare of workers and non-workers is equal, no matter what the proportion of workers and non-workers in the society. Compared to this proposal, "Lassallean" socialism (with a wage (x)) is too generous to the workers, and communism (with a zero wage) is too generous to the non-workers.[1] We can also compare the mechanisms with respect to justice. Gotha programme socialism is, so to speak, just through-and-through (as if justice were lettered in it like a stick of seaside rock) because everyone always receives exactly what they are entitled to – compensation for work, equal reward for need. However equal welfare, and hence justice, is a property only of the equilibrium outcome under either Lassallean socialism or communism. The latter are just in the outcome perhaps, but not in all the makings of the outcome.

To formalize Gotha programme socialism, we observe that the level of Basic Income depends jointly on the productivity of the economy and the number of people who work. If there are c workers, each worker receives

$$f(c) = (x - 1)c/N + 1 - 1$$
$$= (x - 1) c/N \qquad\qquad\qquad (17.1)$$

and this is the same as the amount received by the non-workers in a society containing c workers. But the value of the function $g'(c)$ is the amount received by non-workers when there are $(c - 1)$ workers in the society (since the effect of the defection of a C-playing worker will be to reduce the number of workers by one). So

$$g'(c) = (x - 1)(c - 1)/N \qquad\qquad\qquad (17.2)$$

Comparison of (17.1) and (17.2) shows that $f(c)$ exceeds $g'(c)$ for all values of c. The payoff functions are as depicted in Figure 17.1, with a corresponding equilibrium in which everyone works. This is to say that in an economy capable or producing a surplus (net of labour costs), the introduction of compensating wage payment is sufficient to restore a positive incentive to work. The reason this occurs (the reason that $f(c) > g'(c)$) is that each member of society will receive a proportion $1/N$ of the enhanced net social output consequent upon the member's decision to become a worker. The result is that everyone works, and therefore receives gross income x, equal to an income of $(x - 1)$ net of unit labour cost. This is evidently an egalitarian solution, unlike the supergame solution. Of the gross income x, an amount 1 is paid in recognition of labour contribution, and an amount $(x - 1)$ in recognition of equal need. So it might be said that as the productivity x tends to infinity, the society is becoming progressively more communist (in the somewhat misleading usage of Van der Veen and Van Parijs) because the "needs" element of gross income is growing at the expense of the "contribution" element.

There is, however, one major snag in this solution. The incentive to work, as measured by $f(c) - g'(c)$, is equal to $(x - 1)/N$ and this quantity tends to zero as N tends to infinity (the two payoff lines in Figure 17.1

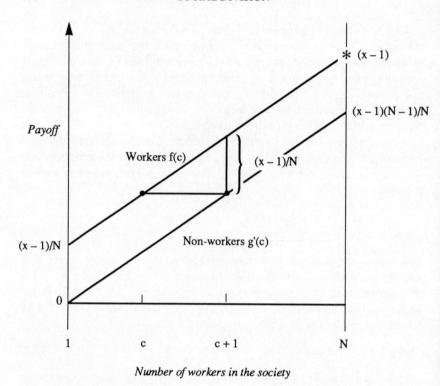

Number of workers in the society

* Boundary equilibrium

Figure 17.1 The Gotha Programme Solution to BIG

will become closer together and eventually merge). The larger the society
is, the less likely it is that people will be motivated to work simply because
of the cooperative share they receive of their own output. The latter
will increasingly appear to them like a drop in the ocean of the entire
social product. It transpires that there is no equivalent difficulty in our
next possible solution to BIG: the "political" solution.

The curious incident of the vanishing police

"Is there any point to which you would wish to draw my attention?" [asked
Inspector Gregory]
   "To the curious incident of the dog in the night-time."
   "The dog did nothing in the night-time."
   "That was the curious incident," remarked Sherlock Holmes.[2]

A political solution envisages the existence of a *police effect*, orchestrated

by communal or state institutions (that is, by an egalitarian or an egalitarian organization of police). The police effect acts to deter free-riding.
Can the free-rider problem be overcome by the addition of such a political
level to the fundamental economic system of BIG?

The answer is: Yes. For suppose we have some system of police which
changes the incentive structure symmetrically so that everyone works.
Then there is nothing for the police force to do, and the police service
costs no money. So the cooperative outcome is sustained as if by magic,
with exactly the same payoffs as if it were an equilibrium in the underlying
economic game. Each player receives the technologically determined maximum equal payoff $(x - 1)$ because the tax bill for the police is zero –
even though economic distribution still occurs according to need, and
not according to contribution.

This argument shows, I claim, that there is always scope for a socio-
political solution to the problem of social order. But perhaps it is not
always such plain sailing for the police. Suppose that there are a few
recidivists in this perfect society. Then the police (who may of course
be all of us as members of a community rather than some of us as
employees of the state) must seek out the miscreants and impose the
sanctions on them which make their recidivism a less attractive option.[3]
The more recidivists there are, the more expensive this process becomes,
and, what adds salt to the wound, the smaller is the social surplus out
of which the policing operation must be paid. We know that at some
point the police will no longer be effective and a breakdown in law and
order will occur. For if everyone in the society were a recidivist, then
everyone would need to be sanctioned, and yet the social product available
to finance the system of sanctions would be zero, so that no sanctions
could be imposed.

If we thus know that law and order is costlessly enforceable if $c =
N$, and expensively unenforceable if $c = 0$, it remains to examine the
trade-off which happens in between. In what circumstances can the police
uphold a working equilibrium of the society?

We begin by specifying a *police technology* (or police function) which
shows how much sanctioning effect one gets from the unit of police
resource. Accordingly, let each unit spent on the police force create y
units of social sanction. This formulation can include the idea that the
police are not perfectly efficient in detecting anti-social activity. Thus,
if the chance of being caught is a probability p, say, and the level of
punishment is P,[4] we posit a level of expected sanction given by

$$y = pP \qquad\qquad (17.3)$$

It comes as no surprise that the less efficient the police force is at detection, the heavier-handed it is likely to be in meting out punishment (since P varies inversely with p for given y). It is explicit also that there is a linear police technology: the more bobbies on the beat; the more villains in the net. (This theory is therefore not intended to apply within the London Metropolitan Police District, where the linear relation is rather between the number of criminals and the personal incomes of the police).

Assume next that in order to finance the police, a tax t_c is levied on each worker (of whom there are c) and this revenue is all used to impose a sanction s_c on non-workers (of whom there are $(N - c)$). Then the payoff functions of BIG must be modified to read

$$f(c) = (cx/N - 1) - t_c \qquad (17.4)$$

and

$$g'(c) = (c - 1)x/N - s_{c-1} \qquad (17.5)$$

The police budget will balance when the total social sanction applied throughout the society takes up the total tax revenue with a given punitive technology y. Thus

$$(N - c)s_c = y.c.t_c \qquad (17.6)$$

Substitution for s_{c-1} in (17.5) yields

$$g'(c) = (c - 1)x/N - y(c - 1)t_{c-1}/(N - c + 1) \qquad (17.7)$$

We know that the configuration of equilibrium points in the modified BIG society with a police force will depend on the relative values of $f(c)$ and $g'(c)$. We see from a comparison of (17.4) with (17.7) that this balance of utility will depend on the relative values of the tax rates t_c and t_{c-1} (that is, on the variation of the tax rate with the size c of the working class in a given population N). We could explore various relationships of t_c with c. A particularly convenient relationship arises from the intuition drawn upon above that the more workers there are, the lower the tax rate can be, because the less the police force has to do. Accordingly, set

$$t_c = t(N - c) \qquad (17.8)$$

where t is a tax parameter. Tax rate is zero when the whole society works, and is maximized when one person alone is working (and so has to finance single-handed the police effort against every other shirking member of society).[5]

Substitution of (17.8) in (17.4) and (17.7) gives

$$f(c) = c[x/N + t] - [1 + tN] \qquad (17.9)$$

and

$$g'(c) = (c - 1)[x/N - yt] \qquad (17.10)$$

Note that the functions $f(c)$ and $g'(c)$ remain linear in c (this is why (17.8) is an especially convenient form of tax relation). The effect of the introduction of this particular taxation system is to increase the gradient of the function f (because the more workers there are, the lower the tax burden becomes) and to decrease the gradient of the function g' (because the sanction against non-workers is increasing as the smaller police budget is nevertheless spread more thickly among the decreasing number of recidivists).

Recall that the underlying Prisoner's Dilemma problem in the Basic Income Game arises because $g'(c) > f(c)$ for all values of c. There will then be a political solution to BIG if and only if $f(c) > g'(c)$ for at least some values of c. Given the arithmetical forms of (17.4) and (17.10) the existence of the solution requires, in particular, that $f(N) > g'(N)$ (there must be at least sufficient deterrent to make the all-worker society an equilibrium). The condition $f(N) > g'(N)$ is

$$(x - 1) > (N - 1)[x/N - yt]$$

or

$$yt > (N - x)/N(N - 1) \qquad (17.11)$$

In this case, the functions f and g' are as depicted in figure 17.2. They intersect in the open interval $(1, N)$, but there is no internal equilibrium, because the functions intersect from the "wrong" directions (falling g' is crossing rising f). The intersection is a point of dispersion, and there are two equilibria in the game – one at each boundary.[6]

If we call the value of c at the intersection c_{crit}, then the behaviour of the system depends also on the initial value of c (that is, the initial number of persons working in the society). Call this value c_{init}. If c_{init} is greater than c_{crit}, a virtuous circle is established: non-workers join the work force, taxes are lowered and sanctions against non-working increase so that the incentive to work is yet further enhanced. Hence the society rapidly migrates to an all-worker society (at the right-hand boundary of Figure 17.2). But if c_{init} is less than c_{crit}, the circle turns vicious: police taxes are so high, and police action so ineffective against the large number

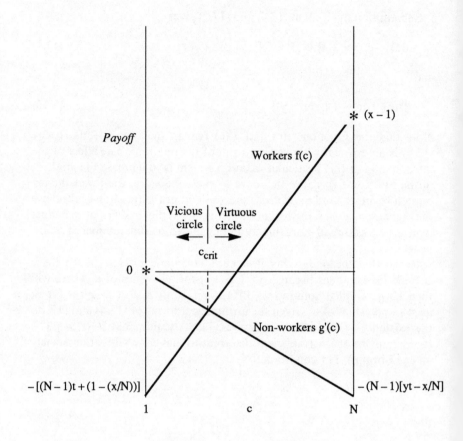

Number of workers in the society

Figure 17.2 The Curious Incident of the Vanishing Police

of free-riders, that it is crazy to be a worker. People leave the work force, which intensifies the tax burden on the remaining workers. Pretty soon, the economy collapses.

The value of c_{crit} (that is, the location of the point of dispersion in Figure 17.2) varies with all the parameters of the model. It is clear to begin with that c_{crit} varies inversely with y (for given N, x and t). This means that the more effective the police technology, the lower the number of workers necessary to sustain cooperation. Less obviously, it can be shown that c_{crit} varies inversely with t (for given N, x and y).[7] This means that the size of the critical complement of cooperative workers is lowered by raising the tax impost parameter t. Increasing the police budget will therefore always bring results. There are however two qualifications to this apparently infallible strategy for creating law and order.

The first problem is that the taxes imposed may be so high that they depress workers' welfare at the coordinate c_{crit} below the level it would have attained if the economy had collapsed instead: police action may be so excessive that the police budget eats up the entire social product produced by workers at c_{crit}. The second, related, problem is that there is a positive lower bound to the value of c_{crit}, regardless of the size of the police budget. It can be shown that, as t increases, c_{crit} tends asymptotically from above to the value $(N + y)/(1 + y)$.[8] Note that if $y = 0$ (and the police is totally inefficient) the asymptote is at $c = N$, whereas if y is infinite (and the police infinitely productive – as I suppose a communist police should be), the asymptote is at $c = 1$. In the latter case the existence of just one worker will start the ball rolling towards the all worker equilibrium. It seems to follow that there is no substitute for efficiency in the police force, since the better the force, the lower is the value c_{crit} at which a virtuous circle of law and order sets in.

Yet whatever the finite positive efficiency of the police, it remains true that there will be some critical mass of workers whose existence is sufficient to trigger the virtuous circle which leads to an equilibrium in which everyone works. This is obviously an egalitarian equilibrium, like the one given by the "Gotha programme" solution to the Basic Income Game. I noted above, however, that the incentive to work attenuates as the "Gotha Programme" society grows in size: the worker's marginal share x/N is less of a motivating factor for large N. So the Gotha programme solution is not so efficacious in a large society.[9]

The "police" solution seems by contrast to work better as society expands. The key condition which makes the all-worker society an equilibrium is condition (17.11). Notice that the r.h.s. of (17.11) is always positive (since $N > x$), but that it tends to zero as N tends to infinity, which means that (17.11) would be satisfied for all positive values of y and t. Thus, in a Basic Income society which is effectively infinitely large, there can be a stable egalitarian political resolution to the Prisoner's Dilemma problem even when the police force is almost totally inefficient and the police tax is negligibly small. The reason for this is not hard to find. If everyone is working, then the whole weight of social disapprobation falls on the first person to step out of line, and this is a crushing deterrent, even if upright members of society contribute very little *per capita* to a rather inept machinery of discouragement.

The overall conclusion of this section is rather surprising. It looks as if it is almost a piece of cake to arrange a solution to the N-person Prisoner's Dilemma in a very large society by positing the existence of a

distinct political apparatus of deterrence. The solution works by transforming the N-person Prisoner's Dilemma into a pure N-person assurance
game lacking the admixtures of Chicken which dogged the Taylor solution.[10]

The unsympathetic critic will say nevertheless that I have scored an
own goal: I have appeared to prove that socialism is either (i) unviable
(because the underlying structure of BIG is an N-person Prisoner's
Dilemma), or (ii) hard to distinquish from an egalitarian form of capitalism
(because the payoff functions of Lassallean, "big wage" socialism are
identical to those of the Basic Wealth model of popular capitalism), or
(iii) applicable only in a relatively small society (because of the attenuation
of incentives under Marx's *Gotha Programme* socialism), or (iv) tyrannical
in the way it must impose a work ethic by external sanction on a reluctant
work force (because of the stabilizing function of the deterrent apparatus
in the "vanishing police" solution to BIG).

I have three responses to this hypothetical criticism. The first is that
it is unsurprising that an egalitarian form of capitalism satisfies the socialist complaint against actually existing capitalism that actually existing
capitalism is inegalitarian (there are other complaints, such as that capitalist property relations are undemocratic, which not even an egalitarian
form of capitalism will satisfy). The second response concedes that my
exposition of the case of the vanishing police may have been provocatively
authoritarian. But the substance of the case may be less so, since we
have not specified either the form of the police system (whether it is
centralized in a state or dispersed in a community) or the content and
severity of the sanctions it imposes (whether these are moral or material
and need be mild or harsh). My third response is that whatever degree
of authoritarianism is entailed by the case of the vanishing police is the
degree of authoritarianism which will in principle be entailed by the stabilizing element in any system of market relations, since the operation of
markets was shown in chapter 8 to involve an exactly analogous problem
of social order. It is therefore my hypothetical pro-capitalist critic who
has really scored the own goal, for if the case of the vanishing police
entails an authoritarian solution to the problem of social order, then
capitalism is an inherently authoritarian system.[11]

Although Basic Income is not nearly as unworkable in theory as Elster
believes, nor as authoritarian in its working as anti-socialist critics might
suppose, one other political implication of the solution given here should
nevertheless be made clear. It seems very unlikely that a Basic Income
scheme is workable without some system of sanctions against free-riders.
This will not punish or stigmatize claimants *per se* (since everyone is
a claimant), but it will punish or stigmatize those who claim without
working. Whatever social apparatus is devised to administer these sanc-

tions – formal or informal, moral or material, centralized or decentralized – there will have to be externally applied discipline in the society. This considerably reduces one of the attractions of the unconditional version of Basic Income compared with its conditional alternatives. Stigma will remain, even if its locus will have changed.

17.2 On Superstructural Explanation

I have argued that it is sufficient for the solution of BIG that a political system exists which makes the cooperative outcome an equilibrium of rational action (we also need a condition on the initial state of the system: $c_{init} > c_{crit}$). This result has established the *possibility* of cooperation (to borrow a phrase from the title of Mike Taylor's book). I have, moreover, taken this political solution to BIG as a prototype of all political solutions to the N-person Prisoner's Dilemma, and hence to the problem of social order. We have already appealed to this mechanism in connection with the problem of contract compliance studied in chapter 8 and the problem of collective action studied in chapter 14. Suppose, then, that we observe that the problem of social order has been solved in some domain of interest. We do not have an explanation for the *actuality* of cooperation unless we have an explanation for the establishment of the political system which, we guess, enables the problem of social order to be solved by rational actors.

So how could such a political system come about? We know that, given the existence of the political system, the equilibrium occurs because of rational behaviour. But is rational behaviour likely to have led to the creation of the political system? Will people have got together to establish a political system for the very reason that the existence of such a political system would resolve their problem of social order? There is a certain logic to this proposal. If actors look at Figure 16.2, they can label the left-hand boundary Warre and the right-hand boundary Peace, and each can reckon that she or he would be better off if all cooperated under a Hobbesian Sovereign than if none cooperated without. And since each can reason that all will so reckon, then all would decide in favour of the rule of a cooperative law enforced by the Sovereign. Yet to say that this is what actors faced with such a choice would decide is not to give an explanation of how the Sovereign power in fact becomes established. And it is extremely doubtful that there is a rational-choice explanation for such a piece of social engineering. For one thing, Sovereign-building is a collective action, and collective action to establish a political system requires the resolution of just such a problem of social order as the political system is designed to overcome.

If rational choice does not offer a very good explanation of the genesis of the political system, another and somewhat more plausible view is that the political system may have come about through a process of social selection. This can occur because the difference between having and not having a political system is the difference between the payoff $(x - 1)$ and the payoff zero in this model. (In general N-person Prisoner's Dilemma terms, it is the difference in the individual payoff at the non-cooperative equilibrium compared with the payoff at the fully cooperative outcome.) This is a big difference – even a BIG difference.

Yet we know we must set out our stall carefully in this area to take account of the variety of distinct claims we might be making about the nature of the explanatory connection between the political system and its underlying economic system (that is, the underlying N-person Prisoner's Dilemma). We can begin by distinguishing between two claims:

Claim 1: the cooperative equilibrium is bound to occur in the economic system, because the economic system will always be stabilized by the provision of an appropriate political system.

Claim 2: whenever the economic system is at a cooperative equilibrium, there must exist an appropriate political system acting to stabilize the economic system.

These two claims differ in what they claim will exist. The first predicts the existence of the cooperative equilibrium, whereas the second only predicts the existence of the political system *given* the existence of the cooperative equilibrium. The claims differ correspondingly in their strength: the first is absurdly strong and the second is not quite ridiculously weak.

To show how strong the first claim is we may refer to the discussion of ethnic division in chapter 14. Suppose that there is a disjoint and exhaustive partition of society between two ethnic groups A and B. Then according to our analysis there can be a stable equilibrium of the society with a monopoly formation in favour of ethnic group A. This monopoly represents the realization of a collective gain for the members of group A, compared to the egalitarian alternative in which all members of the society are treated alike. We also envisage that this monopoly formation is secured by the provision of a political system which enforces the collection of taxes among group A, resists the opposition of group B to the monopoly arrangement, and administers or guarantees the mechanisms of unequal distribution to members of the respective groups.

We have just envisaged a monopoly regime that favours group A. There is however another monopoly regime of which group B rather than group

A is the beneficiary, and we know that circumstances can exist in which this alternative system of discrimination is also a stable equilibrium, with collective gains to members of group B. Yet it is impossible for there to be a political system which simultaneously stabilizes the monopoly position of group A and the monopoly position of group B, for the distributions guaranteed by the respective monopolies are incompatible. The first of the two claims just considered is shown to be untenably strong, since it claims that every possibility of cooperative gain will be realized whereas some possibilities are mutually exclusive.

The second claim is by contrast so weak that it might appear tautological: if one accepts the framework of rational-choice theory, the only way in which a cooperative equilibrium could have come about is because the incentive structure of the underlying Prisoner's Dilemma must have changed. In the case of the A, B ethnic society, for instance, the second claim is only that if the monopoly regime favours group A, there must be a political system which changes incentives to stabilize the A-regime, whereas if there is a monopoly which favours group B, there must be a (different) political system to stabilize the B-regime.

Yet this claim does have a certain content, both because it rules out certain alternatives to rational-choice behaviour, and because the wording is intended to restrict the range of sources from which the stabilizing incentives can arise. Exclusively moral reasons for cooperative behaviour are ruled out, as is the type of conditional cooperation relied upon by Taylor. The claim intends to convey that the N-person Prisoner's Dilemma can only be resolved in general by the provision of a system of sanctions external to the individual, even though these sanctions may interact with internalized norms and values. Thus, if we turn to the discussion of market relations in chapter 8 as an example, we expect that the market system is stabilized by a norm of bargain-keeping, backed by a system of sanctions against those who are shown to break their bargains (some of which sanctions may only be effective because the bargain-breakers have also internalized the bargain-keeping norm).

Such a political system is liable to contain an *educational* element (which creates certain norms and values in the individual), a *surveillance* element (which detects infringements), and an *enforcement* element (which applies sanctions against delinquents). But the second claim does not specify the types of sanction or the precise form of their administration. The different varieties of sanction apparatus – market-like, state-like or community-like – may be said to represent *functionally equivalent* ways of solving the problem of social order. This is a permissible locution, so long as it is understood to mean only that the various political systems are alike in having a stabilizing effect upon (which equals a stabilizing function for) their underlying economic systems.

A distinct, and distinctly stronger, claim would be that the existence of some political apparatus of sanctions is *functionally explained*. Such an explanatory connection is asserted in

Claim 3: whenever the economic system is at a cooperative equilibrium, there must exist a stabilizing political system, whose existence is explained by the stabilizing function that it has.

The difference between this claim and the previous one can be judged by considering the case of a religion which inculcates and enforces a generalized norm of promise-keeping. The existence of the religion – more strictly, the existence of the promise-keeping aspect of the religion – will stabilize any economic system of exchange relations because it will enable co-religionists to trust their partners in exchange transactions.[12] Yet it may well be that this very useful economic function of the religion is simply a by-product of a theology of social behaviour which has come about for very different reasons: the economic function may only be, so to speak, an appendix of the religious practice. To establish that (the promise-keeping aspect of) the religion is explained by its economic effect, it must at the very least be shown that (the promise-keeping aspect of) the religion would not exist unless it had that particular economic effect.[13]

This is a strong claim, though not absurdly strong. If it is accepted that without the religion people would never engage in exchange, and hence not realize any of the cooperative gains to be made from exchange, then it would follow that their welfare might fall below some survival threshold. And if they all died, they would hardly be in a fit state to practise the promise-keeping aspect of their religion. Perhaps it is especially appropriate to look for functional explanations of the ideologies which stabilize fundamental economic arrangements precisely because the effects of failure to stabilize such relations tend to be so devastating. In this view, the existence of the morality that must be possessed by all survivors is explained by the fact of survival, since the amoral never survive to enjoy their amoral condition.

The problem with this view is that the amoral may not in fact always perish. Rather than wither away in normless isolation, amoral individuals may establish two-person Taylorian households whose internal arrangements are secured by conditional threats arising purely from the logic of cooperative benefits.[14] This kind of economic system is, so to speak, self-stabilizing, so that one cannot appeal to the unviability of the unstabilized system as part of the functional explanation of the existence of any stabilizing political element of the stabilized system. It seems wise, then, to step back from our third claim, in favour of the weaker

Claim 4: whenever the economic system is at a cooperative equilibrium, there may exist a stabilizing political system, whose existence is sometimes explained by the stabilizing function that it has.

A functional explanation of the political system will be appropriate only when there are no equilibria of conditional cooperation in the underlying game, and there is a clear survival threshold of some kind between the cooperative and non-cooperative payoffs in the underlying game.[15]

If any Marxists have been itching to translate the foregoing into the language of base and superstructure, I will now help them scratch. It is natural to regard what I have called "the economic system" as the economic *base*, which will be said to be *viable* when the cooperative equilibrium is achieved within it, and unviable otherwise. It will be recalled from chapter 1 that, strictly speaking, a base has a *superstructure* only where the superstructure is *explained* by its relationship to the base. Thus, not every political system is superstructural. There is a distinction, which I have tried to respect in the formulation of the four claims just examined, between noting the stabilizing effect a political system may have, and explaining it by that effect.

The superstructure is a roof which protects its underlying building. But a genuine superstructure must also rest upon the very building it protects, in such a way that the crumbling of the foundations would bring the roof crashing through the floor: the superstructure cannot, for instance, be a canopy attached to a neighbouring house. Construed in this way, the family of Marxian base-superstructure claims has the following membership:

Claim 1: All bases are viable, because all bases will find stabilizing political systems.

Claim 2: All viable bases have stabilizing political systems – but a stabilizing political system is not necessarily superstructural.

Claim 3: All viable bases have superstructures.

Claim 4: Some viable bases have superstructures.

I have resisted claims 1 and 3 as being too strong, and rejected claim 2 as lacking explanatory ambition. I plump for claim 4 as modest but not vacuous: sometimes there are superstructural solutions to the problem of social order.

There will of course be a narrative history of any such solution: a causal story which dwells on inspired leadership, commitment against all the odds to the success of the superstructural project, luck and opportunity. This story will yield a causal explanation for the existence of a given superstructure of sanctions. But such a causal explanation will not be the real explanation we want, for the real explanation we want is that, however it was achieved, the political system exists by virtue of the function it has of resolving the problem of social order. Any old system will do for this purpose – here it will be a system of wage incentives or moral inducements, there it will be gossip or the boys in blue. Communities, states or the more political parts of the economy may all be functional equivalents in this respect. All that matters is that rational actors should be much better off receiving their equilibrium payoffs in the game with a political system than they would be in the game without a political system: so much so that the underlying unpoliticized economy is unviable without its political superstructure. And this superstructural narrative will imply at bottom a functional explanation, and not a rational-choice explanation, for the resolution by rational actors of a generic problem of rational interaction.[16]

Notes

1. These assertions depend on the usual assumptions about the uniformity of the relation between income and welfare for everyone in the society. Note also that I am using the term "Gotha programme socialism" to describe the proposals put forward by Marx in his *Critique of the Gotha Programme* rather than the Gotha proposals themselves, which I describe as "Lassallean socialism". This is on the grounds that the critique is more famous than what it critiqued.

2. Sir Arthur Conan Doyle, "Silver Blaze" in *The Complete Sherlock Holmes* (New York: Doubleday and Co., 1988), p. 347. I am obliged to Ed Reiss for his detective work on this reference.

3. See Michael Taylor, *Community, Anarchy and Liberty* (Cambridge: C.U.P., 1982), pp. 65–90 for the host of social sanctions available to a stateless society. The argument of this chapter is intended to be neutral between state and communal solutions to the problem of social order, and is thus a contribution to anti-Hobbesian anarchism.

4. I ignore stochastic effects. Miller envisages an identical formula in *Market, State and Community* (Oxford: Clarendon Press, 1989), p. 41, n. 17.

5. If we want to arrange an equilibrium of an all-worker society in which there is still an embryonic police force, we must either attribute fixed costs to the policing operation, or assume a probability that the police punish the innocent, with the result that the police budget is greater than zero even at $c = N$. (This is different from the probabilistic interpretation of (17.3), which gives the guilty a chance to escape.) If the theory of deterrence advanced in this section seems fanciful, it is interesting to recall that it was held by the earliest proponents of a Metropolitan police in England, and is partly responsible for the still existing distinction between the uniformed branch and the Criminal Investigation Division. See Dick Hobbs, *Doing the Business* (Oxford: O.U.P, 1989), p. 29.

6. See "Symmetry and Social Division", Behavioral Science, 34, No. 3 (1989) section 9, for a discussion of dispersion points in symmetric games.

7. $c_{crit} = (N + y)/(1 + y) + [1 - (x/N)]/(1 + y)t$, which varies inversely with t, since $1 > x/N$.

8. This result follows immediately from the formula given in the previous note.

9. Though if wages are greater than unity (but no more than x), there is a positive incentive to work no matter how large the society. In this sense, there is always a wage incentive solution to BIG, though it must in general *overcompensate* the worker, if it is to operate effectively in a very large society. I am grateful to Philippe van Parijs for discussion bearing on this point, which is relevant also to egalitarian proposals on which John Baker is working.

10. The two-person assurance game is the prototype of an N-person game with a single point of dispersion, like that depicted in Figure 17.2.

11. In fact, I think neither type of society need be excessively authoritarian, since both can work by reinforcing moral commitments to a contract – in the case of markets a contract between individuals; in the case of socialism, what might be called a social contract between each individual and all other individuals.

12. Compare Michael Mann's comment on early medieval Europe that "the normative pacification of Christendom was a precondition of the revival of markets": *The Sources of Social Power* (Cambridge: C.U.P., 1986), p. 396. For Chris Wickham's reservations about Mann's argument see "Historical Materialism, Historical Sociology", *New Left Review*, 171 (1988), pp. 68–73.

13. I am not certain if the establishment of such a counterfactual is a sufficient condition for the success of a functional explanation of religion by economics, but I am clear that it is a necessary condition.

14. Although such individuals do not need external sanctions in order to cooperate, they must be able to defer gratification, and also hold certain theories about social causation (especially in trusting each other to retaliate in the game of tit-for-tat) as explained in chapter 8.

15. I have taken survival to mean physical survival in the main discussion. If this criterion were relaxed, the scope for functional explanations would be correspondingly increased.

16. This position may be compared with that most recently argued by Jon Elster in *The Cement of Society* (Cambridge: C.U.P., 1989). If Elster's previous position was characterized by "methodological individualism plus rational choice", he has now conceded slightly on rational choice without giving much away on methodological individualism. He avers that "the power of norms derives from the emotional tonality that gives them a grip on the mind" (p. 128) while confessing: "I do not know why human beings have a propensity to construct and follow norms, nor how specific norms come into being and change" (p. 125). In particular, he rejects the kind of explanation advanced in claim 4 for the existence of cooperative norms: "I find it as hard as the next person to believe that the existence of norms of reciprocity and cooperation has *nothing* to do with the fact that without them civilization as we know it would not exist. Yet it is at least a useful intellectual exercise to take the more austere view and to entertain the idea that civilization owes its existence to a fortunate coincidence" (p. 149, original emphasis). I find it rather baffling that Elster should resist the temptation to pursue an intuitively promising line of reasoning in favour of a rather unpromising agnostic exercise. Does the fear of functionalism perhaps enjoy too strong a grip upon his mind?

PART VIII

Conclusion

18

Rational Choice and Social Division

The utilitarian actor is not a charming beast. Amartya Sen has called such a person a "rational fool"; a one-dimensional caricature of the uniquely complex entity each human individual is.[1] What possible reason could one have for trying to build a theory on such an impoverished foundation? I think there are several reasons, the first two of which are somewhat opportunistic.

Mainstream economics, based on rational-choice assumptions, has tended to be used in ways that give comfort to the political right – especially in singing the praises of free market capitalism. The echoes of praise reverberate widely, even if the underlying theories are not widely understood. So even if rational-choice theory were fundamentally mistaken, it would be important politically and ideologically to know that it could be used in different ways, to substantiate Marxist, feminist or anarchist conclusions. I hope to have used it in support of all three types of conclusion, and I believe that this alone would justify the uses of rational-choice theory made in this book.

I also believe that a stronger case can be made in favour of the theory. The rational-choice approach seems to compensate for the relative poverty of its cognitive psychology by its uniquely powerful grasp of social interaction. We seem, in the current state of knowledge, to face something of a trade-off: theoretical complexity is located in either the individual or the society. The formula for Freud, say, is "complex individual, simple society" whereas for economics it is "simple individual, complex society". Sociology seems poised uneasily between the economic devil and the psychoanalytic deep blue sea. Opportunism in social theory recommends the rational-choice approach since, for all its shortcomings, it is about the best theory of social interaction we have. (Perhaps that makes it the rational choice.)

A more positive defence of the theory is that some, possibly large, part of human action surely is captured by the rational-choice assumption: people do conceive alternatives, envisage consequences, weigh up different courses of action and then choose what is best. Those who deride the rational-choice approach (the non-economists, let us say) must nonetheless be shown how far the rational-choice approach will go. The characteristics of social classes, domestic divisions of labour and ethnic groupings, as well as states, can in some measure be illuminated using the sparse data of the theory. If rational fools would arrange themselves in some of the social patterns we recognize, then maybe we are rational fools – or at least more foolish than we like to think.

The further beyond the market place and the conclusions of the political right the rational-choice approach will go, the more likely it appears to be that its taps some aspect of human nature, and the less obviously true are the challenges made as to its partiality. It cannot apply to one class alone, if all classes are understood to arise as a consequence of its application; it cannot apply just to markets if it works for feudal lords and households; it cannot apply just to the capitalist West if it helps to explain the incentive problem under socialism; it cannot apply to one ethnic group alone if it clarifies the patterns of migration between ethnic groups, or the problems of mobilization faced by all ethnic minorities.[2] Rational-choice Marxism is not a contradiction in terms, despite what Marx said about Bentham, and Marx did not in his practice deny its applicability.[3] Nor likewise is it in my view a contradiction in terms to speak of rational-choice feminism, rational-choice anti-racism, or rational-choice socialism.

Yet I am aware of many limitations of the theory too. If I would insist to the sociologically-minded that the rational-choice approach is necessary to any adequate theory of social division, I would insist as strongly to the economically-minded that it is not sufficient for an adequate theory of social division. It is not just that functional explanation is an admissible alternative to rational-choice explanation; in many important applications it seems to be preferable to rational-choice explanation. I found to my surprise in chapter 3 that a functional explanation of the transition to capitalism might be true as well as merely possible; I have just argued that functionalism is well suited to resolve the N-person Prisoner's Dilemma. Even Brenner's Axiom was shown to admit a functional construal. In chapter 12, the relationship between domestic organization and gender ideology appeared most likely to be a functional one, and rational choice seemed better equipped to explain the incidence of long-term pressures to reorganize the home than to play the micro-foundational role Elster had reserved for it.

Rational choice is sometimes radically indeterminate, as in the outcome of the Chicken game; sometimes it depends for its explanatory power on the existence of preference schedules which themselves above all need to be explained; often it requires auxiliary beliefs, not deducible from the payoff structure, in order to interpret the payoff structure. Thus I argued in chapter 8 that the characterization of a particular outcome as an equilibrium will depend on the beliefs about social causation (that is, the social theories) entertained by the actors. Later in the same chapter, the outcome required a certain sense of longevity in an interpersonal relationship, and by implication an extended sense of self. Obligation, too, was deemed irreducible to prudential conduct. Throughout parts V and VI, my emphasis lay as much on the existence of belief systems as on rational action, given belief. Nor did the notion of explaining belief systems directly by rational choice seem promising. In all these fields, rational choice has a role to play, sometimes perhaps a leading role; but it never makes up the whole cast of explanation.

Such thoughts perhaps govern my personal attitude to rational choice as well. The reader will know by now that I am intrigued and puzzled, and no doubt a trifle obsessed, by rational choice. I believe it to be a permanent feature of human conduct; I do not think there is a single area of social life which lies beyond its jurisdiction. It must always be reckoned with, and designers of social institutions will ignore it at their peril. But I do not like rational choice, not one little bit. It does not present a pretty picture of human motivation, not one that warms my heart or lifts my soul. Behaviour strikes me as admirable largely as it transcends the predictions of rational-choice theory. What one admires is behaviour beyond the remit of this book: action more courageous and just, more compassionate and less self-seeking than one has any right to expect. Who knows but that it is within these greater kinds of conduct, and our general feelings about them, that we must also seek some necessary counterpoise to rational choice, and social division.

Notes

1. Amartya Sen, "Rational Fools", *Philosophy and Public Affairs*, 6 (1977).
2. The most persuasive argument I know in favour of the claim refuted by Roemer's work that rational-choice theory applies to one class alone – the petty bourgeoisie – is contained, ironically enough, in an early article by John Roemer: "Neoclassicism, Marxism and Collective Action", *Journal of Economic Issues*, 12 (1978).
3. See chapter 15, note 7.

Bibliography

Abell, Peter. "Rational Equitarian Democracy, Minimax Class and the Future of Capitalist Society: A Sketch towards a Theory." *Sociology* 21 no. 4 (November 1987), pp. 567–90.

Abercrombie, Nicholas, Stephen Hill and Bryan S. Turner. *Sovereign Individuals of Capitalism*. London: Allen and Unwin, 1986.

Aigner, Dennis and Glen Cain. "Statistical Theories of Discrimination in Labor Markets." *Industrial and Labor Relations Review*, 30, no. 2(1977), pp.175–87.

Alchian, A.A. and Harold, Demetz. "The Property Rights Paradigm." *Journal of Economic History*, 33 (1973), pp. 16–27.

Allen, Sheila and Diane Barker, eds. *Dependence and Exploitation in Work and Marriage*. London: Longman, 1976.

Anderson, Benedict. *Imagined Communities: Reflections on the Origin and Spread of Nationalism*. London: Verso, 1983.

Anderson, Perry. *Passages from Antiquity to Feudalism*. London: New Left Books, 1974.

——*Considerations on Western Marxism*. London: Verso, 1979.

Anderson, W., H. Locke and Frank W. Thompson. "Neoclassical Marxism." *Science and Society*, 52, no. 2 (Summer 1988), pp. 215–28.

Assister, Alison. "Did Man Make Language?" *Radical Philosophy* 34 (1983), pp. 25–9.

Aston, T.H. and C.H.E. Philpin, eds. *The Brenner Debate: Agrarian Class Structure and Economic Development in Pre-industrial Europe*. Cambridge: C.U.P., 1985.

Atkinson, J. *A Handbook for Interviewers*. London: H.M.S.O., 1977.

Axelrod, Robert. *The Evolution of Cooperation*. New York: Basic Books, 1984.

Baker, Derek, ed. *Medieval Women*. Oxford: Blackwell, 1978.

Baker, John. *Arguing for Equality*. London: Verso, 1987.

Banton, Michael. "Categorical and Statistical Discrimination." *Ethnic and Racial Studies*, 6, no. 3 (1983), pp. 269–83.

—— *Racial and Ethnic Competition*. Cambridge: C.U.P., 1983.

419

——"Mixed Motives and the Processes of Rationalization." *Ethnic and Racial Studies*, 8, no. 4 (1985), pp. 534–47.

Barrett, Michèle. *Women's Oppression Today: Problems in Marxist Feminist Analysis*. London: Verso, 1980.

——"Rethinking Women's Oppression: A Reply to Brenner and Ramas." *New Left Review*, 146 (July/August 1984), pp. 123–8.

"The Soapbox." *Network: Newsletter of the British Sociological Association*, no. 35 (May 1986), p. 20.

Barrett, Michèle and Mary McIntosh. "The 'Family Wage': Some Problems for Socialists and Feminists." *Capital and Class*, 11 (Summer 1980), pp. 51–72.

—— "Narcissism and the Family: A Critique of Lasch." *New Left Review*, 135 (September/October 1982), pp. 35–48.

—— *The Anti-Social Family*. London: Verso, 1982.

Becker, Gary S. *The Economics of Discrimination*. Chicago: University of Chicago Press, 1971.

Beechey, Veronica. *Unequal Work*. London: Verso, 1987.

Beechey, Veronica and Elizabeth Whitelegg, eds. *Women in Britain Today*. Milton Keynes: Open University Press, 1986.

Beechey, Veronica and Tessa Perkins. *A Matter of Hours: Women, Part-time Work and the Labour Market*. Cambridge: Polity Press, 1987.

Bell, Alan P. and Martin S. Weinberg. *Homosexualities: A Study of Diversity Among Men and Women*. New York: Simon and Schuster, 1978.

Berk, Sarah Fenstermaker. *The Gender Factory: The Apportionment of Work in American Households*. New York: Plenum Press, 1985.

Berk, Sarah Fenstermaker, ed. *Women and Household Labor*. Beverly Hills: Sage, 1980.

Bernard, Jessie. *The Future of Marriage*. New York: Bantam, 1973.

Bertram, Christopher. "International Competition as a Remedy for Some Problems in Historical Materialism." *New Left Review*, 182 (July/August 1990), pp. 116–28.

Bowles, Samuel and Herbert Gintis. *Schooling in Capitalist America*. London: Routledge and Kegan Paul, 1976.

Braham, Peter, Ed Rhodes and Michael Pearn, eds. *Discrimination and Disadvantage in Employment: The Experience of Black Workers*. London: Harper and Row, 1981.

Braverman, Harry. *Labor and Monopoly Capital: The Degradation of Work in the Twentieth Century*. New York: Monthly Review Press, 1974.

Brenner, Johanna and Maria Ramas. "Rethinking Women's Oppression." *New Left Review*, 144 (March/April 1984), pp. 33–71.

Brenner, Robert. "The Origins of Capitalist Development: A Critique of Neo-Smithian Marxism." *New Left Review*, 104 (July/August 1977), pp. 26–93.

Brod, Harry, ed. *The Making of Masculinities: The New Men's Studies*. Winchester, Mass.: Allen and Unwin, 1988.

Brown, Colin. *Black and White Britain: The Third Policy Studies Institute Survey*. Aldershot: Gower, 1985.

Burawoy, Michael and Theda Skocpol, eds. *Marxist Inquiries*. Chicago: Chicago University Press, 1982.

Burgess, Robert G. *Sociology, Education and Schools: An Introduction to the Sociology of Education*. London: Batsford, 1986.

Callinicos, Alex. *Making History: Agency, Structure and Change in Social Theory*. Oxford: Polity Press, 1989.

Callinicos, Alex, ed. *Marxist Theory*. Oxford: Oxford University Press, 1989.

Campbell, Richmond and Lanning Sowden, eds. *Paradoxes of Rationality and Cooperation: Prisoner's Dilemmas and Newcomb's Problem*. Vancouver: University of British Columbia Press, 1985.

Carling, Alan. "Value and Strategy." *Science and Society*, XLVIII, no. 2 (Summer 1984), pp. 129–60.

—— "The Forms of Value and the Logic of Capital." *Science and Society*, L, no. 1 (Spring 1986), pp. 52–80.

—— "Rational Choice Marxism." *New Left Review*, 160 (November/December 1986), pp. 24–62. Reprinted in *Approaches to Marx*, ed. Mark Cowling and Lawrence Wilde. Milton Keynes: Open University Press, 1989, pp. 185–227.

—— "Exploitation, Extortion and Oppression." *Political Studies*, XXXV, no. 2 (1987), pp. 173–88. Reprinted in *Rational Choice Theory*, ed. Peter Abell. Upleadon, Glos: Edward Elgar, 1991, pp. 313–28.

—— "The Schelling Diagram: On Binary Choice with Externalities." *Behavioral Science*, 32, no. 1 (Jan 1987), pp. 4–18.

—— "Symmetry and Social Division: More on Binary Choice with Externalities." *Behavioral Science*, 34, no. 3 (July 1989), pp. 161–75.

—— "In Defence of Rational Choice: A Reply to Ellen Meiksins Wood." *New Left Review*, 182 (July/August 1990), pp. 21–33.

Carter, Alan B. *Marx. A Radical Critique*. Brighton: Wheatsheaf, 1988.

Cashmore, Ellis. *The Logic of Racism*. London: Allen and Unwin, 1987.

Castles, Stephen and Godula Kosack. *Immigrant Workers and the Class Structure in Western Europe*. Oxford: Open University Press, 1973.

Central Statistical Office. *Social Trends 18*. London: H.M.S.O., 1988.

Chapman, Rowena and Jonathan Rutterford, eds. *Male Order: Unwrapping Masculinity*. London: Lawrence and Wishart, 1988.

Cohen, Anthony P., ed. *Symbolizing Boundaries: Identity and Diversity in British Cultures*. Manchester: Manchester University Press, 1986.

Cohen, G.A. *Karl Marx's Theory of History: A Defence*. Oxford: Clarendon Press, 1978.

—— "The Labour Theory of Value and the Concept of Exploitation." In *The Value Controversy*, ed. Ian Steedman et al., London: Verso, 1981, pp. 202–23.

—— "Reply to Elster on 'Marxism, Functionalism and Game Theory'." *Theory and Society*, 11, no. 4 (1982), pp. 483–95.

—— "Functional Explanation, Consequence Explanation and Marxism." *Inquiry*, 25 (1982), pp. 27–56.

—— "Reply to Four Critics." *Analyse und Kritik*, 5 (1983), pp. 195–222.

—— "Nozick on Appropriation." *New Left Review*, 150 (March/April 1985), pp. 89–105.

——— "Restricted and Inclusive Historical Materialism." In *The Prism of Science,* ed. E. Ullmann-Margalit, Dordrecht: D. Reidel, 1986, pp. 57–83.

——— "Self-Ownership, World Ownership and Equality: Part II." In *Marxism and Liberalism*, ed. Ellen Frankel Paul et al., Oxford: Basil Blackwell, 1986, pp. 77–96.

——— *History, Labour and Freedom: Themes from Marx.* Oxford: Oxford University Press, 1989.

Cole, G.D.H. *The Next Ten Years in British Social and Economic Policy.* London: Macmillan, 1929.

Cowling, Mark and Lawrence Wilde, eds. *Approaches to Marx.* Milton Keynes: Open University Press, 1989.

Crompton, Rosemary and Michael Mann, eds. *Gender and Stratification.* Cambridge: Polity Press, 1986.

Crow, Graham. "The Use of the Concept of 'Strategy' in Recent Sociological Literature." *Sociology*, 23, no. 1 (1989), pp. 1–24.

Cunningham, Frank. *Democratic Theory and Socialism.* Cambridge, C.U.P., 1987.

Cutler, Anthony, Barry Hindess, Paul Hirst and Athar Hussain. *Marx's 'Capital' and Capitalism Today.* 2 Volumes. London: Routledge and Kegan Paul, 1977; 1978.

Dale, Angela, Nigel Gilbert and Sara Arber. "Integrating Women into Class Theory." *Sociology*, 19, no. 3 (1985) 384–408.

Dale, R. et al., eds. *Schooling and Capitalism.* London: Routledge and Kegan Paul, 1976.

Daly, Mary. *Gyn/Ecology.* London: The Women's Press, 1979.

Demuth, Clare. *'Sus': A Report on the Vagrancy Act 1824.* London: Runnymede Trust, 1978.

Dench, Geoff. *Maltese in London: a Case Study in the Erosion of Ethnic Consciousness.* London: Routledge and Kegan Paul, 1975.

Dex, Shirley. "The Use of Economists' Models in Sociology." *Ethnic and Racial Studies*, 8, no. 4 (1985), pp. 516–35.

——— *Women's Occupational Mobility: A Lifetime Perspective.* London: Macmillan, 1987.

Doyle, Sir Arthur Conan. *The Complete Sherlock Holmes.* Garden City, New York: Doubleday and Company Inc., 1988.

Dummet, Michael. *Immigration: Where the Debate Goes Wrong.* London: Action Group on Immigration and Nationality, 1978.

Dworkin, Andrea. *Intercourse.* London: Secker and Warburg, 1987.

Dworkin, Ronald. "What is Equality? Part 1: Equality of Welfare; Part 2: Equality of Resources." *Philosophy and Public Affairs*, 10 (1981), pp. 185–246; 283–345.

Ehrenreich, Barbara. *The Hearts of Men: American Dreams and the Flight from Commitment.* London: Pluto, 1983.

Elster, Jon. "Review of Cohen." *Political Studies*, 28 (1980), pp. 121–8.

——— "Marxism, Functionalism and Game Theory: The Case for Methodological Individualism." Theory and Society, 11, no. 4 (1982), pp. 453–81. Reprinted in *Marxist Theory*, ed. Alex Callinicos, Oxford: Open University Press, 1989, pp. 48–87.

——"Roemer vs. Roemer: A Comment on 'New Directions in the Marxian Theory of Exploitation and Class'." *Politics and Society*, 11, no. 3 (1982), pp. 363–73.

—— *Explaining Technical Change: A Case Study in the Philosophy of Science.* Cambridge: C.U.P., 1983.

—— *Sour Grapes.* Cambridge: C.U.P., 1983.

—— *Making Sense of Marx.* Cambridge: C.U.P., 1985.

—— *An Introduction to Karl Marx.* Cambridge: C.U.P., 1986.

—— "Reply to Comments." *Inquiry*, 29 (1986), pp. 65–77.

—— "Three Challenges to Class." In *Analytical Marxism*, ed. John E. Roemer. Cambridge: C.U.P., 1986, pp. 141–61.

—— "Comment on Van Der Veen and Van Parijs." *Theory and Society*, 15 (1987), pp. 709–21.

—— *The Cement of Society.* Cambridge: C.U.P., 1989.

—— *Nuts and Bolts for the Social Sciences.* Cambridge: C.U.P., 1989.

—— *Solomonic Judgements: Studies in the Limitations of Rationality.* Cambridge: C.U.P., 1989.

Elster, Jon ed. *Rational Choice.* Oxford: Basil Blackwell, 1986.

Emmanuel, Arghiri. *Unequal Exchange: A Study of the Imperialism of Trade.* Trans. Brian Pearce, London: New Left Books, 1972.

Engels, Frederick. *The Origin of the Family, Private Property and the State.* London: Lawrence and Wishart, 1972 [1884].

Erikson, Robert. "Social Class of Men, Women and Families." *Sociology*, 18, no. 4 (1984), pp. 500–514.

Ewen, Stuart. *Captains of Consciousness: Advertising and the Social Roots of the Consumer Culture.* New York: McGraw-Hill, 1976.

Fevre, Ralph. "Racial Discrimination and Competition in British Trade Unions." *Ethnic and Racial Studies*, 8, no. 4 (1985), pp. 563–80.

Fine, Bob et al., eds. *Capitalism and the Rule of Law: From Deviancy Theory to Marxism.* London: Hutchinson, 1979.

Firestone, Shulamith. *The Dialectic of Sex: The Case for Feminist Revolution.* London: The Women's Press, 1979.

Ford, David and Jeff Hearn. *Studying Men and Masculinity: A Sourcebook of Literature and Materials.* Publication 1. University of Bradford: Department of Applied Social Studies, 1988.

Foster, John. *Class Struggle and the Industrial Revolution: Early Industrial Capitalism in Three English Towns.* London: Weidenfield and Nicolson, 1974.

Foucault, Michel. *Discipline and Punish: The Birth of the Prison.* Harmondsworth: Penguin, 1975.

French, Marilyn. *Beyond Power: On Women, Men and Morals.* London: Abacus, 1986.

Friedman, James W. *Game Theory with Applications to Economics.* New York: Oxford University Press, 1986.

Gauthier, David. *Morals By Agreement.* Oxford: Clarendon Press, 1985.

Gavron, Hannah. *The Captive Wife: Conflicts of Housebound Mothers.* Harmondsworth: Pelican, 1968.

Gellner, Ernest. *Nations and Nationalism.* Oxford: Basil Blackwell, 1983.

Geras, Norman. "The Controversy about Marx and Justice." *New Left Review*, 150 (March/April 1985), pp. 47–88. Reprinted in *Marxist Theory*, ed. Alex Callinicos, Oxford: Open University Press, 1989, pp. 211–68.

Goffman, Erving. "The Arrangement between the Sexes." In *Women and Symbolic Interaction*, ed. Mary Jo Deegan and Michael Hill, Boston: Allen and Unwin, 1987, pp. 51–80.

Goldthorpe, John. "Women and Class Analysis: In Defence of the Conventional View." *Sociology*, 17, no. 4 (1983), pp. 465–88.

—— "Women and Class Analysis: A Reply to the Replies." *Sociology*, 18, no. 4 (1984), pp. 491–9.

Gould, Bryan. *Socialism and Freedom*. London: Macmillan, 1985.

Graham, Keith. *The Battle of Democracy*. Brighton: Wheatsheaf, 1986.

Gray, Robert. *The Aristocracy of Labour in Nineteenth-century Britain, c. 1850–1900*. London: Macmillan, 1981.

Hakim, Catherine. *Occupational Segregation*. Research Paper no. 9. Department of Employment, 1979.

Halfpenny, Peter. "A Refutation of Historical Materialism?" *Social Science Information* 22, no. 1 (1983), pp. 61–87. Reprinted in *Marx and History*, ed. Paul Wetherly, Aldershot: Avebury, 1992.

Hamilton, Roberta and Michèle Barrett, eds. *The Politics of Diversity*. London: Verso, 1986.

Hammond, Peter. *Her Majesty's Royal Palace and Fortress of the Tower of London*. London: Department of the Environment, 1987.

Hampton, Jean. *Hobbes and the Social Contract Tradition*. Cambridge: C.U.P., 1986.

Hardin, Russell. *Collective Action*. Baltimore: The Johns Hopkins Press, 1982.

Harding, Sandra, ed. *Feminism and Methodology: Social Science Issues*. Milton Keynes: Open University Press, 1987.

Harris, C.C. *The Family and Industrial Society*. London: George Allen and Unwin, 1983.

Harris, Rosemary. *Prejudice and Tolerance in Ulster: A Study of Neighbours and 'Strangers' in a Border Community*. Manchester: Manchester University Press, 1972.

Hakim, Catherine. *Occupational Segregation*. Department of Employment, 1979.

Hart, Nicky. "Gender and the Rise and Fall of Class Politics." *New Left Review*, 175 (May/June 1989), pp. 19–47.

Hearn, Jeff. *The Gender of Oppression: Men, Masculinity and the Critique of Marxism*. Brighton: Wheatsheaf Books, 1987.

Heath, Anthony. *Rational Choice and Social Exchange: A Critique of Exchange Theory*. Cambridge: C.U.P., 1976.

Heath, Anthony and Nicky Britten. "Women's Jobs Do Make a Difference: A Reply to Goldthorpe." *Sociology*, 18, no. 4 (1984), pp. 475–90.

Heath, Stephen. *The Sexual Fix*. London: Macmillan, 1982.

Hechter, Michael, Debra Friedman and Malka Appelbaum. "A Theory of Ethnic Collective Action." *International Migration Review*, 16 (1982), pp. 412–33.

Hilton, R.H., ed. *The Transition from Feudalism to Capitalism*. London: New Left Books, 1976.

Hindess, Barry. *Choice, Rationality and Social Theory*. London: Unwin Hyman, 1988.

Hobbs, Dick. *Doing the Business: Entrepreneurship, the Working Class, and Detectives in the East End of London*. Oxford: O.U.P., 1989.

Humphries, Jane. "Class Struggle and the Persistence of the Working-Class Family." *Cambridge Journal of Economics*, 1, no. 3 (1977), pp. 241–58.

Ingham, Mary. *Men: The Male Myth Exposed*. London: Century Publishing, 1984.

James, Philip S. *Introduction to English Law*. 10th Edition. London: Butterworth, 1979.

James, Susan. *The Content of Social Explanation*. Cambridge: C.U.P., 1984.

Jordon, Bill. *Paupers: The Making of the New Claimant Class*. London: Routledge and Kegan Paul, 1973.

—— *The State: Authority and Autonomy*. Oxford: Basil Blackwell, 1985.

Katz, Claudio J. *From Feudalism to Capitalism: Marxian Theories of Class Struggle and Social Change*. New York: Greenwood Press, 1989.

Keane, John. *Public Life and Late Capitalism: Towards a Socialist Theory of Democracy*. Cambridge: C.U.P., 1985.

Keating, Peter. *Into Unknown England 1966–1913: Selections from the Social Explorers*. Glasgow: Fontana, 1976.

Kelley, Jonathan and Ian McAllister. "The Genesis of Conflict: Religion and Status Attainment in Ulster, 1968." *Sociology*, 18, no. 2 (1984), pp. 171–87.

Kieve, Donald A. "From Necessary Illusion to Rational Choice? A Critique of Neo-Marxist Rational Choice Theory." *Theory and Society*, 15, no. 4 (1986), pp. 557–83.

Lash, Scott and John Urry. "The New Marxism of Collective Action: A Critical Analysis." *Sociology*, 18, no. 1 (February 1984), pp. 33–50.

Lebowitz, Michael A. "Is 'Analytical Marxism' Marxism?" *Science and Society*, 52, no. 2 (Summer 1988), pp. 191–214.

Lenin, V.I. *Imperialism: The Highest Stage of Capitalism*. Peking: Foreign Languages Press, 1965.

Levi, Margaret. *Of Rule and Revenue*. Berkeley: University of California Press, 1988.

Levine, Andrew. *Arguing for Socialism*. London: Verso, 1988.

Levine, Andrew and Erik Olin Wright. "Rationality and Class Struggle." *New Left Review*, 123 (September/October 1980), pp. 47–68. Reprinted in *Marxist Theory*, ed. Alex Callinicos, Oxford: O.U.P., 1989, pp. 17–47.

Levine, Andrew, Elliott Sober and Erik Olin Wright. "The Limits of Micro-Explanation." *New Left Review*, 162 (March/April 1987), pp. 67–84.

Lewis, David. *Convention: A Philosophical Study*. Cambridge, Mass.: Harvard University Press, 1969.

Lindley, Richard. *Autonomy*. Basingstoke: Macmillan, 1986.

Livingstone, Ken. *If Voting Changed Anything, They'd Abolish It*. Glasgow: Fontana, 1988.

Lundahl, Mats and Eskil Wodensjo. *Unequal Treatment: A Study in the Neo-classical Theory of Discrimination*. Beckenham: Croom Helm, 1984.

Lyon, Michael. "Banton's Contribution to Racial Studies in Britain: An Over-view." *Ethnic and Racial Studies*, 8, no. 4 (1985), pp. 471–83.

McCarney, Joseph. "A New Marxist Paradigm?" *Radical Philosophy*, 43 (Summer 1986), pp. 29–31.

Macdonald, Graham and Philip Pettit. *Semantics and Social Science*. London: Routledge and Kegan Paul, 1981.

Macdonald, Graham. *Special Explanations*. Oxford: Basil Blackwell, forthcoming.

McDowell, Linda, Philip Sarre and Chris Hamnett, eds. *Divided Nation: Social and Cultural Change in Britain*. London: Hodder and Stoughton, 1989.

Mack, Joanna and Stewart Lansley. *Poor Britain*. London: Allen and Unwin, 1985.

Macmillan Student Encyclopedia of Sociology. London: Macmillan, 1983.

Macpherson, C.B. *The Political Theory of Possessive Individualism*. Oxford: O.U.P., 1962.

—— *The Life and Times of Liberal Democracy*. Oxford: O.U.P., 1977.

McRae, Susan. *Cross-Class Families: A Study of Wives' Occupational Superiority*. Oxford: Clarendon Press, 1986.

Maguire, John. "Contract, Coercion and Consciousness." In *Rational Action: Studies in Philosophy and Social Science*, ed. Ross Harrison, Cambridge: C.U.P., 1979.

Mann, Michael. *The Sources of Social Power*, Vol. 1, *A History of Power From the Beginning to A.D. 1760*. Cambridge: C.U.P., 1986.

Marshall, Gordon, David Rise, Howard Newby and Carolyn Vogler. *Social Class in Modern Britain*. London: Unwin Hyman, 1988.

Martin, Bill. "How Marxism Became Analytic." *Journal of Philosophy*, 86, no. 11 (1989), pp. 659–66.

Marx, Karl. *Capital: A Critique of Political Economy*, Vol. 1. Trans. Ben Fowkes. Harmondsworth: Penguin, 1976 [1867].

—— *Capital: A Critique of Political Economy*, Vol. 3. *The Process of Capitalist Production as a whole*. Ed. Frederick Engels. London: Lawrence and Wishart, 1974 [1894].

—— *Critique of the Gotha Programme*. Peking: Foreign Languages Press, 1976 [1875].

—— *The Eighteenth Brumaire of Louis Bonaparte*. Moscow: Progress Publishers, 1934 [1852].

Marx, Karl and Frederick Engels. *The German Ideology*. Ed. C.J. Arthur. London: Lawrence and Wishart, 1970 [1846].

—— *Manifesto of the Communist Party*. Moscow: Progress Publishers, 1953. [1848].

Mayer, Thomas F. "In Defense of Analytical Marxism." *Science and Society*, 53, no. 4 (Winter 1989/90), pp. 416–41.

Meikle, Scott. "Making Nonsense of Marx." *Inquiry*, 29 (1986), pp. 29–43.

Meissner, Martin, Elizabeth W. Humphreys, Scott M. Meis and William J. Schau. "No Exit for Wives: Sexual Division of Labour and the Cumulation of Household Demands." *Canadian Review of Sociology and Anthropology*, 12, no. 4. (November 1975), pp. 424–39.

Metcalf, Andy and Martin Humphries, eds. *The Sexuality of Men*. London: Pluto Press, 1985.

Midgley, Mary and Judith Hughes. *Women's Choices: Philosophical Problems Facing Feminism*. London: Weidenfeld and Nicolson, 1983.

Miller, Anne Glenda, ed. *Basic Income*. Proceedings of the First International Conference on Basic Income, Louvain-La-Neuve, Belgium, September 1986. Antwerp: Basic Income European Network, 1988.

Miller, David. *Market, State and Community: Theoretical Foundations of Market Socialism*. Oxford: Clarendon Press, 1989.

Milsom S.F.C. *Historical Foundations of the Common Law*. 2nd Edition. London: Butterworth, 1981.

Morishima, Michio. *Marx's Economics*. Cambridge: C.U.P., 1973.

Mueller, Dennis. *Public Choice*. Cambridge: C.U.P., 1979.

Newby, Howard, Janet Bujra, Paul Littlewood, Gareth Rees and Teresa L. Ress, eds. *Restructuring Capital: Recession and Reorganization in Industrial Society* London: Macmillan, 1985.

Norman, Richard. *Free and Equal: A Philosophical Examination of Political Values*. Oxford: Oxford University Press, 1987.

Norris, Pippa. *Politics and Sexual Equality: The Comparative Position of Women in Western Democracies*. Brighton: Wheatsheaf, 1987.

North, Douglass C. "Is It Worth Making Sense of Marx?" *Inquiry*, 29 (1986), pp. 57–63.

Nove, Alec. *The Economics of Feasible Socialism*. London: George Allen and Unwin, 1983.

—— " 'A Capitalist Road to Communism': A Comment." *Theory and Society*, 15 (1987), pp. 673–87.

Nozick, Robert. *Anarchy, State and Utopia*. Oxford: Basil Blackwell, 1974.

Oakley, Ann. *Housewife*. Harmondsworth: Penguin, 1974.

—— *Subject Women*. Glasgow: Fontana, 1982.

O'Brien, Mary. *The Politics of Reproduction*. London: Routledge and Kegan Paul, 1981.

Offices of Population Censuses and Surveys. *Census 1981: Definitions, Great Britain*. London: H.M.S.O., 1981.

—— *General Household Survey*. London: H.M.S.O., 1984.

Olson, Mancur. *The Logic of Collective Action*. Cambridge, Mass.: Harvard University Press, 1965.

Orbach, Susie and Luise Eichenbaum. *What Do Women Want?* Glasgow: Fontana, 1984.

Ordeshook, Peter C. *Game Theory and Political Theory: An Introduction*. Cambridge: C.U.P., 1986.

Pahl, Jan. "The Allocation of Money Within the Household." In *The State, the Law and the Family: Critical Perspectives*, ed. Michael D. Freeman, London: Tavistock, 1984, pp. 36–51.

Parkin, Frank. *Marxism and Class Theory: A Bourgeois Critique.* London: Tavistock, 1979.

Pateman, Carole. *The Sexual Contract.* Cambridge: Polity Press, 1988.

Pettit, Philip. "Free Riding and Foul Dealing." *Journal of Philosophy.* LXXXIII, no. 7 (July 1986) pp. 361–79.

—— "The Prisoner's Dilemma is an Unexploitable Newcomb Problem." *Synthese*, 76, no. 1 (July 1988), pp. 123–34.

Phillips, Anne and Barbara Taylor. "Sex and Skill." In *Waged Work: A Reader*, ed. *Feminist Review*, London: Virago, 1986, pp. 54–66.

Piore, Michael J. *Birds of Passage: Migrant Labour and Industrial Societies.* Cambridge: Cambridge University Press, 1979.

Pleck, Joseph H. *Working Wives/Working Husbands.* Beverly Hills: Sage, 1985.

Popper, Karl. *Unended Quest: An Intellectual Autobiography.* Glasgow: Fontana, 1986.

Przeworski, Adam. "Marxism and Rational Choice." *Politics and Society*, 14, no. 4 (1985), pp. 379–409.

Rapoport, Anatol and Melvin Guyer. "A Taxonomy of 2 × 2 Games." *General Systems*, 11 (1966), pp. 203–14.

"Rational Choice Revisited: A Critique of Michael Banton's 'Racial and Ethnic Competition'." *Ethnic and Racial Studies*, 8, no. 4 (October 1985). Special Issue.

Reeve, Andrew, ed. *Modern Theories of Exploitation.* London: Sage, 1987.

Reid, Ivan and Eileen Wormald, eds. *Sex Differences in Britain.* London: Grant McIntyre, 1982.

Reid, Ivan. *Social Class Differences in Britain.* 3rd Edition. Glasgow: Fontana, 1989.

Reid, Margaret G. *Economics of Household Production.* New York: John Wiley, 1934.

Rex, John. "Kantianism, Methodological Individualism and Michael Banton." *Ethnic and Racial Studies*, 8, no. 4 (October 1985), pp. 548–62.

Rex, John and David Mason, eds. *Theories of Race and Ethnic Relations.* Cambridge: C.U.P., 1986.

Rigby, S.H. *Marxism and History: A Critical Introduction.* Manchester: Manchester University Press, 1987.

Roemer, John E. "Neoclassicism, Marxism and Collective Action." *Journal of Economic Issues*, 12 (1978), pp. 147–61.

—— "Divide and Conquer: Microfoundations of a Marxian Theory of Wage Discrimination." *Bell Journal of Economics*, 10, no. 2 (Autumn 1979), pp. 695–705.

—— *Analytical Foundations of Marxian Economic Theory.* Cambridge: C.U.P., 1981.

—— *A General Theory of Exploitation and Class.* Cambridge, Mass.: Harvard University Press, 1982

—— "New Directions in the Marxian Theory of Exploitation and Class." *Politics and Society*, 11, no. 3 (1982), pp. 253–87. Reprinted in *Analytical Marxism*, ed. John E. Roemer, Cambridge: C.U.P., 1986, pp. 81–113.

—— "Property Relations vs. Surplus Value in Marxian Exploitation." *Philosophy and Public Affairs*, 11, no. 4 (1982), pp. 281–313.

—— "R.P Wolff's Reinterpretation of Marx's Labor Theory of Value: Comment." *Philosophy and Public Affairs*, 12, no. 1 (1982) pp. 70–83.

—— "Are Socialist Ethics Consistent with Efficiency?" *Philosophical Forum*, 14, nos. 3/4 (1983), pp. 369–88.

—— "Unequal Exchange, Labour Migration, and International Capital Flows: A Theoretical Synthesis." In *Marxism, Central Planning and the Soviet Economy: Economic Essays in Honor of Alexander Erlich*, ed. P. Desai, Cambridge, Mass.: MIT Press, 1983, pp. 34–60.

—— "Equality of Talent." *Economics and Philosophy*, 1 (1985), pp. 151–87.

—— "Rationalizing Revolutionary Ideology: A Tale of Lenin and the Tsar." *Econometrica*, 53, no. 1. (Jan 1985), pp. 85–108. Reprinted in *Rationality and Revolution*, ed. Michael Taylor, Cambridge: C.U.P., 1988, pp. 229–45.

—— "Should Marxists Be Interested in Exploitation?" *Philosophy and Public Affairs*, 14, no. 1 (1985), pp. 29–65. Reprinted abridged in *Analytical Marxism*, ed. John E. Roemer, Cambridge: C.U.P., 1986, pp. 260–82.

—— "Equality of Resources Implies Equality of Welfare." *Quarterly Journal of Economics* (November 1986), pp. 751–84.

—— *Value, Exploitation and Class*. Chur: Harwood Academic Publishers, 1986.

—— "History's Effect on the Distribution of Income." *Social Science Information*, 26, no. 2 (1987), pp. 403–15.

—— *Free to Lose: An Introduction to Marxist Economic Philosophy*. London: Radius, 1988.

—— "Second Thoughts on Property Relations and Exploitation". In *Canadian Journal of Philosophy* (1989), Supplementary Volume 15, *Analysing Marxism*, ed. Robert Ware and Kai Neilsen, pp. 257–66.

Roemer, John, E., ed. *Analytical Marxism*. Cambridge: C.U.P., 1986.

Ross, Edward Alsworth. *Principles of Sociology*. 3rd Edition. New York: D. Appleton-Century, 1938 [1920].

Routh, Guy. *Occupation and Pay in Great Britain 1906–60*. Cambridge: C.U.P., 1965.

Rubery, Jill, ed. *Women and Recession*. London: Routledge and Kegan Paul, 1988.

Runnymede Trust and the Radical Statistics Race Group. *Britain's Black Population*. London: Heinemann Educational Books, 1980.

Rustin, Michael. *For a Pluralist Socialism*. London: Verso, 1985.

Samuelson, Paul A. "The Pure Theory of Public Expenditure." *Review of Economics and Statistics*, 36 (1954), pp. 387–9.

—— "Diagrammatic Exposition of a Theory of Public Expenditure." *Review of Economics and Statistics*, 37 (1955), pp. 350–56.

—— "Aspects of Public Expenditure Theories." *Review of Economics and Statistics*, 40 (1958), pp. 332–8.

—— "Pure Theory of Public Expenditure and Taxation." In *Public Economics*, ed. J. Margolis and H. Guitton, London: Macmillan, 1969, pp. 98–123.

Sayer, Derek. *The Violence of Abstraction: The Analytic Foundations of Historical Materialism*. Oxford: Basil Blackwell, 1987.

Sayers, Sean. "Marxism and the Dialectical Method: A Critique of G.A. Cohen." *Radical Philosophy*, 36 (1984), pp. 4–13.

Schelling, Thomas C. "Dynamic Models of Segregation." *Journal of Mathematical Sociology*, 1 (1971), pp. 143–86.

—— *Micromotives and Macrobehaviour*. New York: W.W. Norton, 1978.

Schick, Frederic. *Having Reasons: An Essay on Sociality and Rationality*. Princeton: Princeton University Press, 1984.

Schofield, Norman. "Anarchy, Altruism and Cooperation: A Review." *Social Choice and Welfare*, 2 (1985), pp. 207–19.

Schultz, T.W., ed. *Economics of the Family*. Chicago: University of Chicago Press, 1974.

Segal, Lynne. *Is the Future Female?: Troubled Thoughts on Contemporary Feminism*. London: Virago, 1987.

Sen, Amartya K. "Isolation, Assurance and the Social Rate of Discount." *Quarterly Journal of Economics*, 81 (1967), pp. 112–24.

—— "Rational Fools: A Critique of the Behavioral Foundations of Economic Theory." *Philosophy and Public Affairs*, 6 (1977), pp. 317–44.

—— "Equality of What?" In *The Tanner Lectures on Human Values*, ed. S. McMurrin. Cambridge: C.U.P., 1980, pp. 195–220.

Seton-Watson, Hugh. *Nations and States: An Enquiry into the Origins of Nations and the Politics of Nationalism*. Cambridge: C.U.P., 1977.

Shubik, Martin. "Game Theory, Behaviour, and the Paradox of Prisoner's Dilemma: Three Solutions." *Journal of Conflict Resolution*, 14 (1970), pp. 181–93.

Slaughter, Cliff. "Making Sense of Elster." *Inquiry*, 29 (1986), pp. 45–56.

Smith, Anthony D. *The Ethnic Origins of Nations*. Oxford: Basil Blackwell, 1986.

Smith, David J. *Racial Disadvantage in Britain: The PEP Report*. Harmondsworth: Penguin, 1977.

Smith, M.G. "Race and ethnic relations as matters of rational choice." *Ethnic and Racial Studies*, 8, no. 4 (October 1985), pp. 484–99.

Smith, Tony. "Roemer on Marx's Theory of Exploitation: Shortcomings of a Non-Dialectical Approach." *Science and Society*, 53, no. 3 (Fall 1989), pp. 327–40.

Spender, Dale. *Man Made Language*. London: Routledge and Kegan Paul, 1980.

Stanley, Liz and Sue Wise. *Breaking Out: Feminist Consciousness and Feminist Research*. London: Routledge and Kegan Paul, 1983.

Steedman, Ian. *Marx after Sraffa*. London: New Left Books, 1977.

—— et al. *The Value Controversy*. London: Verso, 1981.

Steiner, Hillel. "The Natural Right to the Means of Production." *Philosophical Quarterly*, 27 (1977), pp. 41–49.

—— "Land, Liberty and the Early Herbert Spencer." *History of Political Thought*, 3 (1982), pp. 515–34.

—— "Three Just Taxes." In *Arguing for Basic Income*, ed. Philippe Van Parijs, London: Verso, 1992.

Tajfel, Henri. *The Social Psychology of Minorities*. Minority Rights Group Report no. 38. London: Minority Rights Group, 1978. Reprinted in *'Race' in Britain: Continuity and Change*, ed. Charles Husband, London: Hutchinson, 1982, pp. 216–58.

Taylor, Michael. *Anarchy and Cooperation*. London: John Wiley, 1976.

—— *Community, Anarchy and Liberty*. Cambridge: C.U.P., 1982.

—— "Elster's Marx." *Inquiry*, 29 (1986), pp. 3–10.

—— *The Possibility of Cooperation*. Cambridge: C.U.P., 1987.

—— "Structure, Culture and Action in the Explanation of Social Change." *Politics and Society*, 17, no. 2 (1989), pp. 115–62.

Taylor, Michael and Hugh Ward. "Chickens, Whales and Lumpy Goods: Alternative Models of Public Goods Provision." *Political Studies*, XXX, no. 3 (1982), pp. 350–70.

Taylor, Michael, ed. *Rationality and Revolution*. Cambridge: C.U.P., 1988.

Tormey, Judith Farr. "Exploitation, Oppression and Self-Sacrifice." *Philosophical Forum*, 5, nos. 1/2 (Fall/Winter 1973–4), pp. 206–21.

Tucker, R.C., ed. *The Marx–Engels Reader*. NewYork: W.W. Norton, 1972.

Van der Veen, Robert J. and Philippe Van Parijs. " A Capitalist Road to Communism." *Theory and Society*, 15 (1987), pp. 635–55.

—— "Universal Grants versus Socialism: Reply to Six Critics." *Theory and Society*, 15 (1987), pp. 723–57.

Van Parijs, Philippe. *Evolutionary Explanation in the Social Sciences: An Emerging Paradigm*. Totowa, N.J.: Rowman and Littlefield, 1981.

—— "Exploitation and the Libertarian Challenge." In *Modern Theories of Exploitation*, ed. Andrew Reeve, London: Sage, 1987, pp. 111–31.

—— "In Defence of Abundance." *In Canadian Journal of Philosophy* (1989), Supplementary Volume 15, *Analyzing Marxism*, ed. Robert Ware and Kai Nielsen, pp. 467–95.

—— "A Revolution in Class Theory." In *The Debate on Classes*, ed. Erik Olin Wright, London: Verso, 1989, pp. 23–41.

—— "On the Ethical Foundations of Basic Income." In *Arguing for Basic Income*, ed. Philippe Van Parijs, London: Verso, 1992.

Van Parijs, Philippe, ed. *Arguing for Basic Income*. London: Verso, 1992.

Von Neumann, John and Oskar Morgenstern. *The Theory of Games and Economic Behaviour*. Princeton: Princeton University Press, 1945.

Walby, Sylvia, ed. *Gender Segregation at Work*. Milton Keynes: Open University Press, 1988.

Walczak, Yvette. *He and She: Men in the Eighties*. London: Routledge, 1988.

Walker, Pat, ed. *Between Labour and Capital*. Hassocks, Sussex: Harvester Press, 1979.

Ward, Hugh. "Behavioural Models of Bargaining." Ph.D. Thesis, University of Essex, 1979.

—— "The Risks of a Reputation for Toughness: Strategy in Public Goods Problems Modelled by Chicken Supergames." *British Journal of Political Science*, 17 (1987), pp. 23–52.

Ware, Robert and Kai Nielsen, eds. "Analysing Marxism : New Essays on Analytical Marxism." *Canadian Journal of Philosophy*, Supplementary Volume 15 (1989).

Weeks, Jeffrey. *Sex, Politics and Society*. London: Longman, 1981.

Weinberg, Julius. *Edward Alsworth Ross and the Sociology of Progressivism*. Madison, Wisc. : State Historical Society of Wisconsin, 1972.

Weinreich, Peter. "Psychodynamics of Personal and Social Identity." In *Identity; Personal and Social:A Symposium*, ed. A. Jacobson-Widding, Stockholm: Almqvist and Wiksell International, 1983, pp. 159–85.

Weldes, Jutta. "Marxism and Methodological Individualism: A Critique." *Theory and Society*, 18 (1989), pp. 353–86.

West, David. *Authenticity and Empowerment: A Theory of Liberation*. Hemel Hempstead: Harvester Wheatsheaf, 1990.

West, Jackie, ed. *Work, Women and the Labour Market*. London: Routledge and Kegan Paul, 1982.

Wetherley, Paul, ed. *Marx and History: Essays in Base and Superstructure*. Aldershot: Avebury, 1992.

Whyte, John H. "How is the Boundary Maintained between the Two Communities in Northern Ireland?" *Ethnic and Racial Studies*, 9, no. 2 (April 1986), pp. 219–34.

Wickham, Chris. "Historical Materialism, Historical Sociology." *New Left Review*, 171 (September/October 1988), pp. 63–80.

Williams, Raymond. *Keywords: A Vocabulary of Culture and Society*. Glasgow: Fontana, 1976.

—— *Democracy and Parliament*. London: Socialist Society, 1982.

Willis, Paul E. *Learning to Labour: How Working-Class Kids Get Working-Class Jobs*. Aldershot: Gower, 1978.

Wolff, Robert Paul. "Reply to Roemer." *Philosophy and Public Affairs*, 12, no. 1 (1982), pp. 84–8.

Wood, Allen. "Historical Materialism and Functional Explanation." *Inquiry*, 29 (1986), pp. 11–27.

Wood, Ellen Meiksins. "Rational Choice Marxism: Is the Game Worth the Candle?" *New Left Review*, 177 (September/October 1989), pp. 41–88.

Wright, Erik Olin. *Class, Crisis and the State*. London: New Left Books, 1978.

—— "The Status of the Political in the Concept of Class Structure." *Politics and Society*, 11, no. 3 (1982), pp. 321–41.

—— *Classes*. London: Verso, 1985.

—— "What is Middle about the Middle Class?". In *Analytical Marxism*, ed. John E. Roemer. Cambridge: C.U.P., 1986, pp. 114–40.

—— "Why Something Like Socialism is Necessary for the Transition to Something Like Communism." *Theory and Society*, 15 (1987), pp. 657–72.

Wright, Erik Olin, ed. *The Debate on Classes*. London: Verso, 1989.

Young, Michael and Peter Willmott. *The Symmetrical Family*. Harmondsworth: Penguin, 1973.

Index